Revitalizing the Classics

Revitalizing the Classics

What Past Social Theorists
Can Teach Us Today

Tony Simmons

Fernwood Publishing
Halifax & Winnipeg

Editing and text design: Brenda Conroy
Cover design: John van der Woude
Printed and bound in Canada by Hignell Book Printing

Published in Canada by Fernwood Publishing
32 Oceanvista Lane, Black Point, Nova Scotia, B0J 1B0
and 748 Broadway Avenue, Winnipeg, Manitoba, R3G 0X3
www.fernwoodpublishing.ca

Fernwood Publishing Company Limited gratefully acknowledges the financial support of the Government of Canada through the Canada Book Fund and the Canada Council for the Arts, the Nova Scotia Department of Communities, Culture and Heritage, the Manitoba Department of Culture, Heritage and Tourism under the Manitoba Publishers Marketing Assistance Program and the Province of Manitoba, through the Book Publishing Tax Credit, for our publishing program.

Library and Archives Canada Cataloguing in Publication

Simmons, Anthony M. (Anthony Michael), 1945-
Revitalizing the classics: what past social theorists can teach us about today / Tony Simmons.

Includes bibliographical references and index.
ISBN 978-1-55266-555-8

1. Social sciences—Philosophy.   2. Social sciences and history.
3. History, Modern--21st century.   I. Title.

H61.S585 2013   300.1   C2012-908252-X

Contents

To my comrades Rick, Dave, Rob and Ihor (and Marek), of the Bear Clan hiking group, who saved me from a cold and lonely end in the Canadian Rockies.

Acknowledgements

I thank my publisher, Wayne Antony, for his encouragement and for his sage and surgical advice throughout the writing of this book, and also Debbie Mathers, Brenda Conroy, Beverley Rach, John van der Woude at Fernwood Publishing, who magically transformed my manuscript into a real book. Thanks as well as to the taxpayers of Alberta for subsidizing the sabbatical leave that allowed me to complete this project. I also thank my wife, Sybil, who remains the lighthouse in my life.

Chapter 1

The Theoretical Imagination

Life is far more precarious than most of us care to admit. From the shelter of our living room cocoons, we watch the epic stories of our times unfold on our television and computer screens: the fall of the Soviet Union and end of apartheid in South Africa; the break-up of Yugoslavia; the invasions of Afghanistan and Iraq; the genocides in Cambodia and Rwanda; the Arab Spring; the environmental disasters of Hurricane Katrina, the Indian Ocean tsunami, the Haitian and Japanese earthquakes, and the BP oil spill in the Gulf of Mexico. On top of all this, we also witnessed the economic meltdown in the United States and Europe, and the global financial crisis in 2008. And, of course, there was 9/11.

These socially produced calamities and natural disasters disrupted, damaged, bankrupted, uprooted or obliterated the lives of countless individuals. Sometimes, we are personally touched by these stories, either through our own direct involvement, or indirectly,

> ### Figure 1-1 Lord of the Flies
>
> He paused and stood up, looking at the shadows under the trees. His voice was lower when he spoke again.
>
> "But we'll leave part of the kill for..."
>
> He knelt down again and was busy with his knife. The boys crowded round him. He spoke over his shoulder to Roger.
>
> "Sharpen a stick at both ends."
>
> Presently he stood up, holding the dripping sow's head in his hands.
>
> "Where's that stick?"
>
> "Here."
>
> "Ram one end in the earth. Oh — it's rock. Jam it in that crack. There."
>
> Jack held the head and jammed the soft throat down on the pointed end of the stick which pierced through into the mouth. He stood back and the head hung there, a little blood dribbling down the stick. Instinctively the boys drew back too; and the forest was very still. They listened, and the loudest noise was the buzzing of the flies over the spilled guts."
>
> William Golding, *Lord of the Flies,* 1972: 150–151.

through friends or relatives who have, themselves, suffered these experiences. For the most part, though, those of us who reside in the safer and more affluent parts of the world — North America and Europe — are far less likely to be personally acquainted with the raw experience of a major disaster. The greater risks to life are disproportionately borne by the most vulnerable sections of our own populations — such as First Nations people and those who are homeless, destitute or disabled — and by many who live in the less developed countries. Of course, exceptional events may affect us, either directly or indirectly — such as the attacks of September 11, 2001. But the very rarity of these catastrophes in the Global North makes them

1

all the more shocking when they do occur. By contrast, inhabitants of the Global South experience disasters with much greater frequency (see Beck 1992; Caplan 2000).

One lesson to be learned from these events, be they natural or socially produced, is that the structure of society is far more fragile than we usually recognize. While the normal routines of everyday life may persuade us that our society is a relatively permanent and durable structure, a major crisis can quickly disrupt this structure and shatter our illusion of security. But, as we shall see, the fragility of societies and their institutions is the very stuff of social theory. Social theorists are alert to this fragility and have sought to explain why societies normally remain fairly stable, but why they sometimes undergo rapid — and occasionally violent — change. And in most cases of radical social change, the factors of power, inequality and conflict have played important roles. Thereby hangs the tale of classical social theory.

Fact Is Always Stranger than Fiction

Anything that can be imagined has probably already happened somewhere, at some time, for fiction invariably follows in the footsteps of fact. The opening highlight is taken from the novel *Lord of the Flies* by William Golding.[1] This is a story of a group of English schoolboys who, after surviving a mid-flight plane crash, are marooned on a tropical island. At first, the survivors organize themselves into an orderly mini-society. A popular boy, Ralph, is elected as leader of the group and is able to ensure that meetings and other group activities on the island are run fairly and equitably. After a while, however, divisions begin to emerge between boys from different schools, and as a result of these tensions the more affluent "public school" boys break away from the original group to form their own "tribe" — under the autocratic leadership of their head boy, Jack. (In the United Kingdom, the term "public school" paradoxically refers to elite private schools). The novel then recounts in harrowing detail how the members of Jack's tribe swiftly degenerate into a state of savagery. Indeed, the book suggests that the veneer of civilization most of us take for granted is only skin deep. Beneath the surface of our socialization and training lies our primordial animal nature — aggressive, competitive, territorial, hierarchical and strongly patriarchal. The primary message of this story seems to be that when reduced to a state of nature, people regress to their primal selves, and human society reverts to a primitive state of a "war of all against all," in the words of the seventeenth-century English political philosopher Thomas Hobbes (1651, Chapter 13: paragraph 9). It is a familiar parable.

Today, we can think of many parallels — some false and some true — to the loss of innocence and humanity depicted in *Lord of the Flies*. After the devastation of Hurricane Katrina in 2005, initial reports painted an horrific picture of anarchy and depravity among the survivors who had congregated at the Louisiana Superdome in New Orleans. Early media coverage of conditions inside the Superdome carried a number of alleged eye-witness accounts of muggings, rapes and even murder. The makeshift community appeared to degenerate into a human jungle in which only the fittest and most ruthless could hold their own. The fact that most of these accounts were later found to be false has done nothing to lessen their hold on the popular imagination. Even as an urban legend, the parable of the Superdome lives on — appearing to confirm our worst suspicions about the fragility of our institutions and the shallowness of our civilization.

Unfortunately, there are many well documented examples of situations in which a total breakdown of law and order and a collapse of civilized norms and values have occurred. In addition to the Holocaust, the genocides in Cambodia (1975–1979) and Rwanda (1994) are stark reminders of just how fragile our social structures are and how easily our civilized rules of conduct may be swept away on a tide of fanaticism and violence. Wars in Bosnia, Kosovo, Chechnya, Sierra Leone, Liberia and the Congo — among other places — have also harvested a crop of horror stories of what can happen in "failed states" and collapsed societies. Even Canada has its own legacy of brutal skeletons in the closet. The physical and sexual abuse of First Nations children in residential schools and the earlier compulsory sterilization of individuals classified as "mentally unfit" are only two examples of historical horror stories from the home front. Beneath the outward cloak of civility, it seems, the beast is always lurking.

In the face of disaster, most of us experience a strong need to find meaning. Some may turn to our religious faith or political convictions in order to find answers to the question of why such events occur. Others may turn to science for less ideological answers. But it seems natural to us as rational beings to seek explanations for catastrophic events and, indeed, for less dramatic occurrences in our everyday lives. We are all, in our various ways, "thinking reeds" — according to the philosopher Blaise Pascal (1995: 347).[2] We need theories in order to impose some meaning on the chaos of our raw experiences. Humans have theorized since the dawn of time.

Most of the classical social theories covered in this book arose in response to the human disasters of war, revolution and the rollercoaster of social and technological change. All of the theorists tried to explain the transformative events that had influenced their lives and the lives of those around them. Classical social theories still carry the birthmarks of their origins: the social upheavals that changed the course of history. For this reason, we still have much to learn from these theories. Although times have changed since the classical theorists first advanced their ideas, some things — such as war, revolution, violence and human cruelty — have never really changed. In fact, as the old French proverb suggests: "The more things change, the more they stay the same" (*plus ça change, plus c'est la même chose*).

Theorizing *Lord of the Flies*

Although the classical theories of society originated during times of conflict and rapid social change, each theorist provided their own account and explanation of these events. Their perspectives differed from each other according to the nationality, ethnicity, social class and gender of the theorist. These perspectives would have been apparent had these theorists accounted for the events portrayed in *Lord of the Flies*. Let us, as an hypothetical exercise, ask some of the classical theorists to explain the main events of this story.

For Thomas Hobbes, the seventeenth-British philosopher, this novel would doubtless have vindicated his belief that humankind, in its natural state, inevitably descends into a war of all against all, a condition in which life becomes "solitary, poor, nasty, brutish, and short" (Hobbes 1651, Chapter 13: paragraph 9). Hobbes believed that without a sovereign power to regulate and contain the "natural passions" of humans, society would always be brutish and uncivilized. In his view, "war was natural while peace was social." In other words, Jack and his tribe of neo-savages simply reverted to their essential primitive natures once civilized rules of conduct became unenforceable. Left alone, Jack would probably have emerged as the sovereign power on the island and would have eventually imposed his own brutal version of law and order on the schoolboy society.

Jean-Jacques Rousseau, the eigthteenth-century French political philosopher, on the other hand, held opposite views on human nature. Although Hobbes and Rousseau were both social contract theorists, Rousseau believed that the natural state of humankind was one in which early humans enjoyed peaceful, if isolated, relations with each other. In other words, the origins of human society are to be found in those primordial bands of independent hunters and gatherers who met the challenges of life, and the needs of subsistence, largely through their own self-sufficient efforts. According to Rousseau, it was only with the growth of social inequality, despotic monarchy, corrupt clergy and privileged aristocracy that the evils of war, conflict, oppression and exploitation first appeared in human society. Unlike Hobbes, Rousseau believed that "peace was natural and war was social." For this reason, Rousseau would have explained the reversion to savagery in *Lord of the Flies* as an expression of the oppressive class divisions and colonial culture of contemporary British society. Far from representing a return to the primitive, Rousseau would probably have argued that the aggression, competition, territoriality and hierarchy of Jack's tribe of elite public school boys simply reflected the traditional values of the British ruling class. In other words, the descent into savagery was conditioned more by socialization than by some primal genetic inheritance. Jack and his tribe, therefore, are best understood as products of the society that raised and educated them.

For Harriet Martineau, Charlotte Perkins Gillman and other classical feminists, the horrors of *Lord of the Flies* would probably have been explained by reference to gender differences. In their view, if the plane crash survivors had been girls, the events would likely have unfolded very differently. Unlike boys, who — in a patriarchal society — are trained to be competitive, aggressive, independent and forceful, girls are typically socialized into the values of sharing and cooperation, nurturing and networking, diplomacy and peace (see Gilligan 1993). From a feminist perspective, the horrors of *Lord of the Flies* derive from the socialization of young males into the predatory practices and values of the dominant patriarchal society.

Finally, to end this flight of fancy, as a social evolutionist, nineteenth-century sociologist Herbert Spencer would undoubtedly have reaffirmed his belief that social life is always a struggle for existence, one which always ends with the survival of the fittest. Spencer would have seen the division between Ralph's civilized group and Jack's tribe of warriors as a competition between what he called an "industrial" versus a "militant" society. The industrial society is organized around production and social welfare, while the militant society is organized around warfare and conquest. For Spencer, the outcome of the conflict between these two types of society would be determined through the process of natural selection. The society most adapted to its environment would be the one that survived and prevailed.

Why Study Classical Social Theory?

Although we have used *Lord of the Flies* to show how the meaning of the story may be interpreted and deconstructed in different ways depending upon which theoretical perspective is adopted, we could just as easily have used a current affairs news item. After all, social theories are frameworks for interpreting, explaining and understanding our social world. They provide us with narratives that can clarify and simplify some of the significant events of our own lives and the lives of those around us.

This is a book about classical social theory. The term "classical" for sociologists refers to those past social theorists and social thinkers whose works have made important historical contributions to the development of the discipline. The standard list of works of classical writers is known as the "cannon"; the cannon includes those texts that sociologists have come to revere as the most authoritative and influential in the history of the discipline. However, as we shall see, the recognition of what constitutes a classical text may change from one generation to the next. More to the point, who is included and who is excluded from the cannon of classical social theorists tells us more about the changing tastes and sensibilities of sociologists than it does about the merit of past theorists. For most of its history, the classical cannon of social theory included only works by white, middle-class, heterosexual, European male theorists. Today, the scope of the classical cannon has begun to broaden, and this book includes non-European male and female theorists in its definition of "classical."

One important lesson from the study of classical social theory is that none of the problems we face in today's global society are unprecedented. Although we live in a time of breathtaking social change, this was also true for theorists who lived through the revolutionary changes of the eighteenth, nineteenth and early twentieth centuries. Each of the three great classical theorists—the Holy Trinity of Marx, Durkheim and Weber—struggled to make sense of the ways in which the lives of ordinary people had been transformed by the industrial, agricultural, demographic and political revolutions of their times. The attempts of these theorists to understand, describe and explain these societal changes offer us important lessons in how to analyze the transformations in our own societal and global landscapes. The social problems that currently preoccupy us — such as war, inequality, tyranny, hunger, disease, religious, sexual and racial persecution, rapid technological change, financial debt and even environmental degradation —are neither new nor unprecedented. Indeed, many of our current problems were also faced by the classical theorists. Many of the issues that trouble and perplex us today are variations upon earlier themes.

No matter what our field of study, we need to know about those who went before us on the path of learning and discovery. This is true for engineers, physicians, scientists, artists, poets—and even sociologists. All branches of knowledge are built upon the achievements of past thinkers. Only by learning about these achievements are we able to extend the horizons of our knowledge and contribute to our chosen field of study. "If I have seen further," wrote Isaac Newton in 1676, "it is by standing on the shoulders of Giants" (Maury 1992). For Newton, Plato and Aristotle were the giants, whereas for us, the giants are the theorists covered in this book. So what exactly is the value of learning about past theories of society? How can these theories help us to understand our contemporary social worlds? Several reasons come to mind.

Theories give us new powers of social observation: Theories provide us with languages to talk about our social worlds in new ways, and also to observe our social worlds in unaccustomed ways. As a result of talking about and seeing our worlds in new ways, we are able to act and interact within our worlds in innovative ways. Classical theories of society have provided us with a rich vocabulary of basic terms and key concepts that are still in use today. Karl Marx's critical analysis of capitalism and commodity production gave us terms like "class struggle," "alienation," "exploitation," "surplus value," "ideology," "false consciousness" and so on. Similarly, from Emile Durkheim, we inherited such concepts as "anomie," "altruism" and "fatalism"; and from Max Weber, "rationalization" and "Protestant ethic."

To fully understand these terms and concepts, we need to return to their intellectual roots. Nowhere is the power of theory over observation — and over action — more apparent than in the realm of social theory. Social theories have periodically changed the ways we perceive our social worlds and have also changed the ways we act and interact within these worlds. When Europe and North America still subscribed to a theory of social Darwinism — namely, the belief that "white races" were more highly evolved than "non-white races" — this belief affected the ways in which non-Europeans — especially First Nations — were perceived and treated. Indeed, the doctrine of social Darwinism became institutionalized in the colonization and immigration policies of many nations — including those of Canada. It was only with the introduction of the points system in Canada, during the mid-1960s, that non-(Western) Europeans ceased to be classified as "non-preferred immigrants."

New theories change the way we look at and talk about people — even in official documents, such as census classifications. Old terms such as "negro," "oriental" and "Indian" have been discarded in favour of "African Canadian," "Asian" and "First Nations." The difference between these earlier and later terms is that whereas the former terms designated only the (supposedly) "racial" characteristics of particular minority populations, the latter terms designated their "ethnic" or cultural heritage. Underlying this transformation in terminology was a theoretical (indeed, ideological) sea change: a paradigm shift from a "biological" to a cultural definition. There are many other examples that show the power of theories over our beliefs, perceptions and actions. Far from being inconsequential and superfluous, theories play an important role in our lives and in our relationships with others.

Theories help us understand influential political ideologies: The official communist ideology of the former USSR and of present-day China, Cuba, North Korea and Vietnam was largely inspired by Marxism. Similarly, the rise of right-wing extremist movements such as fascism and Nazism were influenced by the extreme reactionary writings of the romantic conservatives of the Counter-Enlightenment, who opposed and criticized the rationalism of the French Revolution (1789). More recently, the neoliberalism of the Reagan (1981–1989) and George W. Bush (2001–2009) administrations in the U.S., the Thatcher (1979–1990) and Blair (1997–2007) governments in the U.K., the Harper government in Canada and international agencies such as the International Monetary Fund, the World Bank and the World Trade Organization has been justified in terms of the classical political economic theories of Adam Smith, Herbert Spencer and Frederick Von Hayek, among others. Classical social theory has played a vital role in the formation of the major political ideologies of the twentieth and twenty-first centuries — including conservatism, liberalism, socialism, communism, anarchism, fascism, feminism and humanism.

Theories provide us with possible explanations for social events: Medieval Arab scholar Ibn Khaldun believed that all Arab civilizations pass through an inevitable historical cycle that accounts for the rise and fall of these societies. In his view, the decline and fall of these Arab cultures was explained by the gradual erosion of social cohesion (or loss of *asabiyya*), which leads to the breakdown of a society and renders it vulnerable to re-conquest by an external, more vigorous culture. Ibn Khaldun would probably have used this theoretical perspective to explain the current rise and fall of autocratic regimes — both royalist and republican — throughout the Middle East and North Africa.

Other theorists have suggested different explanatory models of how societies work. Marx proposed that the "mode of production" (or how people made their living) determined how other parts of society — including the state, the legal system and even the prevailing sets of political and religious beliefs — functioned. For Durkheim, on the other hand, the glue that held society together was "social solidarity" — much like Ibn Khaldun's *asabiyya* (or social cohesion). Once this social solidarity was weakened by the growth of hyper-individualism (as in our own contemporary culture), the resultant state of "anomie" led to social problems. All theories worth their salt always contain a deep (sometimes concealed) causal mechanism that explains social events.

Theories provide us with ideas for research: Although we may no longer agree with all of the conclusions reached by the classical theorists, we have built upon their ideas. From Marx, we have developed studies of social inequality, ideology, the state, capital accumulation and imperialism. From Durkheim, we have developed studies of religion, social organization, suicide, crime and deviance. From Weber, we have developed studies of comparative religion, industrialization, rationalization, modernization and bureaucratization. The early theorists handed down to us their desire to understand the causes and consequences of major social problems, as well as their commitment to study these problems in a rigorous manner. The classical theorists also showed us that a good theory is one that is (1) formulated as a systematic set of ideas (ideas that are logically related to each other); (2) testable (through the methods of empirical social research); and (3) proposes a causal hypothesis (a causal mechanism responsible for producing particular social phenomena). The best of the classical theorists provided examples — admittedly imperfect — of testable social theories. Each of these theories has helped to lay the foundations for future generations of theorists and researchers. This spirit of learning and discovery has been the greatest gift bestowed upon us by the classical theorists

Theories help us see our own personal problems in a social context: Sociological thinking helps people understand their "private troubles" (for example, the tragedies of a broken marriage, unemployment, financial debt, depression, suicide, workplace injury or substance abuse) as "public issues," with sociological causes that often transcend individual causes. This function of social/ sociological theory was most eloquently expressed by C. Wright Mills in his book *The Sociological Imagination* and was first explored by Durkheim, who argued that the phenomenon of suicide could be understood not as an idiosyncratic act of an individual but as a social trend resulting from the failure of modern societies to provide individuals with any real sense of meaning in their lives. This remains the great promise of sociology: to help people understand how their own personal or community problems are often conditioned by factors in the larger society. People can often use this knowledge to regain control over their lives. This emancipatory project — begun by the classical theorists — lies at the heart of the "sociological imagination."

The chapters in this book show how the voices of past social theorists can still speak to us today — often with surprising urgency. Social theories are mini-languages that have, over the years, introduced bold new ways of speaking about and observing the social world. They have periodically transformed our perceptions of social reality. They have also catalyzed masses of people into political action and have contributed to profound — even revolutionary — social change.

The chapters herein all follow a similar outline. After opening with a contemporary illustration, they unpack the main ideas and "conceptual toolbox" of each theoretical perspective. The section on "settling accounts" traces the influence that other thinkers have had on the particular theorist. Every chapter identifies some of the main criticisms that have been made of each theory before concluding with a brief review of the contemporary relevance of each theorist in the world today.

Notes

1. *Lord of the Flies* is also available as a movie; the best version to watch is the original (black and white) British version directed by Peter Brook in 1963.
2. The full quotation is: "Man (*sic*) is but a reed, the most feeble thing in nature, but he is a thinking reed. The entire universe need not arm itself to crush him. A vapor, a drop of water suffices to kill him. But, if the universe were to crush him, man would still be more noble than that which killed him, because he knows that he dies and the advantage which the universe has over him, the universe knows nothing of this."

References

Beck, Ulrick. 1992. *Risk Society: Towards a New Modernity*. New Delhi: Sage.

Caplan, Pat. 2000. "Introduction: Risk Revisited." In Pat Caplan (ed.), *Risk Revisited*. London: Pluto Press.

Gilligan, Carol. 1993. *In A Different Voice*. Boston: Harvard University Press.

Golding, William. 1972. *Lord of the Flies*. London: Faber & Faber.

Hobbes, Thomas. 1962 [1651]. *Leviathan, or The Matter, Forme and Power of a Common Wealth Ecclesiasticall and Civil*. London: Collier-MacMillan.

Maury, Jean-Pierre. 1992. *Newton: Understanding the Cosmos*. Translated by I. Mark Paris. London: Thames & Hudson.

Mills, C. Wright. 1959. *The Sociological Imagination*. New York: Oxford University Press.

Plato. 1966. "Apology" 38a. *Plato in Twelve Volumes*, Vol. 1. Translated by Harold North Fowler, Introduction by W.R.M. Lamb. Cambridge, MA: Harvard University Press.

Pascal, Blaise. 1995. *Pensees. Harmondsworth, UK:* Penguin.

Said, Edward. 1996. *Representations of the Intellectual*. New York: Vintage.

Chapter 2

The Historical Ecology of Ibn Khaldun

The Eurocentrism of Classical Social Theory

One of the great failings of many texts on classical social theory is their tunnel vision — in particular, their failure to include the contributions made by theorists who were women or non-European. Thus, the classical canon of social theory — at least in North America and Europe — has remained resolutely androcentric and Eurocentric, that is, only "dead white males" have received recognition and acknowledgement as classical social theorists. While this myopic record of our intellectual past reflects the patriarchal and colonial origins of social theory, in some areas, the tunnel vision of earlier generations is being successfully challenged and corrected. The rise of feminism — as Chapter 7 exemplifies — has led to the inclusion of the work of many more women in the annals of classical social theory. But the recognition of those social thinkers who lived beyond the borders of Europe has been slower and is still in its early stages. Although ritual recognition is sometimes extended to the ancient Greeks (Socrates, Plato, Aristotle, Herodotus, Thucydides, Thrasymachus and Heraclitus), to selected early Christian writers (Augustine and Thomas Aquinas) and to the occasional Asian philosopher (Lao Tzu and Confucius), most social theory textbooks have yet to undertake any serious review of non-European social theorists. Ibn Khaldun is one of the few non-Western social thinkers whose

> ### Figure 2-1 Fourteenth-Century Muslim Sage Has Much to Teach Us
>
> Ibn Khaldun (1332–1406) was no less distinguished as a statesman and judge than as a scholar, but it is as the author of a colossal Universal History (Kitab al-'Ibar)... that he is remembered. His family were refugees from the Reconquista, the Christian reconquest of Spain, and Ibn Khaldun served various rulers of North Africa and Granada.
>
> His last adventure was an encounter in Damascus with Tamerlane, the last of the great Mongolian-Tartar conquerors who destroyed so much of the classical Islamic civilisation
>
> Ibn Khaldun is a useful antidote to the... theories that hold sway today. He reminds us that all civilisations decline, with a chilling evocation of the impact of the Black Death: "It was as if the voice of existence in the world had called out for oblivion and restriction, and the world had responded to its call." Yet that devastation in turn brought "a new and repeated creation, a world brought into existence anew." Muslims and non-Muslims alike may take courage from this Sufi sage, who lived in a period of even greater instability than ours.
>
> Daniel Johnson, *Telegraph*, Oct. 26, 2001 <www.telegraph.co.uk/comment/4266452/14th-century-Muslim-sage-has-much-to-teach-us.html>.

original insights into the workings of societies and civilizations have received attention by Western scholars. One of the earliest social theory texts to have recognized the contributions of Ibn Khaldun was by Barnes and Becker (1938). As Alatas (2006: 796) notes, "Becker and Barnes, in their *Social Thought from Lore to Science*, first published in 1938, devote many pages to a discussion of the ideas of Ibn Khaldun, recognizing that he was the first to apply modern-type ideas in historical sociology."

Besides the obvious intellectual and scholarly benefits of tracing the diverse origins of social thought, there are also practical political gains to be had from adopting a more multicultural perspective on the history of social theory. Indeed, at a time when several influential conservative theorists — such as Samuel Huntington (1998) and Bernard Lewis (2003) — have suggested that the West is on a collision course, in a "clash of civilizations," with resurgent Islam across the Middle East, Asia and North Africa, the work of Ibn Khaldun has much to teach us. Although he wrote nearly seven centuries ago, his observations on Arab and Muslim cultures are full of valuable insights that even today may both clarify contemporary Western misunderstandings and misconceptions of these cultures and help us better understand the dynamics of our own societies.

Reconstructing Ibn Khaldun

The current Western view of Arab and Muslim cultures is the product of many centuries of conflict, conquest and colonization. Since the time of the Crusades in the eleventh and twelfth centuries, when Western nations first invaded and occupied the "Holy Land," the historical relations between the West and the Arabs has remained that of the colonizer to the colonized. Arabs and Muslims have for centuries been seen, for the most part, as colonial caricatures, as products of the Western colonial imagination. The term that is often used to describe the oversimplified and largely fictitious Western colonial view of Eastern cultures is "Orientalism." If the critique of this view can be traced to a single event, that event was probably the publication of the book *Orientalism* (1978), by the late Palestinian-American scholar Edward Said. Said's study revealed in a startling way the extent to which Western attitudes towards the East have been constructed from ethnocentric (i.e., Eurocentric) and racist generalizations and stereotypes. Since 9/11, Muslims have often become the "folk devils" of the mass media and popular culture in the West. Ahmed (2002: 23) suggests: "The years of negative press, news of hijacking or hostage taking or honor killings, reinforced by big budget, mainstream Hollywood films like *True Lies*, *Executive Decision* and *The Siege*, had conditioned the public to expect the worst from a civilization widely viewed as "terrorist," "fundamentalist," and "fanatic." Given the current Islamophobia of many in the West, the early

Arab scholar Ibn Khaldun has much to teach us

Unlike most textbooks on the history of social thought, which typically begin with the European Enlightenment, this book argues that one of the earliest general theories of social change — and the rise and fall of societies and dynasties — is found in the work of Ibn Khaldun. Figure 2-2 conveys the essential details of Khaldun's life, which have been compiled from a number of sources, including his auto-biography.

It is obvious from even a cursory review of his biography that Ibn Khaldun led an active, nomadic and adventurous life. He experienced imprisonment for his politics; refuge in a monastery; success as a diplomat for local rulers and sultans; and the challenge of negotiating with the brutal Mongol conqueror, Timur, (or Tamberlane) over the fate of the city of Damascus. Both his parents died from the bubonic plague, and his wife and children were all drowned at sea. That he faced both triumph and disaster with apparent resignation and equanimity is a perspective that one commentator (Anderson, 1983: 271) has labelled "tragic realism." He spent much of his professional life shuttling between North Africa (the Maghreb), Spain (Andalusia)

Figure 2-2 Ibn Khaldun's Biography

1332: Ibn Khaldun, born in Tunis to a family that had migrated from Andalusia in Spain after the Christian Reconquest of Seville.

1349: At the age of 17, Ibn Khaldun lost both his parents to the Black Death, an intercontinental epidemic of the plague that hit Tunis between 1348–1349.

1352: At the age of 20, he began his political career at the Chancellery of the Tunisian ruler Ibn Tafrakin

1357: Ibn Khaldun, then 25 years old, was sentenced to a 22-month prison sentence for engaging in political intrigue, although he was released in 1358. He then decided to move (in Spain).

1364: the Sultan of Granada, the Nasrid Muhammad V, entrusted him with a diplomatic mission to the King of Castile, Pedro the Cruel to endorse a peace treaty. He was later sent back to North Africa.

1368–69: Ibn Khaldun entered a monastery, and occupied himself with scholastic duties.

1375: he was sent by Abu Hammu, the Abdu I Wadid Sultan of Tlemcen, on a mission to the Dawadida Arabs tribes of Biskra.

1378: he returned to his native Tunis

1384: a ship carrying his wife and children sank off the coast of Alexandria.

1401: Ibn Khaldun took part in a military campaign against the Mongol conqueror Timur (Tamerlane), who besieged Damascus. Ibn Khaldun was lowered over the city wall by ropes in order to negotiate with Timur for the safety of Damascus. He subsequently recorded an account of this meeting in his autobiography.

1401–05: Ibn Khaldun spent the following five years in Cairo completing his autobiography and his history of the world. He was also salaried as a teacher and a judge.

1406: Ibn Khaldun dies in Cairo.

Wikipedia

and the Middle East (the Mashreq). Besides being a scholar, judge, translator, teacher and diplomat, he was a practical man of action rather than just a contemplative thinker. Today he would be called a "shuttle diplomat" — a person who travels from country to country trying to resolve disputes and negotiate agreements between nations.

The project of recovering Ibn Khaldun as a seminal figure in the history of social thought is not without its challenges, Perhaps the greatest of these challenges is to resist the temptation to assimilate his ideas into the contemporary discourse of Orientalism — with its Eurocentric biases, its historical fixations, and its colonial representations of the Arab/Muslim "Other." As Hannoum (2003) shows, the French translation of Ibn Khaldun's *History of the Berbers* involved a subtle yet wholesale transformation in the meaning of the original Arabic text. Whereas Khaldun describes how the conquered Berbers were similar in disposition and courage to their Arab conquerors, the French translation of his work exaggerates the cultural and "racial" differences between Berbers and Arabs. In other words, the local knowledge of Ibn Khaldun is replaced — in translation — with the colonial knowledge of the translators. "Such a discourse contradicts the narrative of Ibn Khaldun on the origins of the Berbers, but it does fit nicely with the translated text of de Slane that makes the history of North Africa the history of a struggle between Arabs and Berbers" (Hannoum 2003: 80). Such a reconstruction serves, of course, to justify the French colonial policy of divide and rule, portraying this policy as a "natural" outcome of long term "racial" differences between these two peoples.

In a similar vein, Anderson (1983) warns of the dangers of trying to assimilate Ibn Khaldun's ideas into a contemporary theoretical narrative.

Figure 2-3 Forerunners of Ibn Khaldun

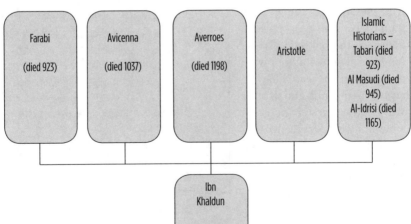

Such recontextualizations invariably take Ibn Khaldun out of his own time and turn him into a solitary figure — unconnected to a past or present — and without any antecedents or contemporaries. Thus, although the eminent historian Arnold Toynbee (1935: 322) paid tribute to the work of Ibn Khaldun by describing his book *The Muqaddimah* as "a philosophy of history which is undoubtedly the greatest work of its kind that has ever yet been created by any mind in any time or place," another commentator (Katsiaficas 1996: 4) notes that "Toynbee fails to comprehend Ibn Khaldun's continuity with Hellenistic and Byzantine philosophy, or with Islamic historians who produced comprehensive world histories." Other interpretations have also placed Ibn Khaldun in an historical vacuum, impervious to the real world in which he actually lived and worked.

The dangers of assimilating Ibn Khaldun can also be seen in the frequent attempts to compare his ideas with those of later social and economic theorists. While there is nothing inherently wrong in making cross-cultural and trans-historical comparisons, it is important not to strip Ibn Khaldun of his historical context in a way that does violence to his ideas and intentions. In Ibn Khaldun we have a man whose scholarly ideas and social theories grew out of his own experiences as a seasoned diplomat and a practical politician — as well as a judge, teacher and translator. And although his work contains occasional sacred references to Allah, most of his writing refers to secular events and historical processes. He was one of the earliest scholars to consciously strive for impartiality in his accounts of different societies and civilizations even though, as Ahmed (2002: 25) emphasizes, Ibn Khaldun was a believer and his work contains a strong moral imperative (see also White, 2009). Besides seeing himself as an historian and chronicler of past events, he also considered himself what we would call a social scientist; he sought to uncover the underlying causes that drove the mechanisms of human history. While he drew upon the best of Islamic historical scholarship, he remains unique in providing a comprehensive and analytical history of his own and other cultures and civilizations.

At a time when the religion of Islam is the centre of so much controversy, the rediscovery of Ibn Khaldun is significant, above all, because he reacquaints us with the rich traditions of Islamic humanism and scholarship Like many other scholars of his generation, Ibn Khaldun was a cosmopolitan thinker who travelled extensively throughout the continental Islamic caliphate of the fourteenth century. His autobiography reveals that Islamic scholars were often at the leading edge of scientific discovery and humanistic knowledge in such areas as mathematics, astronomy, medicine, geography, chemistry, architecture, history, language and poetry, as well as in studies of the Qur'anic scriptures. Other writers have also acknowledged the extent to which the Muslim Arab cultures of the first millennium enriched our knowledge of the sciences and the humanities — as well as of trade, commerce and manufacturing (Maalouf, 1984: 264). In these respects, Islam offered enlightenment to many of the traditional cultures of the Middle East and North Africa. It was an inspiration for the growth of knowledge and social justice and often combated local superstition and prejudice.

From History to Historiography

One of the great achievements of Ibn Khaldun was his transformation of "history" into "historiography" — that is, a transformation from the naive study of the past into the critical study of how the past is chronicled. By introducing critical distance between the past and the methods used to study it, Ibn Khaldun hoped to improve the reliability of historical accounts and to draw attention to the methodological weaknesses of many standard histories of his own time. He was, therefore, an innovator in the attention he gave to historiographic methods of research and scholarship. In the foreword to his *Muqaddima,* which was itself a "prolegomenon" (introduction) to his monumental work *The Kitābu l-ibār (Book of Evidence, Record of Beginnings and Events from the Days of the Arabs, Persians and Berbers and their Powerful Contemporaries,* usually abbreviated to *l-ibār),* Ibn Khaldun makes clear his intention to move beyond a simple chronology of past events to a deeper understanding of history. He suggests that to fully appreciate the past, it is necessary to probe beneath the level of surface appearances (*zahir*) in order to explore the underlying causes and origins (*batin*) of these events (Alatas, 2006: 784). He also insists that any responsible study of history has to critically examine the methods of study used to document historical "facts." For Ibn Khaldun, as for many later writers, "facts" do not speak for themselves; they are always products (or artefacts) of particular ways of observing, speaking and theorizing about past events. "The inner meaning of history, on the other hand, involves speculation and an attempt to get at the truth, subtle explanation of the causes and origins of existing things, and deep knowledge of the how and why of events. History, therefore, is firmly rooted in philosophy. It deserves to be accounted a branch in it" (Ibn Khaldun, cited in Abdo, 1996: 37).

Besides reflecting on some of the theoretical presuppositions and scholarly methods typically used to research and document past events, Ibn Khaldun also identified what we would today call the "sources of bias" that invariably contaminated the work of historians of his own day. In Book 1 of *The Kitābu l-ibār,* Ibn Khaldun lists at least seven sources of bias, which, he concludes, can introduce significant error (or "untruth") into "historical information."

Figure 2-4 Ibn Khaldun's Historiography

Sources of Bias	Description
Partisanship	Historians' own prejudices and predispositions in favour of, or against, a cause may incline them to accept or reject information without sufficient critical examination.
Unreliability of Sources	Historians often fail to scrutinize the reliability of informants (or "transmitters") whose accounts provide the basis of historical information.
No Subjective Meaning	Historians often accept at face value, eye witness accounts of events from an observer who may not have fully understood the subjective meaning of these events from the perspective of those who participated in them.
No Independent Verification	Historians need to independently verify or confirm all accounts provided by single informants, as these accounts may prove to be unreliable without corroboration.
Appearance versus Reality	Historians need to acquaint themselves with the basic laws of nature in order to competently judge whether or not an informant's account is realistic and credible.
Power and Privilege	Historians and informants seeking to please or ingratiate themselves with the powerful and the privileged may collect information which favours social elites or political leaders.
Ignorance of Natural Causes	Historians need to discover the underlying (necessary and sufficient) causes of the event.

Ibn Khaldun was one of the earliest historians to recognize that "history" is never a simple empirical record of past events. He understood that history is always a product of (often unacknowledged) methods of study, societal conventions and human nature. The goal of his studies was to introduce a discipline of historical and social scholarship that would be more transparent, accountable and reflexive than any that had preceded it. He strove, above all, for greater impartiality, objectivity and universality in his pursuit of knowledge than had any previous scholar. This was the moral and methodological mission behind his conception of socio-historical knowledge, or what he termed *Ilm Al 'Umran (The New Science)*. With a sensibility ahead of his time, Ibn Khaldun expressed skepticism that any historian could ever acquire a complete or absolute knowledge of historical events or societal processes. He expressed this in the language of his day: "God is the ultimate repository of all knowledge. Man is weak and deficient. Admission [of one's ignorance] is a specific religious duty." (Ibn Khaldun (2005) *The Muqaddimah*, Ch. 2: Sec. 30).

The Historical Ecology of Human Societies

Since Western sociologists and anthropologists first discovered Ibn Khaldun, they have sought in different ways to assimilate his ideas into their respective disciplines. For some (Katsiaficas, 1996), he was a very early pre-Marxist philosopher; whereas for others (Honigmann, 1976), he was a kind of cultural anthropologist. Some (Anderson, 1983) saw him as a "tragic realist," and others have even claimed him as an early forerunner of the liberal economist Adam Smith (Karatas, 2004). For our purposes, the most characteristic aspect of Ibn Khaldun's theories of history and society is his conviction that the life cycle of all living things — which encompasses the stages of birth, growth, maturation, decay and death — applies equally to the history of human societies and civilizations. It is clear from his writings that Ibn Khaldun recognized that the process of social and historical change was driven not simply by internal factors inherent in the human condition, but also by external factors — of climate, environment, weather and other extra-social conditions which help to shape the course of human history. Unlike later European theorists — from the Enlightenment onwards — who began to separate the rational from the sensual, the individual from the social, the cognitive from the affective and the human from the animal nature of "Man," Ibn Khaldun retained an holistic and symbiotic perspective on human society and insisted that nations and cultures should always be studied in the context of their natural environment. This ecological perspective is evident throughout Ibn Khaldun's studies of nations, cultures and civilizations and from his cyclical theories of social organization and state formation. The ecological approach to the study of human society is most apparent in the persistent analogy of the organic life cycle, which frequently reappears in the *Muqaddima* and in other writings. For this reason, labelling Ibn Khaldun's social theory as the "historical ecology of human society" seems appropriate.

> The world of the elements and all it contains comes into being and decays. Minerals, plants, all the animals including man, and other created things come into being and decay, as one can see with one's own eyes. The same applies to the conditions that affect created things, and especially the conditions that affect man. Sciences grow up and then are wiped out. The same applies to crafts and to similar things. (Ibn Khaldun (2005) *The Muqaddimah*, Ch. 2: Sec. 14)

Ibn Khaldun understood the course of human history in much the same way he understood the life cycle of living species. Human societies begin as simple decentralized families, clans and tribes, often living in nomadic conditions far from permanent settlements. Over time, these peoples migrate to centres of greater population density, where they become urbanized, settled and sedentary. Eventually, these towns and cities grow larger and more complex, and begin to form stable and long-term civilizations with cultural inheritances transmitted from one generation to the next. But within these mature civilizations lie the seeds of their own destruction. As civilizations reach a final stage of decay, they become ripe for overthrow by more "primitive," virile and robust cultures — driven from the harsh nomadic life of the wilderness and drawn to the relative comfort and security of urban life. And thus the cycle of social life begins anew.

While he may not have been the first, Ibn Khaldun remains the best known of the pre-modern scholars to have expounded a cyclical theory of history and social change. For Ibn Khaldun, the cycle of historical change was a natural process, inherent in the nature of all living things. In this respect, he paved the way for later historians and philosophers — Giambattista Vico, Edward Gibbon, Oswald Spengler, Vilfredo Pareto and Arnold Toynbee, among others — to recount the rise and fall of countless cultures and civilizations. At the same time, notwithstanding the universal implications of his social thought, the primary focus of Ibn Khaldun's historical studies was on the peoples of the Maghreb (North Africa) and neighbouring regions. In outlining his cyclical theory of social change, Ibn Khaldun distinguished three different stages in the development of Arab society. The first stage was nomadism (*badawa*) — best exemplified in the desert peoples of North Africa and the Middle East: the Bedouin. The next stage was permanent settlement in towns and cities: urbanism (*tamaddun*). The final stage was marked by the rise of civilizations (*hadara*) — stable and sophisticated cultures transmitted from one generation to the next. Some commentators (Dhaouadi, 1990: 323) have remarked that this passage from nomadism though urbanism to civilization reflects a strong evolutionist theme in the social thought of Ibn Khaldun.

Many later social thinkers identified underlying mechanisms that they believed drove the course of human history. For Karl Marx, it was the

Figure 2-5 Ibn Khaldun's Typology of Social Organization

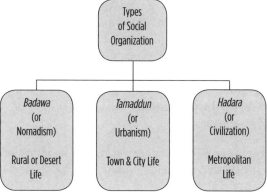

mode of production; for Max Weber, it was the historical drive towards greater "rationalization" and modernization. For Ibn Khaldun, the driving force of human history was that sense of social cohesiveness, or solidarity, which binds social groups together: strong among kinship and tribal groups but gradually weakened among larger, more complex and more sedentary groups. According to Ibn Khaldun, the strongest social bonds were to be found among those primitive — often nomadic — peoples whose tribes and nations were bound together by blood relations and common descent. With the migration of these elementary groups into centres of permanent settlement, however, the cohesion that once unified and integrated these groups is progressively weakened. By the time these sedentary groups morph into larger and more complex civilizations, their original spirit of cohesion and solidarity is, in all likelihood, lost forever. Once a civilization loses its internal cohesion, it becomes vulnerable to corruption, degeneration and destruction — and ripe for overthrow.

The term Ibn Khaldun uses to describe the social cohesion he believes is the source of group energy and solidarity is *asabiyya*. He perhaps even romanticizes this quality as the essence of a vigorous, virile and robust culture. The attributes of *asabiyya* represent the traditional virtues of hardiness, self-reliance and independence, as well as a puritanical capacity for hard work and asceticism. *Asabiyya* is the power that unites and integrates nomadic groups in their hostile and often unforgiving wilderness environments. When these groups migrate into urban settlements and adjust to a more sedentary lifestyle, their *asabiyya* may begin to weaken, or it may be sustained in different ways "The things that go with luxury and submergence in a life of ease break the vigor of the *asabiyya* which alone produces superiority." (Ibn Khaldun (2005) *The Muqaddimah* 1, 286–87; 1, 296–97; 1, 317; I, 344; 2, 118–19). For Ibn Khaldun, the preservation of *asabiyya* is essential for the growth of a royal dynasty (a *mulk*) and for the consolidation of a strong pattern of centralized and stable government. The loss of *asabiyya* always spells the decline and fall of a civilization and its replacement by a more robust culture.

From his historical studies of the Maghreb (North Africa) and the Mashreq (the Middle East), Ibn Khaldun concluded that most dynasties had a life expectancy of four generations, after which time they lost their *asabiyya* and, thereby, their power to rule. Narratives of the rise and fall of dynasties were not unknown among ancient thinkers. A thousand years earlier, Plato also speculated on the decline of states in the *Republic*. In his own writings, Ibn Khaldun refers to this prediction of the life expectancy of Arab dynasties as "the rule of four generations."

> The rule of four [generations] with respect to prestige usually holds true. It may happen that a "house" is wiped out, disappears, and

collapses in fewer than four, or it may continue unto the fifth and sixth generations, though in a state of decline and decay. The four generations can be defined as the builder, the one who has personal contact with the builder, the one who relies on tradition and the destroyer. (Ibn Khaldun (1958) *The Muqaddimah*, Ch. 2: Sec.14)

Interestingly, Khaldun identified what we might call (and what Emile Durkheim — see Chapter 10 — called), "excessive individualism" as the greatest threat and the most likely destroyer of social solidarity (Katsiaficas, 1996: 15). One example of a nation in which individualism predominated over group feeling, or *asabiyya*, according to Ibn Khaldun, was the Arabs. He provides a harsh description of a nomadic people he believed was lacking in social solidarity and collective consciousness: "Because of their savagery, the Arabs are the least willing of nations to subordinate themselves to each other, as they are rude, proud, ambitious, and eager to be the leader. Their individual aspirations rarely coincide. But when there is religion among them, through prophecy or sainthood, then they have some restraining influence in themselves" (Ibn Khaldun, 1986: 1: 305).

A final example of Ibn Khaldun's ecological approach to history and society may, perhaps, be seen in his concept of "invasion economy" (Dhaouadi, 1990: 328). Just as one species may invade and succeed the environmental niche of another, so a nation or culture may also invade and displace another. This analogical reference to the invasion and succession of populations within a given territory is another indication of how Ibn Khaldun's thinking emphasized the holistic and environmental dimensions of inter-cultural and inter-civilizational contact, conflict and eventual accommodation.

The Bedouin Code

Like some philosophers before him, and many after, Ibn Khaldun was inclined to glorify and romanticize "primitive" peoples — those "noble savages" who dwelt in the wilderness and who represented the pristine qualities of hardiness, self-reliance and independence. For Ibn Khaldun, the nomadic Bedouin best exemplified the virtue of *asabiyya*. Unlike the soft and sedentary town and city folk, who had lost their instinct for survival and self-preservation, the Bedouin still represented the primal values of a vigorous and robust culture. Their nomadic bands were bound together by consanguinal ties of family and by social ties of loyalty and hospitality. The harsh desert environment only served to reinforce these ties of kinship and tribal solidarity. "The respect for blood ties leads to affection for one's relations and blood relatives, the feeling that no harm ought to befall them nor any destruction come upon them" (Ibn Khaldun (2005) *The Muqaddimah*, Ch. I, p. 264).

While Ibn Khaldun is far from uncritical of Bedouin culture, he clearly

Figure 2-6 The Bedouins According to Ibn Khaldun

5. Bedouins are more disposed to courage than sedentary people.
The... reason for this is that sedentary people have become used to laziness and ease. They are sunk in well-being and luxury. They have entrusted defense of their property and their lives to the governor and ruler who rules them, and to the militia which has the task of guarding them. They find full assurance of safety in the walls that surround them, and the fortifications that protect them. No noise disturbs them, and no hunting occupies them. They are carefree and trusting, and have ceased to carry weapons. Successive generations have grown up in this way of life. They have become like women and children, who depend upon the master of the house. Eventually, this has come to be a quality of character that replaces natural (disposition).

The Bedouins, on the other hand, live separate from the community. They are alone in the country and remote from militias. They have no walls and gates. Therefore, they provide their own defense and do not entrust it to, or rely upon others for it. They always carry weapons. They watch carefully all sides of the road. They take hurried naps only when they are together in company or when they are in the saddle. They pay attention to every faint barking and noise. They go alone into the desert, guided by their fortitude, putting their trust in themselves. Fortitude has become a character quality of theirs, and courage their nature ... This is an observed fact ... "God creates whatever He wishes."

Ibn Khaldun (2005) *The Muqaddimah* Ch. 2: Sec. 5

admired their strong sense of common identity and their deep allegiance to norms and values. Like many other warrior cultures, the Bedouin emphasized the virtues of courage and fortitude and derided cowardice and weakness as vices. All were expected to uphold the values of honour, loyalty and hospitality, and any perceived dishonour or shame was met with swift revenge or protracted feud. As Ibn Khaldun noted, these primal values stood in sharp contrast to the compromised and corrupted morals of the urban populations.

While Ibn Khaldun lauded the noble qualities of the Bedouin, he also insisted that the moral structure of their society and culture could only be upheld and maintained through the beneficent influence of religion — that is, of Islam. He believed that, without the strong moral precepts and practices of Islam, the nomadic and decentralized cultures — or what, as a medieval writer, he referred to as the "barbarians" — would rapidly degenerate into anarchy and chaos.

Today, the closest approximation to the Bedouin code is still to be found among the Pashtun tribes in the border areas of Afghanistan and Pakistan. The Pashtun have long upheld a set of ethical beliefs and traditional practices commonly known as *pashtunwali*. Like the Bedouin code, the precepts and practices of *pashtunwali* place strong emphasis on the importance of hospitality for all guests (even enemies); revenge for perceived injustices or dishonour; and protection of land and property (including women); as well as on the martial virtues of strength, courage, fortitude, independence and self-reliance. In Afghanistan, the Pashtun have formed the backbone of resistance to the U.S./NATO 2003 invasion and occupation, much as they had resisted the Soviet invasion during the 1980s and the British invasions of the nineteenth century. Respect for the traditions of *pashtunwali* obliged the Afghan Pashtun to guarantee protection and security to Osama Bin Laden after 9/11 and to resist U.S. demands for his immediate capture and surrender. Indeed, so strong is the norm of hospitality that the Pashtun have on occasion offered protection and medical care to wounded U.S. service people, even though they had been fought as the enemy (see Luttrell and Robinson, 2007). The laws of revenge also begin to explain the fierceness of the Taliban resistance to the Western invasion of Afghanistan and the persistence of suicide attacks and other forms of retaliation against the "Crusader nations" (see Ahmed, 2002: 38).

The traditional moral codes of desert peoples such as the Bedouin, and mountain peoples such as the Pashtun, may appear harsh and inhumane to Western eyes. Although they prize the values of generosity and hospitality, the Pahstun (and Bedouin) codes also prescribe harsh punishments for those who offend or transgress these codes. Thus, women could be stoned to death for adultery; "honour killings" could be carried out against "disgraced" women; men could lose their limbs for theft or deceit; apostates and heretics could be beheaded; and family conflicts could escalate into long-standing blood feuds. Tribal codes of justice are often harsh and unforgiving, and implacably patriarchal in their beliefs and practices.

For Ibn Khaldun, the desert culture of the Bedouin represented the strongest and purest expression of *asabiyya* — the powerful sense of group identity and social cohesion that enabled a vigorous people to conquer and dominate more sedentary and less robust cultures. However, once a strong nomadic or tribal people — such as the Bedouin — migrated into the towns and cities, the strength and power of their *asabiyya* would often weaken and dissipate. While Ibn Khaldun acknowledged that new expressions of *asabiyya* could emerge in urban environments — especially under the influence of charismatic leaders (see Gierer, 2001: 4; Stowasser, 2011) — he remained convinced that most established civilizations lose their *asabiyya* and ultimately succumb to corruption and cultural decay. At the same time, as Katsiaficas (1996: 15) notes, Ibn Khaldun harboured few illusions about the impact of the Bedouin Arabs upon those cultures and civilizations they came to dominate. While he may have praised their desert toughness and resilience, he was unsparing in his criticisms of their poor administrative and political abilities.

Besides the similarities already mentioned between Ibn Khaldun's cyclical theory of history and those of writers such as Vico, Gibbon, Spengler, Pareto and Toynbee, other parallels between Ibn Khaldun and later Western thinkers have been noted (Alatas, 2006: 788; Ahmed, 2002: 25; Stowasser, 2011). In some cases, theorists have readily acknowledged his influence on their

Figure 2-7 European Echoes of Ibn Khaldun's Ideas

Ibn Khaldun	Henry Maine	Emile Durkheim	Ferdinand Toennnies	Charles Horton Cooley	Robert Redfield	Daniel Lerner	Howard Becker
Badawa or Nomadism	Status	Mechanical Solidarity	Gemeinschaft	Primary Group	Folk	Traditional	Sacred
Tamaddun or Urbanism	Contract	Organic Solidarity	Gesellschaft	Secondary Group	Urban	Modern	Secular

ideas, but in most cases, the parallels have only been detected in retrospect. However, the sheer number of these European echoes of his ideas indicates that — in his own way and time — Ibn Khaldun had stumbled upon some of the enduring themes in the history of social thought and some of the timeless aspects of the universal human condition.

Ibn Khaldun's Conceptual Toolbox

Science of Society (Ilm al `umran)

Although *The History of the Berbers* (Kitab al-'Ibar) was Ibn Khaldun's histori-cal masterpiece, many commentators agree that *The Muqaddima* remains his most significant sociological work. This work, which was really an introduc-tion to the historian's craft, shows that Ibn Khaldun was one of the earliest recorded thinkers to discuss the methods used by historians in their chronicles of past events. Indeed, Ibn Khaldun was one of the first writers to question the objectivity, logical coherence and accuracy of many previous historical accounts and the first to emphasize the need for proper verification of all sources of historical information. He was also one of the first to introduce explicitly theoretical and analytical ideas into his historiographic narratives. In this respect, he was as much an epistemologist as he was an historian. One biographer (Y. Lacoste, 1966: 187) remarked: "If Thucydides is the inventor of history, Ibn Khaldun introduces history as a science."

Alone amongst the scholars of his day, Ibn Khaldun questioned the veracity of many historical studies and also rejected the purely speculative thinking of much Islamic philosophy. He was, for all intents and purposes, the progenitor of a new empirical and universal science of society — a seminal figure in the evolution of modern sociology. In these respects, Ibn Khaldun prefigured the later works of the French sociologists Henri de Saint-Simon and Auguste Comte. Their program for a "positive philosophy" also rejected traditional speculative philosophy in favour of universal and empirical sci-ence of society (sociology) in which all ideas would be subject to the tests of reason and experience.

Figure 2-8 Ibn Khaldun's Conceptual Toolbox

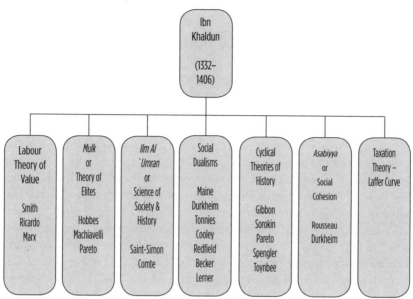

Social Cohesion (*Asabiyya*)

One of the most important ideas to appear in Ibn Khaldun's work is *asabiyya*, or social cohesion. This concept provided Ibn Khaldun with a thematic idea that he effectively used to bring theoretical coherence to his historical studies. Throughout much of his scholarly career, Ibn Khaldun remained preoccupied with the causes of the decline of civilizations. His work may be read as an exploration into the rise and fall of — mostly Arab Muslim — civilizations and a theoretical explanation for this cycle of events. He sensed the approaching end of his own civilization, and although he was unable to avert this coming catastrophe, he struggled to comprehend and explain it. The concept of *asabiyya* provides a key to Ibn Khaldun's theory of historical change. For while the strongest and purest expressions of *asabiyya* are to be found in the "primitive" tribes of the desert, and other wilderness regions, the eventual weakening and loss of *asabiyya* in urban populations is, according to Ibn Khaldun, a major cause of the decline and fall of civilizations.

It is not hard to find some striking parallels to the idea of *asabiyya* in later social thought. Indeed, it resembles the notion of *volunte generale* (or "general will") in the writings of Jean-Jacques Rousseau and also the concept of *consensus universalis*, introduced by Auguste Comte. But by far and away the strongest European parallel is the concept of "mechanical solidarity," introduced by French sociologist Emile Durkheim.

As we shall see more clearly in a later chapter, Durkheim also concluded that traditional societies were bound together by powerful collective sentiments and strict moral codes. The mechanical solidarity of a traditional society was reinforced through a powerful set of collective beliefs and practices (*conscience collective*) and a simple division of labour. The harsh codes of morality and justice often practised in these societies was described by Durkheim as "repressive law" — based more on the desire for vengeance and retribution against the offender than on restitution for the victim. Much like Ibn Khaldun, Durkheim believed that this strong sense of mechanical solidarity is eventually weakened when rural or tribal populations migrate to towns and cities. Although he conceded that a new form of social solidarity — "organic solidarity" — could emerge in urban settings, he shared with Ibn Khaldun the belief that the excessive individualism of city life could lead to the collapse of social solidarity and to the rise of abnormal or pathological forms of behaviour. This striking resemblance between the ideas of Durkheim and Ibn Khaldun is probably more than accidental. Hannoum (2003: 67) states in a revealing footnote (#29): "In addition to the fact that the work of Ibn Khaldun was available by mid-nineteenth century, Durkheim also had an Egyptian doctoral candidate, Taha Hussein, working on the Muqaddima."

Social Dualisms

Another aspect of Ibn Khaldun's work that is often compared to the writings of later European social thinkers is his sharp distinction between the nomadic cultures (*badawa*) of the Bedouin, and the urban (*tamaddun*) and civilized (*hadara*) cultures of town and city dwellers. This stark dichotomy between nomadism and urbanism is central to Ibn Khaldun's theory of historical change, and, as Dhaouadi (1990: 329) suggests, it can also be compared to other famous dualisms in the history of social thought. For Ibn Khaldun, the difference between nomadism and urbanism was more than a simple academic distinction. He was aware of the growing signs of cultural decay that presaged the impending decline of his own Arab Muslim civilization. For him, the contrast between nomadism and urbanism was deeply personal; these were not neutral sociological categories.

> On the emotional level the author of Al'Ibar had more sympathy with the Bedouin life-style. He saw the Bedouin as good by nature as well as moderate in his materialistic orientation. These Bedouin traits are similar to those of the Islamic religion…. With this background in mind, one could also explain Ibn Khaldun's well-known unfavorable attitude toward the sedentaries. He found that the sedentary over-materialistic environment corrupts human nature's goodness and consequently, undermines the basis of Islamic values. Dhaouadi, 1990: 331)

For European theorists of the nineteenth and twentieth centuries, the dichotomies between rural and urban, sacred and secular, community and society — among many other dualisms — represented the decline of traditionalism and the birth of modernity. As we shall see in later chapters, these dualisms were all expressions of what some of these commentators termed the "transition crisis" of European societies: the rapid shift from traditional to modern lifestyles. Many later theorists also speculated on the social and moral consequences of urbanization and constructed their own theoretical interpretations of these historical changes. But Ibn Khaldun was one of the earliest thinkers to relate these demographic shifts to the rise and fall of civilizations.

Royal Dynasties (*Mulk*)

Although many of Ibn Khaldun's ideas may appear relevant to the study of modern societies, his intention was to produce a universal history of the Arab Muslim civilizations of his own time. Indeed, his historical theory of the rise and fall of Arab civilizations remains unrivalled even to this day in the scope of its ambition and the breadth of its coverage. Dhaouadi (1990: 332) remarks: "No contemporary Arab social scientist has yet developed an articulate social theory of contemporary Arab society comparable to that of Ibn Khaldun of Arab society before and during his own time." The historically specific nature of his work is most apparent in his theory of *mulk*, or royal dynasties. According to Ibn Khaldun, the rise of a royal dynasty often coincided with the conquest of a decadent and decaying culture by a more vigorous one. But in order to produce a durable and lasting dynasty, the rulers of any society needed to create a government that integrated and regulated the population in a way that only a renewed *asabiyya* could achieve — through the power of religion (Islam). Even then, as we have already noted, Ibn Khaldun predicted that any royal dynasty would likely exhaust its *asabiyya* within four generations, if not earlier, whereupon it would become vulnerable to eventual overthrow by a new resurgent outsider culture.

Ibn Khaldun's preoccupation with the role of royal authority in establishing social order has prompted some comparisons with the ideas of social thinkers such as Thomas Hobbes and Nicolai Machiavelli (Stowasser, 2011). According to Katsiaficas (1996: 6), it is likely that Machiavelli knew of Ibn Khaldun's work, as well as that of other European thinkers. There are several passages in the works of Ibn Khaldun that seem to foreshadow later pages from Hobbes' *Leviathan*. Consider the following:

> By dint of their nature, human beings need someone to act as a restraining influence and mediator in every social organization, in order to keep its members from (fighting) with each other. That person must, by necessity, have superiority over the others in the

matter of group feeling… Such superiority is royal authority… Royal authority means superiority and the power to rule by force. (Kitab Al-'Ibar, Book 1; Ch. 2: 16, cited in Abdo, 1996: 88)

However, as Gierer (2001: 5) points out, according to Ibn Khaldun, force alone is no guarantee of authority. In order to secure a stable leadership and durable dynasty, an effective ruler must also display the qualities of wisdom, beneficence and empathy

The Economics of Ibn Khaldun

Like many great scholastic works of the ancient and medieval worlds, Ibn Khaldun's ideas traverse a number of modern academic disciplines. He was not simply an historian but also a philosopher, sociologist and economist, as well as something of a theologian and interpreter of the Qur'an. But it is only in recent years that his economic ideas have attracted serious attention. As is often the case, many writers, including myself, compare Ibn Khaldun's ideas with those of more recent social thinkers.

Historical Materialism

Some commentators represent Ibn Khaldun as an early historical materialist —a pioneer of the tradition later immortalized by Karl Marx and Friedrich Engels. Although there is no definite evidence to show that Marx was acquainted with Ibn Khaldun's ideas, several writers suggest that both Marx and Engels may have seen the French translation of *The Muqaddimah* (Katsiaficas, 1996: 6; Alatas, 2006: 786). In any event, there are superficial similarities between Marx's historical materialism and the economics of Ibn Khaldun. Unlike his contemporaries — but like Marx and Engels — Ibn Khaldun explained the general social and economic condition of different peoples in relation to how they produced their livelihood rather than in terms of any inherent "racial," "national" or "mental" qualities. And even though there are some decidedly racist passages in his writings (see, for example, his disparaging comments on "Negroes" — Abdo, 1996: 98; Katsiaficas, 1996: 16), Ibn Khaldun primarily sought to explain cultural and behavioural differences between peoples in terms of their material conditions of existence. "It should be known that the differences of condition among people are the result of the different ways in which they make their living. Social organization enables them to cooperate toward that end and to start with the simple necessities of life, before they get to conveniences and luxuries" (Ibn Khaldun (2005) *The Muqaddima*, Ch. 2: Sec. 1)

Value of Labour

Some enthusiasts have gone even further, suggesting that Ibn Khaldun be credited with an early exposition of the "labour theory of value," which was later associated not only with Marx, but also with Adam Smith, David Ricardo and other classical political economists of the eighteenth and nineteenth centuries (Cosma, 2009: 53). In strictly economic terms, the classical labour theory of value states: "The value of any commodity is equal to the amount of [socially necessary, or average] labour time used to produce it" (Marx, 1967: 39). In other words, everything that is bought or sold acquires its value — as opposed to its price — from the amount of human labour required to produce it. According to this theory, the value of all products comes from the labour of those who produce them. Marx and Engels later extended this thesis into their own original "theory of surplus value," whereby the accumulation of capital and the creation of profit is only made possible through the "exploitation" of the working class. This controversial idea gave birth to Marxism as an economic doctrine and to revolutionary socialism as a global political movement. The rest, as they say, is history.

However, according to Karatas (2004), although Ibn Khaldun subscribed to an early version of the labour theory of value, he did not intend it to be a critical or revolutionary doctrine. Unlike the socialists who came four centuries later, Ibn Khaldun also acknowledged the "labour" of entrepreneurs, merchants and traders, and recognized that the law of supply and demand could always trump the law of value. "Ibn Khaldun... clearly indicated that 'the profit human beings make is the value realized from their labour.' However, Ibn Khaldun considered not only the activities of the workers, but of the entrepreneurs to be productive as well.... Ibn Khaldun considers both workers and the entrepreneurs as respected members of the society who try to maximize the return for their activities in the form of wages and profits" (2004: 5–6).

Thus, while acknowledging that all value derives from labour, Ibn Khaldun insisted that the labour of the entrepreneur, along with that of the merchant and the trader, were equally important elements in the process of production. For him, the successful economy — much like the successful polity or royal authority — rested on the principles of *asabiyya* — a generic ideology which emphasized the importance of cooperation and coordination of individuals in all aspects of social life, including the economy. In the hands of modern, neoliberal economists, therefore, it is hardly surprising that Ibn Khaldun begins to sound like a neoliberal.

Economy and the State

If it is true that every age reinvents its past, then the Ibn Khaldun of today carries the heavy imprint of our present passions and preoccupations. Under the influence of neoliberalism, which has infiltrated into the hegemony of many Western governments and most global financial institutions, any re-discovery of Ibn Khaldun is bound to be affected by this ideological climate. This is not to say that contemporary interpretations of his ideas are deliberate distortions. However, any review of his social or economic thought will always be influenced by the prevailing academic biases and popular sentiments.

Today, Ibn Khaldun's economic theories and policies strike a responsive chord in many nations of the global economy, and nowhere more so than in the Arab economies of the Maghreb and Middle East. Many of Ibn Khaldun's observations on economic policy seem particularly relevant to the post–Cold War economic climate of the second millennium. He was, among other things, opposed to government (i.e., royal) intervention into the private sector. He believed that trade, commerce and manufacturing were best left to the merchants, artisans and craftspeople, as they had the knowledge and experience to run these enterprises most efficiently. He was similarly opposed to attempts by the royal authority to regulate prices or to interfere in other way with the free play of market forces. He believed that the natural operation of the law of supply and demand would best ensure the satisfaction of basic human needs. And although the struggle of merchants and traders against royal absolutism in the fourteenth-century Islamic world was very different from ideological conflicts of the modern world, several recent commentators (Karatas, 2004; Cosma, 2009) claim Ibn Khaldun as a distant forerunner of classical economic theory.

At the same time, Ibn Khaldun did not entirely discount government in administering the economic affairs of the nation. It was, he felt, the re-sponsibility of the state through its stabilization policies to increase output and employment, to protect property rights, to establish a stable monetary policy and to protect trade routes by ensuring peaceful relations with trading partners. His advocacy for the role of government in stabilizing the economy, especially in raising what we would today call "consumer demand and in-vestor confidence," has led some commentators to embrace Ibn Khaldun as a precursor of John Maynard Keynes and neoclassical economics. "The concept of the role of the government in stabilization policy to generate excess demand was formulated by Ibn Khaldun five centuries before Keynes got the attention of the whole world on stressing the importance of excess demand to increase output and create public works and confidence in order to increase employment" (Karatas, 2004: 3).

Ibn Khaldun's most important observation on the economy related to taxation policy. He was among the very first of the early social thinkers to warn against the over-taxation of populations. Indeed, he predicted that although heavy taxation may at first generate huge revenues for the royal coffers, these revenues will soon decline over time. The long-term results of over-taxation will be to stultify trade, commerce and manufacturing and to depress consumer demand and investor confidence — resulting in a lower tax base. In other words, Ibn Khaldun predicted centuries ago that over-taxation would precipitate a cycle of economic recession. His recipe for a healthy economy was to restrain government spending, especially in the areas of military and bureaucratic expenditures, and to keep taxes as low as possible. He suggested that, by stimulating the economy in these ways, a government was more likely to increase its tax revenues over time. This formula for allowing low levels of taxation to stimulate consumer demand and investor confidence — thereby leading to higher tax revenues — is known in modern economic parlance as the Laffer Curve. On this platform, Ibn Khaldun could run as a conservative politician in many Western nations today. Looking back on his economic observations and opinions, we now recognize Ibn Khaldun as one of the most original thinkers of the ancient world. In his own way, he anticipated many of the ideas of later economists: "What is clear is that Ibn Khaldun had 'discovered a great number of fundamental economic notions a few centuries before their official births. He discovered the virtues and the necessity of a division of labor before Smith and the principle of labor value before Ricardo' and the role of government in stabilization policy before Keynes" (Karatas, 2004: 10, citing Boulakia, 1971).

Ibn Khaldun's views on the economy mirror his views on the polity and on society in general. While he emphasized the need for stable royal dynasties to ensure peace, order and cohesion in the Arab nations of his time, he also insisted that these dynasties rule with benevolence and justice. He opposed despotic and tyrannical regimes not only because they oppressed religious and civic freedoms but also because they suffocated economic enterprise. All such regimes were, he concluded, destined for decay and destruction. His call for moderation in taxation echoed his call for moderation in religious and civic affairs. He was, after all, an advocate of *asabiyya* in the matter of governance and public policy. In the final analysis, he was not simply a social scientist, but an Islamic humanist, driven by a passion for justice and universalism.

Lessons from Ibn Khaldun

The recent rediscovery of Ibn Khaldun comes at a critical time in relations between the West and the Islamic world. In many ways, the historical mistrust that has existed between these cultures since the Crusades has been exacerbated by recent events. The founding of the State of Israel (1949) and the subsequent partition and occupation of much of Palestine; the anti-colonial wars of independence fought in Algeria and other nations of the Maghreb;

the Suez crisis (1956); the Israeli-Arab wars and conflicts throughout the mid-twentieth century; and the Iranian Revolution (1979) all contributed to a climate of suspicion and mistrust. And then came 9/11. Since then, there has been a rising tide of anti-Arab sentiment and Islamophobia in the West. The aftermath of 9/11, as we know, led to wars in Afghanistan and Iraq, and to the destabilization of Pakistan, Somalia, Yemen and other nations. Since 2010, the Arab Spring has been followed by counter-revolution and repression in many Middle Eastern states and the NATO (2011) military intervention in Libya. What does Ibn Khaldun have to teach us about relations between Arab and Western civilizations?

Settling Accounts

Ibn Khaldun is able to correct the distorted images of Arab/Muslim civilizations held by many Western scholars over the years. As we have seen, the history of Western social thought has long been plagued by an Orientalism that has privileged Western civilization and denigrated the cultures of the Near and Far East. (Indeed, the very terms of this present discussion are coded in the discourse of Orientalism, inasmuch as the "Far East," "Middle East" and "Near East" all presuppose a Eurocentric point of reference). Even as radical a thinker as Karl Marx fell prey to prevailing prejudices about the cultures of Asia and the Middle East. His "Asiatic mode of production" misrepresented Eastern cultures as static and passive — with neither a recorded history nor a capacity for modernization. Although a fierce critic of Western colonialism, Marx suggested that only through their own colonization could Eastern cultures emancipate themselves from their backwardness and achieve modernization and full human development. "The assumed absence of classes or objective conditions capable of internally producing the bourgeois class led Marx to the logical conclusion that change in Asia is only possible if induced or imposed from the outside. This logic appears to advocate a developmental/progressive role for colonial capitalism" (Abdo, 1996: 17). But if Marx's view of Eastern civilizations was limited by the ignorance of his generation, an even more distorted picture emerged from the pen of Max Weber. Although a student of comparative religion, Weber reproduced some of the worst caricatures of Islam and the Eastern Muslim civilizations. His generalization of these societies as "oriental despotisms" and his indiscriminate allegations of the rampant sensuality of Islam and its rapacious desire for conquest and conversion — along with his demonization of the Prophet Mohammad — are in retrospect patently absurd. "Weber does not only paint a distorted picture of Islam, or in his words, 'the national Arabic warrior religion.' In fact, he goes so far as describing Islam as a monster threatening to swallow up the world — i.e., Weber's world" (Abdo, 1996: 24).

There can be little doubt, therefore, that a familiarity with Ibn Khaldun's historical studies could go a long way towards correcting some of these misapprehensions. Not only did he describe the great diversity that existed between the different nations of the Maghreb and the Mashreq, he also documented the dynamism of these societies — their propensity for transformation. Moreover, Ibn Khaldun reminds us that the Arab Muslim civilizations were great centres of science and learning at a time when much of Europe remained in the Dark Ages. It was only during the Crusades —known to the Arabs as the Frankish Wars — that Europeans first came into contact with the great Arab libraries of medicine, astronomy, chemistry, geography, mathematics and architecture. These were the sources of knowledge that the Europeans began to imitate, assimilate and then surpass — in their own Renaissance of higher learning. As many historians (Maalouf, 1984: 264) note, the legacy of Arab learning remains with us still: "Many words bear testimony to this even today: zenith, nadir, azimuth, algebra, algorithm, or more simply, cipher." The dynamism and intellectual vitality of the Arab civilizations ended with the Frankish conquests and the occupations that followed these wars. It was only then that the Islamic world entered a frozen period of stagnation and insularity.

Strong Attachments and Historical Memory

One of the most important lessons to be learned from Ibn Khaldun is that the traditional codes of conduct among nomadic, tribal, religious or ethnic groups such as the Pashtun in Afghanistan and Pakistan, the Shia of South Lebanon, the Kurds of Turkey, Syria, Iraq and Iran, and the Bedouin of the Middle East express great solidarity and loyalty towards insiders, and great hostility and antagonism towards invaders. These traditional groups are, after all, united and integrated by strong ties of *asabiyya*. The Pashtunwali is a case in point. According to this code, the norm of hospitality ensures that all guests fall under the protection of the tribe against outsiders. This is the main reason that the Taliban government of Afghanistan was unwilling to capture and deliver Osama bin Laden into American hands immediately after 9/11 — even under the threat of war. Besides his acclaim as a war hero in the Afghan resistance to the former Soviet invasion, Osama bin Laden was also a guest of the nation. His extradition would have brought shame upon the Taliban and upon the Pashtun people. Ahmed (2002: 38) makes this point:

> The laws of hospitality and revenge dominate the code. Pukhtunwali explains why the Taliban would not surrender their guest Usama bin Ladin even though they faced death and destruction. It also suggests that the laws of revenge will be activated and individuals or groups will extract vengeance for what they have suffered as a result of the war in 2001.... The tribal interpretation of Islam explains

why there is a sympathy for the Taliban in those parts of Muslim society where tribalism is strong, as in some parts of Saudi Arabia; it also explains the aversion to them where it is not, as in the middle class sections of society in Cairo or Karachi.

Ibn Khaldun would not only have understood this response; he would have predicted it. Among tribal peoples, or those recently descended from them, there is still a strong sense of group solidarity throughout the Muslim world. *Asabiyya*, which has been lost among the affluent urbanized middle classes of many Middle Eastern states, remains strong on the Arab street and, of course, in the desert. This sense of an international Muslim community — or *ummah* — has no real equivalent in the West, where most people identify first and foremost as citizens of separate nation-states with distinct cultural and linguistic traditions. In the Arab world, however, strong attachments among co-religionists still exist, and these attachments traverse national borders and engender international religious solidarity. This explains, in part, why global organizations — such as Al-Qaeda — are successful in recruiting fighters from so many different Muslim nations.

Pan-Islamic solidarity across the Maghreb, the Mashreq and throughout Central Asia reinforces the collective memory of many Muslims of their historical struggles against the West. This sense of history partly explains why Islamic resistance and jihadist movements such as the Taliban, Al-Qaeda, Al-Shabaab, Jemaah Islamiah and even Hezbollah often refer to the "Crusader nations" in their diatribes against the U.S. and its Western allies. The history of the Crusades has been kept alive over the centuries partly through the religious fervour of radical Muslim clerics and activists and partly through the Western geopolitics of militarism, greed and cultural imperialism. In an eerily prophetic forecast, written almost twenty years before the 9/11 attacks, a twentieth-century Arab historian (Maalouf, 1984: 266) concluded his study with an ominous outlook:

> In a Muslim world under constant attack, it is impossible to prevent the emergence of a sense of persecution, which among certain fanatics takes the form of a dangerous obsession … it seems clear that the Arab East still sees the West as a natural enemy. Against that enemy, any hostile action — be it political, military, or based on oil — is to be considered no more than legitimate violence. And there can be no doubt that the schism between these two worlds dates from the Crusades, deeply felt by the Arabs, even today, as an act of rape.

The Arab Spring

The closing month of 2010 saw the start of political upheavals in North Africa and the Middle East which together have become known as the Arab Spring. Since the removal of President Zine El Abidine Ben Ali, President Hosni Mubarak and Muammar Gaddafi — as the leaders of Tunisia, Egypt and Libya respectively — popular struggles for freedom and democracy in the Arab world have spread to many other countries, including Bahrain, Yemen and Syria. This unprecedented turmoil in a region of great geopolitical significance for the West promises to redraw the political map in a number of different ways. The rise to power of nationalist, socialist or Islamic governments in other Arab nations could lead to a profound realignment of politics in the region. The fall of Hosni Mubarak ended Egyptian support for the Israeli blockade of Gaza. Further changes could follow the fall of other pro-Western regimes — such as those in Jordan, Saudi Arabia and the Persian Gulf states. We have entered a time of great instability for Western geopolitical and energy interests.

It is unlikely that Ibn Khaldun would have been greatly surprised by the current political unrest in the Middle East and North Africa. He long ago conceptualized the history of the Arab world as the rise and fall of civilizations and societies in an endless cycle of conquest, decay and reconquest. He concluded that the average life expectancy of any royal dynasty would not exceed four generations, and he likely would have extended this four-generation rule to republican regimes. Indeed, given the secular nature of many republican regimes and their ambivalent relationship to Islam, he may well have predicted a shorter lifespan for them. For Ibn Khaldun, the incipient decline and fall of dynasties was brought about by a loss of *asabiyya* — the social glue that binds people together and legitimizes their leaders. In our own time, Ahmed (2002: 31) observes that many Arab societies are experiencing a rapid loss of *asabiyya* in a number of different ways:

Figure 2-9 The Rise and Possible Fall of the Syrian Dynasty

The great Arab philosopher of history Ibn Khaldun's... concept of *asabiyya* — variously translated as clannism or group solidarity... provides a more adequate explanation of the political systems operating in many Arab countries than notions... such as communism, nationalism, and socialism.... As Albert Hourani explained in his magisterial *History of the Arab Peoples* "*asabiyya* is a force that informs the patriarchal family order that still underpins the structure of power in many Arab societies."... But in Ibn Khaldun's time every dynasty bore within itself the seeds of decline, as rulers degenerated into tyrants or became corrupted by luxurious living.... The rise and possible fall of the Assad dynasty (in Syria) would provide a perfect illustration of the Khaldunian paradigm under recent postcolonial conditions.

Malise Ruthven, "Storm Over Syria." *New York Review of Books*, June 9, 2011, <www.nybooks.com/articles/archives/2011/jun/09/storm-over-syria/?page=2>.

Asabiyya is breaking down in the Muslim world because of the following reasons: massive urbanization, dramatic demographic changes, a population explosion, large-scale migrations to the West, the gap between rich and poor which is growing ominously wide, the widespread corruption and mismanagement of rulers, the rampant materialism coupled with the low premium on scholarship, the crisis of identity and, perhaps most significantly, new and often alien ideas and images, at once seductive and repellent, instantly communicated from the West which challenge traditional values and customs. This process of breakdown is taking place when a large percentage of the population in the Muslim world is young, dangerously illiterate, mostly jobless and therefore easily mobilized for radical change.

Ibn Khaldun would certainly have seen the writing on the wall. And after the repressive and corrupt republican regimes in Tunis, Cairo and Tripoli had been swept away by the tides of history, along with the kingdoms and sultanates in the Gulf, he would have predicted several generations of cultural and political regeneration under new Arab regimes. But he would have concluded that in time these too would succumb to a decline of aba-siyya — leading to their inevitable decay and displacement. And thus the cycle would be repeated — endlessly.

References

Abbadi, Suleiman. 2004. "Ibn Khaldun Contribution to the Science Economics." *Journal of Al Azhar University-Gaza* 7, 1: 41–48.

Abdo, Nahla. 1996. *Sociological Thought: Beyond Eurocentric Theory*. Toronto: Canadian Scholars' Press.

Ahmed, Akbar. 2002. "Ibn Khalldun's Understanding of Civilizations and the Dilemmas of Islam and the West Today." *Middle East Journal* 56, 1: 20–45.

Alatas, Syed Farid. 2006. "Ibn Khaldun and Contemporary Sociology." *International Sociology* November 21, 6: 782–95.

Anderson, Jon W. 1983. "Conjuring with Ibn Khaldun: From an Anthropological Point of View." *Journal of Asian and African Studies* 18, 3/4 (July/Oct.): 263–73.

Barnes, Harry Elmer, and Howard Becker. 1938. *Social Thought from Lore to Science*. Boston, New York; London: D.C. Heath.

Boulakia, Jean David C. 1971. "Ibn Khaldun: A Fourteenth-Century Economist." *Journal of Political Economy* 79, 5 (Sept.-Oct.): 1117.

Cosma Sorinnel. 2009. "Ibn Khaldun's Economic Thinking." *Ovidius University Annals of Economics* (Ovidius University Press) 14: 52–57.

Danner, M. 2004. *Torture and Truth: America, Abu Ghraib, and the War on Terror*. May 12. New York: New York Review of Books.

Dhaouadi, Mahmoud. 1990. "Ibn Khaldun: The Founding Father of Eastern Sociology." *International Sociology* 5, 3: 319–35

Gierer, Alfred. 2001. "Ibn Khaldun on Solidarity ('Asabiyya') — Modern Science on Cooperativeness and Empathy: A Comparison." *Philosphia Naturalis* 38, 4: 91–104.

Hannoum, Abdelmajid. 2003. "Translation and the Colonial Imaginary: Ibn Khaldûn Orientalist." *History and Theory* 42, 1 (Feb.): 61–81.

Honigmann, John J. 1976. *The Development of Anthropological Ideas.* Homewood, IL: Dorsey Press.

Huntington, Samuel. 1998. *The Clash of Civilizations and the Remaking of the World Order.* New York: Simon & Schuster.

Ibn Khaldun. 1958. *The Muqaddimah: An Introduction to History.* Translated by Franz Rosenthal. (Bollingen Series XLIII.) New York: Pamtheon Books.

____. 1986. *The Muqaddimah.* Translated by F. Rosenthal. 3 vols. London: Routledge and Kegan Paul.

Karatas, Selim Cafer. 2006. *Economic Theory of Ibn Khaldun and Rise and Fall of Nations.* May 18. At <uned.es/congreso-ibn-khaldun/pdf/11%20Selim%20Karatas.pdf>.

Katsiaficas, George. 1996. *"Understanding the Dialectical Thought of Ibn Khaldun: Toward an Analysis of the Role of the Individual and the Place of the Group in History."* Pan African Conference on Philosophy, Addis Ababa, December 1996: 4. In its original form, this paper appeared in Claude Sumner and Samuel Yohannes (eds.). *Perspectives in African Philosophy*, Addis Ababa: Rodopi Publishers, 1997).

Lacoste, Yves. 1966. *Ibn Khaldoun, naissance de l'histoire, passe du tiers-monde*, Paris: F. Masppero. (A brilliant Marxist interpretation, to be used with caution: cf. review in *Times Literary Supplement*, 8 August 1968, p. 853).

____. 1984. *Ibn Khaldun: The Birth of History and the Past of the Third World.* Translated by David Macy. London: Verso.

Lewis, Bernard. 2003. *What Went Wrong? The Clash Between Islam and Modernity in the Middle East.* San Francisco: Harper Perennial.

Luttrell, Marcus, and Patrick Robinson. 2007. *Lone Survivor.* New York and Boston: Little, Brown.

Maalouf, Amin. 1984. *The Crusades Through Arab Eyes.* New York: Shocken Books.

Marx, Karl. 1967 [1967]. *Capital: Volume I.* New York: International Publishers.

Ruthven, Malise. 2011. "Storm Over Syria." *New York Review of Books.* June 9.

Said, Edward W. 1978. *Orientalism.* New York: Pantheon.

Stowasser, Dr. Barbara Freyer. 2011. *Religion and Political Development: Comparative Ideas on Ibn Khaldun and Machiavelli.* Center for Contemporary Arab Studies: Edmund A. Walsh School of Foreign Service.

Toynbee, Arnold. 1935. *A Study of History* Vol. 3. Second edition. London: Oxford University Press.

Warner, Marina. 2011. *Stranger Magic: Charmed States and the Arabian Nights.* London: Chatto & Windus.

White, Ali. 2009. "An Islamic Approach to Studying History: Reflections on Ibn Khaldun's Deterministic Historical Approach." *Intellectual Discourse* 1.17, 2: 221–44.

Chapter 3

The Rationalism of the Enlightenment

The Ambiguous Legacy of the Enlightenment

Most of the classical social theories outlined in this book can be traced back to the period of European history known as the "Enlightenment," or "Age of Reason." The Enlightenment was a period of exceptional intellectual creativity and social upheaval, which lasted from the mid-seventeenth to the late eighteenth century. During this time philosophers began to critique many of the established doctrines of their day — especially those long sanctified by religious faith or tradition. The appearance of the Enlightenment philosophers was a sign that imminent historical changes would soon reshape the landscape of the old world and usher in a new age of modernity. This tide of intellectual controversy and criticism, which swept across Europe and America, was followed by a century of political unrest, a century that witnessed uprisings, rebellions, revolts

> **Fig 3-1 The End of Optimism**
>
> Can we still have faith in an idea of progress when the very inventions and ways of life that were thought would bring it about — market capitalism and individual freedom — are wreaking unprecedented environmental destruction?
>
> There is a deeper problem about anchoring the effort to defend progress in the 18th-century Enlightenment: it lands you squarely in a fraught argument about Eurocentrism. Too often citing the Enlightenment is a precursor to an attack on other systems of thought — such as Islam; too often appeals to an Enlightenment legacy are a code for privileging this European period of intellectual creativity. At its crudest, it can amount to a land grab for civilisational superiority in which the west has brought progress to the world.
>
> Madeleine Bunting, "Hail the 21st-century Enlightenment," *Guardian*, June 13, 2010 <www.guardian.co.uk/commentisfree/2010/jun/13/21st-century-enlightenment-revolution-mind>

and revolutions. Many of these social changes were foreshadowed in the social theories of the Enlightenment. In the words of the philosopher Hegel: "When philosophy paints its grey in grey, one form of life has become old, and by means of grey it cannot be rejuvenated, but only known. The owl of Minerva, takes its flight only when the shades of night are gathering" (Hegel 2008 [1821]: xxi). This idea that philosophers can somehow presage, or foretell, the outbreak of momentous historical events in which societies are turned upside down reappears from time to time. Nineteenth-century existentialist philosopher Soren Kierkegaard echoed Hegel's sentiment:

"There is a bird called the stormy petrel, and that is what I am, when in a generation storms begin to gather, individuals of my type appear" (cited in Dru 1958: 95). At the same time, these statements suggest that in the history of social theory, action often precedes thought and that the struggles of real individuals to change their life conditions are only later expressed as philosophical ideas. This is, perhaps, what Karl Marx (1947: 199) meant in his famous aphorism: "The philosophers have only interpreted the world in various ways; the point is to change it."

Most writers unequivocally see the Enlightenment in positive terms. It was the dawn of a new age, in which ancient prejudices and superstitions were suddenly subjected to the critical gaze of reason. All those institutions in society — such as the monarchy, the aristocracy and the church — that derived their legitimacy from traditional authority, rather than from the rational consensus (or social contract) of free "men," were critiqued and condemned. This was an age of unprecedented skepticism and radical doubt, an age that paved the way for the revolutions of the eighteenth century (see Hampson 1968; Hawthorn 1976). But it was also an age of unparalleled innovation and invention — especially in the fields of science and technology. The heliocentric theory of the universe, popularized by Nicolaus Copernicus (1473–1543) and Johannes Kepler (1571–1630), prefigured Isaac Newton's later science of mechanics and his laws of gravitation. Advances in medicine, anatomy and physiology replaced mediaeval medical practices inherited from the time of Galen, the ancient Greek physician. Old schools of thought were displaced by new disciplines. Alchemy was superseded by chemistry; astrology by astronomy; numerology by mathematics; and the theory of humours by modern germ theory. Along with the birth of modern science came revolutionary developments in technology — the microscope, the telescope, the pendulum clock, the thermometer and barometer, the guillotine and perhaps most significantly, the internal combustion engine. (For a discussion of how the development of the telescope transformed the theory and observation languages of astronomy, see Koestler 1959, and Feyerabend 1975.)

The vision that produced the discoveries of modern science, the inventions of modern technology and the power of rational thought was described by one historian as the "mechanization of the world picture" (Dijksterhuis 1986). Since the early rationalism of Rene Descartes and Francis Bacon, scientists and philosophers of the Enlightenment studied all forms of life as "systems" — that is, sets of mutually interrelated parts in which a change in one part would lead to a change in the entire system. The solar system was seen as a system made up of interrelated planetary objects. The human body was seen as a system made up of interrelated vital organs. Even societies came to be seen as systems made up of freely associating individuals. Moreover, the philosophers of the Enlightenment believed that societies, like machines, could be stripped down and reassembled — according to the principles of reason. The Enlightenment was nothing less than an great leap forward for all humanity. Or was it?

The excerpt in Figure 3-1 makes clear that not everyone has viewed the Enlightenment as a one-way milestone in humanity's march of progress. Alongside the advances in art, science, literature, medicine, life- and labour-saving technologies, there was also a dark side to this time period. Perhaps no one has offered a more critical reappraisal of the Enlightenment than twentieth-century French social theorist Michel Foucault (1975, 1971). In much of his published work, Foucault reflected on some of the more sinister outcomes of the Age of Reason. Foucault showed how the much vaunted power of rational thought was applied not only to the "emancipatory project" of the Enlightenment, but also to the increased control and confinement of individuals — especially those considered to be part of the "problem populations" in society. Such populations included not only criminals and social deviants, but also the mentally ill, the homeless and destitute, gypsies, orphans, beggars, vagrants and other marginalized elements in society. Foucault describes the Enlightenment as the "Great Confinement," a time when increasing numbers of people were kept in "carceral institutions": mental hospitals and lunatic asylums, houses of correction, prisons and penitentiaries, workhouses and poor houses, orphanages and compulsory military service. It was also a time when new disciplinary practices were introduced by medical, custodial and state authorities to control various forms of "social deviance." Whereas in previous times, "lunatics" were allowed to roam free and orphans left to their own devices, the Enlightenment began to deal with these social problems in a more "scientific" and disciplined way. Thus, the traditional freedoms of individuals were often replaced with confinement and regulation (see, for example, Gutting 1989; Canguilhem 1998: 313–29). New methods of psychiatry were used to "govern" the innermost aspects of the individual personality (see, for example, Rose 1989). New methods of confinement and surveillance were used to control prisoners. The panopticon was a new type of prison, designed by English philosopher Jeremy Bentham, which allowed the authorities to observe prisoners without their knowledge. This method of constant surveillance reduced the costs but also induced prisoners to exercise greater self-discipline as they never knew when they were under observation. In this and other ways, the Enlightenment declared war on "unreason" and "idleness," and in its zeal to reform "problem populations," it laid the foundations for the rise of totalitarian states in the twentieth century. Many of the carceral institutions founded during the Enlightenment survived well into the Victorian period, as this famous passage from *The Christmas Carol* by Charles Dickens reminds us.

"At this festive season of the year, Mr. Scrooge," said the gentleman, taking up a pen, "it is more than usually desirable that we should make some slight provision for the Poor and destitute, who suffer greatly at the present time. Many thousands are in want of common necessaries; hundreds of thousands are in want of common comforts, sir."

"Are there no prisons?" asked Scrooge.

"Plenty of prisons," said the gentleman, laying down the pen again.

"And the Union workhouses?" demanded Scrooge. "Are they still in operation?"

"They are. Still," returned the gentleman, "I wish I could say they were not."

"The Treadmill and the Poor Law are in full vigour, then?" said Scrooge.

"Both very busy, sir."

"Oh! I was afraid, from what you said at first, that something had occurred to stop them in their useful course," said Scrooge. "I'm very glad to hear it." (Dickens 1843: 16–17)

The study of "exotic" human populations — at least in Enlightenment Europe — was very much a by-product of the expansion of European colonialism — the conquest and occupation of foreign lands. Indeed, these studies played an important part in the process. On the one hand, they produced data that was used by colonial authorities for more efficient administration and control. On the other hand, the racist assumptions and conclusions of these studies served to "legitimize" the colonial enterprise as a mission to "civilize" native populations. In this respect, early anthropology and sociology, which originated during the Enlightenment, were the handmaidens of colonialism (see for example, Gough 1960; Asad 1973; Kuper 1985). These Enlightenment social sciences helped to consolidate and perpetuate the racial prejudices of their age. Following taxonomies developed by botanists, zoologists and biologists, Enlightenment anthropologists produced an hierarchical classification of humans into three major "racial" groups — Caucasoid, Negroid, and Mongoloid — and later, Australoid and others. This classification remained popular long after it had been discredited by population biologists and geneticists. Enlightenment anthropologists also subscribed to human evolutionist theories that inevitably placed Europeans at the top of the evolutionary scale, while other populations were defined as "primitive" and less evolved. Enlightenment psychologists measured and compared cranial development in members of different "race" (as well as gender and class) groups — always to the advantage of (upper class, male) Europeans. "In the 1860's, the founder of the British Anthropological Institute, John Beddoe, developed an 'Index of Nigressence' based on cranial characteristics, which he used to support the claim that the Irish were 'Africanoid.' In the twentieth century, 'craniometric' techniques were used by the Nazis to distinguish 'Aryans' from 'non-Aryans'" (Gray 2009: 270).

These examples illustrate that the traditional image of the Enlightenment as a gilded age of increasing liberty, equality and progress is only one side of the picture. While the Age of Reason contributed to the sum of human happiness through its development of science and technology and a new spirit of humanism, it also laid the foundations for new forms of domination and destruction — the legacies of which remain with us today. The lesson to be learned from this is an old one: the discovery and application of new knowledge is always something of a Faustian pact. Once the genie is out of the bottle, there is no knowing what it will do. (See Saul 1993, for a passionate, if conservative account of how some philosophical ideas — especially the idea of "Reason" — have left a heritage of dogma and dictatorship. See also Gray 2007.)

The Spirit of the Enlightenment

The Enlightenment spanned the turbulent century from the English Revolution in 1689, through the American Revolution in 1776, to the French Revolution in 1789. During this time of political and social upheaval, social philosophers became increasingly critical of the medieval regimes of Europe. Much of this social criticism was directed at the established institutions of traditional societies — especially the monarchy, the nobility and the clergy. In place of the old values of duty, loyalty and "fealty" — which the lower classes "owed" to their "betters" — the rationalist philosophers preached new values of reason, liberty, equality and progress. These ideas gained currency and popularity throughout Europe during this period.

In England, the revolution resulted in the overthrow of James II and the peaceful installation of a constitutional monarch (William III, or William of Orange). For the first time, the power of a monarch was based upon the consent of a parliament — even though the seventeenth-century parliament was not democratic in any modern sense. The only people allowed to vote were prosperous male property owners. A century later, in 1789, the French Revolution overthrew the old regime (*ancien regime*) and installed a revolutionary government (the Jacobins), led by Robespierre, Danton and Saint-Just, among others. Between these dates, in 1776, the American Revolution saw the breaking away of the new world from England. Without doubt, the Enlightenment represented a period of great political and social change in Europe and North America.

In philosophical terms, the Enlightenment represented the rise of rationalism in European social thought. Rationalism argued that the power of reason could overcome superstition and prejudice in the realm of ideas, and tyranny and despotism in the realm of politics. All aspects of social life became subject to critical examination. Nothing traditional was considered sacred to the rationalist thinkers: certainly not religion, or metaphysics or — for that matter — aesthetics, education or anything else.

In social terms, the Enlightenment corresponded to the rise of new social classes in European societies. These classes were composed of merchants, traders and manufacturers — the *bourgeoisie*, who were frustrated by the constraining regulations imposed on trade and industry by the institutions of the old order. In many ways, the ideas of the Enlightenment were an expression of the class struggle in the eighteenth century, between the rising industrial and commercial *bourgeoisie* on the one hand, and the old order of landed aristocracy, hereditary privilege and absolute monarchy, on the other. Thus, the popular revolutionary struggles were based upon demands for greater freedom, and these demands, centred on social, political and economic life, arose from the fundamental ideas associated with the Enlightenment social philosophers.

The Enlightenment Conceptual Toolbox

The following list provides examples of the most basic values of the Enlightenment thinkers and how these translated into philosophical and political criticism of the established power structures of European societies:

- *Freedom from arbitrary power*: Opposition to the power of the British government to tax without representation in the American colonies; opposition to royal absolutism and hereditary privilege in France and other European societies.
- *Freedom of speech*: Opposition to constraints on political publishing; opposition to the sedition laws.
- *Freedom of association*: Opposition to legislation such as the Combination Acts and conspiracy laws, which were designed to prevent the formation of trades unions, political parties, dissenting religious groups, and cooperative and mutual aid societies. The lifting of the prohibitions on these and other voluntary organizations eventually laid the foundation for the growth of a civil society.
- *Freedom of trade*: Opposition to mercantilist laws, which privileged royal monopolies — such as the British East India Company and the Hudson's Bay Company — and regulated trade (through the Navigation Acts and the Corn Laws). In Britain, Adam Smith was the most celebrated advocate of free trade.

- *Freedom to realize one's potential*: Opposition to the traditional belief that the liberties of ordinary individuals were granted as "privileges" by the ruling classes. Enlightenment thinkers asserted their liberties as universal and inalienable "natural rights" based on reason rather than on tradition or authority. The best example of this value is to be seen in the American Declaration of Independence (see Figure 3-2).

> **Figure 3-2 U.S. Declaration of Independence**
>
> We hold these truths to be self-evident, that all men are created equal; that they are endowed by their creator with inherent and inalienable rights, that among these are life, liberty and the pursuit of happiness; that to secure those rights governments are instituted among men, deriving their just powers from the consent of the governed; that whenever any form of government becomes destructive of these ends, it is the right of the people to alter or abolish it, and to institute new government.
>
> — United States Declaration of Independence, second paragraph

Settling Accounts

As we have noted, the Enlightenment gave birth to a new movement of critical thought — commonly referred to as "rationalism." For the rationalists, no source of authority was acceptable unless it could pass the test of reason. All traditional ideas and institutions were criticized by the rationalists if they were not based on the principles of reason. The following were the main targets of rationalist criticism:

- *Traditional religious systems of belief*: Rejection of all systems of thought based upon revelation, faith or other non-rational authorities and sources of evidence. Rationalists questioned the value of the "holy scriptures."
- *Traditional authorities*: Criticism of all institutions and authorities that were not based upon popular consent and that restricted the rights of the people to investigate and verify the truth of popular received doctrines — especially the authorities of the crown, the church and the nobility. These institutions were criticized as tyrannies, or despotisms.
- *Speculative thinking*: Opposition to highly abstract metaphysical, religious or philosophical systems of thought which could not be verified through observation or experience. These systems included such traditional schools of thought as the scholarly logical works of Thomas Aquinas and pre-Newtonian "sciences" such as alchemy, astrology and numerology.

The key ideas advanced by the Enlightenment thinkers were those of reason, liberty, equality, social contract and progress. And even though there were significant differences between Enlightenment thinkers — especially those from different European nations — most critical thinkers of this period emphasized the importance of these key ideas. All of the Enlightenment thinkers believed that society — and the governance of society — should be based upon reason, observation and experience. They were especially opposed to the old theory of the "Great Chain of Being," which asserted that the traditional hierarchies of the monarchy, the church and the aristocracy were ordained by God. Under the old system, any revolt against these traditional authorities was seen not only as unlawful sedition and treason, but also as unnatural sacrilege and heresy (as an offence against the divine order of things and thus against "nature"). A classical account of these ideas is provided by Lovejoy (1936); see also Danby (1949).

The eighteenth-century rationalists also explored the question of "human nature" — or more exactly, what humans were like when "in a state of nature." The rationalist philosophers asked what is primary, necessary or "natural" about humans in society, and what is secondary, contingent or artificial. Different philosophers gave different answers to this question. As we saw in the first chapter — around our discussion of *Lord of the Flies* — Thomas Hobbes believed that humans, in a state of nature, lived in a state of "war of all against all" (or *omni bellum omni*). However, other philosophers, such as Jean-Jacques Rousseau and John Locke, saw humans in a state of nature as peaceful, passive and cooperative. For Hobbes, "war was natural, and peace was social." In other words, Hobbes believed that in a natural (uncivilized) state, humanity existed in a brutal, competitive and aggressive state of violence and warfare, which could only be ended through the imposition of social order by a powerful sovereign authority. For Rousseau and Locke, "peace was natural and war was social." Rousseau believed that while the original (or natural) state of humanity had been peaceful and self-sufficient, the growth of social inequality and tyrannical government had led to conflict, violence and war. For Rousseau (and other *philosophes* of the French Enlightenment), the solution to social problems lay in the eradication of corrupt institutions and their replacement by institutions based on reason and justice.

> **Figure 3-3 Human Nature: Benign or Malign?**
>
> The old debate between Hobbes and Rousseau on what humans were like in a state of nature has spilled over into modern disagreements between social anthropologists and sociobiologists regarding the origins of human society. For some anthropologists — such as Ashley Montagu, *The Human Revolution*, and Gordon Childe, *Man Makes Himself*, the earliest humans were tool-making cooperative social beings. However, for sociobiologists — such as Lionel Tiger, *The Imperial Animal*, Desmond Morris, *The Naked Ape*, Robert Ardrey, *The Territorial Imperative* and Konrad Lorenz, *On Aggression*, the earliest humans were aggressive, territorial, warlike beings. Like many debates which started as philosophical disagreements, this one has grown into a modern social scientific controversy.

For both Hobbes and Rousseau, however, the basis of human society lay in the "social contract," which defined social relationships and produced social order. For Hobbes, the social contract required that individuals surrender their natural freedoms to a powerful sovereign ruler, who could then impose social order — by force, if necessary — on the anarchy of pre-social existence. For Rousseau, on the other hand, the social contract needed to be based upon the free consent of the governed.

This notion of the power of reason to solve all social problems gave the Enlightenment thinkers their belief in "human perfectibility and progress." They believed that reason could overcome the prejudices and superstitions of the past and ensure the progressive development and evolution of human society. The Enlightenment was, therefore, characterized by a strong optimism regarding human "evolution."

The Enlightenment in Different Nations

Although most social thinkers of the Enlightenment subscribed in one way or another to beliefs in reason, liberty, equality and progress, there were some important national differences between thinkers from different countries. In America, the Revolutionary War was seen as a popular revolt against the arbitrary power of the British colonial government to impose taxes on the American colonists without their representation in the British parliament. The battle cry of the colonists was "no taxation without representation." However, the more important sentiments of the American Revolution related to ideas about individual liberty, equality and the necessity for government to be based upon the consent of the governed. At the same time, these democratic sentiments of the American colonists were not extended to the interests of slaves, indigenous peoples, women or men "of no property." Democracy and self-government were only intended for white, middle-class, Anglo-Saxon, protestant males.

In France, where the unrestrained power of the absolute monarchy was matched by the extravagant wealth of the nobility and the clergy, the oppressive weight of the *ancien regime* (the old order) was deeply resented by the general population. For this reason, the social criticism directed against the French establishment was far more radical than in Britain, where the power of the monarchy — at least since 1689 — had been constitutionally restrained by Parliament. Many of the French Enlightenment thinkers were political radicals who paved the way for the French Revolution. They opposed royal absolutism, and the theocratic links between the crown, church and nobility, and they sought the complete overthrow of the political and religious establishment. The prevailing philosophy of the French Enlightenment thinkers was that of "materialism" — the view that all our ideas are reflections of the material world, which exists independently of our ideas. One of the most important traditions to emerge from the Enlightenment in France was that of positivism — the belief that there are laws of society in much the same way that there are laws of nature. Once these laws of society are discovered through social science, knowledge of these laws can be used to predict and explain the occurrence of social events. Today, however, "positivism" refers more to a broad philosophical tendency than to a rigorously formulated theory of knowledge. It has often been used to refer inclusively to classical positivism, classical empiricism, logical positivism, logical empiricism and critical rationalism (among others, see L. Kolakowski 1968, 1972; for sociological positivism, see Zetterberg 1954; Lundberg 1939).

The main tradition of French social thought was also strongly influenced by "holism" (sometimes known as "realism") — the belief that the structures of society exist *sui generis*, that is, above and beyond the sum of the individuals who compose these structures. In Britain, however, the main tradition of social thought was influenced by "individualism" (sometimes known as "nominalism") — the belief that the structures of society (or the economy) are fully reducible to the individuals who compose these structures. These two distinct intellectual traditions have shaped the growth of social theory in their respective nations.

In Britain, the presence of a constitutional monarchy, as well as a class system that was more open to the rising expectations of the new industrial capitalist class, defused some of the more extreme social criticism associated with the Enlightenment in France. Unlike many of their French counterparts, the British philosophers were reformers rather than revolutionaries. Far from being radicals, these thinkers contributed to the rise of liberalism, utilitarianism and — as we shall see — empiricism. After the "Glorious Revolution" of 1689, civil society began to develop in Britain. With the establishment of a constitutional monarchy and a parliament, there was greater participation by "the people" in the process of government and more opportunity for peaceful social change. These constitutional changes opened the way for a gradual incorporation of the new commercial/industrial classes — the *bourgeoisie* — into the political establishment without any need for revolution and without any real broadening of democratic structures. Most thinkers in Britain believed that gradual improvements to society were both possible and desirable. In order to ensure that piecemeal reforms were carefully introduced into society, emphasis was placed upon observation and experience. The Enlightenment in Britain, therefore, gave birth to several important traditions, one of which was "empiricism" — the belief that knowledge of the world can only be gained through sensory experience. Another was "utilitarianism" — the belief that the greatest good for the largest number of people is best advanced through the unregulated pursuit of individual self-interest (through the market). This is sometimes known as the doctrine of *laissez-faire* (or non-intervention). This doctrine is the basis for the political philosophy of liberalism — the ideology that proclaims individual freedom and the power of reason as the principles best suited to promote political liberty and economic efficiency (or utility) — and the guiding principle for advocates of free trade.

In Germany, the situation was again different. Because of the harsh autocratic power exercised in the independent states, or principalities, that preceded the rise of a modern unified Germany, the critical ideas of Enlightenment philosophers were more muted. Instead of proposing revolutionary changes to the establishment, as in France, or social reforms, as in Great Britain, the German philosophers took the safer course of focusing on the internal and historical aspects of their society and culture. Politics was volatile and dangerous. The real bonds between individuals and communities were seen as cultural — through language, music, folklore, literature, tradition and history — rather than through a political state. In Germany, therefore, the ideas of the Enlightenment found expression in the philosophical traditions of historicism and idealism. German thinkers — such as Kant, Hegel, Fichte and Schelling — focused on the inner development of society through history and culture, and developed a philosophy of "idealism" — the belief that the reality of the world is based upon our ideas, that only ideas are real. These traditions were later to play an important role in the rise of German social theory.

Although the Enlightenment is often portrayed as a period in which old superstitions and prejudices finally gave way to science and reason, we should not allow ourselves to be completely swept away by the propaganda of these times. The Age of Reason, as we have already seen, had its dark side. It was, for example, a time when "scientific" justifications for racial prejudice and racial exploitation first emerged. Although some of the Enlightenment thinkers — such as John Stuart Mill in his pamphlet, *The Negro Question* (1850) — attacked the institution of slavery and argued for the full equality of all peoples, other thinkers developed racial typologies and classifications that formed the basis for racist theories. Thus, eminent philosophers such as Voltaire, Hume and Kant contributed to the pernicious idea that Africans represented a lower stage of evolutionary development than that achieved by Europeans (see Davis 2006).

Montesquieu — The French Liberal

An important figure of the French Enlightenment was the Baron de Montesquieu. Although he was not as well-known as other French thinkers of this period, Montesquieu's ideas helped to shape the development of sociological theory. Among Montesquieu's most useful contributions to social theory were his attempts to classify and analyze different types of society. Montesquieu was one of the earliest social theorists to construct what later came to be known as "ideal types." These are representations of social structures, social processes or social events based upon a description of their typical characteristics. However, although ideal types may help us to compare and contrast societies in different ways, no real society or institution completely conforms to any ideal type, which are only ever approximations of reality. And although their use was pioneered by Montesquieu, they were later employed to greatest effect by the German sociologist Max Weber in his comparative historical studies of religion and social organization.

In many ways, Montesquieu's ideas were more closely related to the liberalism of the British Enlightenment than to the radicalism of the French. Along with his countrymen Alexis de Tocqueville and Emile Durkheim, Montesquieu represents the relatively minor tradition of French liberalism. This liberal influence may be seen in his classification of different types of government. Although he acknowledged that some forms of republic may constitute extremely democratic states (ensuring the maximum amount of equality between citizens), he suggests that only monarchies can best protect the individual liberties of all citizens. For Montesquieu, the best guarantee for the protection of individual liberties is the existence of "checks and balances" within the state. In this respect, Montesquieu advanced similar ideas to those of English political philosopher Jeremy Bentham. In monarchies, according to Montesquieu, the existence of several different constituencies, or estates (such as the crown, the nobility, the church and the people), provides a buffer between the citizen and the state, whereas in a fully democratic republic, the citizen is more directly exposed to the unchecked — and potentially totalitarian — power of the state. Montesquieu would probably have applauded the sentiments of the bumper sticker that was spotted in San Francisco a few years ago: "Practice Safe Government — Use Kingdoms."

While some of us today may not share Montesquieu's preference for the monarchy over the republic, his discussion raises interesting questions for us: for example, to what extent is there always a trade-off between equality and freedom? In societies that strongly proclaim the value of equality (such as the socialist/communist states of China, Cuba and North Korea), the value of individual freedom is invariably sacrificed. In societies that strongly proclaim the value of individual freedom (such as the capitalist states of the United States and the United Kingdom), the value of equality is invariably sacrificed. These questions would have intrigued Montesquieu, although he probably would have pointed out that full equality between citizens was only possible in those democratic republics with relatively small populations.

The final point that we need to remember about Montesquieu (and the other classical theorists) is that he was a product of his times. Although Montesquieu was more thoughtful and fair-minded in his social analysis than many of his contemporaries, he was still influenced by the popular prejudices of his age. In his portrayal of Eastern societies as "Oriental despotisms," Montesquieu had clearly internalized the commonly held Eurocentric and racist assumptions about non-European societies. Montesquieu's discussion of "savage" and "barbarian" societies also shares some of the Eurocentric prejudices of his contemporaries. However, these inevitable limitations should not blind us to the pioneering spirit of Montesquieu's works — especially *Persian Letters* (1721) and *The Spirit of the Laws* (1748) — or to the formative value of his attempts to classify and analyze the societies of his time. Without Montesquieu, there likely would have been no Saint-Simon, no Comte and no Durkheim.

Rousseau — Radical or Romantic?

Perhaps the most popular and influential *philosophe* of the French Enlightenment was Jean-Jacques Rousseau. Although Rousseau was the centre of much discussion and debate in France and throughout the capitals of eighteenth-century Europe, he was actually a citizen of Switzerland. And, in the sense that all theorists are products of their places and times, Rousseau's Swiss origins may be discerned in his view that democracies are best suited to relatively small societies — such as the city states of ancient Greece and the small decentralized cantons of his native Switzerland.

Rousseau's ideas proved important to the development of social theory for a number of reasons. Rousseau believed strongly in the power of reason, both as a way to scientifically understand society and as a way to reform society. He believed that reason would enable us to discover the laws of society in much the same way as Newton had discovered the laws of nature. In his view, many of the problems of society (such as inequality, tyranny, war and conflict) could be solved if the principles of reason were used to organize and govern societies. Like most Enlightenment thinkers, Rousseau believed that social problems were caused by insufficient knowledge and education. The problems of unjust governments and corrupt institutions could be solved if reason were applied to the conduct of human affairs. Rousseau subscribed to the doctrine of "human perfectibility" — the belief that through the application of reason to human affairs, humanity possesses an infinite capability for "progress."

As we suggested in our discussion of *Lord of the Flies*, Rousseau saw the primal natural state of humans as largely solitary and self-sufficient. Without the constraints of civilization, humans foraged for food and sustenance in small autonomous groups. Above all, humanity in a state of nature was essentially peaceful. The problems of inequality, tyranny, war and conflict only began with the rise of organized society, privileged classes and centralized government. This sentiment is clearly expressed in the famous opening sentence of Rousseau's greatest work, *The Social Contract*: "Man is born free, but everywhere he is in chains" (2008: 14).

Although Rousseau has been criticized for invoking an image of the "noble savage," much of this criticism is misplaced. Any conception of a pre-social natural human, living in a "state of nature," was only ever intended by Rousseau as a heuristic device. He never claimed that human groups had ever actually existed without language, culture or social organization; the "state of nature" was simply a hypothetical construct arrived at by bracketing all the socio-cultural attributes of "civilization" in order to hypothesize a "natural human." Rousseau's purpose in such theorizing was primarily critical. He wanted to show that the severe inequalities that characterized the European societies were social rather than natural in origin. This willingness to examine the social basis of human inequality made Rousseau one of the earliest pioneers of social theory. He was among the very first thinkers to suggest that social inequality is not natural but rather a socially produced condition.

Rousseau believed that in order for humans to live cooperatively in large numbers, it was necessary for them to sacrifice some of the individual liberties they had formerly enjoyed when living separately in a state of nature. Individual liberties had to be sacrificed in order to ensure the greater good of the larger society. According to Rousseau, however, the social contract should be based upon reason and justice rather than tradition and authority. In other words, the social contract should be based upon the "general will" and not on the Divine Right of Kings or the Great Chain of Being. All governments should be based upon the consent of the governed. Rousseau believed that any society guided by reason would necessarily be a just society. A just and reasonable society was one in which the social contract was based upon the general will of its members. According to Rousseau, in order for authority to be legitimate, the individual must freely submit to the general will. Any authority which exacted the submission of individuals through coercion, force or fraud was dismissed by Rousseau as tyranny or despotism. Rousseau used his theory of society as a trenchant critique of the established political and social order of his day — the *ancien regime*. He was particularly critical of the profound inequalities that existed between the different estates — especially between the privileged nobility and the oppressed peasantry. Because he believed that his society was based upon unreasonable — and therefore unjust — principles, he maintained that existing inequalities were the result of corrupt institutions rather than of natural differences. He also concluded that the conflicts and wars that resulted from competition and inequality were caused by corrupt institutions and not by any natural inclinations towards war, aggression or territoriality. For Rousseau, "peace was natural and war was social."

However, unlike Marx, Rousseau did not call for the abolition of private property. He was not a revolutionary theorist in this respect. While he railed against the excesses and self-indulgence of the landed gentry, he was not opposed to the private ownership of property. And, unlike Marx and the socialist, communist and anarchist thinkers, Rousseau favoured slow, gradual and moderate social change. His advice to the Polish authorities was to emancipate the serfs only when they had shown their fitness for freedom. He may well have given this same advice to the slave-holders of the American South had he been around then.

There are always many ways in which the work of any social theorist can be interpreted, or "deconstructed." The French revolutionary *philosophes* chose to read Rousseau as a radical or revolutionary thinker because of his emphasis on reason, equality and progress. But the later writers of the Counter-Enlightenment considered him a conservative and a romantic because he also emphasized the importance of living with nature and the power of sentiment and feeling. And although Rousseau, in *Emile*, envisioned the possibilities of social change through educational reform, he was unwilling to extend his demand for educational equality to women. For this reason, his ideas were challenged by Mary Wollstonecraft and later feminists. But, when all is said and done, Rousseau was one of the earliest theorists to suggest that social inequalities were not simply a reflection of natural differences. This was, in itself, a revolutionary observation. And today, because of his emphasis on the importance of nature, Rousseau is sometimes seen as a great-grandfather of the green movement (Edmond and Eidinow 2006: 330)

Hobbes — Hard-Headed Realist

The ideas of Thomas Hobbes are often contrasted to those of Jean-Jacques Rousseau. The two men came from different countries and lived in different centuries. Whereas Rousseau was a major figure of the eighteenth century, Hobbes was born into the late sixteenth century and died well into the last part of the seventeenth. Rousseau was a citizen of Switzerland and was influenced by the democratic potential of small states. Hobbes lived through the English Civil War and was influenced by the turbulence and unrest of those times. Despite their differences, both men are recognized as important Enlightenment figures, Hobbes in the British Enlightenment and Rousseau in the French. As Enlightenment thinkers, they both believed in the prevailing values of Enlightenment thought — reason, liberty, equality and progress. But although Hobbes started from similar premises to those of Rousseau, he often arrived at different conclusions.

Like Rousseau, and other Enlightenment thinkers, Hobbes speculated on what humanity had been like in a state of nature — or, to put it another way, what were the essential characteristics of human nature. However, unlike

Rousseau, Hobbes believed that the natural condition of equality generated competition, conflict, aggression and war among pre-social humans. The main causes of conflict were, according to Hobbes, "First, Competition, Secondly, Diffidence, Thirdly, Glory." Whereas for Rousseau, natural humans lived in a state of relative peace and isolation, for Hobbes, natural humans lived in a state of conflict and violence, or in his own words, in a "war of all against all" — *omni bellum omni*. Because Hobbes and Rousseau differed in their assumptions about humanity's natural state, they also reached different conclusions regarding the ideal form of government. For Hobbes, a powerful sovereign authority was necessary in order to bring an end to humans' natural state of competition, conflict and violence. In other words, it is only through the surrender of individual freedoms through a social contract with a powerful sovereign authority that peace and social order can be imposed from above — by force if necessary — on the natural state of competition

Figure 3-4 The Enlightenment: Different National Traditions

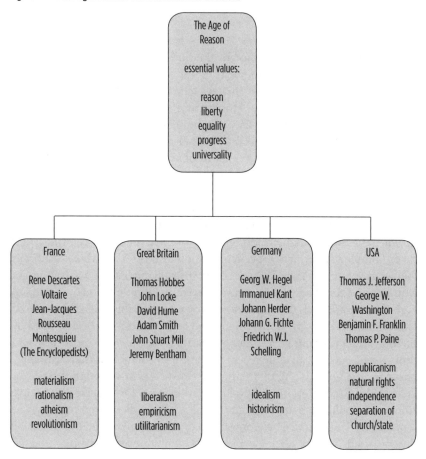

and conflict. Whereas Rousseau believed that the power of traditional authority had brought poverty, inequality and social injustice, for Hobbes, the power of traditional authority was an absolute prerequisite for social order. Hobbes presents his basic argument in the following way: Because people exist in a natural state of equality (their natural differences are equally distributed throughout the population), this equality results in a competition for resources — for wealth, for security and for prestige (or honour). This natural competition for resources leads ultimately to a war of all against all. In such a state of violent anarchy, there are no common standards of right or wrong. The only law that is respected is that of "might makes right." The only way in which this state of competition and conflict may be ended is through the emergence of a powerful sovereign authority, to which all must become subservient. Only then will the natural state of conflict be overcome, and only then will peace finally prevail.

Figure 3-4 illustrates that the rationalism of the Enlightenment was expressed differently by thinkers from different European countries.

The Enlightenment Today

Before we conclude our discussion of the Enlightenment, we need to reflect upon the relevance of these theorists to our own times and circumstances. What would Hobbes and Rousseau have to say about contemporary politics in the early twenty-first century? Hobbes may well have argued that the need for a powerful sovereign authority can be seen in the chaos that followed the fall of Josef Tito (Yugoslavia) and other dictators of the Soviet Union and Eastern Europe in 1989, as well as of Saddam Hussein (Iraq), Hosni Mubarak (Egypt) and Muammar Gaddafi (Libya). At least Saddam Hussein was able to impose — an admittedly brutal — social order on the mixed volatile population of Sunnis, Shia and Kurds in Iraq. But once the U.S. deposed Hussein, Iraq quickly reverted back to a state of war of all against all, in which the lives of many Iraqis became "solitary, poore, nasty, brutish and short." Similar consequences occurred after the end of Tito, whose death was followed by a war of Yugoslav succession — involving Serbs, Croats, Bosnian Muslims and Kosovars. These wars of all against all resulted in the break-up and disintegration of the state. Hobbes would probably conclude that the anarchy and conflict of many "rogue and failed states" has been caused by the downfall of strong governments. On the other hand, Rousseau would probably have celebrated the recent birth of more democratic governments, based on the general will of the people, in such post-communist states as Poland, the Czech Republic, Slovakia, Slovenia and (former) East Germany. Rousseau would have argued that the fall of these dictatorial regimes was replaced by voluntary social contracts based upon the popular consent of the governed. Most of all, he would have championed the uprisings that led to the Arab Spring of 2011. He undoubtedly would have applauded the overthrow of royalist and military despotisms throughout the Middle East and North Africa, and he would have hoped for the emergence of democratic republican governments based upon popular rule.

But in the real world, the truth is never black or white, but always some variable shade of grey. Unfortunately, many of the so-called popular uprisings or "democratic revolutions" in post-Soviet Eastern Europe have failed to secure the social contracts that would have appealed to Rousseau. It is now apparent that the so-called the "rose revolution" in Georgia (November 2003–January 2004), the "orange revolution" in Ukraine (January 2005) and the "tulip revolution" Kyrgyzstan in (April 2005) were spearheaded by the American democratization International NGOs working at the behest of the U.S.foreign policy establishment. Indeed, it has become increasingly evident that the main causes of these revolutions in Eastern Europe and Central Asia were closely aligned to U.S. foreign-policy interests (strategic expansion, energy security and the war on terrorism). While the evidence of this type of geo-political manipulation cannot be used to discredit all popular uprisings — many of which were authentic grassroots struggles for democracy and social justice — knowledge of the extent of superpower manipulation makes it imperative to study each case on its own merits. Many of these uprisings have ended in the installation of new strongmen, who have reimposed dictatorships on their subjugated populations. In Belarus, Alexander Lukashenko has steadily consolidated his power through authoritarian means. In the Ukraine, the "orange revolution" seems to have collapsed with the growing power of the autocratic President Viktor Yanukovych. Other post-Soviet

Figure 3-5 Differences between Rousseau and Hobbes

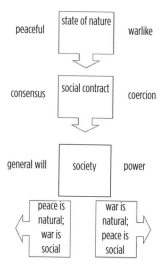

dictators include Islam Karimov of Uzbekistan, Nursultan Nazarbayev of Kazakhstan and Emomalii Rahmon of Tajikistan. The list is a long one. We can only assume that Hobbes would have felt vindicated while Rousseau would have felt betrayed. Time alone will tell us the fate of the Arab Spring.

References

Ardrey, Robert. 1961. *African Genesis: A Personal Investigation into the Animal Origins and Nature of Man.* New York: Atheneum.

___. 1966. *The Territorial Imperative: A Personal Inquiry Into the Animals Origins of Property and Nations.* New York: Atheneum.

Asad, Talal (ed). 1973. *Anthropology and the Colonial Encounter.* London: Ithaca Press.

Canguilhem, Georges. 1998. " The Decline of the Idea of Progress." Translated by David Macey. *Economy and Society* 27, 2–3 (May): 313–29.

Childe, Gordon. 1936. *Man Makes Himself.* Oxford: Oxford University Press.

Danby, John F. 1949. *Shakespeare's Doctrine of Nature — A Study of "King Lear."* London: Faber and Faber.

Davis, David Brion. 2006. "Blacks: Damned by the Bible: Review of *The Curse of Ham: Race and Slavery in Early Judaism, Christianity, and Islam,* by David M. Goldenberg." *New York Review of Books,* November 16.

Dickens, Charles. 184.3 *A Christmas Carol.* London: Chapman and Hall.

Dijksterhuis, Eduard Jan. 1986. *The Mechanization of the World Picture.* Princeton, NJ: Princeton University Press.

Dru, Alexandra (ed.). 1958. *The Journals of Soren Kierkegaard, 1834–1854.* London: Fontana Books.

Edmond, David, and John Eidinow. 2006. *Rousseau's Dog: Two Great Thinkers at War in the Age of Enlightenment.* London: Faber & Faber.

Feyerabend, Paul K. 1975. *Against Method: Outline of an Anarchistic Theory of Knowledge.* London: Verso.

Foucault, Michel. 1971. *Madness and Civilization: A History of Insanity in the Age of Reason.* New York: Pantheon Books.

___. 1975. *Discipline and Punish: The Birth of the Prison.* New York: Random House.

Gough, Kathleen 1960 *Anthropology and Imperialism.* Ann Arbor, MI: Radical Education Project.

Gray, John. 2007. *Enlightenment's Wake: Politics and Culture at the Close of the Modern Age.* Oxford: Routledge.

___. 2009. *Gray's Anatomy: Selected Writings.* Toronto: Anchor Canada.

Gutting, G. 1989. *Michael Foucault's Archaeology of Scientific Reason.* Cambridge/New York: Cambridge University Press and Canguilhem.

Hampson, Norman. 1968. *The Enlightenment.* Harmondsworth, Middlesex: Penguin Books.

Hawthorn, Geoffrey. 1976. *Enlightenment and Despair: A History of Sociology.* Cambridge: Cambridge University Press.

Hegel, Georg. 2008 [1821]. "Preface." *Philosophy of Right.* New York: Cosimo Classics.

Koestler, Arthur. 1959. *The Sleepwalkers: A History of Man's Changing Vision of the Universe.* London: Hutchinson.

Kolakowski, Leszek. 1968. *The Alienation of Reason: A History of Positivist Thought.* Translated by Norbert Guterman. Garden City, NY: Doubleday.

___. 1972. *Positivist Philosophy from Hume to the Vienna Circle.* Translated by Norbert Guterman. Harmondsworth: Penguin Books.

Kuper, Adam. 1985. "Anthropology and Colonialism." *Anthropologists and Anthropology: The Modern British School.* Second edition. London: Routledge & Kegan Paul.

Lorenz, Konrad. 1966. *On Aggression.* New York: Harcourt, Brace & World.

Lovejoy, Arthur. 1936. *The Great Chain of Being: A Study of the History of an Idea.* Cambridge, MA: Harvard University Press.

Lundberg, George. 1939. *Foundations of Sociology.* New York: Macmillan.

Marx, Karl, and Friedrich Engels. 1947. *The German Ideology*: Parts 1 & 3. (Theses on Feurabach No. 11). New York: International Publishers.

Mill, John Stuart. 1984 [1850]. "The Negro Question." In John M. Robson (ed.), *The Collected Works of John Stuart Mill, Volume XXI — Essays on Equality, Law, and Education.* Introduction by Stefan Collini. Toronto: University of Toronto Press; London: Routledge and Kegan Paul.

Montagu, Ashley. 1965. *The Human Revolution.* New York: Bantam Books.

Montesquieu, Baron Charles de. 1973 [1721]. *Persian Letters.* Translated by C.J. Betts. Harmondsworth & New York: Penguin Books.

___. 1989 [1748]. *The Spirit of the Laws.* Translated and edited by Anne M. Cohler, Basia Carolyn Miller, and Harold Samuel Stone. Cambridge: Cambridge University Press.

Morris, Desmond. 1967. *The Naked Ape, A Zoologist's Study of the Human Animal.* New York: McGraw-Hill.

Rose, Nikolas. 1989. *Governing the Soul: The Shaping of the Private Self.* London: Routledge.

Rousseau, Jean-Jacques. 2008 [1962]. *The Social Contract.* New York: Cosimo Inc.

Saul, John Ralston. 1993. *Voltaire's Bastards: The Dictatorship of Reason in the West.* New York: Vintage.

Tiger, Lionel, and Robin Fox. 1971. *The Imperial Animal.* New York: Holt, Rinehart and Winston.

Zetterberg, Hans. 1954. *On Theory and Verification in Sociology.* Stockholm: Almquist and Wiksell.

Chapter 4

The Conservatism
of the Counter-Enlightenment

The Modern
Conservative Backlash

One lesson that history teaches us is that periods of rapid social and technological change often produce strong movements of resistance to that change. Times of accelerated innovation and transformation may also become times of great backlash— commonly referred to today as "pushback." Nowhere is this tendency more noticeable than in the world of politics and ideology. This historical lesson offers a simple social analogy to Isaac Newton's third law of motion, namely that any action is accompanied by a reaction of opposite and equal magnitude.

Figure 4-1 describes a large public rally organized by conservative TV talk-show host Glen Beck. This rally, named "Restoring Honor," was a quintessential conservative event inasmuch as it was held to publicize and promote core conservative values and beliefs. In calling for a return "to God," Beck and other speakers addressed the popular sense of discomfort that many in the audience experienced as a loss of national purpose and personal faith. Among the grievances felt by conservatives in

Figure 4-1 "Restoring Honor" Rally

The media and celebrity power exerted by some contemporary American conservatives could be seen in Washington on August 27, 2010, when conservative commentator, Glen Beck organized a "Restoring Honor" rally that was reportedly attended by around 100,000 people. Among the speakers at this rally was Sarah Palin, the former Vice-Presidential candidate for the Republican Party. The rally was controversially held on Martin Luther King Day — at the Lincoln Center, where Martin Luther King delivered his "I have a dream" speech forty-seven years earlier. The rally presented a classic agenda of conservative values. Listeners were warned of the decline of patriotism in America — as well as the erosion of such basic institutions as the family, the church and the community. Beck and other speakers urged the crowd to return the core values of America — and most importantly, to re-embrace religious faith and reject the creeping secularism of American society.

"Beck urged the country to 'turn back to God.'... Beck [said] the rally was meant to reclaim the U.S. civil rights movement 'from politics,' arguing that the movement was about 'people of faith who believe you have an equal right to justice.'"

Adapted from CNN Politics online, <http://articles.cnn.com/2010-08-30/politics/glenn.beck.rally.monday_1_conservative-commentator-glenn-beck>

the U.S., the following are particularly current: the growing secularization of American society and the decline of Judeo-Christian values; the corruption and immorality of corporate executives and high public officials (the disgraced list is a long one and includes Michael Milken, Bernie Madoff, Bernie Ebbers, Kenneth Lay, Conrad Black, Eliot Spitzer, Scooter Libby and Rod Blagojevich ... among others); the eclipse of "traditional" family values; and the loss of national prestige — with military defeats/stalemates in Vietnam, Afghanistan and Iraq. Besides a return to religious values, the Restoring Honor rally also called for a return to patriotism and respect for military service, some of the most fundamental conservative values of the present age.

As we shall see throughout this chapter, the beliefs expressed by conservatives have varied according to the time and place in which they lived and wrote. In this sense, the beliefs of conservatives have always remained "situational" in content. Thus, while eighteenth- and nineteenth-century European conservatives defended the aristocracy, nobility and monarchy against the destabilizing changes of capitalism, today's economic conservatives strongly identify themselves with the virtues of "free enterprise" and the autonomy of the market against the threats of "government intervention," socialism and the welfare state. Today, conservatives who are strong advocates of an unregulated private sector and who campaign for free trade, competition, privatization and deregulation are often referred to as "neoliberals." Neoliberals are economic conservatives; they seek a return to a world unfettered by government intervention, in which economic and social life is wholly determined by the autonomous market forces of supply and demand. Although some commentators have referred to a neoliberal "revolution" in domestic and foreign policy, neoliberalism remains, at heart, a conservative movement that seeks to restore the economic principles of a past — and mythologized — golden age.

Similarly, today's social conservatives often campaign against what they see as threats to public morality: such as crime, abortion, same-sex marriage and illegal immigration. It is difficult to enunciate a general conservative ideology, as the specific beliefs of conservatives have always been shaped in response to particular events within their own societies. In the eighteenth and nineteenth centuries, conservatism was largely "elitist" in its appeal to the privileged classes; today, it is more "populist" in its appeal to disaffected elements of the general population. What, then, is the underlying thread that allows us to include these disparate examples under the general classification of "conservative"? The answer to this question can only be stated in the most general terms. Conservatives — both past and present — have all claimed to defend those customary beliefs and practices that have proven their value over time against the encroachments of new or novel innovations which threaten

Figure 4-2 British National Party Manifesto: Combating the Erosion of British Culture

The character of daily life in Britain is becoming corroded by the gradual but inexorable loss of many of those things that made Britain civilised.

Culture, tradition, civility and heritage cannot be reduced to issues of economics or distorted by politically correct interference.

The people of England, Scotland, Wales and Ireland are bound together by blood and this close connection ensures an overlap of culture, heritage and tradition.

Our national character and native institutions are a precious heritage which reflect our origins and are an expression of our genetic identity.

We support a return to the traditional standards of civility and politeness in British life.

Courtesy, which is about consideration for others, should be taught in school, and demanded of government employees in their interactions with the public.

BNP *Manifesto 2010 : Culture, Traditions and Civil Society,* <www.general-election-2010.co.uk/bnp-manifesto-2010-general-election/bnp-manifesto-2010-culture-traditions-and-civil-society>.

to destabilize the traditional social order. This is why the nineteenth-century conservatives opposed the French Revolution, and this is why twenty-first-century conservatives oppose same-sex marriage, health-care reform and mass immigration. For most conservatives, the history of their societies is seen as a gradual retreat from an earlier golden age — or as a fall from grace. Their ideological battles are undertaken to preserve the best of the old and to resist the worst of the new. At heart, they remain nostalgic for a simpler age governed by traditional beliefs and practices that have stood the test of time.

In other Western societies that have experienced rapid (and often disruptive) social, cultural and technological changes, similar conservative sentiments are often expressed by politicians, clergy, journalists, pundits and media celebrities. For example, the excerpt in Figure 4-2 is taken from an election manifesto of the ultra-nationalist, far-right party in Great Britain — the British National Party (BNP).

The Conservative Code

The growth of far-right political parties and grassroots organizations in North America and Europe feeds off popular grievances and concerns that frequently receive sensational exposure in the conservative print media, Internet blogs, talk radio and cable TV news, and among conservative commentators and political pundits. A theme that appears in many conservative manifestos and policy statements is the perceived need for stronger expressions of patriotism or nationalism — declarations of love for the motherland, fatherland or homeland. Because of the greater porousness of international borders and national frontiers, as well as the greatly increased mobility of workers, strong expressions of patriotism may also be read as anti-immigrant sentiments. In many Western nations, fears about global terrorism have helped to channel anti-immigrant sentiment into outright Islamophobia — intolerance towards

Muslim immigrants. In the BNP election manifesto excerpt in Figure 4-2, anti-immigrant rhetoric is expressed in carefully coded language. The manifesto authors are concerned about "threats" to British identity, culture and heritage, and — most blatantly — genetic identity. "Traditional standards of civility and politeness" are subtly juxtaposed to the presumed, although unstated, rudeness of immigrants and "foreigners." Another far-right political group has recently emerged in the U.K. — the English Defence League — also with a strong anti-immigrant, anti-multicultural and anti-Muslim agenda.

These sentiments reveal an important aspect of conservative ideology, namely nostalgia for the "good old days," regret over the passing of a simpler and more secure time, the longing for a lost sense of community and for a lost national identity. Indeed, a strong sense of nostalgia for lost institutions and values has been an enduring theme in expressions of conservative ideology. It is the golden thread that connects the call for a return to family values and the traditional family, for a recommitment to our Judeo-Christian heritage in schools and in public life, for a return to common decency and public civility, for renewed expressions of patriotism and national pride, and for a restoration of respect for tradition. Traditional conservatism remains, at its root, an appeal for the return of the past.

Although conservative traditions share a common set of beliefs and values, each national movement displays the birthmarks of its own particular origins. Thus, conservatism in Great Britain differs in some ways from that in France, Germany and other nations. Likewise, notwithstanding its similarities, U.S. conservatism has remained distinct from other conservative traditions and has evolved in its own independent and separate direction. Because of the historical victory of the Enlightenment over conservative doctrines — and the triumph of reason, liberty and progress over tradition and nostalgia — conservative values are often relegated to the back burner in contemporary societies. At times of crisis and upheaval, however, conservative ideas sometimes reappear on the political horizon, often as sources of resistance to contemporary politics and ideology. At such times, conservative ideas may not always be expressed openly and directly, but more often in coded messages which can be easily deciphered by their intended audiences.

Thus, during the late 1950s and mid-1960s, in the heat of the civil rights protests and demonstrations in the U.S., southern politicians would frequently reaffirm their commitment to uphold "states' rights." This coded message referred to the constitutional right of individual American states to maintain their own racially segregated institutions — schools, restaurants and other public facilities such as toilets, drinking fountains, etc. — without any federal "interference." It required the passage of the *Civil Rights Act* in 1964 to finally outlaw racial segregation in both public and private sectors. Today, when conservatives talk about the "traditional family," they are offering a critique of same-sex marriages/unions and single-parent households. The expression "family values" becomes a critique of feminism and pro-choice abortion rights, as well as reproductive rights associated with stem cell research and in vitro fertilization, and pornography. Concerns over a perceived loss of "national identity" may be read as an attack on the policies of multiculturalism and cultural diversity. Policy recommendations for "health-care reform," "social welfare reform," "educational reform" and greater "consumer choice" are coded messages for the policies of privatization, de-regulation and full marketization.

Conservatism today is made up of a number of different intersecting and sometimes contradictory movements. Secular conservatives range from the economic libertarians of the small business classes to the neoconservatives (or neocons) with transnational corporate interests. Secular conservatives also include the militarist and national security lobbies of the nation state. However, the Christian right (sometimes referred to as "theo-cons") is also a formidable part of modern conservatism — especially in the U.S. The media of televangelism have mobilized a powerful religious lobby group that has often succeeded in imposing its priorities onto national domestic and foreign policy agendas. And beyond the margins of religious and secular conservatism lie the politics of the far right. This motley assortment of ultra-nationalist and xenophobic conservatives includes white supremacists and also — at least in the U.S. — patriot and armed militia groups, as well as neo-Nazis, all with strong anti-government ideologies and beliefs. At this extreme end of the political spectrum, the traditions of conservatism begin to merge with those of outright fascism. The horrific attacks in Norway by Anders Breivik, a fanatical far-right anti-immigrant, anti-Muslim ideologue who detonated a car bomb in Oslo in July 2011 which killed eight people, before travelling to the island of Utøya, where he randomly shot to death eighty-nine young people attending a youth camp, show the violent lengths to which some far-right ideologues may go to resist what they regard as the "corrupting influences" of multiculturalism, feminism and socialism. These attacks were "justified" in his manifesto, *2083: A European Declaration of Independence*.

The Roots of Modern Conservatism

The historical roots of modern conservatism extend back to the French Revolution, which, more than any other single event in European history, was a watershed in modern political thought — a watershed which serves to differentiate the competing ideologies of liberalism, socialism and conservatism. In many ways, the French Revolution was the culmination of other social and economic changes (such as the Agricultural and the Industrial Revolutions) that were transforming traditional European societies into modern nation states. As sociologist Robert Nisbet (1953, 1970, 1986) recognized, many of the central ideas of the early classical social theorists were directly related to the "transition crisis" — the transformation of traditional into modern societies. "The fundamental ideas of European sociology are best understood as responses to the problem of order created at the beginning of the nineteenth century by the collapse of the old regime under the blows of industrialism and revolutionary democracy" (Nisbet 1966: 21).

After the French Revolution, nothing was ever the same again. This event polarized social classes throughout Europe as nothing had ever done before. After the fall of the old regime and the execution of the French king, Louis XVI, and his queen, Marie Antoinette, the monarchs and aristocrats of other European nations went on the defensive. They had begun to feel the winds of change blowing through their own societies. Post-revolutionary Europe in the nineteenth century continued to be a hotbed of social unrest and political change. It was against this landscape of class war and revolutionary politics that the origins of modern conservative thought first emerged. Conservatism was born of a profound distrust of the abstract, universal ideas of the Enlightenment thinkers and of, what seemed to some as, the catastrophic consequences of these ideas. Indeed, it seemed to the conservative writers of the late eighteenth and early nineteenth centuries that the world had been turned upside down (see Hill 1972; Laslett 1965; Berman 1988). In France, the monarchy was overthrown and a totalitarian administration, the Committee for Public Safety, was formed by the new revolutionary government. For several years after the Revolution (1793–1794), the Committee for Public Safety imposed the Reign of Terror on the general population, during which priests, aristocrats, foreigners and political opponents were murdered — often guillotined — with impunity. For the landed nobility and the propertied classes in France, a traditional way of life had come to an end. Across Europe, the governments of kingdoms, dukedoms and other principalities braced themselves to confront a new threat that had arisen from the ashes of the French Revolution — the coronation of Napoleon as Emperor of France and a period of French military expansionism as the Napoleonic armies sought to spread their revolutionary doctrines across Europe. No wonder the conservatives hated the Enlightenment and all it stood for.

Conservatives at the Crossroads of History

If the Enlightenment philosophers believed that they spoke with the voice of reason, the conservative thinkers believed with equal fervour that they spoke with the voice of experience — indeed, with the wisdom of the ages. The French Revolution became many different things to many different people. For the Enlightenment *philosophes*, it was a time of emancipation and unprecedented promise. Humanity had finally been released from the shackles of prejudice, superstition and oppression. The possibilities for the progressive development of humanity seemed endless; the optimism of the times seemed boundless. However, as the political storm clouds began to darken over France, some of the most influential minds in Europe and America expressed their horror at what they perceived as the rise of terror and totalitarianism in France and their apprehensions for the future of civilized society.

Although the conservative thinkers shared many beliefs and values, there were also significant distinctions between thinkers from different national and cultural backgrounds. (One writer who has attempted to trace some of the leading patterns of conservative thought is Russell Kirk [1953; 1982]).

Two of the leading romantic conservative thinkers of the French Counter-Enlightenment were Louis de Bonald and Joseph de Maistre. In most respects, the French romantic conservative were far more extreme in their views than were such British conservatives as Edmund Burke. For this reason, the French thinkers may better be defined as "reactionaries" than as simple conservatives (cf. Robin 2011). They tended to idealize and roman- ticize the past and would have been happy to have re-imposed mediaeval social relations onto what they saw as the degenerate, corrupt and anarchic state of modern French society. Besides being strong traditionalists, however, the French romantic conservative were also theocratic thinkers who sought to re-establish the power and privilege of the Catholic Church in French society, and the supremacy of the Pope in all spiritual matters. (For recent commentaries on the French ultra-conservatives see Tarrago 1999: 167–77; Blum 2006: 23–30; Berlin 2005; Bradley 1999.)

Reactionary thinkers, rulers and politicians may be distinguished from conservatives by the extremism of their views. Whereas conservatives have sought to preserve the best of the past in an effort to slow or reverse the pace and extent of social change, reactionaries have often sought to forcibly restore the past and to reinstate traditional institutions. In post-revolutionary France, the French reactionaries fought to restore the power and privileges of the monarchy, aristocracy and clergy, and to re-impose feudal social relations on the general population. While conservatives may appear "gradualist" in their politics and opposed to sudden transformations in societal beliefs and practices, reactionaries may appear "revolutionary" in their desire to turn back the clock and re-impose a *status quo ante* (a previous state of affairs). This has been the case with many right-wing extremist parties — e.g., fascist, Nazi and neo-Nazi — all of which celebrate nationalism, racial purity, traditional authority and hierarchy, and an appeal to a romanticized or mythologized historical past.

The most extreme of the nineteenth-century conservative thinkers were often members of the overthrown French nobility who were united in their opposition to, and abhorrence of, the French Revolution and its aftermath. In their writings, they supported the restoration of an absolute monarchy, the return of the landed gentry to prominence and the re-establishment of the Catholic Church to its former position of authority. Some writers — such as the arch-conservative, Joseph de Maistre — called for the re-imposition of a theocratic state in France and the reconstitution of feudal social relations. Unlike many other conservatives of his time, de Maistre acquired a reputation for glorifying power and violence in bloodthirsty passages that have survived the test of time (see Figure 4-3).

The conservatism of Edmund Burke was more moderate than that of his French counterparts. Burke was not opposed, in principle, to all or any changes in social or political institutions. While he roundly condemned the "excesses" of the French Revolution, he took a different view of the earlier American Revolutionary War. For Burke, it was the British colonial government's unjust imposition of taxation without representation on the American colonies that precipitated the War of Independence. He considered the American Revolution a natural response to a colonial administration that had broken with tradition, abused its authority and flouted long established standards of natural justice. The American revolutionaries, unlike the French, fought in a just cause.

> ### Figure 4-3 The Violence of Reaction
>
> A Power, a violence, at once hidden and palpable… has in each species appointed a certain number of animals to devour the others…. And who [in this general carnage] exterminates him who will exterminate all others? Himself. It is man who is charged with the slaughter of man…. The whole earth, perpetually steeped in blood, is nothing but a vast altar upon which all that is living must be sacrificed without end, without measure, without pause, until the consummation of things, until evil is extinct, until the death of death….
>
> War is thus divine in itself, since it is a law of the world. War is divine through its consequences of a supernatural nature which are as much general as particular. War is divine in the mysterious glory that surrounds it and in the no less inexplicable attraction that draws us to it. War is divine by the manner in which it breaks out.
>
> Excerpt from the St. Petersburg Dialogues, Dialogue 7, Joseph de Maistre, 1971: 252–54.

There were other ways in which some of Burke's political conclusions departed from those of the French romantic conservatives. Burke was deeply opposed to the "peculiar" institution of slavery in the Americas. He also campaigned for an end to convict transportation to Australia. And, as an Irishman, he strongly supported Catholic Emancipation and remained a critic of British (mis)rule in Ireland. None of these concerns were typical of a hard-nosed, dyed-in-the-wool conservative. However, Burke remained true to his own conservative principles; his social criticism was based on his belief that the time-honoured traditions of natural and prescriptive justice and *noblesse oblige* had been violated by the irresponsibility of absentee landlords (in Ireland) and by the arbitrary brutality of plantation slavery (in the American colonies).

In the German principalities, conservative political opinion was represented in the writings of such thinkers as Justus Moser, Adam Muller, Karl von Haller and Georg Hegel (in his later years). Each of these thinkers in his own way strongly opposed the doctrines of the Enlightenment and the revolutionary changes that had occurred in France and other places. Von Haller's writings included a trenchant critique of Rousseau's conception of the social contract, while Moser and Muller idealized medieval social relations to the detriment of modern urban/industrial societies. In common with most conservative theorists, these thinkers strongly favoured a natural organic development of the state. Consequently, they opposed any arbitrary laws — whether legislated by monarchies or by republics — that would artificially interfere with the "natural processes" of social development. The most distinctive aspects of German conservatism were its "historicism" and its "idealism." German conservatives focused on the historical, cultural and inner "spiritual" development of their nations. Ironically, in his later years, Georg Hegel became known as one of the great conservative thinkers of his generation, although his earlier work was often seen as radical and revolutionary in its impact on popular political opinion.

The Conservative Conceptual Toolbox

The ideas of the romantic conservatives were far from monolithic in content. However, most conservatives shared a set of beliefs. The following list describes how these commonly held beliefs constituted the core of conservative social theory.

- *Anti-utopianism:* The conservatives profoundly distrusted the Enlightenment rationalists for their worship of abstract concepts such as reason, liberty, equality and progress. The rationalists believed that society could be reconstructed along such universal principles as the "natural rights of man" and the social contract. Conservatives dismissed these plans to reorganize society as dangerous utopian fantasies and feared that they would lead to new tyrannical forms of government. Conservative essayists Jonathan Swift and Daniel Defoe parodied the plans of social reformers in such books as *Gulliver's Travels* and *Robinson Crusoe*, while cartoonist James Gilray satirized the horrors of the French Revolution in the pages of *Punch* magazine. In the twentieth century, this tradition of conservative political satire was continued by writers such as C. S Lewis in *The Screwtape Letters*, Anthony Burgess in *The Clockwork Orange*, William Golding in *Lord of the Flies* and Aldous Huxley in *Brave New World*.
- *Importance of the irrational*: For the conservatives, any conception of human nature had to include irrational as well as rational factors. They believed

that human conduct is governed not only by reason and reflection but more often by sentiment, habit, custom and tradition — everything that the Enlightenment dismissed as prejudice and superstition. Prejudice, for conservatives, was the basis of social life and morality. It was the social cement that bonded together what would otherwise be only a conglomeration

Figure 4-4 Dangers of Abstraction

There are no men in the world. I have seen Frenchmen, Italians, Russians in my life… I even know, owing to Montesquieu, that one can be a Persian. But when it comes to man, I state I have never met him; even if he exists, I know nothing about him.

Joseph de Maistre [1796](1994) *Considerations on France, p. xxiii.*

of atomized individuals. "Man" as a thinking being (as emphasized by Descartes and Pascal) was replaced in conservative — and especially romantic — thought by "man" as a feeling being. The conservatives juxtaposed the importance of "needs" to the rationalists' insistence on "rights."

- *Rejection of abstractions:* Conservative thought was hostile to the idea of an abstract universal conception of human nature. Conservatives insisted that humankind is always defined in concrete rather than abstract terms, with particular rather than general characteristics. Real individuals are always associated with particular statuses in society defined by family, race, nation, "blood and soil" — such as father, son, lord, serf, French or English. Unlike the Enlightenment rationalists, who described humans in abstract slogans — such as "the citizen," "humanity" or the "universal brotherhood of man" — conservative thinkers strongly emphasized the importance of history, nationality, culture and homeland when talking about real individuals.

- *Anti-individualism*: One of the crucial aspects of conservative thought for the later development of sociological theory was its anti-individualism. Conservative thinkers rejected outright the (rationalist) view that society was nothing more than the sum (or aggregate) of naturally independent individuals who had come to a voluntary agreement on how to organize their society — the doctrine of the social contract. Instead, conservatives believed that each society had a life of its own which was greater than simply the sum of its parts. This idea is known as the "holistic," or "realist," perspective. Conservative thinkers reasoned that individuals are naturally dependent upon society for everything — for their identities, culture, nationality, language and social rank. In other words, individuals are products of a society that existed before them and which will continue exist long after them. None of us chooses which language we grow up speaking or with which currency we pay our bills. These things, like other aspects of our culture, are handed down to us from previous generations. They are products of a society that pre-dates us and will probably outlive us. For these reasons, conservatives saw society as an unbroken chain of events linking past to present to future generations. These considerations led conservative thinkers to conclude that society was best seen as a social organism made up of a number of vital parts, or institutions. Each of these institutions was presumed to have naturally evolved over many generations in order to satisfy some basic human needs. From these ideas, the analogy of

> ### Figure 4-5 The Web of Time
>
> It [the state] is a partnership in all science; a partnership in all art; a partnership in every virtue, and in all perfection. As the ends of such a partnership cannot be obtained in many generations, it becomes a partnership not only between those who are living, but between those who are living, those who are dead, and those who are to be born. Each contract of each particular state is but a clause in the great primeval contract of eternal society.
>
> Edmund Burke, *Reflections of the Revolution in France* 1959: 117.

society as a "social organism" was born, a view that has greatly influenced the development of sociological theory. This early "organicism" of the conservative thinkers set the stage for the later tradition of "structural functionalism," which was to dominate sociology for the greater part of the twentieth century. During the nineteenth century, however, the organic view of society provided conservative thinkers with an ideological weapon to use against the arguments of the rationalists. They argued that, if society was really an organism, it could not be rationally reconstructed along the lines proposed by the *philosophes*. The social organism was not a machine, and its vital parts could not be removed or replaced without inflicting serious injury, or even death, to the organism. In other words, it was necessary to nurture and preserve the major institutions of society as they embodied the legacy of countless previous generations and the inheritance for many future generations.

- *Importance of groups and sub-units*: Conservatives also insisted that people were primarily incorporated into society through small groups and associations. Unlike the rationalists, who proclaimed that individuals were, first and foremost, all equal citizens of the state, conservatives emphasized that real individuals found their social identities through membership in institutions — the family, community, church, occupation group and nation. Many conservative thinkers warned of the dangers facing individuals who were totally dependent upon the state. In order to prevent the kind of state tyranny that had accompanied the French Revolution, conservative theorists stressed the importance of pluralistic institutions in society that could shield, or buffer, the individual from the power of the state. In their own way, the conservatives provided us with an early critique of totalitarianism. They also warned of the dangers of excessive individualism. Over time, some of these ideas were taken up by social theorists who were far from being ideological conservatives. Auguste Comte, for example, believed that the decline of traditional religion required the growth of a new secular religion that could provide a rational basis for integrating and regulating individuals in society. Indeed, he proposed that sociology — the science of society — be adopted as the new secular religion. Even the great nineteenth-century sociologist Emile Durkheim was convinced that only by joining associations such as occupational corporations could individuals recover a sense of community and solidarity in the impersonal landscapes of the modern urban-industrial society.

- *Interdependence of social institutions*: Conservatives also believed, as part of their view of society as a social organism, that all parts of society are interdependent and interrelated. Any change in one part of society — such as the abolition of the monarchy — would affect the total social organism. For this reason, all attempts to bring about social change should be viewed with great caution.

- *Importance of basic needs*: In contrast to the Enlightenment emphasis on the "natural" or "universal" rights, Conservative thinkers insisted on the importance of the basic needs of members of society. According to their view, humankind has long experienced certain constant and unalterable needs, which have always been satisfied by particular social institutions. Among the most important of these needs are social order and moral regulation, needs that have traditionally been met by the institutions of government and the church. Conservatives feared that if the basic institutions of society were radically disrupted — by revolution or social unrest — then only misery and disorder would result. They were concerned that society — as a social organism — was vulnerable to "infection" from subversive ideas, much as the human body was vulnerable to infection, ill-health and death.

- *Importance of moral order and moral community:* The conservatives viewed the French Revolution as a major historical catastrophe. From their perspective, the Revolution had resulted in the social and moral disintegration of French society, which had descended into a state of moral anarchy. Not only had the subversive revolutionary doctrines of the Enlightenment successfully challenged long-held beliefs and traditions, but the growth of Protestantism — with its emphasis on individualism — had also undermined the spiritual unity of society. The conservatives looked with horror on the encroaching forces of urbanization, industrialization and secularization. They saw post-revolutionary society as a disorderly collection of egotistical individuals engaged in the pursuit of their own selfish ends. In this respect, nineteenth-century conservative thinkers were eloquent critics of capitalism. They compared the deepening divisions that existed in industrial society between the bourgeoisie and the working class with what they portrayed as the far more harmonious relations that had existed in earlier agrarian society between lord and peasant, monarch and subject. Indeed, much of their thinking and writing was centred on the need to re-establish an organic and moral community. There has always been a strong nostalgic tendency in conservative thought to idealize, or romanticize, past societies. This was clearly the case for the American pro-slavery writers of the ante-bellum literature of the nineteenth century. Example of this tradition are the book *The Passing of the Great Race* by Madison Grant (1916) and the movies *The Birth of a Nation* by D.W. Griffith (1915) and *Gone With the Wind* (1939), based on the 1936 book by Margaret Mitchell. Today, as already indicated, conservatives have been transformed from critics into apologists for capitalism. Whereas earlier conservatives saw capitalism as a serious threat to a social order based upon hereditary privilege and traditional authority, today's conservatives see capitalism as their best hope for preserving basic freedoms (of speech, assembly, trade and commerce) from the encroachments of government intervention, the indolence of the welfare state and the dangers of totalitarianism. But as always, conservatives see themselves as protecting the stability of the past from the perils of the future.

- *From anti-theory to social theory*: Although nineteenth-century conservative thought was motivated, above all, by the need to prevent revolutions, to restore old regimes, or to reinstate traditional principles in post-revolutionary regimes, the conservative tradition eventually acquired a life of its own. It became more than simply a rearguard action against the Enlightenment. Over time, its main ideas crystallized into a coherent worldview and a programmatic set of ideas that influenced other theorists, many of whom were neither, themselves, conservatives nor opponents of the bourgeois social order. Conservative thought has played an important role in the historical development of sociological theory. The organic analogy has proven to be a durable one. In retrospect, we can now see how the nineteenth-century tradition of organicism evolved into the twentieth-century theory of structural functionalism. Many other key conservative concerns — such as the significance of historicism, irrationalism, small groups and a strong moral community — influenced later social theorists, including, among others, Montesquieu, de Tocqueville, Le Play, Le Bon, Saint-Simon, Comte, Durkheim, Tonnies and Pareto. The conservative tradition bequeathed an enduring legacy of political and social thought that continues to the present day.

Two Faced Philosophers

To avoid oversimplifying the politics and ideologies of conservatism, several points should be emphasized. For a start, some of the thinkers normally classified as Enlightenment philosophers also had intellectual affinities with the romantic conservative writers. This was certainly the case for Rousseau, Hume, Kant and the later Hegel. It is always a mistake to try and pigeon-hole social theorists into "water-tight," or mutually exclusive, compart-ments. These writers were complex personalities and thinkers whose work defies easy classification. Second, considerable diversity existed among the Enlightenment writers and among the romantic conservative writers of the Counter-Enlightenment.

Indeed, there were several important Enlightenment thinkers whose work inspired later currents of romantic conservative thought. This was certainly true of Rousseau. For the educated classes of the later eighteenth century, Rousseau was celebrated by some, and vilified by others, as a radi-cal opponent of the old regime. His philosophical works on the origins of inequality and the social contract secured his reputation as a revolutionary thinker. However, other aspects of Rousseau's social thought — his worship of nature and his elevation of feeling and "sensibility" over reason — were to later endear him to some of the romantic conservatives.

Scottish philosopher David Hume was another Enlightenment thinker who inspired the romantic conservatives . Although Hume was a skepti-cal rationalist who openly questioned many things, including the need for religion, he differed from other Enlightenment thinkers on the question of "causality." Many Enlightenment rationalists believed that the natural world was constructed as a machine and operated according to the law of cause and effect. Instead of seeing the relationship between cause and effect as inherent in "nature," Hume believed that this relationship was a product of the human mind — a way of thinking about the relations between things. In acknowledging the power of the mind to actively create ideas — such as causality — Hume parted company with those Enlightenment thinkers who believed that the mind simply reflected sensations from the external world (Copleston 1964: 90–93). For another British philosopher, John Locke, the mind at birth was a blank, or empty, slate — a *tabula rasa* — which was gradu-ally filled with sensory experiences, or representations of the external world (Locke 1996: 7, 33). The belief that all knowledge is based upon sensations from the external world is known as "empiricism."

Besides questioning the philosophy of empiricism, Hume also questioned the philosophy of "deductivism" — the idea that all knowledge is based upon the logical relations between cause and effect. Instead, Hume pioneered a new philosophy of "inductivism" — the idea that knowledge was based not on the logical relations between things, but on the pattern of past, or customary, relations. In other words, Hume proposed that the best way to understand/predict future relations between things, or events, is to study the pattern of past relations. For Hume, understanding was a psychological rather than a logical process. As one commentator observed, "Hume's account of belief illustrates his tendency to confuse logic and psychology. For he gives a psychological answer to the logical question about the grounds of that assurance which he calls belief" (Copleston 1964: 93).

Hume's groundbreaking reflections on the active processes of the mind were further refined by the German philosopher Immanuel Kant. Indeed, Kant went beyond Hume in outlining the categorical frameworks — such as space, time and causality — that are necessary for us to organize and interpret our perceptions of "reality." Kant has often been categorized as a major Enlightenment thinker. Both he and Hegel contributed to the German philosophical tradition of idealism. However, Kant has also been seen as a critic of the Enlightenment concepts of "reason" and "experience." Because of this, he was eventually embraced by some of the romantic conservative thinkers.

Much the same could also be said of the ideas of Georg Hegel, one of the most influential philosophers of the twentieth century. Today, Hegel's philosophy presents us with some intriguing paradoxes. To the question of whether Hegel was an Enlightenment or a romantic conservative thinker, our answer must be both. On the one hand, the young Hegel was celebrated for introducing the tradition of "historical idealism," which viewed the historical process as the progressive realization of reason in the world. Hegel believed that history could be understood as the process whereby reason was able to overcome ignorance and superstition and thereby bring the impersonal forces of "nature" under conscious rational human control. It is easy to see why Hegel's theory of history appealed to many Enlightenment rationalists and revolutionary thinkers. Hegel pioneered a "dialectical" theory of history — the idea that historical change results from the gradual accumulation of minor changes, which lead eventually to sudden major transformations. The historical process that drives these revolutionary changes is not a straightforward or unilinear one. Rather, it develops through a series of internal oppositions, or "contradictions," which bring to a close one form of life and lay the ground for its transformation into a new form. It was this dialectical theory of history that endeared Hegel to the Enlightenment radicals and that later attracted Karl Marx to a dialectical theory of society. However, in his later years, Hegel was often viewed as a conservative thinker, largely based on Hegel's belief that the German state should be seen as the supreme incarnation of "historical reason." His idealization of the German state lost him many former admirers, but won over many former critics. More recent and more cynical writers have sometimes observed that Hegel's later ideas represented a retreat from the politics of the French Revolution and a step towards the future politics of the Third Reich.

New World versus Old World Conservatism

In contrast to the romantic conservatives of France and Germany and the constitutional conservatives in Great Britain, all of whom were Counter-Enlightenment thinkers, U.S. conservatism originated under somewhat different circumstances. The distinctive character of American conservatism reflects its particular historical and cultural origins and its own ideological evolution. One of the earliest differences was American conservatism's attitude towards the monarchy — and by extension, to the whole system of inherited wealth and privilege. European conservatives — and even the constitutionally minded Edmund Burke — regarded the monarchy as a sacred institution, the centrepiece of an organic system of inherited privilege in which rank, hierarchy and authority were divinely ordained and enforced through custom and tradition. Insurrection, rebellion, revolt or revolution against the monarchy was seen, not simply as treason, but as an attack against the natural order of things. The traditional conservative sanctification of the monarchy was inspired by the Divine Right of Kings and the Great Chain of Being (see Lovejoy 1936 and Danby 1948 for a literary application of these ideas).

For the American colonists, 1776 was the year in which they broke their connection with the British monarchy. "No taxation without representation" was the battle cry of the American Revolution — an event which shaped the course of U.S. politics for many years to come. Some of the land-owning elites — the Loyalists and the Tories — supported the British Crown, and an estimated 20 percent of the population of the colonies left the U.S. for Canada or for Mother England. This haemorrhage of landed gentry, rich merchants, old families and colonial officials led to a "decapitation" of the leadership which had presided over the American colonies. In this respect, the slate was wiped clean, with the removal of the old representatives of the crown, the hereditary aristocracy and the established church. In other words, the very elements that formed the backbone of the romantic conservative reaction in Europe were swept away by the revolutionary broom of history in America. However, the old elites were soon replaced by new elites — with the rise of a new commercial and industrial bourgeoisie. But unlike the European aristocratic elites, which remained staunchly monarchist in their political ideologies, the new American elites were — for the most part — passionate republicans. Even the most conservative American political thinkers shared strongly republican sentiments.

This republican pedigree, which conservatives share with all other political persuasions in the U.S., has given a confusing twist to American conservatism. In an important sense, all American political parties are descendants of republicanism. For this reason, it is sometimes difficult to decide whether or not particular individuals or organizations should be classified as conservative or liberal in their political orientation. Whereas in Europe and Britain these opposing political philosophies were sharply separated from each other, in the U.S., many conservatives appeared to hold liberal views on a number of particular issues. John Adams, who is often cited as a conservative thinker, advocated free trade on the one hand, but a strong federal government, on the other. Today, these would probably be seen as contradictory political positions. Thomas Jefferson was a strong advocate for religious freedom and toleration, but an equally strong partisan for small government. He also is normally recognized as a conservative thinker. When compared to their European counterparts, the Americans appear — in some respects — more like liberals than traditional conservatives. None of the European conservatives, with the exception of Edmund Burke, would have supported free trade — an ideology closely associated with Adam Smith, a pre-eminent thinker of the Enlightenment. Most European conservatives strongly endorsed the royal monopolies and the navigation acts that regulated trade, commerce and industry well into the nineteenth century.

At the same time, post-revolutionary America was hardly a classless or egalitarian society. Besides the widespread practice of the "peculiar institution" of slavery, other traditional forms of social inequality and stratification continued to divide the population. Independence and the demise of the colonial aristocracy simply led to a rearrangement of class domination. The new home-grown elite was, if anything, more rapacious than the old — in its ruthless expropriation of "Indian" land and its exploitation of the domestic and immigrant working class. After independence, many political divisions in America were more personal than political — such as the parting of the ways between Thomas Jefferson and James Madison in 1824 with the breakup of their Democratic-Republican Party. Other divisions were to prove more fundamental, especially those around the issue of slavery. When, in the 1830s, the southern conservative Dixiecrat John Calhoun formed the Whig party, which supported the Union and opposed abolitionism, the political division over slavery became more fully institutionalized.

Ironically, in view of the course of twentieth and twenty-first century politics, in the nineteenth century it was the Republican Party rather than the Democratic Party that opposed slavery and supported the cause of abolitionism — with the slogan "free land, free labor and free men." And it was, of course, the Republican Party under Abraham Lincoln that fought against the secessionists of the southern slave states during the American Civil War. Indeed, the closest that any American politician

Figure 4-6 The Conservatives: Different National Traditions

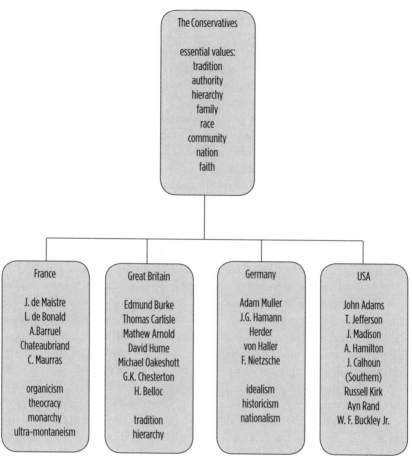

came to emulating the die-hard conservatives of the European romantic conservatives was John Calhoun, who defended slavery against what he perceived as the corrupting forces of modernization. For him, the white plantocracy represented a natural elite in an organic society dominated by landed property and inherited wealth and based upon a hierarchy of racial and class privilege. The Old South — as portrayed in the movie *Gone With the Wind* — symbolized for Calhoun the same set of values that the *ancien regime* symbolized for Louis de Bonald and Joseph de Maistre. The apologists for the southern plantocracy were as close as America ever came to the Counter-Enlightenment reaction.

Conservatism Today

Conservatism today, as a political brand, is far from being a single homogenous movement in either North America or Europe. In fact, conservatism in most Western societies covers a broad spectrum of orientations, some of which come close to contradicting each other. The most obvious tension that exists on the political right is that between economic and social conservatives. Economic conservatives (or neoliberals), for the most part, favour free market policies (those that emphasize privatization, de-regulation and full marketization), reduced social spending, low taxes and limited central government. Social conservatives, on the other hand — especially those informed by the Christian right — are far more concerned with what they define as a return to traditional standards of public and private morality. In their promotion of "family values," social conservatives are strongly opposed to such current "permissive" practices as pro-choice abortion rights, same-sex marriage rights and legally available pornography. They also campaign for the return of school prayer, greater law-and-order legislation and the restoration of capital punishment, in those jurisdictions that have abolished the death penalty.

While many voters embrace both social and economic conservatism, this has not always been the case. Indeed, it has become increasingly apparent that while economic conservatism — at least in North America — appeals to the larger business community, the appeal of social conservatism is strongest among voters in the more marginalized or more traditional regions of society. In Canada, for example, the basis of support for socially conservative parties such as the Conservative Party of Canada (and its predecessors, the Reform Party and Canadian Alliance) was in the "Bible Belt" — the rural west — especially Alberta, British Columbia and other Prairie Provinces. Similarly, in the U.S., much of the support for the grassroots Tea Party that surfaced in 2010 appeared to come from the more marginalized regions — from the south, from Appalachia and from the decaying rustbelt towns strewn across the country. Like its grassroots (or "populist") counterparts elsewhere, the Tea Party targeted the politics of the "elitist establishment." However, the rise of grassroots social conservative movements has sometimes produced tensions with other conservative interest groups. While social conservatives often campaign for a return to traditional morality and family values, they also embrace anti-immigrant and xenophobic views. Although this kind of narrow parochialism reflects working-class fears of job losses — arising from privatization, domestic downsizing, overseas out-sourcing and increased global competition — these grassroots concerns can sometimes run counter to the business interests of the corporate agenda. Thus, the social conservatism of conservative populists may coexist uneasily with the economic conservatism of the corporate conservatives. In other words, conservatism is not immune to the class divisions that have produced tensions and splits in other political constituencies. These tensions are sometimes apparent in the uneasy alliance that exists between social conservatives and economic conservatives in the Conservative Party of Canada. In the U.S., similar tensions can be observed within the Republican Party. Today, more than ever, the legacy of traditional conservatism is split between interest groups with differing political agendas.

References

Berlin, Isaiah. 2005. *Two Enemies of the Enlightenment: The Second Onslaught: Joseph de Maistre and Open Obscurantism.* The Isaiah Berlin Virtual Library At <http://berlin.wolf.ox.ac.uk/lists/nachlass/maistre.pdf>.

Berman, Marshall. 1988. *All That Is Solid Melts into Air: The Experience of Modernity.* Harmondsworth, Middlesex: Penguin (Non-Classics).

Blum, Christopher Olaf. 2006. "On Being Conservative: Lessons from Louis de Bonald." *The Intercollegiate Review* 41: 23–31.

Bradley, Owen. 1999. *Modern Maistre: The Social and Political Thought of Joseph de Maistre.* Lincoln: University of Nebraska Press.

Burgess, Anthony. 1962. *The Clockwork Orange.* New York: WW Norton.

Burke, Edmund. 1959. *Reflections on the Revolution in France.* Edited by William B. Todd. New York: Holt, Rinehart and Winston.

Copleston, Frederick. 1964. *A History of Philosophy.* Vol. 5 (Part 2). Garden City, NY: Image Books (Doubleday).

Cukor, George, Sam Wood, and Victor Fleming (directors). 2000 [1939]. *Gone With the Wind.* Warner Home Video.

Danby, John. 1948. *Shakespeare's Doctrine of Nature — A Study of King Lear.* London: Faber.

Defoe, Daniel. 2003 [1719]. *Robinson Crusoe.* Harmondsworth: Penguin Classics.

Golding, William. 1954. *Lord of the Flies.* London: Faber and Faber.

Grant, Madison. 1916. *The Passing of the Great Race; or, The Racial Basis of European History.* New York: Charles Scribner's Sons.

Griffith, D.W. 1998 [1915]. *The Birth of a Nation* (originally called The Clansman). Image Entertainment DVD.

Hill, Christopher. 1972. *The World Turned Upside Down: Radical Ideas During the English Revolution.* Harmondsworth: Penguin Books.

Huxley, Aldous. 1962 [1932]. *Brave New World.* New York: Vintage Paperbacks.

Kirk, Russell. 1953. *The Conservative Mind: From Burke to Eliot.* Washington, DC: Regnery Publishing.

___. 1982. *The Portable Conservative Reader.* NJ: Viking/Penguin.

Laslett, Peter. 1965. *The World We Have Lost: England Before the Industrial Age.* New York: Charles Scribner's Sons.

Lewis, C.S. 2001 [1942]. *The Screwtape Letters.* San Francisco: HarperCollins.

Locke, John. 1996 [1689]. *An Essay Concerning Human Understanding.* Abridged and edited by Kenneth P. Winkler. Indianapolis/Cambridge: Hackett Publishing.

Lovejoy, Arthur. 1936. *The Great Chain of Being: A Study of the History of an Idea.* Cambridge, MA: Harvard University Press.

Maistre, Joseph de. 1971. *The Works of Joseph de Maistre.* Translated by Jack Lively
    New York: Schocken Books.

___. 1994 [1796]. *Considerations on France.* Edited by Richard Lebrun. Oxford: Oxford
    University Press.

Mitchell, Margaret. 1936. *Gone With the Wind.* New York: Macmillan Publishers.

Nisbet, Robert. 1953. *The Quest for Community: A Study in the Ethics of Order and Freedom.*
    New York: Oxford University Press.

___. 1966. "The Two Revolutions." Chap. 2 in *The Sociological Tradition.* New York:
    Basic Books.

___. 1970. *The Social Bond: An Introduction to the Study of Society.* New York: Alfred A.
    Knopf.

___. 1986. *Conservatism: Dream and Reality.* Minneapolis: University of Minnesota Press.

Robin, Corey. 2011. *The Reactionary Mind: Conservatism from Edmund Burke to Sarah Palin.*
    New York: Oxford University Press.

Swift, Jonathan. 1996 [1726]. *Gulliver's Travels.* Mineola, NY: Dover Publications.

Tarrago, Rafael E. 1999. "Two Catholic Conservatives: The Ideas of Joseph de
    Maistre and Juan Donoso Cortes." *Catholic Social Science Review* 4: 167–77.

Chapter 5

The Positivism of Auguste Comte

Technocracy and Its Discontents

According to Fischer (1990: 17), "Technocracy, in classical political terms, refers to a system of governance in which technically trained experts rule by virtue of their specialized knowledge and position in dominant political and economic institutions." Today, we live in an age in which the promises of science and technology to solve our problems and add to our happiness have never been greater. Science and technology have already sent us to the moon — and on to outer space. They have genetically modified our crops for increased productivity and greater resistance to disease. They have revolutionized our information, communication and transportation systems. They have pioneered new surgical procedures, new therapeutic drugs and new medical advances. They have rebuilt our cities and transformed our landscapes. Future green technologies promise to solve the problems of climate change, much as new biotechnologies promise to find new cures for systemic diseases through genetic engineering and stem cell research. The promises of science and technology are apparently limitless. And to the extent that we continue to trust these promises, we remain children of the Enlightenment — firm optimistic believers in the inevitability of progress. But as Figure 5-1 makes clear, not everyone believes in the promise

<table>
<tr><td>

Figure 5-1 The Technocrats

"We're Embarking on a Progressive Experiment with High Stakes for the Nation"

When historians look back on the period between 2001 and 2011, they will be amazed that a nation that professed to hate bureaucracy produced so much of it... they will see it as another progressive era... based on the faith in government experts and their ability to use social science analysis to manage complex systems.

This progressive era is being promulgated without much popular support. It's being led by a large class of educated professionals, who have been trained to do technocratic analysis, who believe that more analysis and rule-writing is the solution to social breakdowns, and who have constructed ever-expanding networks of offices, schools and contracts....

If the reforms fail... large sectors of the population... will feel as if their country has been hijacked by a self-serving professional class mostly interested in providing for themselves.

If that backlash gains strength, well, what's the 21st-century version of the guillotine?

David Brooks, July 19, 2010, "The Technocracy Boom," *New York Times* <http://www.nytimes.com/2010/07/20/opinion/20brooks.html?_r=0>.

</td></tr>
</table>

of this brave new world. Ever since the Enlightenment, skeptics, cynics and satirists have ridiculed the exaggerated claims of technocrats that they can rationally reshape our world and solve society's most pressing problems.

English literature is replete with such portraits of scientists and technocrats. In *Gulliver's Travels*, Jonathan Swift satirized a visit he had paid to the Royal Society of London in 1710. His comical account describes the professors at the Grand Academy of Lagado engaged in such projects as extracting sunbeams from cucumbers, pumping farts from dead dogs and converting human excrement into food Later allegories of technocratic societies — such as *Brave New World* by Aldous Huxley, *1984* by George Orwell and the dark fantasies of Kurt Vonnegut — were written more as warnings of things to come rather than as exercises in the absurd. Much of the fictional literature on technocratic societies is fixated on dark themes, most of which reflect common apprehensions about the power of technology to dominate and control our lives. The ambivalence expressed in earlier literature towards science and technology reappears in much contemporary science fiction. Technology, it seems, brings forth not only dreams of utopias but also nightmares of dystopias.

Among the many nightmare visions that have appeared both in print and on screen, two themes in particular seem to speak to the fears of past and present generations. The first relates technocracy to totalitarianism: a technocratic society that totally dominates, regulates and manipulates its members. Examples of these dystopic visions of technocracy are legion — ranging from Huxley's and Orwell's books, mentioned above, to such movies as *The Matrix*, *Blade Runner*, *Gattaca* and *V is for Vendetta*, among others. The second theme, closely related to the first, is the alienation of humans from the machine. More than simply a protest against totalitarianism, this theme suggests that the mechanized, automated, engineered, cybernetic and robotic societies of the future — and, increasingly, of the present — are, in some important ways, contrary to "human nature." They are, in the strongest possible sense, "unnatural." The image of human heroes fighting to retain their humanity in a world in which machines and cyborgs threaten to destroy or alter human nature is a haunting and pervasive theme in science fiction nightmares. This theme clearly speaks to popular fears about the future impact of technocracy on our moral, as much as on our physical, survival as a species.

Over the past fifty years or so, there has been no shortage of critical accounts of the failures or dysfunctions of technocratic — including industrial, military, municipal and even psychotherapeutic — projects. Most of these cases have revealed the limitations of technocratic pipe-dreams, as well as the hubris of those technocrats who have sought to re-engineer the core elements of human nature. One of the early examples of a technocratic regime was the system of scientific management introduced by Frederick

Winslow Taylor in the opening decade of the twentieth century. Although this system laid the foundations for mass production in many industries — most notably in the automobile industry under Henry Ford — it also generated new problems of worker alienation, boredom and resistance on the assembly line (see, for example, Blauner 1964; Chinoy 1955; Shepard 1971; Braverman 1974). In time, "Taylorism" became a synonym for mechanized forms of exploitation, alienation and de-skilling in the workplace and has now been largely displaced by new production technologies and new management strategies. Further examples of the unintended dysfunctional consequences of technocracy may be seen in the massive urban development (and slum clearance) schemes undertaken in many inner city neighbourhoods throughout the 1960s and 1970s. Most of these projects were designed and implemented by technical experts without any grassroots community consultation or involvement. Consequently, old neighbourhoods with established communities were often destroyed and replaced by anonymous housing estates which rapidly degenerated into high crime areas and no-go zones (see, for example, Jacobs 1961; Wirth 1938; Mumford 1961). In Canada, an early victim of urban renewal was the Black community of Africville within the city of Halifax. Once again, the hubris of the technocratic planners had overlooked basic human needs — in this case, the need for a sense of community and neighbourhood identity (Clairmont and Magill 1999).

Figure 5-2 Technocracy and War

A dramatic example of how the best-laid plans of technocrats can go awry comes out of the Vietnam War. Back then, the US Secretary of Defense, Robert McNamara brought into his department a new generation of scientifically trained experts to run the war as rationally and efficiently as possible. Many of these experts were recruited from the Rand Corporation and became known as McNamara's "whiz kids." With their systems analyses, time and motion studies and precise cost-benefit calculations, they promised to win the war in record time and at minimum cost. They applied the latest techniques of economic analysis, operations research, game theory and computing to the war effort, and introduced modern management systems to coordinate the Planning, Programming and Budgeting Systems of the Department of Defense. Together they devised a modern defence strategy for the Nuclear Age that seemed — from their own glowing accounts — invincible. But as we now know — forty years later — all the social science, organizational research and technological hubris in the world was not enough to defeat the enemy in combat. Precision-guided missiles, toxic jungle defoliants, "psychological operations" and U.S.-led "agrarian land reform programs" all failed to break the will of the Vietnamese combatants, and at the end of the day, the Americans were ignominiously defeated. The Vietnam War proved beyond any doubt that political problems require political, not technocratic, solutions. Four decades later, we are still learning that lesson. (See Halberstam,1993; Hendrickson, 1997; Wright, 2012.)

Some of the most dramatic examples of technocratic hubris are to be seen in the inflated, and often unrealistic, expectations placed by government defence and security agencies in new military technologies and planning strategies. Although the application of science to military technology has produced a formidable hardware of nuclear and conventional weapons of mass destruction, the military-industrial technocracy, at least in the U.S. and other NATO states, continues to reveal its limitations and vulnerabilities on the battlefield. Nowhere was the gap between the inflated promises and the failed outcomes of the American military technocracy more apparent than in the case of the Vietnam War. Notwithstanding their superior weaponry, their control of the air space and their use of social science in counter-insurgency and pacification programs, the U.S. military was unable to achieve a final victory in this war. Robert McNamara (secretary of defence under Presidents John F. Kennedy and Lyndon B. Johnson from 1961–1968) and his "whiz kids" were soon to learn that the application of reason to the conduct of war was no guarantee of "success," "victory" or "progress." Indeed, the lesson to be learned from these examples is that there are no simple technological solutions to complex political problems.

More recently, similar examples of technocratic hubris have been seen in American announcements of a "revolution in military affairs" (RMA) resulting from the application of information technology (IT) to military hardware. The promise of an RMA led Donald Rumsfeld, Defense Secretary under George W. Bush, to pronounce a "military transformation" in the U.S. invasion and occupation of Iraq in 2003. This military transformation emphasized the use of high altitude "smart" bombs and precision-guided missiles instead of the — more conventional — heavy deployment of ground troops. Once again, the inflated promises of the technocrats — often opposed by conventional military commanders — have proven to be hollow. The war in Iraq has not been "won" by superior military technology and may well have been "lost" through technocratic hubris. The war in Afghanistan appears to be headed for a similar outcome. Today, more than ever before, we have become painfully aware that technocratic solutions often rebound in the form of new problems. In other words, we have learned that big technology — whether mechanical or organizational — is not the answer to every question. Technology has its limits, and technocracy, its own dysfunctions.

The Original Technocrats

The promises and limitations of technocracy are exemplified in the work of Auguste Comte. In some ways, Comte was — or aspired to be — a nineteenth-century technocrat. He was, along with his mentor and teacher, Henri de Saint-Simon, one of the earliest thinkers of the modern age to openly campaign for the application of social science to the solution of societal problems. For this alone he deserves our attention as a prototypical technocrat. He wrote at a time when popular expectations of the power of reason to solve social problems were at their highest, and when many of the resultant problems of social engineering had yet to become apparent.

Comte's relationship to his mentor appears in retrospect to have been a parasitic and unprincipled one. Although Comte was greatly influenced by the political and social theories of Saint-Simon, and served as his secretary for several years (1819–1822), Comte took full credit in his later writings for many of Saint-Simon's ideas and hardly acknowledged any influence from his former teacher. For this reason, Comte has sometimes been accused of plagiarism (see Zeitlin 2001: 69, 77).

Saint-Simon introduced many of the basic ideas that Comte later developed more fully. It was Saint-Simon who first coined the expression "social physics" to designate the scientific study of society. Saint-Simon was also the first to analyze the division of labour in industrial societies when he referred to the "bees" (workers, industrialists, scientists, artists, merchants, traders, etc), who worked and produced, versus the unproductive "drones" (rentiers, landlords, aristocrats, clergy and monarchy), who did not. Saint-Simon further distinguished between what he regarded as the two quintessential types of society: the feudal (or military) system versus the industrial system. This dualism was later appropriated by the British social theorist Herbert Spencer, for whom it became a central typology.

Saint-Simon was one of the forerunners of modern socialist thought — inasmuch as he advocated public rather than private ownership of the means of production in society and an end to capitalism. He was a pre-Marxist socialist. Marx ridiculed Saint-Simon and other earlier socialist thinkers, such as Charles Fourier, Pierre-Joseph Proudhon and Robert Owen, as "utopian socialists." (This term was popularized by Friedrich Engels in his book *Socialism: Utopian and Scientific*, 1892, which was extracted from his earlier text *Anti-During*, 1878.) For both Marx and Engels, utopian socialists were those whose idealist conception of socialism remained grounded in a moralistic and regressive model of society. Utopian socialists, not unlike their conservative adversaries, continued to hope that history could somehow be put into reverse gear; that the clock could somehow be turned back to an era of pre-industrial harmony. According to Marx, the utopian socialists believed that socialism could be achieved simply through the application of (social) science to society — without any political struggle by the working class for revolutionary change. They failed to recognize that modern capitalism had changed forever the rules of the game for everyone.

> They still dream of experimental realization of their social Utopias, of founding isolated phalansteries, of establishing "Home Colonies,"

of setting up a "Little Icaria" — duodecimo editions of the New Jerusalem — and to realize all these castles in the air, they're compelled to appeal to the feelings and purses of the bourgeois. By degrees they sink into the category of the reactionary conservative Socialists depicted above, differing from these only by more systematic pedantry, and by their fanatical superstitious belief in the miraculous effects of their social science. They, therefore, violently oppose all political action on the part of the working-class; such action, according to them, can only result from blind unbelief in the new Gospel. (Marx and Engels 1992 [1848]: 36–37)

At the same time, however, Marx learned much from the utopian socialists, and some of his key concepts — notably that of "class conflict" — were borrowed (although later adapted) from these early socialist traditions.

In some respects, Saint-Simon was more forward-thinking than many of his contemporaries. Whereas most of the nineteenth-century utopian socialists conceived of building a socialist society in local terms — factory by factory and village by village — Saint-Simon envisaged socialism on a national scale, with a centralized mode of production. In this sense, he helped to blaze the trail that Marx and Engels later trod when they dreamed of the revolutionary conquest of state power by an awakened proletariat.

It is in his national and centralized vision of the new society that Saint-Simon reveals his credentials as an original technocrat. Unlike previous socialist thinkers, Saint-Simon believed that the future administration of a socialist society should be run by (social) scientists and industrialists — a new technocracy in all but name. He felt that the authority of the new state should be centralized and that economic production should be centrally planned and regulated by the state. It was this vision of the new social order that led Durkheim to distinguish Saint-Simon's ideas of socialism from those of other contemporary socialists. Whereas other socialists relied on the authoritarian power of the state to administer the new society, Saint Simon placed all of his hopes on the new science of society to educate and uplift the masses:

At first such a conclusion may be surprising, for it seems to contradict the authoritarian character which the Saint-Simonian system presents in certain passages. For have we not seen Saint-Simon demand that a national catechism be established and that all contrary instruction be prohibited? But what makes this contradiction disappear — at least what lessens it — is that, if Saint-Simon does recognize an authority, it is exclusively that of science, and this authority, having no need of force to be accepted, impresses him.... Force is unnecessary where attraction suffices, and consequently the role of the managers of society is needed only to apprise men

> where their advantage lies, that is to say, what modes of conduct are implied in the nature of things. (Durkheim 1959: 98)

Although most of Saint-Simon's ideas for social reform and reconstruction now appear hopelessly antiquated and outdated, he deserves recognition as one of the early pioneers of social science, and as one of the forerunners of the independent discipline of sociology. It was, Saint-Simon — and not Comte — who first proposed that the scientific study of society should be divided between the study of social statics (order) and the study of social dynamics (progress). It was also Saint-Simon — and not Comte — who first enunciated the law of the three stages: the periodization of history into three evolving stages of human consciousness — the Theological, the Metaphysical and the Positive (or Scientific) stages. And it was also Saint-Simon rather than Comte who, in his doctrine of the New Christianity, first promulgated a new secular religion based on science and the "positive philosophy." These ideas later inspired social engineering projects that continued well into the twentieth century — and beyond.

Settling Accounts

Today, the main claim to fame of Auguste Comte is for popularizing the term "sociology" and for advocating sociology as the scientific study of society. And while Comte is still honoured as a founding father of sociology, most modern commentators have found little to applaud and much to criticize in his ideas. However, students should resist the temptation to dismiss Comte because of some of his more bizarre and outdated ideas. Instead, we should try to understand him against the background of the of the times in which he lived. Indeed, the golden rule for understanding all the social theorists is to contextualize them — to place them firmly within their historical context. Comte's view of society as an organism constitutes an important link in the chain of social thought that that can be traced back through the Enlightenment to Ibn Khaldun and all the way to the ancient Greeks (Rigney 2001: 17).

Comte was a social thinker who set himself some very ambitious goals. In his main work, *The Course of Positive Philosophy*, he wanted to create a comprehensive intellectual system that would synthesize all available knowledge. His positive philosophy was designed as a treatise on the proper method for acquiring knowledge, as well as a program for the improvement of society. Comte's hope was to find a way to preserve the unity of knowledge at a time of growing specialization and fragmentation.

Comte was deeply shocked by the aftermath of the French Revolution. He believed that the Revolution had rocked the foundations of French society and had destabilized the political and moral order. As previously mentioned, the French Revolution was followed by a Reign of Terror — from 1793 to 1794 — when thousands of opponents or suspected opponents of the new regime were guillotined or shot. It was a time of unprecedented civil unrest and mass executions.

For these reasons, Comte set himself the task of developing a science of society which could be used to reconstruct a new moral order — or *consensus universalis* — in France. This concern over the collapse of the moral order was shared by many other thinkers of this era. Some, like de Bonald and de Maistre, were outright conservatives, whereas others, like Emile Durkheim, were more liberal thinkers. But for many theorists of the post-revolutionary period, the reconstruction of the moral order in France became one of the most urgent and pressing issues of the age.

Although Comte shared the concerns of the conservatives about the apparent breakdown of the political and moral order, he was optimistic that science could solve the major social problems. In Comte's view, the fall of the *ancien regime* had left French society without any shared moral basis. The new institutions had failed to create any stable or durable social bonds. Post-revolutionary society in France was divided by the ongoing conflicts between radicals, liberals and conservatives.

Faced with these problems, Comte eventually concluded that only a new type of secular religion could provide an effective basis for re-integrating the individual into society. According to Comte, the new religion — what he was later to call the "religion of humanity" — should be based upon a scientific understanding of society. This new science of society could then be used to reconstruct the political and moral order and to solve the outstanding social problems of the day. One of Comte's more controversial opinions was that the new society should be governed by social scientists — a social technocracy

Figure 5-3 Nineteenth Century Political Ideologies

Conservatism	Liberalism	Socialism & Communism
Hierarchy	Individualism	Class polarization (i.e. pauperism &
Traditional authority	Utilitarianism	immiseration)
Social order	Spontaneous social order	Social (and economic) planning
Organic community	Universalism	Redistribution of wealth
Nation	Self-regulating market economy	Abolition of private property
Race	Non-interference	Self-governing communities & industrial
Status	Laissez-faire	enterprises
Family	Free trade	Socio-economic reforms
Non-Rational (Romantic) factors	Maximal utility	Universal franchise
Ritual, Ceremony & Worship	Representative government	Revolutionary change
	Political reforms	
	Limited franchise	
	Piece-meal social reform	

in all but name. In his view, only social scientists had the knowledge to guide the process of social reconstruction and to inform the process of government.

Comte's Theory of Positivism

In many ways, the cornerstone of Comte's social thought is to be found in his positive philosophy, or his theory of positivism. It is worth recalling that this theory, like so many of Comte's ideas, first originated in the work of Saint-Simon. For Comte, the theory of positivism entailed both a theory of knowledge and a theory of society. As a theory of knowledge, positivism emphasized the importance of observation, experiment and comparison as essential methods for the scientific study of society. Positivism sought to discover the natural laws that governed social development and to introduce social reforms that were consistent with these laws. The goal of positivism was to bring together the intellectual traditions of rationalism (Descartes, Voltaire, etc) and empiricism (Galileo, Newton, Bacon, Locke, etc) into a powerful new scientific synthesis. Comte wanted to combine the best of both worlds — reason and experience — into the scientific study of society.

Comte chose the term "positivism" to distinguish his philosophy from what many critics had labelled the "negative philosophy" of Hegel because of its critical tendencies. "Positive philosophy" was a conscious reaction against the critical and destructive tendencies of French and German rationalism, a reaction that was particularly bitter in Germany., Contemporaries recognized that the principles Hegel enunciated in his philosophy led him "to a critique of everything that was hitherto held to be the objective truth." His philosophy "negated" — namely, it repudiated any irrational and unreasonable reality" (Marcuse 1960: 325). In contrast to Hegel, who emphasized the changing, contradictory and dialectical nature of "reality," Comte believed in a stable reality made up of verifiable facts which were discoverable through observation and experience. In place of dangerous "metaphysics," Comte pioneered the scientific study of society. The following were some of the main characteristics of Comte's theory of positivism:

Anti-critical: Positivism was opposed to all systems of thought that it regarded as unsound or undesirable, especially religious and metaphysical systems. It was particularly opposed to all forms of critical thought that sought to contrast "what is" with "what could, or should be." Positivism remained resolutely "presentist" in orientation, that is, strongly anchored in the present and opposed to the utopianism and radicalism of the Enlightenment, to the negativism of Hegel and to revealed "faith" of traditional religions.

- *Scientistic*: Another characteristic of Comte's positivism was its scientism — the belief that only the natural sciences provided an appropriate model for all other disciplines of inquiry. Positivists believed that knowledge is a unified whole and that the methods of acquiring knowledge are the same for all fields of human inquiry. The appeal of the scientific model was based on the track record of science (from Galileo to Newton), on the need for effective social reforms (or social engineering) and on science as the best model for education.

- *Sociologism*: Social phenomena are real things. Comte believed that social objects (social structures, social processes and social events) had an independent existence that could not be reduced to, or explained away by, psychological or biological explanations; they had an existence and reality that were independent of the observer. In other words, for Comte, all social structures (nations, communities, neighbourhoods) were more than simply the sum total of the individuals who composed them. Societies had their own form of social reality. They were *sui-generis* — which is to say, they were all self-produced, self-sufficient and independent forms of reality. This belief in the autonomous nature of social reality is sometimes known as "sociological realism," "sociological holism" or "sociologism." This idea was later developed by Emile Durkheim into a method for empirical social research.

- *Social engineering*: The dream of positivism was to discover the laws of society in much the same way that natural scientists (like Newton) had discovered the laws of nature. Comte believed that an understanding of social laws would enable social scientists to predict and control societal processes and to eliminate the wholly unplanned and sometimes disruptive consequences of these processes — such as revolutions. For Comte, knowledge of social laws was a necessary prerequisite for any effective administration and governance of society. Positivism proposed a program of piecemeal social reform (or social engineering) rather than revolutionary social change and total social transformation. Unlike the early socialists (such as Saint-Simon, Proudhon and Fourier), positivism was more concerned with solving existing social problems than with utopian political projects. In this respect, positivists such as Comte saw themselves as scientists who were far removed from the ideological battles of their day. They were opposed to all ideologues — both revolutionaries (those who wished to re-engineer society into something new) and reactionaries (those who wished to restore a previous social system) — and believed themselves to have progressed far beyond ideology. Ironically, they never recognized that positivism had become, for all intents and purposes, a new ideology in its own right.

Figure 5-4 Comte's Classification of the Sciences

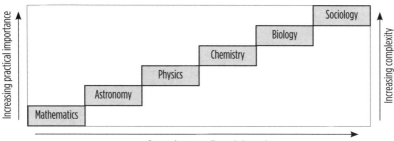

Decreasing generality and abstraction

Comte's Conceptual Toolbox

For Comte, the sciences formed both an historical and a logical hierarchy of knowledge. The historical hierarchy was based on the order in which the sciences first developed. The early physical sciences laid the foundations for the later development of the biological and social sciences. On the other hand, the logical hierarchy was based on the different levels of generality and abstraction of each of the sciences (see Figure 5-4).

By including sociology (or "social physics," as it was first called), as the "queen of the sciences," Comte emphasized that the study of organisms — whether biological or social — required a distinctive scientific method of inquiry. Therefore, Comte drew a sharp line of demarcation through his classification between those sciences concerned with the study of inorganic matter and those concerned with the study of living organisms, whether these were biological or social. Because Comte was strongly committed to an holistic (or realist) view of social reality and because he rejected individualist (or reductionist) views, he excluded both psychology and economics (or "political economy," as it was called in his day), as well as philosophy and theology, which were both considered "sciences" in an earlier (medieval) age, from his hierarchical table of the sciences. In order for sociology to develop into a positive science, Comte believed that it needed to (1) overcome theological and metaphysical thought, (2) accumulate empirically verifiable knowledge and (3) discover social laws which could lead to the prediction of social processes and social events.

As we have already suggested, Auguste Comte was far from being an original theorist. Many of his ideas were begged, borrowed or stolen from other social thinkers — most notably from his erstwhile mentor, Henri de Saint-Simon. Saint-Simon had already formulated — although only in outline form — such concepts as "positiveness," "social physics," the "law of the three stages," as well as the idea that that social reconstruction should be based upon knowledge derived from a new secular religion of science. It was

Figure 5-5 Comte's Division of the Subject Matter of Sociology

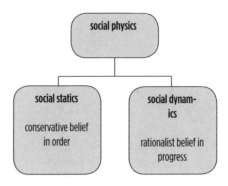

left to Comte to expand upon these ideas and to integrate them more fully into a comprehensive theory of knowledge and society. Indeed, all things considered, perhaps the only original contribution that Comte made to the study of society was that of its name. As far as we know, Comte coined the term "sociology" after he discovered that his original term, "social physics," had been appropriated by the Belgian statistician Adolphe Quetelet. Much of his subsequent reputation appears to rest upon this invention.

Comte divided the study of society into two distinct parts — the study of social statics and the study of social dynamics (see Figure 5-5). Even this division of the subject matter of sociology was partly driven by political considerations. Comte's system was designed as a way to reconcile the warring ideological parties of his day — the romantic conservatives and the Enlightenment radicals. The study of social statics (or social order) appealed to the conservatives, who wished to re-establish conditions of harmony and order in post-revolutionary society. On the other hand, the study of social dynamics (or social change) appealed to the radicals, who rejected any return to the *ancien regime* and who believed in the doctrine of human perfectibility — the possibility for constant change and perpetual progress in society. Comte's vision of sociology drew equally from the traditions of order and progress. Indeed, "Order and Progress" became the official motto for the positive science of society, and the expression remains to this day emblazoned on the national flag of Brazil (see Nachman 1977).

For Comte, the study of social statics involved the methodical study of social order. This aspect of Comte's social physics emphasized the interrelations between the different parts of society. Comte was particularly interested in knowing how each social institution — such as the family, the division of labour, language and religion — contributed to the maintenance of social order. Wherever there was a breakdown — or disruption — of harmony between these institutions, Comte concluded that this was evidence of a sickness, or pathology, within society. This view of society as a social organism made up of a set of interrelated parts, or vital organs, was based on the analogy of a biological organism — in particular the human body. For this reason, this view of society became known as "organicism."

One of the most important institutions in society, according to Comte, was the family. He insisted that it was the family rather than the individual that was the most elementary unit in society. It was through families that individuals were born and acquired their identities and social roles. In this respect, Comte did not believe that society was — even in theory — reducible to the individuals that composed it. He was opposed to the individualist arguments of some Enlightenment thinkers, especially those influenced by the British traditions of liberalism and utilitarianism. At the same time, Comte also emphasized the importance of religion as an institution that provided social unity and solidarity. He believed that the church, even a secular scientific church, was necessary for social integration. Comte's views regarding the importance of religion as a source of social integration were later developed more fully by the next generation of nineteenth-century social theorists — especially Emile Durkheim.

Comte's views on "social dynamics" can be illustrated in his Law of Human Progress, better known as the law of the three stages. This law was intended to govern the development of consciousness (that is, through knowledge, or "reason") as well as the development of society (and social organization). Comte believed that all forms of social development are

Figure 5-6 Comte's Law of the Three Stages

Stage	Consciousness	Period	Leaders	Social Integration
Theological	Religious ideas focused on unobservable forces that are interpreted as spirits and other supernatural beings.	Fetishistic Polytheistic Monotheistic	Priests	Kinship, small groups and religious communities
Metaphysical	Philosophical ideas focused on the essences of phenomena, and a rejection of all supernatural explanations.	Protestant Deistic	Philosophers	The state, the military and the systems of law
Positive	Scientific ideas derived from reason and experience: from observation and analysis. Rejection of speculative thought that is not based upon empirical observation of confirmed facts.	None given	Scientists	Integration through industry and the specialized division of labor, as well as through the state and the "general will" or the consensus universalis

driven by changes in social consciousness. Moreover, all changes in social consciousness are reflected in corresponding changes in social organization. Thus, during the Middle Ages, "theological" consciousness (which was based upon a closed religious worldview) was reflected in a rigid mediaeval social organization. However, during the Enlightenment, the prevailing "metaphysical" consciousness (which was based upon critical, speculative, radical philosophy) led to a state of social disorganization and political anarchy. As far as Comte was concerned, the development of all living things — personalities, nations, civilizations — could be explained by this law. Finally, Comte believed that under the "positive" stage — when science triumphed over all previous forms of consciousness — history would ultimately lead to a fully developed social order in which the limitations of earlier societies would be overcome and transcended. The new social order would make possible stability without stagnation and evolution without revolution. The new society — under the guidance of the secular religion of humanity — would be the best of all possible worlds. Each stage of development set the conditions for the next stage; no exceptions were admitted, and no stage could be bypassed.

> **Figure 5-7 Comte's Law of the Three Stages Explained**
>
> Each of our leading conceptions — each branch of our knowledge, passes successively through three different theoretical conditions: the Theological or fictitious; the Metaphysical or abstract; and the Scientific or positive.... In the theological state, the human mind, seeking the essential nature of beings, the first and final causes (the origins and purpose) of all effects... supposes all phenomena to be produced by the immediate action of supernatural beings. In the metaphysical state,... the mind supposes... abstract forces, veritable entities (that is, personified abstractions)... capable of producing all phenomena.... In the final, the positive state, the mind has given over the vain search after Absolute notions, the origin and destination of the universe, and the causes of phenomena, and applied itself to the study of their laws — that is, their invariable relations of succession and resemblance.
>
> (Comte, cited in Thompson and Tunstall, 1971: 18).

Comte's Contributions

Although many of Comte's ideas have been dismissed by contemporary critics as absurd, reactionary and often plagiarized from other thinkers, there is still some justification for including him in the pantheon of early classical social theorists. The following list describes some of the enduring contributions Comte has made to the history of social theory.

- *Comte argued strongly for the irreducibility of "social objects" to other fields of study, whether to psychology, biology or economics (political economy)*: He insisted on the intellectual autonomy of sociology. Society, according to Comte, was *sui generis*. Among the next generation of nineteenth-century sociologists and social theorists, Emile Durkheim was greatly influenced by these ideas.

- *Comte advanced an organismic conception of society:* This view — which was also strongly endorsed by the conservative theorists — emphasized, among other things, the interdependence of the different parts of society. The organismic view was based upon the assumption of sociological realism — that the social whole is greater than the sum of its parts. This view was further developed by Emile Durkheim and Herbert Spencer and was a forerunner of the twentieth-century theory of structural functionalism.
- *Comte's interest in social science was directly related to his positive program for social reconstruction*: Comte's "positive philosophy" was intended as both a theory of knowledge and as a theory of society.
- *Comte influenced later social thinkers with his emphasis on the "scientific" study of society*: He promoted the use of "scientific methods" of observation, experimentation and comparison, and he popularized the discovery of "scientific laws" of society — those observed relationships between recurrent events. Both Durkheim and Spencer were influenced by these conceptions of sociology as the "scientific" study of society.

Criticizing Comte

For most of us today, and even to some of his own contemporaries, Comte's view of a technocratic society run under the benevolent dictatorship of social scientists seems totalitarian and open to obvious abuses. The idea that the administration of the new technocratic order should be entrusted to a new secular priesthood (of social scientists) with Comte, himself, installed as the first Pope of Humanity is easily dismissed as anachronistic and even as megalomaniacal. However, the historical study of Comte's ideas does help to make some things more transparent. It is clear, for example, that the origins of sociology as the "scientific" study of society were directly related to the political needs of the new industrial bourgeoisie for greater social order and social control during a time of civil unrest and political revolution. The intellectual and practical reconstruction of society promoted by Comte and his followers was designed to counter and suppress the rising tide of revolutionary ideas — particularly those of socialism, communism, trade unionism, early feminism and anarchism. As Comte, himself, wrote: "It is only by the positive polity that the revolutionary spirit can be restrained, because by it alone can the influence of the critical doctrine be justly estimated and circumscribed" (Comte, [1896] 2000: 155).

Even John Stuart Mill, a liberal utilitarian, once an admirer of Comte, was later to describe Comte's program for social reconstruction as: "The most complete system of spiritual and temporal despotism that ever issued from the brain of any human being — except perhaps, Ignatius Loyola, a system by which the yoke of general opinion, wielded by an organized body of spiritual teachers and rulers, would be made supreme over every action, and as far as is in human possibility, every thought, of every member of the community" (Mill 2001 [1909–14]: 15). Another erstwhile defender of Comte's thought, Thomas Huxley, was later to offer this critical opinion: "M. Comte's philosophy in practice might be compendiously described as Catholicism minus Christianity" (Huxley, Barker et al. 1872: 28).

> Comte found himself in opposition to all trends in the social thought of his times. He was against conservatism, as he declared himself in favour of the new industrial society; he was against liberalism, as he was very critical of the actual state of that society; and he was against socialism, as he refused in his criticism of the new society, to go beyond capitalism. This resulted in his isolation, which was increased by the fact that even many positivists turned their backs on him because they thought that Comte's competing with the prophets of the ideal society was reneging on the calling of scientist. (Szacki 1979: 191)

Comte Today

Comte presents a somewhat paradoxical historical figure. On the one hand, his reputation has undoubtedly suffered from the knowledge that some of his most "original" ideas — the law of the three stages, positive philosophy, social physics and the hierarchy of the sciences — were strongly influenced by, if not actually plagiarized from, Saint-Simon. Added to this controversy is the fact that many of his later preoccupations — the universal religion of humanity, his own secular version of the papacy and his peculiar advocacy of "cerebral hygiene" — appear today as bizarre and eccentric. John Gray provides the following example of how eccentric the early positivists appeared — even to their contemporaries:

> The Positivists approached the construction of the new religion with an obsessive concern for detail. New forms of clothing were invented. Waistcoats were designed with the buttons on the back, so that they could be put on and taken off only with the assistance of other people. The aim was to provoke altruism and co-operation. Sadly, the result was to provoke raids from the police, who — taking Saint-Simon's talk of "the rehabilitation of the flesh" literally — suspected his disciples of taking part in orgies. (Gray 2009: 267)

However, these eccentricities cannot totally efface the contributions that Comte made to the formulation of a new science of society, nor can they diminish his historical significance as a social reformer and early ambassador of sociology.

In the overall cost accounting of the liabilities and assets of Comte's legacy, the verdict of history — the history of ideas — has been to recognize him as a pioneer and popularizer of early positivism and as a founder of the academic discipline of sociology. For these reasons, at least, Comte retains his place in the pantheon of nineteenth-century social thinkers. Beyond the historical reckoning of his strengths and weaknesses, however, there is a more troubling aspect of Comte's legacy that should provide us with a warning and teach us a disturbing lesson. That lesson, to revisit the start of this chapter, pertains to the hubris of technocracy. Of all the many concerns that have been expressed over the years regarding the exalted hopes and expectations of technocratic experts and planners, one concern has proven particularly telling. It is that many technocrats continue to harbour the delusion that there is always a technical solution for any political problem that may arise in human society. This belief in the efficacy of technical solutions for political problems has had a long and inglorious history — and continues to haunt us.

The search for technical solutions to political problems has sometimes led to the abandonment of diplomacy in favour of technology in order to re-solve conflicts of interest, national rivalries and political confrontations. Thus Ronald Reagan, while still president of the U.S., hoped that the development of an anti-ballistic missile defence shield around the country (the Strategic Defense Initiative or, more popularly, "Star Wars") would reduce the need for immediate agreement with the U.S.S.R. on a strategic arms limitation treaty (SALT). In other words, it was hoped that the technology would "trump" the need for diplomacy. Indeed, this very point was made by physicist Hans Bethe, who had worked on both the nuclear bomb and the hydrogen bomb at Los Alamos and who argued that diplomacy was the best defence against nuclear war. He rejected the idea of a technical solution to the Cold War and suggested that a defence shield could be viewed as threatening to the U.S.S.R. because it would limit or destroy Soviet offensive capabilities while leaving American offensive capabilities intact. (See, for example, his letter, written with Carl Sagan and other scientists, to the *Wall Street Journal*, cited in Bethe et al. 1985). But as other writers have noted, the myth of technological invincibility has always appealed to public opinion in the U.S. and has often paid rich political dividends: Thus Reagan's unfulfilled promise of a Star Wars program proved popular and — for a time — politically expedient:

> A perfect anti-ballistic missile defense was beyond the reach of technology. It was just a story, and yet to trust the polls, the idea had great popular appeal in the mid-eighties, and many Americans believed such a thing could be built…. The fact that the program did not produce a single weapon only helped Reagan, for had it produced some sort of ABM system, the story with all of its mythic overtones would have given place to a piece of technology with a

lot of practical difficulties attached. Politically at least, anti-missile defenses were better air than metal. (Fitzgerald 2000: 38)

The idea that most human problems are amenable to technical solutions is a seductive belief and one that increasingly holds sway in our high technology world. But as we have already suggested, technology frequently makes promises it cannot keep. Ronald Reagan's Strategic Defense Initiative was derisively labelled "Star Wars" by its critics in order to ridicule its unrealistic, utopian and phantasmagorical nature. The exaggerated claims that US Secretaries of Defense Robert McNamara and Donald Rumsfeld made for the ability of advanced military technology to secure quick military victories — in Vietnam and in Iraq, respectively — all ran aground on the hard reality of human resistance. On many occasions, the promises of advanced technology have proven unrealistic — and even arrogant in their expectations.

Similarly, the high hopes of city planners for urban renewal during the 1960s were also often shipwrecked on the quicksands of social reality. The removal of the "slums" — those inner-city low-income neighbourhoods and communities — and the transfer of their inhabitants to the new high-rise public housing "projects" only succeeded in exacerbating rather than eliminating the problem of urban crime and "social disorganization."

By the mid-twentieth century, the social technocrats were promising a brave new world free from ideological and political division. Many of these so-called "end-of-ideology" theorists claimed that, through a combination of technological progress and enlightened policies, Western capitalist societies had pioneered a new age of political convergence in which the old ideological differences between the superpowers had become increasingly redundant (see, for example, Bell 1960; Lipset 1960; Shils 1968; Touraine 1971; Fukuyama 1989, 2006). After the fall of communism in the last decade of the twentieth century, many social technocrats trumpeted their belief that Western capitalism was now the only viable paradigm to bring peace and prosperity through a combination of political democracy and competitive markets.

Today, more than a decade into the twenty-first century, these claims appear ludicrous, if not downright risible. The 2008 global recession and the resulting instability of international currencies and economies have shaken public confidence in the ability of Western capitalism to solve its own problems. Moreover, the widening global gap between rich and poor suggests that the panaceas of capitalism — free trade, privatization, deregulation, low taxes, reduced government spending and full marketization — are more often the causes rather than the solutions to the problems of global poverty and insecurity. At the same time, the wealthiest nations appear unable or unwilling to seriously address the pressing environmental problems of climate change, global warming and their addiction to a carbon-based economy.

The 9/11 attacks on the World Trade Center also demonstrated that the forces of Western modernization and corporate globalization were far from unopposed in some parts of the world. The counter-insurgency wars that followed the invasions of Afghanistan and Iraq have further shown that these military interventions — and the so-called "humanitarian" liberal values they claim to represent — can be fiercely resisted when imposed upon the recalcitrant populations of foreign lands. Even in Western nations, evidence suggests that ideological divisions have widened rather than narrowed (see Jost 2006). Time has not been kind to the end-of-ideology ideologues and the social technocrats. Perhaps one important lesson to be learned from these recent experiences is that the exaggerated claims of Western technocrats should always be treated with caution and never taken at face value. The promises of technocrats to trump ideology and to solve political, economic and environmental problems have invariably proven unrealizable. Contrary to the earlier expectations of Saint-Simon and Comte, technocracy has failed to become a universal panacea for social problems. Indeed, on many occasions, technocracy, itself, has become the problem.

References

Bell, Daniel. 1960. *The End of Ideology.* Glencoe, IL: Free Press.

Bethe, Hans A. et al. 1985. "Why Star Wars Won't Work." At <nybooks.com/articles/archives/1985/feb/14/why-star-wars-is-dangerous-and-wont-work/on> January 2.

Blauner, Robert. 1964. *Alienation and Freedom: The Factory Worker and His Industry.* Chicago: University of Chicago Press.

Braverman, Harry. 1974. *Labor and Monopoly Capital: the Degradation of Work in the 20th Century.* New York: Monthly Review Press.

Chinoy, Eli. 1955. *Automobile Workers and the American Dream.* Garden City, New York: Doubleday.

Clairmont, Donald, and Dennis Magill. 1999. *Africville: The Life and Death of a Canadian Black Community.* Toronto: Canadian Scholar's Press.

Comte, Auguste. 1912. *Systeme de Politique Positive.* 4 vols, fourth ed. Paris: Georges Crès & Cie.

____. 2000 [1896]. *The Positive Philosophy of Auguste Comte.* Translated by Harriet Martineau. [London: George Bell & Sons] Kitchener, ON: Batoche Books.

Durkheim, Emile. 2009 [1959]. *Socialism and Saint Simon.* [London: Routlege & Kegan Paul] Taylor & Francis e-Library.

Engels, Friedrich. 1969 [1878]. *Anti-Dühring.* Moscow: Progress Publishers.

____. n.d. [1892]. *Socialism: Utopia and Scientific.* Moscow: Progress Publishers.

Fischer, Frank. 1990. *Technocracy and the Politics of Expertise.* Newbury Park, CA: Sage Publications.

Fitzgerald, Frances. 2000. *Way Out There in the Blue: Reagan, Star Wars and the End of the Cold War.* New York: Simon and Schuster.

Fukuyama, Francis. 1989. "The End of History?" *National Interest* 16 (Summer): 3–18.

___. 2006. *The End of History and the Last Man*. New York: Free Press.

Gray, John. 2009. "The Original Modernizers." Chapter 19: *Selected Writings*. Mississauga, ON: Anchor.

Halberstam, Robert. 1993. *The Best and the Brightest*. New York: Ballantine Books.

Hendrickson, Paul. 1997. *The Living and the Dead: Robert McNamara and Five Lives of a Lost War*. New York: Vintage.

Huxley, Aldous. 1962 [1932]. *Brave New World*. New York: Vintage Paperbacks.

Huxley, Thomas H.; G.F. Barker, et al. 1872. *Half Hours with Modern Scientists*. New Haven, CT: Charles C. Chatfield.

Jacobs, Jane. 1961. *The Death and Life of Great American Cities*. New York: Random House.

Jost, John T. 2006. "The End of the End of Ideology." *American Psychologist* 61, 7: 651–70.

Lipset, Seymour Martin. 1960. *Political Man*. Garden City, NY: Doubleday.

Marcuse, Herbert. 1960 [1941]. *Reason and Revolution: Hegel and the Rise of Social Theory*. Boston: Beacon Press.

Marx, Karl, and Friedrich Engels. 1992 [1848]. *The Communist Manifesto*. Oxford: Oxford University Press.

Mill, John Stuart. 2001 [1909]. *Autobiography*. Vol. 25, Part 1: Chapter 6: 15 [edited by Charles Eliot Norton, The Harvard Classics. New York: P.F. Collier & Son]. Bartleby.com, Inc.

Mumford, Lewis. 1961. *The City in History: Its Origins, its Transformations, and its Prospects*. London: Penguin.

Nachman, Robert G. 1977. "Positivism, Modernization, and the Middle Class in Brazil." *The Hispanic American Historical Review* 57, 1: 1–23.

Orwell, George. 1949. *Nineteen-Eighty Four*. London: Secker and Warburg.

Rigney, Daniel. 2001. *The Metaphorical Society: An Invitation to Social Theory*. Lanman, MD: Rowman and Littlefield.

Shepard, Jon. 1971. *Automation and Alienation: A Study of Office and Factory Workers*. Cambridge, MA: MIT Press.

Shils, Edward Albert. 1968 [1955]. "The End of Ideology?" In Chaim Waxman (ed.), *The End of Ideology Debate*. New York: Simon & Schuster.

Swift, Jonathan. 1996 [1726]. *Gulliver's Travels*. Mineola, NY: Dover Publications.

Szacki, Jerzy Ryszard. 1979. *History of Sociological Thought*. Westport, CT: Greenwood Press.

Thompson, Kenneth, and Jeremy Tunstall (eds.). 1971. *Sociological Perspectives*. London: Penguin Educational.

Touraine, Alain. 1971. *The Post-Industrial Society. Tomorrow's Social History: Classes, Conflicts and Culture in the Programmed Society*. New York: Random House.

Waxman, Chaim I. (ed.). 1968. *The End of Ideology Debate*. New York: Funk & Wagnalls.

Wirth, Louis. 1938. "Urbanism as a Way of Life." *American Journal of Sociology* 44: 1–24.

Wright, Richard. 2012. "When Systems Thinking Ruled the Pentagon." *Systems Thinking World Journal* 1. 1 (June 18). <http://stwj.systemswiki.org/?p=1067>.

Zeitlin, Irving. 2001. *Ideology and the Development of Sociological Theory*. Seventh edition. New Jersey: Prentice Hall.

Chapter 6

The Social Evolutionism of Herbert Spencer

Welcome to the Jungle

"Welcome to the Jungle" is a song by the U.S. hard rock band Guns n' Roses, popular throughout the late 1980s and the early 1990s. The song's lyrics captured the mood of the times: a sense that social life had degenerated into a stark, competitive struggle for existence and that civil society had descended into the law of the social jungle. Indeed, the sense of alienation, confrontation and defiance expressed by many rock bands of this period — the Clash, Generation X and the Sex Pistols in the U.K. and Guns n' Roses, Nirvana, the Dead Kennedys and Rage Against the Machine in the U.S. — all reflected the raw realities of the neoliberal years. Over the past few decades, the neoliberal policies — pursued by the Reagan, Clinton and Bush administrations in the U.S. and by the Thatcher, Major and Blair governments in the U.K. — of low taxes, reduced government spending, privatization, de-regulation and the replacement of government programs by private-sector, market-driven services, rapidly changed the faces of their respective societies.

Some of the downsides to the politics of privatization have been seen in such areas as military procurement, where huge U.S. companies such as Halliburton (and its subsidiary Kellogg, Brown & Root — KBR Inc), which were contracted to supply basic services to the U.S. military, have been charged with offences ranging from bribery and corruption to workplace sexual assaults and environmental contamination. Also, the privatization of the U.S. military, through the use of private military contractors (PMCs), has resulted in the deployment of U.S. combatants who are not subject to the Uniform Code of Military Justice — and have, as a result, often acted with impunity in the Afghanistan and Iraq combat zones (Singer 2003; David 2002; Scahill 2007). Similar problems of unaccountability have arisen with the rise of private prisons in the U.S.

In the U.K., the privatization of British Telecom and British Gas was undertaken during the 1980s under the Conservative governments of Margaret Thatcher, when many state-run firms were sold off to the private sector. These policies were very unpopular at the time and resulted in greatly increased costs to the consumer. The neoliberal agenda has also been implemented in the private sector, where the corporate strategies of down-sizing and out-sourcing have resulted in massive job losses and stringent wage cuts. In Canada, we have seen the privatization of federal airport security services, provincial and municipal services such as garbage collection and foster child agencies, and the greatly increased use of private security companies. Sometimes, problems and abuses have arisen from these privatization policies. The policies of deregulation have often gone hand-in-hand with those of privatization. It is now generally agreed that the deregulation of the banking and financial services industry in the U.S. (as well as in Ireland, Greece and other European nations) led directly to the financial crisis and recession of 2008, which continues to impact us today. Canada, whose financial sectors are more closely regulated, has managed to avoid some of the worst consequences of deregulation — insider trading, rampant financial speculation, bankruptcies, home evictions and plunging unemployment — but still experiences the indirect effects of the global crisis. Throughout the Global South, the harsh realities of neoliberal policies have been felt for decades in the so-called "structural adjustment" programs imposed by international lending agencies (such as the World Bank, the International Monetary Fund and the World Trade Organization). Unfortunately for many ordinary workers and consumers around the world, the politics of privatization appears

---

Figure 6-1 Reality Bites:
The Cynical Underpinning of Reality TV

From "Survivor" to "The Amazing Race," from "The Apprentice" to "Runway," the ugly truth is that, far from being a competition in which the best contestant wins, Reality TV shows are rife with infighting, political cliques, backbiting, betrayal, and exclusion. Alliances are formed, individuals are targeted for expulsion, and participants often lie about each other in order to put themselves in a better light than their competitors....

All of which says what about American culture? Have we entered an era of social Darwinism in which "the survival of the fittest" rules? Is Reality TV redefining the values of the American people, or are they only reflecting a shift that had already taken place?.... Survival of the fittest. Now think about Katrina, and the woefully inadequate governmental response, and the circling of land speculators around the ruined neighborhoods of New Orleans only days after the hurricane....

We need to take a good look at Reality TV and the morally bankrupt values it is promoting, and ask ourselves this: What do we as citizens want our relationship to be with each other? What do we want our government, which acts as our surrogate, to do to help the poorest and the weakest among us? Are we really committed to the "survival of the fittest" view as expressed by Reality TV, corporate interests, and current government officials, or do we want to create a community which provides a safety net for the vulnerable and help for each other in the event of unexpected misfortune?

Fans may enjoy all the high drama of their favorite reality TV shows, and may laugh at any comparison to our larger social structure. But the grim fact is, Reality TV eerily reflects the cynicism and self-interest that permeates American society today, and the implications of that, should another widespread disaster strike, are not pretty.

Aldene Fredenburg, *Article City*, Dec. 11, 2006 <articlecity.com/articles/music_and_movies/article_791.shtml>.

only to have elevated private greed over public need. Today, we are all living with the results of these policies.

In the U.K., the Thatcher years saw an abrupt increase in social inequality and social conflict. These early years of neoconservatism also witnessed some aggressive foreign policy adventures: for Thatcher it was the War in the Falkland Islands (Malvinas), and for Reagan, the invasion of Grenada. These patriotic military spectacles were designed in part to reprise the lost glory of Empire and in part to distract public attention from deepening social crises at home. Wars against foreign adversaries were followed by wars against domestic adversaries — especially against the labour and trade union movements. While Thatcher broke the back of the miners' union in the U.K., Reagan did the same for the air controllers' union in the U.S. The years of Thatcherism and Reaganism were marked by huge tax cuts for the rich, deep cuts in social services for the poor and unemployed and large increases in military expenditures. These were years that witnessed the dismantling of the welfare state and a widening gap between the rich and poor. For the rich, the era of Thatcherism and Reaganomics was a time of unparalleled accumulation of wealth; for the poor, a time of growing poverty and insecurity. It is hardly surprising, then, that the dark side of neoliberal economics and neoconservative politics has been recorded in the often defiant musical voices of these times — including, among other traditions, punk, new wave, alternative, heavy metal, industrial, grunge and more recently, rap and hip-hop. The bands that performed this music have become icons of popular resistance — as well as symbols of nihilism and apathy — against the authoritarian state, against the triumph of profit over people and against the abandonment of the poor. Indeed, the decline of the welfare state and the breakdown of the social contract can be traced in the lyrics that emerged as musical commentaries on these times.

For the elderly on fixed incomes, the sick, the unemployed and the poor, the period of Thatcherism and Reaganomics signalled a reversion to a harder, meaner and less compassionate society. The postwar period of accessible social services and health care, affordable public housing, collective bargaining rights and progressive taxation gave way to a new era of brash individualism and personal struggle for economic and social survival. For the first time since the end of World War II, ordinary Britons, Americans and Europeans were thrown into a social jungle created by neoliberal policies that most critics derided as "social Darwinism." For many, social life in the jungle became a competitive struggle for existence in which only the fittest could flourish and survive.

Social Darwinism in Everyday Life

Even though these policies originated almost forty years ago, the continuing legacy of neoliberalism still defines our world. We live in social worlds that have been transformed by the policies of privatization and deregulation — most dramatically in the delivery of health care and social services. We continue to witness the erosion of the public sector and the steady expansion of industries dominated by a small number of corporations in the private sector. In many ways, our public identity as "citizens" has been increasingly eclipsed by our private identity as "consumers." The market place — and its hegemonic law of supply and demand — has become the major arbiter of our everyday lives. While financial scandals continue to hit the headlines, and most societies are still reeling from the effects of the financial crisis that broke in 2008, the evidence shows that the gap between the rich and poor is wider now than at any time since World War II.

Does the label of "social Darwinism" apply to our present society; does the law of the social jungle operate everywhere in our daily lives? Has our society has really become a dog-eat-dog world in which all individuals are expected to sink or swim on their own merits. This scenario is the essence of social Darwinism — the ideology that was first most clearly enunciated by Herbert Spencer in the nineteenth century.

As the excerpt in Figure 6-1 suggests, the ideology of social Darwinism is alive and well in contemporary popular culture — at least in reality TV shows. Most of these shows — such as *Big Brother, Survivor, The Amazing Race, Fear Factor, Dragons' Den, The Apprentice* — are based upon the common formula of "competition and selection," and each promotes the value of wining at any cost. Paradoxically, many of the contestants form close personal bonds during these competitions and often express grief when their rivals are finally eliminated. Whether these shows are spontaneous or scripted performances, they clearly promulgate an ideology consistent with the values of social Darwinism: the competitive struggle for existence and the survival of the fittest. That these shows endorse winning as the highest value — even if this requires contestants to break conventional rules of honesty and fairness — is recognized by Aldene Fredenburg in a disquieting revelation:

> In a recent episode of "The Apprentice," one team discovered that the competing team had arranged to purchase every available megaphone from a store chain for an upcoming promotion. The team that made the discovery beat their competitors to the store carrying the equipment, misrepresented themselves to the store clerk, and made off with the other team's megaphones. Donald Trump's response? "Good for them!"

Some of the more thoughtful observers of reality TV shows over the past ten years have commented on the probable influence of these shows on popular culture and public consciousness. Some commentators suggest that the strong emphasis on competition and selection fits well with the competitive values of private enterprise promoted in contemporary capitalist culture — even though the capitalistic marketplace is now characterized more by monopoly and oligopoly than by "perfect competition." Zoë Druick (2010) makes this explicit link: "Today's reality television naturalizes rather than questions the social Darwinism of competitive capitalism and the governmentalized social context of neoliberalism that it exposes."

Besides advertising the values of competition and endorsing situational ethics, commentators point out that reality TV — along with some social media — also contributes to a culture of narcissism, self promotion and instant celebrity status. While criticism of the culture of narcissism is nothing new (see Lasch 1979), the present emphasis on winning at any cost, and eliminating the losers, provides a new legitimacy for self-celebration. The self-advertising possibilities of social media such as MySpace, Facebook, Youtube and Twitter only serve to firmly entrench this culture into the ethos of corporate capitalism. In this sense, narcissism (for the winners) and humiliation (for the losers) may be seen as yet another consequence of the ideology of social Darwinism in popular culture today.

Since the financial recession in 2008, many critics of big business, high finance and neoliberal government policies point to evidence of social Darwinian principles at work. The exorbitant profits pocketed by the CEOs and senior executives of major banks, hedge fund managers, investors, speculative financiers, inside traders and other "masters of the universe" stand in marked contrast to the lay-offs, lockouts, rollbacks, benefits losses and union-busting imposed on the working class — the real victims in this crisis. (For more detailed data on the catastrophic effects of the economic crisis on the working class, see McNally 2010.) And, as some commentators remind us, the law of the social jungle — whereby the rich and super-rich accumulate wealth while the workers face wage cuts and job losses — extends back to the so-called "Gilded Age" of

Figure 6-2 The Law of the Jungle

The Great Recession of 2007–2009 was more than a financial and political crisis. At root, it was a moral crisis. Bernie Madoff and a handful of other racketeers were prosecuted, but all those actively or passively involved in the financial scam were not exposed, let alone legally dealt with.... Social Darwinism defined morality during American capitalism's first stage of global ascendancy. The question haunting America today is whether it defines today's deepening crisis and thus the nation's historical eclipse.

David Rosen, "The Return to Social Darwinism: America's Moral Crisis" *CounterPunch*, January 28, 2011 <www.counterpunch.org/2011/01/28/the-return-to-social-darwinism>.

the late nineteenth century. In order to explore the ideological roots of social Darwinism more closely, we need to turn to the work of Herbert Spencer.

Herbert Spencer and the Rise of Social Evolutionism

If ever the maxim "See how the mighty have fallen" were applied to intellectuals and thinkers, the example of Herbert Spencer is a case in point. Herbert Spencer was one of the most eminent intellectuals of the Victorian era and one of the most influential writers of his age. Celebrated among the intellectual community in Britain, he was personally acquainted with Charles Darwin, Thomas Huxley and George Elliot (the female author of such novels as *The Mill on the Floss* and *Silas Marner*). He also attracted widespread support in the United States among social thinkers and among prominent industrial tycoons (or "robber barons," depending upon your point of view) such as Andrew Carnegie. At the same time, Spencer was reviled by the religious establishment of his time because of his outspoken agnosticism. He is among the few examples in the history of social thought of someone so exalted during his lifetime who passed swiftly into relative obscurity after his death in 1903.

During his lifetime, Spencer's work was regarded as indispensable to scholars and students in such widely disparate fields as biology, psychology, anthropology and sociology. Knowledge of his evolutionist theories was essential for anyone with an interest in educated opinion or in the nineteenth-century world of ideas. Spencer was to nineteenth-century Europe what the French existentialist philosopher Jean-Paul Sartre was to the mid twentieth century, and for what the poststructuralist philosopher Michel Foucault was to the late twentieth century. Soon after his death, however, Spencer's work appeared to lose its relevance, and his popularity rapidly declined. Indeed, this precipitous fall of a "great man" moved twentieth-century American social theorist Talcott Parsons to ask — in his book *The Structure of Social Action* (1937) — "Who now reads Spencer?" In fact, Parsons was repeating a question first asked by his Harvard colleague C. Crane Brinton (1933) and, as some more recent theorists have ironically remarked, may now also be asked of Parsons' own work (see Buxton 1985; Bryant 1983).

Perhaps the greatest irony of Spencer's life was that, in death, his final resting place would be so close to that of his mortal ideological enemy, Karl Marx. Both men are buried at Highgate Cemetery in London: "The headstone of his grave overlooks Marx's tomb, which is situated just to the other side of a path that leads through the graveyard" (Ashley and Orenstein 2005:118).

Since Parsons first consigned Spencer to the dustbin of history in the 1930s, things have changed. In fact, Spencer may have come to agree with the famous cable sent by Mark Twain in response to the mistaken publication of his obituary: "The reports of my death are greatly exaggerated" (White 1897, 1910). Spencer's reputation has been somewhat rehabilitated since Parsons first delivered his own judgement. Indeed, Parsons, himself, helped that process by incorporating ideas from Spencer's evolutionary theory of society into his own theory of social change. A similar rebirth of evolutionism in mid-twentieth-century anthropology also helped to resuscitate the corpse that lay in Highgate Cemetery. This example of the death and resurrection of a major social thinker reminds us once again that intellectual fashions change. What may appear now to be dead and buried in the world of ideas, tomorrow may be reborn and recycled for a new generation of students and scholars.

> **Figure 6-3 The Fallen Superstar**
>
> Who now reads Spencer? It is difficult for us to realize how great a stir he made in the world.... He was the intimate confidant of a strange and rather unsatisfactory God, whom he called the principle of evolution. His God has betrayed him. We have evolved beyond Spencer. Professor Brinton's verdict may be paraphrased as that of the coroner, "Dead by suicide or at the hands of person or persons unknown." We must agree with the verdict. Spencer is dead. But who killed him and how? This is the problem.
>
> Talcott Parsons, *The Structure of Social Action*, 1937, (Free Press, New York: 1968) p. 3.

Settling Accounts

Spencer's social thought reveals some major contradictions. In developing his evolutionary theory of society, Spencer combined intellectual traditions that were often radically at odds with each other and fundamentally irreconcilable. Unlike Comte, who managed to synthesize order and progress within an overall organismic view of society, Spencer's work is riddled with paradoxes. He was never able to fit together the following discrepant parts of his social theory into a logically integrated and unified whole.

- *Organicism*: Spencer incorporated some aspects of the organic view of society into his evolutionary theory. His work emphasized the mutual interdependence of all parts of an organism, whether biological or social. He also introduced, and popularized, such terms as "structure," "function" and "organization." In Spencer's theory, a society was classified as a "super-organism." However, unlike those organicists of the French school, such as Comte and Durkheim, Spencer was not a sociological realist. He did not believe that the whole is greater than the sum of its parts. Instead, Spencer adopted the radical individualist (or nominalist) view — consistent with the British school of liberalism (and utilitarianism) — that the social whole is fully reducible to the sum of its individual parts. As we shall see, this belief led Spencer to advocate a politics that was very different indeed from the social engineering polices advanced by French positivists such as Comte and Durkheim.

- *Positivism*: Spencer believed with Comte that the task of sociology was to discover general laws of society in much the same way that Newton had discovered the physical laws of matter, and Darwin, the biological laws of living organisms. Spencer believed that the principles underlying the explanation of the natural world must also hold true for the social world. In other words, Spencer subscribed to the positivist theory of scientific knowledge. However, Spencer parted company with Comte and Durkheim on the positivist view of social engineering. Whereas the French positivists emphasized the role of the state in bringing about social reform and social reconstruction, Spencer was strongly opposed to almost any form of state intervention into what he regarded as the private lives of individuals. Influenced by the intellectual culture of liberalism and utilitarianism in Britain, Spencer remained a radical individualist (or what we might today call a "libertarian") in his politics and a stalwart *laissez-faire* free-enterpriser in his economics.

- *Evolutionism*: The hallmark of Spencer's sociology was his theory of societal evolution. According to Spencer, all forms of matter were subject to the general laws of evolution. He distinguished between three levels of material reality — inorganic (physical/chemical substances), organic (living organisms) and super-organic (human societies). Everything on earth was governed by the law of evolution. In his own sociological work, Spencer insisted that both the study of social statics (social structures) and the study of social dynamics (social change) were wholly based upon the general theory of societal evolution. For Spencer, evolution was an essentially unilinear process: all organisms (including societies) were evolving from relatively simple to increasingly more complex forms of organization. The process of evolution for all organisms involved the progressive specialization of functions and the greater differentiation of structural parts. As organisms become more complex (i.e., made of a greater number of parts), each of these parts become more specialized in its function. Spencer invoked this fundamental "law" of evolution to explain how lower forms of life, such as single-celled organisms, eventually evolved into higher forms of life, such as the higher primates. He also assumed that the more "highly evolved" industrial societies of Europe and North America had ascended the evolutionary ladder only because they had been successful in the struggle for the "survival of the fittest." In fact, it was Spencer, not Darwin, who introduced and popularized this expression. On the other hand, Spencer saw the non-Western, non-industrialized nations as less evolved human societies and the "primitive" societies of "savages" in far away exotic lands as the very lowest stages of super-organic evolution. However, it was left to later "thinkers" — especially theorists who contributed to the tradition of social thought known as "social Darwinism" — to draw more explicitly racist conclusions from these evolutionist premises.

Although the theory of evolution played a prominent role in Spencer's sociology, his version of evolutionary theory differed greatly from those of his contemporaries Darwin and Comte. Darwin believed the process of evolution was driven by natural selection; changes in the structures of organisms occurred largely through "random mutation" rather than as a result of innovative behaviour. Random mutation produced changes in organisms, and some of these changes proved highly adaptive. Changes which proved the most adaptive were preserved and perpetuated through the process of natural selection. Spencer's interpretation of evolution, however, was decidedly pre-Darwinian and was more directly influenced by French biologist Jean-Baptiste Lamarck (1744–1829). Lamarck believed that organic traits were acquired (or lost) through use (or disuse), and that acquired characteristics could be genetically transmitted from one generation to the next. In other words, giraffes acquired longer necks because they struggled to reach higher food sources than other animals. In this way, they prevailed in the constant competitive struggle for the survival. For Darwin, on the other hand, the longer neck of the giraffe was the result of a random genetic mutation that proved highly adaptive and was thus perpetuated through natural selection. There is a big difference between these two outlooks. Lamarck believed that evolution was driven by necessity, whereas Darwin believed that it was driven largely by chance.

Spencer's version of evolutionism also differed from that of Comte in at least one significant way. Comte, as we have already seen, understood societal evolution primarily in "idealist" terms. He described the evolution of human societies — in his law of progress, or law of the three stages — as progressing through three stages of human consciousness (theological, metaphysical and positive). Spencer, however, understood societal evolution primarily in "materialist" terms. He saw the evolution of human societies as going through different stages of material culture (technology, the division of labour, political and social organization) — as well as human consciousness.

Figure 6-4 Spencer on Comte

What is Comte's professed aim? To give a coherent account of the progress of human conceptions. What is my aim? To give a coherent account of the progress of the external world. Comte proposes to describe the necessary, and the actual filiation of ideas. I propose to describe the necessary, and the actual, filiation of things. Comte proposes to interpret the genesis of our knowledge of nature. My aim is to interpret ... the genesis of the phenomena which constitute nature. The one is subjective. The other is objective.

(Spencer 1904, Vol. 2: 570

Utilitarianism

As we have already seen, there is an uncomfortable fit in Spencer's social theory between his organicism, on the one hand, and his individualism, on the other. Nowhere is Spencer's distance from Comte, Durkheim (and the French school) more apparent than in his radical individualism. Spencer was both a methodological and a political individualist. He believed that societies (and all social structures) were fully reducible to the sum of their individual parts. Individuals were the real building blocks of society. But Spencer's radical individualism was most pronounced in his politics. He was a strong believer in the radical utilitarian principle that had become a trademark of intellectual culture in nineteenth-century Britain. This principle stated: "The greatest good for the largest number is obtained through the unregulated pursuit of individual self-interest." (This principle is sometimes referred to as "rational egoism," see, for example, Internet Encyclopaedia of Philosophy, n.d.). In other words, society and the economy worked most efficiently when individuals were left alone to pursue their own self-interest. Today, this principle is often known as the "market principle," or *laissez-faire* — the principle of non-intervention of the state in the private affairs of individuals. In practice, this principle has been used as a justification to keep government out of the business/private sector and to leave all major economic and other decisions to the marketplace. In practice, the policy of *laissez-faire* in late capitalist societies has meant that most strategic economic decisions are now made by large, powerful corporations, which may only be thought of as "individuals" — or "corporate citizens" — in the most abstract legalistic sense. In any contest between the individual consumer and the individual corporation, the corporation usually triumphs, unless consumers are able to exert some form of collective pressure — through boycotts, class action lawsuits or political intervention.

In Spencer's day, there was no welfare state, no social services and no safety net for the elderly, the sick and the destitute. Because of his politics, Spencer remained a strong opponent of any state intervention to ameliorate the suffering of the lower classes. He was opposed to laws banning child labour, to laws introducing compulsory education and even to laws establishing postal services and lighthouses. He was against all forms of government intervention except those designed for national defence or for the protection of individual — mostly property — rights. Spencer opposed any government assistance for the marginalized in society because he believed that the fate of all depended on the evolutionary struggle — the survival of the fittest. Any attempt to protect the weakest members of society, in Spencer's view, would only serve to weaken society as a whole. The evolutionary process alone should decide which individuals survived and which did not (see, for example, Ashley and Orenstein 2005: Ch. 5; Coser 1977; Ritzer 2008: Ch. 5).

Spencer's Conceptual Toolbox

When we turn to Spencer's principles of sociology and to his classification of human societies, we again confront the apparent similarities, and the evident differences, between his ideas and those of Comte. Like Comte, Spencer embraced a positivist theory of knowledge (although not a positivist theory of social engineering). And also like Comte, Spencer divided his sociology between the study of social statics and the study of social dynamics. But Spencer's understanding of these sociological divisions differed from that of Comte.

In general, Spencer believed that every known society could be analyzed in terms of different systems. Each of these systems was seen by Spencer as a different structure that performed a distinct function for the whole society. The following three systems were the most important:

- *Sustaining system*: The sustaining system involved those groups in society concerned with the production of goods and with the integration and coordination of internal resources.
- *Regulating system*: The regulating system involved those groups in society concerned with maintaining political order, as well as the organization of internal and external security through military, police and other legitimate agencies of coercion.
- *Distributing system*: The distributing system involved those groups in society responsible for linking together the sustaining and regulating systems. The distributing system involves the functions of transportation and communication in society.

Spencer also developed a general classification of all known human societies, based on what were believed to be the four basic evolutionary levels of society. Societies were ranked according to their size and their organizational complexity — from the lowest level of evolutionary development to the highest and most advanced level. It will come as no surprise that Spencer ranked his own society — Great Britain — as an example of the highest level of societal development. His general classification of societies included the following evolutionary types:

- *Simple societies*: Simple societies were generally small, nomadic and without stable leadership. Examples were Eskimos (as Spencer referred to them) and Pueblo Indians.
- *Compound societies*: Compound societies were settled agricultural societies which may also include some industry and some buildings. Examples were the ancient Greeks and the West African Ashanti.
- *Double-compound societies*: Double-compound societies were completely settled societies with a political structure, a religious hierarchy, often a

caste system and a complex division of labour. Examples were eleventh-century England, thirteenth-century France and ancient Peru.

- *Treble-compound societies*: Treble-compound societies were the "great civilized nations." Examples were modern Britain and Western Europe, and the Assyrian Empire.

Finally, in addition to his general classification of human societies, Spencer proposed another typology, which, although borrowed from Comte (and Saint-Simon), became the most well-known of Spencer's classifications. This was his categorical distinction between militant and industrial societies. In proposing this distinction, Spencer was providing an answer to the following question: "What would be the main difference between a society organized for war (against other societies) versus a society organized for production (for the satisfaction of its own members)?" Since the dawn of humanity, societies have differed in their orientations towards war and peace. The most famous example of this distinction from the ancient world was that between the Greek city-states of Sparta and Athens. Sparta was a society dedicated to war, whereas Athens was a centre of learning and civilization. In more recent times, we can think of Nazi Germany as an example of a militant society, fully mobilized and organized for the prosecution of war.

For Spencer, the distinction between militant and industrial societies cut across all the different stages of societal evolution. Thus, militant and industrial societies could be distinguished at simple as well as compound stages of societal development. See Figure 6-5 for the main criteria Spencer used to distinguish militant from industrial societies.

As with all ideal-type classifications, no society ever completely conforms to a particular ideal type. All real societies exhibit a mixture of these characteristics, although some societies are clearly more organized for war than for peace. It could be argued that Canada, with its relatively low defence budgets and relatively small armed forces, is a good example of a contemporary industrial society, in Spencer's sense. On the other hand, although the U.S. has a massive defence budget and large armed forces, it is still far from being a (purely) militant society, in Spencer's sense. Today, there are relatively few societies that can be characterized as purely militant types, with one exception perhaps being North Korea, which appears to be in a permanent state of war preparation. To return to the start of this book, the two tribes that formed among the schoolboys marooned in *Lord of the Flies* — Ralph's tribe and Jack's tribe — could easily be distinguished in terms of Spencer's dualism.

As we have seen in this chapter, Spencer was a controversial and paradoxical figure in the history of social thought. He borrowed some ideas from Comte regarding the principles of sociology and the positive study of society. He advanced a strongly evolutionist theory of society, and he introduced the

Figure 6-5 Militant versus Industrial Societies

Characteristic	Militant Society	Industrial Society
Dominant function or activity	Corporate defensive and offensive activity for preservation and aggrandizement	Peaceful, mutual rendering of individual services
Principle of social coordination	Compulsory cooperation; regimentation by enforcement of orders; both positive and negative regulation of activity	Voluntary cooperation; regulation by contract and principles of justice; only negative regulation of activity
Relations between state and individual	Individuals exist for benefit of state; restraints on liberty, property, and mobility	State exists for benefit of individuals; freedom; few restraints on property and mobility
Relations between state and other organizations	All organizations public; private organizations excluded	Private organizations encourage
Structure of state	Centralized	Decentralized
Structure of social stratification	Fixity of rank, occupation, and locality; inheritance of positions	Plasticity and openness of rank, occupation, and locality; movement between positions
Type of economic activity	Economic autonomy and self-sufficiency; little external trade; protectionism	Loss of economic autonomy; interdependence via peaceful trade; free trade
Valued social and personal characteristics	Patriotism; courage; reverence; loyalty; obedience; faith in authority; discipline	Independence; respect for others; resistance to coercion; individual initiative; truthfulness; kindness

Source: Coser 1977: 95.

concepts of "structure" and "function" into the modern vocabulary of sociology in order to distinguish between the different parts of a social organism, and the actions performed by these parts in helping the organism to adapt and survive in its environment. However, he parted company from Comte (and other French social theorists) on the practical and political implications of his social theory. Although Spencer was an organicist in his theoretical conception of society, he remained a radical individualist in his political orientation. He was opposed to almost any form of state intervention, and he advocated an extreme liberal (and radical utilitarian) political philosophy: that society (and the economy) worked best when individuals were left alone to pursue their own (rational) self-interests. This was a philosophy that greatly appealed to the class of industrial capitalists of the nineteenth century, a class which promoted an ideology of "rugged individualism." Spencer appears to us today as an anachronistic figure, but some of his evolutionary ideas may find a new audience in an age of growing environmental and ecological concerns.

From Social Evolutionism to Social Darwinism

Although Herbert Spencer still occupies a place in the pantheon of nineteenth-century social thinkers, he has — as we have seen — been demonized by many critics on the left as the callous "father" of social Darwinism (Hofstadter 1944). While it is true that Spencer remained strongly opposed to any form of government regulation or economic planning and to any state assistance to the destitute in society, the dark picture often painted of

> **Figure 6-6 The Banquet of Life**
>
> A man who is born into a world already possessed, if he cannot get subsistence from his parents on whom he has a just demand, and if the society do not want his labour, has no claim of right to the smallest portion of food, and, in fact, has no business to be where he is. At nature's mighty feast there is no vacant cover for him. She tells him to be gone, and will quickly execute her own orders, if he does not work upon the compassion of some of her guests. If these guests get up and make room for him, other intruders immediately appear demanding the same favour. The report of a provision for all that come, fills the hall with numerous claimants. The order and harmony of the feast is disturbed, the plenty that before reigned is changed into scarcity; and the happiness of the guests is destroyed by the spectacle of misery and dependence in every part of the hall, and by the clamorous importunity of those, who are justly enraged at not finding the provision which they had been taught to expect. The guests learn too late their error, in counter-acting those strict orders to all intruders, issued by the great mistress of the feast, who, wishing that all guests should have plenty, and knowing she could not provide for unlimited numbers, humanely refused to admit fresh comers when her table was already full.
>
> Thomas Malthus, *An Essay on the Principle of Population* 1803: 531.

Spencer's indifference to human suffering has been overdrawn. One reason for this unbalanced view of Spencer is that most recent accounts fail to situate his work and ideas within the historical and intellectual context of the Victorian era. Historicizing Spencer enables us to see him more clearly as a man of his times, and less as an ideological monster.

Today, Spencer is often reviled for introducing the expression "struggle for existence" into the vocabulary of sociology and — by extension — into the lexicon of conservative politics. However, what many critics have overlooked is that the general ideas of "struggle for existence" and "survival of the fittest" were already entrenched in the Victorian worldview long before Spencer published his *Study of Sociology* (1893), or indeed, before Darwin published his *Origin of Species* (1859). In fact, one of the greatest intellectual influences of the late eighteenth- and mid-nineteenth-century social thought was Thomas Malthus, whose *Essay on Population* was published in 1798. More than any other social thinker of this period, it was Malthus who laid the foundations for what was later to acquire the label of "social Darwinism." It was Malthus who envisaged the social world as a competitive struggle for existence in which only the "fittest" were destined to survive. And it was Malthus who insisted that those least fit for survival — the poor, the unemployed, the sick, the weak, the imbeciles, the indigent, the idle and the unfortunate — should be left to their own devices, to sink or swim, as nature determined. Malthus became the main protagonist of his age against the revolutionaries and reformers of the Enlightenment — those who campaigned for social equality, social justice and recognition of the universal rights of "men," as citizens of the new republics.

Malthus, of course, became famous for his law of population: his prediction that human population growth would inevitably outstrip the available food supply. In other words, while global population growth increases geometrically, the supply of food can only ever increase arithmetically. Consequently, Malthus preached a doctrine of natural selection whereby the inordinate growth of population would ultimately be curtailed by "natural population checks" — positive checks, such as famine, war and pestilence or preventive checks, primarily birth control (through abstinence). Malthus also opposed any attempts (by public or private agencies) to ameliorate the plight of the poor. He concluded that those who were unable to provide for themselves should be allowed to perish — in accordance with the law of the survival of the fittest. This view was clearly enunciated in one of his most infamous passages (see Figure 6-6), a view that was to earn political economy the sobriquet of the "dismal science." It is interesting to note that Malthus withdrew this highly controversial passage from later editions of his essay (Hardin 1998).

Elwell (2001a and 2001b) suggests that Malthus, notwithstanding his later notoriety, was in some respects a social reformer and proposed a number of ways to ameliorate the plight of the destitute of his time. Malthus's ideas of struggle and competition also percolated into the theories of Adam Smith, David Ricardo, John Stuart Mill and other nineteenth-century political economists and philosophers. Indeed, some of the core assumptions of what was later labelled "social Darwinism" were already established before Herbert Spencer published his most important work. According to Claeys (2000), the ideology of social Darwinism may be broken down into the following four basic assumptions:

1. all natural organisms — including humans — are governed by biological laws;
2. all species experience a struggle for existence that arises from the pressure that population growth exerts on the available food supply;
3. highly adaptive traits — physical or mental — which provide a competitive advantage to organisms in their struggle for existence, may be transmitted through heredity to future generations, and thereby spread more widely within the population; and

4.   the hereditary effects of natural selection account for the emergence of new species, and the elimination of other species.

The first three of these assumptions were already commonplace by the time Charles Darwin published his *Origin of Species* in 1859. It is important to recall, therefore, that the Victorian worldview, which emphasized the ideas of competition, the struggle for existence, survival of the fittest, non-intervention or *laissez-faire*, natural laws, etc., was already established by the time Darwin and then Spencer published their major works. Spencer did not invent these ideas; he inherited them from the intellectual culture of his time — and he adapted them to his own particular theoretical vision. The mid-Victorians, who cherished these Malthusian beliefs, also began to translate them into a number of moralistic dualisms: the idle versus the industrious; the deserving versus the undeserving poor; the provident versus the profligate; the productive versus the unproductive. These binary oppositions were important political markers in the emergent narrative of social Darwinism.

By the 1850s, with the publication of *Origin of Species*, the Malthusian worldview of the mid-Victorians was gradually repackaged as an evolutionist doctrine (Claeys 2000: 236–37). This transformation was accomplished in a number of specific ways. New popular opinions emerged proclaiming the following beliefs as established "facts":

1.   Individual or national "character" was shaped not simply by the moral force of individual effort or self-improvement (education), but more importantly through inherited characteristics that passed these mental and moral traits from one generation to the next, and spread them throughout the population.

2.   The principles of natural selection could be applied not only to structural (i.e., morphological) changes in organisms, but also to behavioural changes, and not only to animals, but also to humans (i.e., to social behaviour). The principles of natural selection, therefore, were increasingly used to explain the rise and fall of different human populations in their respective struggles for existence. This extension of evolutionism into social Darwinism also meant that "survival of the fittest" was no longer understood to be driven by breeding capacity (fecundity or fertility), but more by other selective advantages — such as "intelligence," (moral) "character," "civilization," etc. This change of focus opened the door to harsh comparisons between the "depraved" lower-class populations (as well as anachronistic and unproductive aristocracies) versus the more enlightened, productive and evolutionary adapted middle-class populations. The new focus also sharpened invidious comparisons between the presumed "civilized races" of the West versus the "primitive races" of Africa, Asia and South America.

3. Race was an explanation for the struggle of existence and the survival of the fittest. Indeed, the idea of "race" became one of the defining characteristics of social Darwinism. The new mid-nineteenth-century combination of Malthusian and evolutionist ideas became increasingly fixated on the idea of "race" as an explanation. But while Darwin had originally used the term "race" as a synonym for animal "species," later uses of the term by social Darwinists were intended to distinguish between (superior and inferior) human populations. Thus, the poor and indigent were often described by social Darwinists as a "degenerate" race, a definition which eventually lent credibility to later campaigns for selective breeding, sterilization and the practice of eugenics.

4. The major human population groups (Caucasoid, Negroid, Mongoloid and Australoid) could be defined according to strictly biological criteria: skin colour, skull shape, hair texture, eye shape, etc. Thus, finally, the term "race" acquired its more modern meaning. This definition of "race," from a Western ethnocentric viewpoint, served to distinguish the "civilized races" from those considered "savage" or "barbarous." This definition of "race" also provided a convenient ideological rationale for imperial expansion and European colonialism. Further attempts to provide the concept of "race" with scientific legitimacy were found in the efforts of such pseudo-sciences as phrenology and anthropometry to measure and classify the comparative cranial development of different "racial" groups — always to the advantage of white, Western (middle-class) male Europeans.

Several conclusions may be drawn from the forgoing discussion. First, the ideology of social Darwinism emerged as a combination of a number of different intellectual influences: Malthusianism, utilitarianism and evolutionism — all of which converged around the mid-nineteenth century. Together, they came to represent a Victorian worldview that explained the struggle for existence and survival of the fittest as the triumph of "superior races" over "inferior races" — both at home (in terms of class struggle) and abroad (in terms of colonialism).

Second, social Darwinism was, as already mentioned, formed through a combination of shifting and changing intellectual influences. While Charles Darwin initially secured his reputation as an evolutionary biologist, he was later to fall under the spell of the cultural climate that surrounded and enveloped him, which was later labelled "social Darwinism." It is a lesser known fact that, influenced by the prevailing ideas of his era, Darwin eventually became a social Darwinist, himself, inasmuch as he began to apply his original theory of natural selection to human populations — and began to describe the urban underclass as a degenerate "domestic race." As several commentators (Claeys 2000; Leonard 2009) note, Darwin radically reformulated his ideas in subsequent revisions of both his early works (such as *Origins of Species*) and his later works (such as *Descent of Man*). Similarly, Herbert Spencer changed some of his views as he grew older and as his ideas were tested by time. Some of his harsher political positions softened in later years, an important point to realize if we are to render a balanced verdict on his contributions to social theory.

Finally, it should be noted that although social Darwinism is normally seen as a very conservative ideology, one which was used by politicians to rationalize the sterilization, institutionalization and forced emigration of "problem populations" at home and the colonization of indigenous populations abroad, this is not the whole story. In fact, some versions of social Darwinism were more progressive than others (Claeys (2000: 228). Some theorists, such as Walter Bagehot, believed that a liberal democratic society was needed to ensure political freedom and intellectual competition. W.R Greg interpreted the law of survival of the fittest as a radical republican ideal that would bring an end to inherited privilege and eliminate the unproductive aristocracy. Benjamin Kidd and Thomas Huxley concluded that the collectivist power of a benign state was needed to ensure free and equal opportunities for all individuals to fulfill their potentials in the struggle for existence. Furthermore, anarchist Peter Kropotkin applied the law of "survival of the fittest" to human societies and showed that collaboration and "mutual aid" provided a comparative advantage to those communities that cooperated rather than competed with each other. For Kropotkin, and other anarchists and socialists, a more radical version of social Darwinism was used to discredit competitive capitalism as an inefficient and outmoded stage of evolution in favour of a more highly evolved and cooperative society. Social Darwinism, therefore, was an ideology that produced many offspring — most of them to the political right but a few to the political left.

By far the most vehement criticisms of social Darwinism — especially in its original form of Malthusianism — came from the left and ultra-left. Both Marx and Engels were severe critics of Malthus, and they derided his law of population. For them, the problem of "surplus population" was caused by the most predatory aspect of early capitalism, namely, "primary accumulation." This process of land clearances and evictions was undertaken in order to make room for capitalistic agricultural production. It resulted in the dispossession of a landless peasantry, and at the same time, it fed the capitalistic need for a "reserve army" of unemployed workers in order to depress wages. Surplus population, for Marx and Engels, was a by-product of the capitalistic drive for cheap land and labour in order to fuel the factories and ensure the process of capital accumulation. For the anarchist William Godwin — who debated Malthus in a pamphlet entitled *On Population*, the solution to poverty and overpopulation lay in a wholesale reconstruction of society along the principles of natural justice and social equality. This was a viewpoint shared by other anarchists, such as Michael Bakunin and Pierre-Joseph Proudhon.

Was Spencer a Conservative or a Radical?

What should we make of the contested legacy of Herbert Spencer — a social theorist much reviled by the political left and much revered by the political right? Writers from different perspectives have usually taken from Spencer only what they needed to advance their own agendas. Much of the animus directed against Spencer from the political left is derived from Richard Hofstadter's book *Social Darwinism in America*. But some recent commentators (Leonard 2009) show that Spencer's views are often distorted in Hofstadter's interpretations. Consequently, recognition of the complexity and growth of Spencer's social thought has often fallen between the cracks. Was Spencer a callous and uncompromising conservative, or was he an irresponsible libertarian; or should we, perhaps, remain cautious about caricaturing his ideas and oversimplifying his views?

While it is true that Spencer was a rugged individualist and a strong opponent of almost all forms of government intervention or regulation of social life, he was not without social conscience, nor a simple apologist for the status quo. Sometimes Spencer swam against the prevailing intellectual currents of his day — and advanced a progressive (and critical) rather than conservative agenda. His passionate commitment to individualism made him an enemy of all forms of authoritarianism, as well as a strong defender of personal and political liberties. And although his ideas were seized upon by rich capitalists such as Andrew Carnegie — as an intellectual justification for the unregulated pursuit of profit — Spencer still retained the independence of mind to disquiet and disappoint even his most fervent admirers. Thus, as Francis (2007: 103-4) reports, in 1882, at a gala reception in New York, Spencer confounded the local business community with his controversial and unexpected opinions. Among other things, he suggested that government activity should be expanded rather than restricted in its "special sphere, the maintenance of equitable relations among citizens" (Francis 2007: 103). He also downplayed what he called "the gospel of work" in favour of more free time for self-improvement. "There needs to be a revised ideal of life.... Life is not for learning, nor is life for working, but learning and working are for life" (104). One can only imagine how the good burghers of New York responded to this apparent repudiation of the Protestant ethic by their legendary prophet of competitive capitalism.

Spencer is also excoriated for his alleged indifference to the fate of the most vulnerable elements in society, those who were unfit for survival in the competitive struggle for existence. His apparent callousness is often recalled in the notorious passage: "If they are sufficiently complete to live, they do live, and it is well they should live. If they are not sufficiently complete to live, they die, and it is best they should die," (Spencer 1872: 415). However, many of Spencer's critics miss the follow-up sentence: "Of course, in so far as the severity of this process is mitigated by the spontaneous sympathy of men for each other, it is proper that it should be mitigated."

While Spencer opposed any government intervention to reduce poverty, he was in favour of charitable organizations doing everything they could to ameliorate the suffering of the poor. His anti-authoritarianism also distanced him from any state-sponsored schemes for eugenics, to which he is often inaccurately linked. Unlike Francis Galton, Karl Pearson, Charles Darwin and other proponents of eugenics (such as socialists George Bernard Shaw, Sidney Webb and H.G. Wells), Spencer did not support government programs for the compulsory sterilization, selective breeding or forced emigration of "problem populations." He was too much the libertarian to ever endorse such coercive and invasive measures of population control.

Spencer's antagonism to state interventionism and authoritarianism may also be seen in his condemnation of militarism and colonialism. Contrary to many public intellectuals of his era who favoured colonialism and who saw the British Empire as a source of civilization and enlightenment, Spencer remained unconvinced. "Colonial government, properly so called, cannot be carried on without transgressing the rights of the colonists. For if, as generally happens, the colonists are dictated to by authorities sent out from the mother country, then the law of equal freedom is broken in their persons, as much as by any other kind of autocratic rule" (Spencer 1872: 391). While it is unclear whether Spencer is referring to the European colonists or to the indigenous inhabitants, his dislike of overseas dominions is apparent from this passage. What is clear is that Spencer was highly critical of militarism and of overseas colonial adventures. When informed that the British troops engaged in the Second Afghan War (1878–1880) found themselves in danger, his response was unsentimental and decidedly unpatriotic: "When men hire themselves out to shoot other men to order, asking nothing about the justice of their cause, I don't care if they are shot themselves" (Spencer 1902: 126). One can safely assume that he would have been equally unenthusiastic about the recent NATO "mission" in Afghanistan.

Criticizing Spencer

Like Darwin and many other theorists, Spencer's views evolved — and sometimes changed — during the course of his lifetime. In his early writings, he appears as an advocate for the rights of women and opposes any restrictions on their personal or professional freedoms. Spencer supported the right of women to obtain an education, to enter occupations or professions of their choice and to pursue independent careers. He held these opinions at a time when popular (male) support for these rights and freedoms was conspicuously absent in Victorian England. In his later writings, however, Spencer did not support the campaign for the right of women to vote. Unfortunately, by then his views more faithfully reflected the patriarchal and paternalistic attitudes of his times. He came to believe that women were temperamentally unsuited to hold and discharge the responsibilities of government office, and he also felt that it was inconsistent for them to demand the right to vote, on the one hand, but to seek exemption from military office, on the other:

> Herbert Spencer, in his essay on "Justice," says that he once favoured woman suffrage "from the point of view of a general principle of individual rights." Later he finds that this cannot be maintained, because he "discovers mental and emotional differences between the sexes which disqualify women from the burden of government and the exercise of its functions. He also considers it absurd for women to claim the vote and military exemption in the name of equality. (Johnson 1897: Ch. 10 online)

Spencer was, as are most major theorists, a person of passionate beliefs and strong principles. He was also full of inconsistencies and internal contradictions. As he grew older, as we have seen, some of his views became more conservative. But in the interests of fairness and historical accuracy, we need to reject the caricature of Spencer — as a proto-fascist and ideological monster — that has appeared in so many standard textbooks of social theory. If Spencer has something to teach us today, it is perhaps this: that personal freedom is still the most important value to uphold in our society and that all utopian schemes for social transformation are circumscribed by the brute facts of global resources and human nature. In some ways, his message has never been as relevant.

References

Ashley, David, and David Michael Orenstein. 2005. *Sociological Theory: Classical Statements*. Sixth edition. Boston: Pearson Education,

Brinton, C. Crane. 1933. *English Political Thought in the Nineteenth Century*. London: Ernest Benn Ltd.

Bryant, Christopher G.A. 1983. "Who Now Reads Parsons?" *The Sociological Review* 31, 2: 337–49.

Buxton, William. 1985. *Talcott Parsons and the Capitalist Nation-State*. Toronto: University of Toronto Press.

Claeys, Gregory. 2000. "The 'Survival of the Fittest' and the Origins of Social Darwinism." *Journal of the History of Ideas* 61, 2: 223–40.

Coser, Lewis. 1977. *Masters of Sociological Thought: Ideas in Historical and Social Context*.

Second edition. Fort Worth: Harcourt Brace Jovanovich.

Darwin, Charles. 1859. The *Origin of Species by Means of Natural Selection*. London: John Murray.

___. 1871. *The Descent of Man, and Selection in Relation to Sex*. Two vols. London: John Murray.

David, James R. 2002. *Fortune's Warriors: Private Armies and the New World Order*. Vancouver: Douglas & McIntyre.

Druick, Zoë. 2010. "A Married Couple: Reality TV's progenitor turns 40." *FlowTV* 11, 6. At <flowtv.org/?p=4705>.

Eliot, George. 1860. *The Mill on the Floss*. Edinburgh & London: William Blackwood and Sons.

___. 1861. *Silas Marner*. Edinburgh & London: William Blackwood and Sons.

Elwell, Frank W. 2001a. *A Commentary on Malthus' 1798 Essay on Population as Social Theory*. Lewiston, NY: Edwin Mellen Press.

___. 2001b. "Malthus' Social Theory." At <www.faculty.rsu.edu/~felwell/Theorists/Malthus/Index.htm>.

Fredenburg, Aldene. 2006. *Reality Bites: The Cynical Underpinning of Reality TV*. Janury 6. At <articlecity.com/articles/music_and_movies/article_791.shtml>.

Francis, Mark. 2007. *Herbert Spencer and the Invention of Modern Life*. Ithaca, NY: Cornell University Press.

Godwin, William. 1820. *Of Population: An Enquiry Concerning the Power of Increase in the Numbers of Mankind, Being an Answer to Mr. Malthus's Essay on that Subject*. London: Longman, Hurst, Rees, Ornie & Brown.

Hardin, Garrett. 1998. "The Feast of Malthus: Living Within Limits." *The Social Contract* Spring: 181–87. At <http://www.thesocialcontract.com/artman2/publish/tsc0803/article_741.shtml>.

Hofstadter, Richard. 1992. *Social Darwinism in American Thought, 1860–1915*. Philadelphia: University of Pennsylvania Press.

___. 1992 [1944]. *Social Darwinism in American Thought, 1860–1915*. Philadelphia: University of Pennsylvania Press.

Internet Encyclopaedia of Philosophy (IEP). n.d. "Egoism." At <iep.utm.edu/egoism/>.

Johnson, Helen Kendrick. 1897. "Woman's Suffrage and Sex." Ch. 10: *Woman and the Republic*. New York: *D. Appleton & Company*. At <http://www.gutenberg.org/dirs/etext05/7woms10.txt>.

Lasch, Christopher. 1979. *The Culture of Narcissism: American Life in an Age of Diminishing Expectations*. New York: W.W. Norton.

Leonard, Thomas C. 2009. "Origins of the Myth of Social Darwinism: The Ambiguous Legacy of Richard Hofstadter's Social Darwinism in American Thought." *Journal of Economic Behavior and Organization* 71: 37–51.

Malthus, Thomas. 1798. *"An Essay on the Principle of Population, as it Affects the Future Improvement of Society with Remarks on the Speculations of Mr. Godwin, M. Condorcet, and Other Writers."* Second edition. (Book 4, Chap. 6, p. 531.) London: J. Johnson.

McNally, David. 2010. *Global Slump: The Economics and Politics of Crisis and Resistance*. Oakland: PM Press.

Parsons, Talcott. 1968 [1937]. *The Structure of Social Action*. New York: Free Press.

Ritzer, George. 2008. "Herbert Spencer." Chapter 5: *Classical Sociological Theory*. Fifth edition. Boston: McGraw-Hill, Higher Education.

Rosen, David. 2009. *Sex Scandals America: Politics & the Ritual of Public Shaming*. Toronto: Key Publishing House.

___. 2011. "The Return to Social Darwinism: America's Moral Crisis." *CounterPunch* January 28. At <http://www.counterpunch.org/2011/01/28/the-return-to-social-darwinism/>.

Scahill, Jeremy. 2007. *Blackwater: The Rise of the World's Most Powerful Mercenary Army*. Chicago: Nation Books (Division of Haymarket Books).

Singer, Peter W. 2003. *Corporate Warriors. The Rise of the Privatized Military Industry*. New York: Cornell University Press.

Spencer, Herbert. 1872. *Social Statics: or, The Conditions Essential to Human Happiness Specified, and the First of Them Developed*. New York: D. Appleton.

___. 1884. *The Principles of Sociology*. Volume 1. New York: D. Appleton.

___. 1893. *The Study of Sociology*. New York: D. Appleton.

___. 1902. *Facts and Comments*. New York: D. Appleton.

___. 1904. *An Autobiography*. 2 vols. New York: D. Appleton.

White, Frank Marshall. 1897. "Mark Twain Amused." *New York Journal* 2 June.

___. 1910. "Mark Twain as a Newspaper Reporter." *The Outlook* 96, 24 December. At <en.wikiquote.org/wiki/Mark_Twain>.

Chapter 7

First Wave Feminism

Glaring Omission

One of the most glaring omissions from the annals of classical social theory is the contributions made by women. Although the writings of European female social thinkers, philosophers, mystics and moralists extend from the fifteenth century through the Enlightenment, and into the modern age, very little of their work has been recorded in standard accounts of classical social theory. Lewis Coser's androcentric books *Men of Ideas* (1965) and *Masters of Sociological Theory* (1967) only made explicit what had been implicit in most theory textbooks. It has only been in the past forty or so years that serious efforts have been made — mostly by feminist scholars — to recover the lost legacy of women social theorists from the period defined as "classical." Some of these writers have focused on the androcentric (or masculine) bias of classical social theory (Sydie 1987; Clark and Lange 1979), while others have made concerted efforts to bring to light the classics of female social thought (McDonald 1994; Spender 1983; Wallace 1989). But even these works often segregate women theorists into feminist texts rather than integrate them into a more inclusive cannon of classical social theory. While the historical struggles of women in mainstream society — for voting, reproductive and citizenship rights, pay equity, etc. — are now well known and widely celebrated, their struggles for gender justice in the halls of academia have received far less attention. As Young (1989) and others have documented, male prejudice and discrimination at first excluded, and later marginalized, most women in academic disciplines — including sociology — and for many years prevented the recognition of female scholars and researchers.

The Global Gender Gap

While it is true that times have changed in the West (or the Global North), in many other parts of the world, the struggles of women for social justice remain as hard and as desperate as ever. The record of past struggles should remind us of the harrowing narratives of the present. Although this chapter is devoted to the women who pioneered the development of social theory and research during the early period of modernization in the English-speaking societies of North America and Great Britain, perhaps the most appropriate place for us to begin this discussion is in the present. For while we consider these eighteenth- and nineteenth-century women social thinkers as early feminists, it is clear that the social revolution they started is still far from complete; indeed, in many parts of the world, it has barely begun.

Disturbingly, it seems as though many women living in what used to be called the "Third World" — and what is now called the "Global South," the "developing world," the postcolonial world" or even the "G-77" — have been bypassed by the Western feminist revolution. Many of these women remain trapped in what seems to us a time warp, and have yet to experience many of the gains made in Western women's rights or to celebrate many of the political victories won by their Western sisters several generations ago. Women around the world continue to experience widespread forms of gender oppression. They are frequently victims of extreme sexual violence — especially in war and combat zones. In cultures characterized by gender apartheid, young girls are frequently denied the right to education, and adult women are denied the right

> ### Figure 7-1 Global Gender Gap
>
> International Women's Day is celebrating its 100th anniversary in 2013. While it may seem that, in 2013, the need for a day celebrating women and women's rights is no longer necessary, the fact is that women's status is still far from equal to that of men worldwide.
>
> Women remain four times as likely as men to be victims of domestic abuse, while women worldwide still have a 70 percent chance of becoming a victim of physical or sexual abuse from men in their lifetime. Globally, as of 2007, women were still paid 17 percent less than men. Men are nine times more likely to obtain senior management positions than women, despite the fact that the percentage of women attending university rose by 78 percent between 1997/8 and 2000/01. Moreover, 50 percent of women in Canada had a post-secondary degree or certificate in 2001.
>
> Politically, women don't fare much better. In 2008, only 16 percent of ministerial positions in the Canadian Parliament were held by women, and women accounted for only 21.3 percent of elected representatives. At this rate, it will take until 2029 for women throughout the developed world to constitute 40 percent of the elected representatives of national assemblies.
>
> This inequality is reflected in popular culture as well. In 2009, only 24 percent of global news subjects were female, and only 30 percent in Canadian news stories. Of the top 250 domestic grossing films in the United States in 2007, women only made up 21 percent of the directors, executive producers, producers, writers, cinematographers and editors. Twenty-one percent of films released that same year employed no women in any of those roles. When women are featured in American media, they are four times as likely as men to be marketed for their sexuality. Whichever way you look at it, the struggle for gender equality still has a long way to go.
>
> Biggs., Gingell and Downe, *Gendered Intersections*, 2011.

to work outside the home. In many developing nations, women experience high levels of maternal mortality and are often victims of domestic abuse. Notwithstanding the political and constitutional advances made by women in the developed world, throughout much of the Global South, women remain second class citizens

To Western eyes, the list of heinous offences against women is long and covers a wide range of patriarchal abuse. These offences include — among others — the often culturally sanctioned practices of abduction, forced marriage, "honour" killings, genital mutilation and gender apartheid (known as *purdah*). In addition, there are also internationally recognized crimes such as murder, systematic rape, sexual slavery and sex trafficking, as well as the more commonplace institutionalized injustices of gender discrimination in employment, education, law, reproductive rights, property rights and child custody. While Western feminists may still campaign for greater reproductive freedom (in relation to divorce, contraception, abortion, in vitro fertilization, etc), as well as for greater employment equity and increased political representation, these struggles pale in comparison to the ugly landscape of oppression faced by women in many other parts of the world.

From a woman's global perspective, the planet is divisible into two different worlds. On the one hand, there is the Western world of liberal democracies with elected governments, constitutions and charters, independent judiciaries, and open and vigorous civil societies. On the other hand, there is the developing world of authoritarian military, single-party and theocratic dictatorships that are often controlled by paramount tribal, clan, religious, ethnic or other dominant groups. In the developed world, the struggles for gender equality are well advanced, although far from complete.

Notwithstanding progress made on many fronts, Western women still confront resistance and backlash from political conservatives and religious (mainly Christian) fundamentalists on such issues as reproductive rights, employment equity and political representation. But in the developing world, the majority of women face a grimmer and far more brutal existence than their Western sisters. In contemporary war zones — from Central Africa to the Balkans, from South America to South-East Asia and beyond — millions of women have become the victims of widespread and systematic rape, perpetrated as a ruthless and deliberate weapon of war (Askin 1997). In other regions, such as the Middle East, North Africa and Central Asia, countless women exist without human rights, in theocracies based upon gender apartheid. And all around the globe, women remain trapped in various forms of sexual slavery, trafficked from country to country and from continent to continent — for the pleasure and profit of the men who control their lives. And on top of their gender oppression, many women in the developing world also suffer the burdens of class, caste, religion, race, ethnicity, disease and chronic poverty on a scale largely unknown to their Western sisters.

In many ways, the juxtaposition of these two worlds would seem astonishing to an extraterrestrial observer. But to those born into this dual system of development and dependency, the end results can hardly appear surprising. There is a dynamic link between the development of the Global North and the underdevelopment of the Global South. As many writers suggest (Amin 1976; Baran 1957; Cardoso and Faletto 1979; Emmanuel 1972; Frank 1969), these worlds are simply opposite sides of the same coin.

Women Without Borders

Thanks to the past practices of European colonialism, that which has served to enrich and empower the Global North has simultaneously served to impoverish and impede the Global South. From this perspective, the contrast between the relative power and privilege of Western women and the relative deprivation and dependency of women from the developing world is no accident. Rather, it is the logical outcome of a long history of colonialism that has joined the North and the South in an unholy system of exploitation and oppression. Mahua Sarkar (2004: 325) observes:

> One could of course argue … that the so-called "modernisation" of British women in the early nineteenth century and the "lack" of it among women in parts of the world colonised by Britain might just have something to do with each other. Any discussion of developments — economic, political or social — in either of these locations should therefore take into account the relational nature of these processes, especially since the particular definition of "emancipation" being deployed here turns so heavily on the trope of visibility/voice in a "public" sphere that is defined by the condition of colonial domination.

Yet in spite, or because, of the scale and scope of their oppression, the women of the Global South have fought some of the most heroic struggles for women's rights in our time. One such woman hero in the struggle for human rights in former colonial territories is Ellen Johnson-Sirleaf, the first president of an African country (Liberia) and a nominee for the 2011 Nobel Peace Prize. Her triumph over war, imprisonment and exile has made her a shining example not only for African women, but for all women facing the challenges of poverty, ignorance, violence and disease in the developing world. Other women from the Global South have also been honoured for their dedicated work in human rights and conflict resolution. Aung San Suu Kyi was awarded the Nobel Peace Prize in 1991 for her nonviolent work for human rights and independence in Burma/Myanmar. Rigoberta Menchú — from Guatemala — was awarded the Nobel Peace Prize in 1992 for her work for "ethno-cultural reconciliation based on respect for the rights of indigenous peoples." In 2003, the Iranian human rights advocate Shirin

Ebadi was the first person from Iran, and the first Muslim woman, to win a Nobel Prize. The first African woman to be named a Nobel Peace Laureate, in 2004, was Wangari Maathai, honoured "for her contribution to sustainable development, democracy and peace." Wangari Maathai founded the Green Belt movement in Kenya in 1977, a movement which has planted millionsof trees in an effort to prevent soil erosion and provide firewood for cooking fires.

This list of women Nobel Peace Prize Laureates brings us full circle back to the primary focus of this chapter: the women of classical social theory, the first wave feminists. One of the earliest women to win the Nobel Peace Prize was Jane Addams, a social researcher, activist and social reformer who is one of the major personalities profiled in this chapter. Best known as the founder of Hull House, a settlement house in Chicago, Jane Addams was a peace activist during World War I with the International Congress of Women. She also helped to found the Women's International League for Peace and Freedom. And, along with her colleagues in the Sociology Department at the University of Chicago, Jane Addams became a highly respected social researcher and social reformer working in the immigrant communities of Chicago at the turn of the twentieth century.

The Battle of the Sexes

European and North American women in the eighteenth and nineteenth centuries faced many of the challenges that currently confront women in the developing world. Throughout the eighteenth, nineteenth and early twentieth centuries, the social order of virtually all Western countries was divided between two basic spheres of existence. The world of women was centred on the private, or domestic, sphere, and women were charged with household duties and responsibilities such as cooking, cleaning, childcare, managing the servants and providing domestic recreation and entertainment. The world of men, on the other hand, was centred on the public realm of work, property, politics, education, law, government and affairs of state, including war. Only men were expected (and permitted) to enter the professions, to own property, to legislate and enforce the law, to attend university, to enter the military, to vote or run for public office, to become ordained members of the clergy, and — in the most general sense — to exercise their rights as citizens. The world of women in pre-modern Western society was largely divorced from the centres of power, wealth, learning and social influence. And although Western women were spared the more extreme manifestations of gender apartheid — such as the custom of *purdah*, still practised today in some Muslim and Hindu communities — their social world was largely excluded from and subordinated to that of men. Under the rule of unrestrained patriarchy, women of the eighteenth and nineteenth centuries remained fully dependent upon men for their social existence. The only notable exceptions to this dependence were in the traditional authority conferred upon royal personages, such as Queen Victoria of England and other European female sovereigns. But for the general population, the world of women was subordinated to that of men. Thus had it been from time immemorial, and thus would it remain until the biggest upset in the political history of humanity — the French Revolution.

The French Revolution, in 1789, upset the social applecart in many different ways. It overthrew a monarchy, uprooted an aristocracy and over-turned the power and privilege of an established church. But the Revolution did more than simply transform the existing institutions of the *ancien regime*. It shattered the myth that these social hierarchies were in any way based upon "natural" inequalities. For the first time in history, social inequality was seen to be a (literally) "man-made" institution, rather than a natural or a divinely ordained human condition. It was, therefore, inevitable, that amidst the social and intellectual earthquake that reshaped the political landscape of France — and eventually of Europe — that the question of gender in-equality would be raised alongside other forms of inequality in society. The French Revolution — with its appeal to "Liberty, Equality and Fraternity" — ushered in a new age of intellectual and political ferment. It opened the door to fresh ideas. Long lasting institutions came under scrutiny and attack; tradition and custom were held accountable to the universal principle of reason. The times they were indeed a-changing. It was only a matter of time before the impact of the Revolution extended beyond the borders of France. Even though the Revolution failed to secure the right of French women to vote — they did not receive this until the end of World War II — and one of the strongest champions of the rights of women, Olympe de Gouges, was executed during the Reign of Terror in 1793 (see Mousset 2007), it invoked the ideals of human equality and inspired later generations of feminists to campaign for gender equality. These campaigns rapidly caught fire in both Britain and America.

Feminism in Britain

In Great Britain, one of the earliest complaints against the inequality of the sexes, and one of the earliest arguments in favour of women's emancipa-tion, appeared in Mary Wollstonecraft's polemical work, *A Vindication of the Rights of Women* (1792). In this work, Wollstonecraft critiqued the paternalistic educational ideas of Jean-Jacques Rousseau, who, despite his credentials as a revolutionary democrat, believed that the goal of a girl's education should be to equip her to play the supportive roles of wife and mother in society. Although Rousseau appeared to pay lip service to the notion of gender equal-ity, his proposals for educational reform were based upon his conviction that women were not equal to men in their capacities and capabilities:

> In what they have in common, they are equal. Where they differ, they are not comparable. A perfect woman and a perfect man ought not to resemble each other in mind any more than in looks, and perfection is not susceptible of more or less. In the union of the sexes each contributes equally to the common aim, but not in the same way. From this diversity arises the first assignable difference in the moral relations of the two sexes. (1979: 358)

For Rousseau, women were designed to play a very different role in society from that of men — a role that was subordinate to men. He believed that women should be "passive and weak," "put up little resistance" and act in ways "made specially to please man" (358). And as Young (1989: 254) also reminds us, Rousseau believed that "men's desire for women itself threatens to shatter and disperse the universal, rational realm of the public, as well as to disrupt the neat distinction between the public and private. As guardians of the private realm of need, desire, and affectivity, women must ensure that men's impulses do not subvert the universality of reason" (for more on Rousseau's view of women, see Okin 1978; Lange 1979; Schwartz 1984).

Two years earlier, in 1790, Wollstonecraft had already published a strong rejoinder to the conservative Edmund Burke, who, in his own work *Reflections on the Revolution in France*, argued against extending the franchise to women — especially in a period of social unrest and political revolution.

Married eventually to the anarchist William Godwin, but with an illegitimate child from a previous relationship, Mary Wollstonecraft cut an unconventional and controversial figure for her time. In her published work, she was not only an advocate for universal suffrage, but also for other rights that were then denied women — such as divorce, education and sexual freedom. For this, she was reviled by men and women alike. One critic, Horace Walpole, described Wollstonecraft as a "hyena in petticoats" (Grovier 2005).

The campaign for women's suffrage suffered a major defeat in 1832 when the *Great Reform Act* upheld the ban on women voting. But this setback only served to further politicize the growing feminist movement in Britain and led to a proliferation of societies and associations dedicated to the emancipation of women. In 1865, the women's movement was given a major boost when the philosopher John Stuart Mill, an avowed champion of women's rights, was elected as MP to the British parliament. Four years later, in 1869, in close collaboration with his wife, Harriet Taylor Mill, he published his famous work *The Subjection of Women*, which remains to this day one of the most eloquent arguments for the emancipation of women.

The opening decade of the twentieth century saw an intensification of the campaign for women's suffrage and the emergence of such national leaders as Millicent Fawcett and Emmeline Pankhurst (along with her two daughters,

Sylvia and Christabel). These were also years of increased tension within the women's suffrage movement, and splits developed between its moderate and more militant wings. The rise of civil disobedience among the militant "suffragettes" led to an escalation of direct action tactics which included the disruption of public meetings, large street demonstrations, vandalism, arson and bombings, and — towards the end of the decade — hunger strikes. Many of the imprisoned hunger strikers were subjected to brutal force-feeding, a practice that often resulted in permanent injury and sometimes in death. Indeed, at least one historian (Purvis 1995: 122–23) suggests that the brutality of this practice could be likened to rape, especially when forcible feedings were conducted through the rectum or vagina of the prisoners. Force-feeding had already been used against Irish political prisoners by the British authorities and would again be used by the U.S. authorities against Al-Qaeda suspects in the prisons at Guantanamo Bay, Abu Ghraib and many other interrogation sites around the world. The intensified campaign for women's right to vote was further dramatized when a well known suffragette, Emily Davison, threw herself fatally in front of a speeding racehorse — the king's horse — at the Epson Derby in 1913. Eventually, under the *Representation of the People Act* in 1918, women in Britain over the age of thirty who were property owners and university graduates won the right to vote in national elections; under the re-vised Act of 1928, they won full equality with men — the right to vote over the age of twenty-one. The long, hard battle for women's suffrage was finally over.

Feminism in the United States

In the United States, the first major landmark in the struggle for women's emancipation was the Seneca Falls Convention, in 1848. Several women leaders came to national prominence around this time, including Susan B. Anthony and Elizabeth Cady Stanton. In the years that followed this con-vention, a split developed in the women's movement between those, such as Lucy Stone and Julia Ward Howe, who supported the campaign to extend voting rights to African-American men (the Fifteenth Amendment), versus those who were opposed to this amendment because it did not include vot-ing rights for women. Over the next few years, the campaign for women's rights progressed unevenly in the different states of the Union. While some states permitted divorce on numerous grounds, others did not. Thus, in 1862, the chief justice for the state of North Carolina denied an application for divorce on grounds of cruelty, stating: "The law gives the husband power to use such a degree of force necessary to make the wife behave and know her place" (Hemming and Savage 2009: 76–78). In general, the western states and territories were more favourably disposed to women's suffrage than were the eastern states — a trend that also marked the progress of women's rights in the provinces of British North America (later to be the Dominion of Canada). The frontier culture, with its shortage of labour and urgent need for settlement, proved more accommodating to women's rights than the more established and hidebound eastern states (and eastern provinces of Canada). When, in 1918, women finally received the federal vote in the U.S., women from the state of Wyoming had already been voting for half a century.

The issue of whether to prioritize the campaign to enfranchise African-American men over that of women's suffrage divided the women's movement in the U.S. and led to charges of racism against those — such as Susan B. Anthony and Elizabeth Cady Stanton — who opposed the Fifteenth Amendment. Throughout the long struggle for women's suffrage in the U.S., feminists and abolitionists sometimes came into conflict with each other. Although most early feminists were also abolitionists, the campaign to enfranchise African-American free men was often manipulated by national political parties to obstruct the cause of women's suffrage. Similarly, the feminist cause was manipulated by political parties in an effort to deny the vote to African-American free men. It was not until 1890 that the different wings of the feminist movement united under the National American Woman's Suffrage Association. Eventually, at the end of World War I, the U.S. Congress passed the Nineteenth Amendment, which granted women the right to vote in federal elections. It should also be noted that until the nineteenth century, the electoral laws of most Western countries contained various restrictions. Property qualifications were commonly used throughout the British Empire to restrict the vote to those who owned a requisite amount of rateable property or who paid a requisite amount of taxes. Plural voting rights also allowed wealthy property owners to cast several votes according to the value of their property. Needless to say, these qualifications gave an essentially class character to early voting. Although property qualifications were later abolished for national or federal elections, they remained in force for local and municipal elections well into the mid-twentieth century. In some southern states of the U.S., these qualifications were augmented by literacy tests that were used to deny African-American citizens the right to vote. It was only in the wake of the civil rights campaigns of the 1960s that these tests were finally ruled unconstitutional.

Feminism in Canada

In Canada, the right of women to vote in provincial elections was first legislated in 1916, by the provinces of Manitoba, Alberta and Saskatchewan. Other provinces followed suit — Ontario and British Columbia in 1917, Nova Scotia in 1918, New Brunswick in 1919, Prince Edward Island in 1922, and finally Quebec in 1940. Newfoundland, still a colony, gave the right to vote to women in 1925. Women who were both British subjects and close relatives to members of the armed forces were allowed to vote in federal elections in

1917. In 1919, legislation was passed that extended the federal franchise to all women. The first woman to be elected to the Canadian parliament was Agnes MacPhail, in 1921.

One of the landmarks in the history of women's rights in Canada was the case of the Famous Five — Emily Murphy, Henrietta Muir Edwards, Irene Parlby, Louise McKinney and Nellie McClung — women litigants who petitioned the Supreme Court over the restrictive definition of the legal term "persons." Under the *British North America Act*, individuals legally defined as "persons" possessed a number of basic rights — such as the right to own and transfer property, to sue and be sued, to enter into contracts, to incur debt, to attend university, to enter the professions and to stand for public office, including the Canadian Senate. Appointment to the Senate was a burning issue for Canadian feminists at this time because only the Senate had the authority to approve divorces, and amend the divorce laws. But in 1928, the Supreme Court of Canada ruled against the Famous Five, concluding that only men could legally be defined as "persons." The following year, the Famous Five, led by Emily Murphy, appealed the ruling before the Judicial Committee of the Privy Council of London, which reversed the verdict of the Supreme Court. Thereafter, women were legal persons in the Dominion of Canada. Emily Murphy also led the fight for other women's rights in Canada. In 1916, she was the first woman in the British Empire to be appointed as a magistrate. In the same year, in the Alberta legislature, she successfully sponsored the *Dower Act*, which ensured an equal division of matrimonial property between husband and wife upon divorce. The Act prevented the total dispossession of a divorced woman and her children by the former husband and thereby protected them from poverty. However, Emily Murphy's reputation has grown somewhat tarnished over the years. Although she is still primarily remembered as a feminist freedom fighter of the early twentieth century, she also bestowed a less endearing legacy upon posterity. Her political views on some of the pressing social issues of her day now appear unenlightened. In her book *The Black Candle*, for example, Murphy linked what she perceived as the growing menace of narcotics to the arrival of new immigrants from China. Her campaign against "Oriental" drug use helped to mobilize popular opinion in support of the exclusionary *Chinese Immigration Act* of 1923. Although her views on "non-white races" reflect the prejudices of her day, her writings appear to us today as undeniably racist in tone and character. Emily Murphy was also a strong advocate of eugenics and "selective breeding." She campaigned vigorously for the compulsory sterilization of "feeble minded" individuals and families, and helped to sponsor the *Sexual Sterilization Act* in Alberta. This Act remained in force until 1971. As all of us, Emily Murphy was a product of her age, and her views reflected many of the beliefs of her times.

The political landscape for most women in the eighteenth and nineteenth centuries was in many respects dark and dismal territory. Women had little or no control over the most important aspects of their lives. They were unable to vote or stand for public office, to hold property, to divorce, to receive an education, to enter a profession or even to protect themselves from domestic abuse. Moreover, for many women, to the burdens of gender oppression and inequality were added the extra burdens of class, race and ethnicity. This was the background from which the women of classical social theory emerged to fight their ideological and political battles for sexual freedom, justice and social equality.

First Wave Feminists in Theory and Practice

Simone de Beauvoir (1989: 105) wrote that "the first time we see a woman take up her pen in defense of her sex" was at the turn of the fifteenth century, with *The Book of the City of Ladies* by Christine de Pizan (1363–1430). And, there were other European women — such as the mystical holy woman Hildegard von Bingen (1098–1179) — whose writings even predate those of de Pizan. However, what is referred to as "first wave" feminism really began in the late 1800s and early 1900s as a movement that fought for women's rights — especially the right to vote. Many of the early women activists were known as "suffragists" (or "suffragettes") — those who campaigned for "suffrage" — or the right to "vote." The term was coined during the mid-twentieth century in order to distinguish earlier women activists from those of the "women's liberation movement," or second wave feminists. Whereas the first wave feminists were primarily concerned with issues of equality, those of the second wave were primarily concerned with issues of freedom.

Figure 7-2 First Wave Feminists

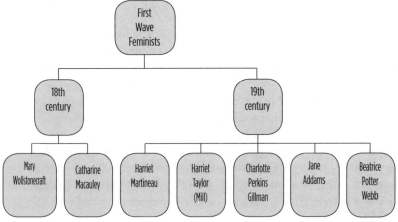

Looking back at the work of early women theorists, it is clear that their subordinate status in society greatly limited the scope and scale of their contributions to social theory. European societies in the eighteenth and nineteenth centuries were strongly patriarchal in structure and ideology and relegated women to the private, domestic world of the family. In contrast, most (white, Western, middle-class, heterosexual) males had access and entry to the public institutions of society and, compared to women, were "masters of the universe." The powers and privileges enjoyed by bourgeois males in a patriarchal capitalist society were also translated into the world of abstract thought and ideas. Men not only had the time, opportunity and resources to engage in speculation and theorizing, they also inherited a world in which this type of activity was regarded as legitimate and appropriate for men. It was generally accepted that some men had the right (indeed the duty) to remake the world in thought and reason, much as other men were remaking the world in terms of their practical activities — in industry, trade, commerce, government and war. Social theory arose, in no small part, as a reflection of the real practical activities of men — in a patriarchal world. What, then, were the most pressing social issues addressed by the early feminist thinkers of the eighteenth and nineteenth centuries? To what extent did their contributions to social thought grow out of their own practical struggles for equality, freedom and social justice?

Social Reform Movements

A characteristic shared by many women social thinkers of the past has been their support for, and involvement in, movements for social reform and political change. Although some of the classical male theorists were also involved in social movements — most notably Marx and Engels, as well as Rousseau and other Enlightenment thinkers — many more were not. Because of their "underdog" subordinate social status, many classical women thinkers were active proponents of one social cause or another, in addition to their own scholarly activities.

Thus virtually all of the eighteenth- and nineteenth-century women discussed in this chapter were strong supporters of the abolitionist movement and harsh critics of the "peculiar institution" of slavery. Both Catharine Macaulay and Harriet Martineau visited the United States and later used their experiences to campaign energetically for the abolition of slavery. Many women thinkers also drew attention to the parallels which existed between the oppression and exploitation of slaves in plantation society and the oppression and exploitation of women in patriarchal society. Many of the early women thinkers also identified themselves with other social movements. In particular, the temperance movement of the nineteenth century was led by women activists, who saw alcohol as a major contributor to domestic violence

Figure 7-3 First Wave Feminists' Movements

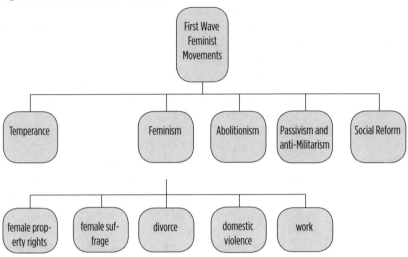

and urban poverty. Many women also supported movements for passivism and anti-militarism. Catharine Macaulay, for example, was outspoken in her contempt for the false patriotism of her age, which glorified the horrors of war: "I know of no real advantages … which can accrue to any people from success in arms but that of political security…. Victory only serves to facilitate the ends of domestic tyranny and is purchased with the addition of accumulated taxes, with public debts, and public slavery" (quoted in McDonald 1994: 9). Even Florence Nightingale, who worked for the British War Office, drew attention to the health problems experienced both by the British soldiers and by the colonized inhabitants of the British Empire. Other women, in their writings and public addresses, initiated and supported early movements for animal rights, for protecting the environment, for compulsory secondary education and for reform of the penal system — especially for an end to capital punishment (or at least an end to public executions).

However, by far the most popular cause supported by all major women social thinkers of the eighteenth and nineteenth centuries was the general concern for women's rights. The key issue of these times was the right to vote, and the cause of women's franchise, or suffrage, was championed by all serious women thinkers of the pre-modern age. Alongside the right to vote, the right of women to independently own property was an important demand of the early (middle-class) women's movement. Other demands included the criminalization of domestic violence, the legalization of divorce and the right to enter professions such as medicine, law and government.

Moderation

Another typical characteristic of the classical women thinkers was the relative moderation of their political and social opinions. In this respect, women thinkers exhibited a greater "realism" in their social thought than many of the leading male theorists of the age. Thus, while both Mary Wollstonecraft and Catharine Macaulay were influenced by the Enlightenment thinkers of their time, each took strong exception to the assumptions of sexual inequality and what we call today sexual stereotyping contained in the social theories of Rousseau and others. Indeed, throughout the eighteenth and nineteenth centuries, women thinkers were often the harshest critics, not only of the conservative defenders of the sexual status quo, but also of those radical and revolutionary patriarchs whose progressive ideas did not extend to the emancipation of women. Perhaps part of the reason for the greater moderation and realism in the social thought of women was that, as the service caste in a patriarchal society, women as workers and activists had to deal with the social problems that often resulted from extreme ideologies and uncompromising social policies enacted by men. For this reason, women thinkers tended to resist political and ideological extremes and tempered their beliefs with the lessons learned from their practical experiences of the world. Thus, although Harriet Martineau was a *laissez-faire* liberal in her political outlook, she was not as extreme in her views as was Herbert Spencer. Unlike Spencer, Martineau was not opposed to all legislation (she accepted some forms of factory legislation), and — under the influence of Comte — she saw some limited role for government in helping to bring about the utilitarian ideal of the greatest good for the largest number of individuals in society.

In a similar vein, Catharine Macaulay also took issue with some of the leading male social thinkers of her day. Like Wollstonecraft, she critiqued Rousseau for advocating a sexist theory of education in his book *Emile* and for propagating the belief that the subordination of women was a result of the natural inequality of the sexes. Macaulay also rejected the extreme view of human society proposed by Thomas Hobbes, ridiculing his argument that human society originated as a "war of all against all." Macaulay, quite reasonably, pointed out that even in a relatively solitary "natural state," parents would almost certainly educate their children in the arts of survival and that bonds of love, morality and obligation would most likely be formed during this early stage of human development. She concluded that Hobbes's cartoon description of early human society was simply designed to justify his androcentric view of government in which the freedom of the individual had to be surrendered to the higher authority of the state (i.e., patriarchal power). Macaulay believed, in contrast to Hobbes, that political equality and good government were not only compatible but were indispensable to each other. Nor were Rousseau and Hobbes the only targets of her criticisms and witticisms. As a republican and ardent anti-monarchist, Macaulay did her best to demolish Edmund Burke's critique of the French Revolution, published in his book *Reflections on the Revolution in France*. She lampooned Burke's defence of custom, tradition and authority and argued that these traditional authorities had been overthrown in France because they were tyrannical and corrupt. She also challenged Burke's assertion that aristocratic governors were needed to control the passions of the common people by asking who would control the passions of the governors. Although Macaulay's political and social views are unknown to most students today, she was in her time unrivalled in her ability to puncture the pomposity and sanctimony of much that passed for serious political opinion.

Practical Knowledge

Most the classical women social thinkers had a strong orientation towards "practical knowledge," which is best defined as knowledge derived from observations of everyday life which can be used to further an understanding of everyday life. Although all of the classical women thinkers were deeply concerned with the social issues, their approach to the study of society was grounded more in the everyday world of their practical experiences than in the abstract realm. This emphasis led many of the early women thinkers to become pioneers in the techniques of empirical social research. Unlike many of their male counterparts who constructed "grand theories" of society, most of the women thinkers turned their attention to how to rigorously observe social phenomena and how to collect valid information about society. Thus, Harriet Martineau, in her book *How to Observe Moral and Manners*, set out what she regarded as the necessary conditions for the recording and reporting of what we would today call sociological data. Among other things, she discussed such topics as social facts, social indicators, objectivity, bias, induction and interviewing, as well as the interaction effects between researchers and their subjects. It is fair to say that Martineau published one of the first methodological manuals in the history of social thought. In later years, her interests in empirical social research led her to collaborate with Florence Nightingale on several research projects. Together, the two women analyzed epidemiological data on diseases among British soldiers. They also campaigned against the *Contagious Diseases Act*, which unfairly targeted and penalized prostitutes.

Other women social thinkers also contributed to the growth of empirical social research and to the methodology of social inquiry. In the United States, the nineteenth-century social thinker and activist Jane Addams introduced a tradition of social research that would later be known as the Chicago School of Sociology. From the living laboratory of her experimental community in Hull House, Addams pioneered techniques for collecting urban ethnographical data on new immigrants and also began one of the first consumer protection movements in America. Around the same time in Great Britain, Beatrice Potter Webb devoted herself, among other things, to extending the techniques of empirical social research. She eventually published some of the first methodological treatises in the United Kingdom.

Ethical Research

Another characteristic of women social thinkers which distinguishes them from many (although not all) of the classical male thinkers was their ethical commitment to social theory and social research. As we have already seen, all of the women reviewed in this chapter were strong proponents of women's rights, and all of them supported the demand for the emancipation of women. At the same time, many of these women were also affiliated with a variety of other social reform movements, including abolitionism, passivism, animal rights, consumerism, environmentalism, penal reform and temperance. For these women, the motivation to study society sprang from deep ethical convictions as well as from intellectual curiosity. In other words, none of these women were content to undertake a study of society for its own sake. All of them wanted to change society in particular ways for particular causes. The commitment to undertake ethical research appears to be an enduring characteristic of women scholars in general and of feminist theorists and researchers in particular. Feminist scholars use the term "standpoint theory" to describe the woman-centred conceptual framework that has often guided the theoretical ideas and empirical observations of past and present women thinkers (see, for example, Harding 2004; Kenney and Kinsella 1997; Crasnow 2009). And although some male classical theorists — such as Marx and Engels, Rousseau, and even Weber and Durkheim — were also strongly motivated by ethical concerns for social justice, the ethical commitment to theory and research remains a hallmark of women's contributions to the history of social thought.

Criticism, Empiricism and Theory

A great amount of feminist scholarship has already been done in recovering the neglected contributions of women social thinkers to the history of classical social thought. As we have seen, Macaulay, Wollstonecraft and Taylor were astute and perceptive critics of many of the leading social theorists of their time. Indeed, some of the most trenchant criticisms of Rousseau, Hobbes, Spencer and other prominent male theorists are to be found in the writings of the classical women thinkers. These women contributed rich and robust analysis and criticism to the theoretical literature. As we have suggested, the contributions and innovations made by the early feminists to empirical social science reflected the practical world of everyday experience in which these women lived, worked and organized. In other words, the subordination and domestication of women in eighteenth- and nineteenth-century society both compelled them, and enabled them, to make the study of everyday life their principal sociological focus. Women were drawn to empiricism because of their status and role within the domestic structures of patriarchal society.

Mary Wollstonecraft: Enlightenment Feminist

Although a strong critic of the patriarchal social order and an early champion of women's rights, Mary Wollstonecraft is often regarded with some ambivalence by contemporary feminists. While most feminists today applaud her commitment to women's rights, many remain ambivalent toward what they perceive as her decidedly middle-class values and her reluctance to radically challenge the system of class privilege that characterized Britain in the eighteenth century.

As we have already seen, Mary Wollstonecraft acquired historical fame through the publication of her major work, *A Vindication of the Rights of Women* (1792), which was addressed as much to the (patriarchal) radicals of the Enlightenment as it was to the conservative defenders of the *ancien regime*. In her family life, Mary Wollstonecraft was at the centre of a circle of radical social thinkers and political activists. She was married to William Godwin, one of the foremost anarchist theoreticians of his day, whose book *An Inquiry Concerning Political Justice* (1793) caused a storm of controversy in Britain for its defence of the French Revolution. Her daughter with Godwin, also called Mary, married the radical poet Percy Bysshe Shelley. Mary Shelley was later immortalized as the author of *Frankenstein*, a novel which can be read as a critique of the dark side of the Enlightenment imagination. In her published work, Mary Wollstonecraft was not only an advocate for universal suffrage but also for other rights that were then denied women, such as divorce, education and sexual freedom. For this, she was reviled by men and women alike.

Mary Wollstonecraft appears now as a middle-class feminist whose progressive ideas about the rights of women were not always matched by her ideas about social class. Although she was unequivocal in demanding universal voting rights, she seemed resigned to social class divisions. Indeed, Wollstonecraft even suggested that the emancipation of (middle-class) women was unattainable without the continued support of a servant class, which could relieve women activists from the burdens of household labour.

> For a woman to discharge "the duties of her station" she requires "merely a servant maid to take off her hands the servile part of the household business." Women's emancipation, then, is utterly dependent upon the prior existence of a class of women whose labour power is available to perform the more menial and mundane

household chores of the middle classes. It is emancipation of the few at the expense of the many. (Ferguson 1999: 441)

To contemporary ears, there is something disquietingly "elitist" about this championing of the rights of middle-class women at the expense of the rights of working-class women. While it may be argued that Wollstonecraft's views about the inevitability of social class divisions were shaped by her historical background and class origins, these views were not held by all middle-class feminists of her generation. As we shall see, the same time period also produced women thinkers and activists who were far more progressive than Wollstonecraft in their views about social and economic inequality.

The most valuable legacy of Wollstonecraft lies in her powerful call for the complete emancipation of women and for an end to the political, economic and legal constraints that prevented the full participation of women in government and in civil society. But in addition to her political activism, Mary Wollstonecraft also deserves to be remembered as a progressive educational reformer. Her views on the education of women were far in advance of her time. Not only did she promote co-educational schooling and favour state schools over elitist private schools, but she also campaigned for women to be taught such traditionally forbidden subjects as anatomy and medicine. Above all, it is for her passionate and articulate critique of the patriarchal status quo of her own time that we remember Mary Wollstonecraft — one of the early voices of social protest and one of the early champions of social and educational reform.

Harriet Martineau: Empirical Feminist

Harriet Martineau represents the next generation of women social thinkers after Mary Wollstonecraft. Although both the eighteenth- and nineteenth-century feminists were equally committed to the emancipation of women in Western societies, there were some subtle differences in the ways in which the major theorists of each time period presented their cases. Eighteenth-century women such as Wollstonecraft still wrote and published under the immediate influence of the Enlightenment and in the shadow of the French Revolution. For this reason, women thinkers of this age presented their ideas in abstract and universal terms, in much the same way as the leading male theorists of the Enlightenment. With the advent of the nineteenth century, however, social commentary and social criticism and other ideas about society began to be formulated more rigorously — with greater attention to theoretical generalization and to empirical observation. In other words, the jump from the eighteenth to the nineteenth century saw the transformation of social philosophy into social theory and, increasingly, into social research. Whereas we may classify Mary Wollstonecraft as a feminist social philosopher, Harriet Martineau is better described as a feminist social theorist and an early social researcher.

For many years, Harriet Martineau's chief claim to fame was as the official translator of Auguste Comte's major work, *The Positive Philosophy*. Some commentators have remarked that Martineau's translation of this work was far superior to the original, and indeed, Comte used Martineau's English translation as the basis for the re-translation of his book back into French. As well, Harriet Martineau wrote many books of her own. She was, among other things, an experienced traveller, an acute observer of social customs and institutions, and a perceptive social critic. Moreover, her numerous publications show that she contributed substantially to the systematic study of society — as a theorist, as a comparative social commentator, as a methodologist and as an empirical observer. Unfortunately, it was a mark of the times in which she lived that the considerable intellectual accomplishments of many women thinkers remained publicly unrecognized. Indeed, there is a whole tradition of "lost scholarship" that needs to be re-excavated and reinstated into the historical canon of social science. Often when such luminary women scholars were acknowledged, it was only as "intellectual servants" of celebrated male thinkers. This was certainly the case with Harriet Martineau, who was the intellectual servant of Auguste Comte, and with Harriet Taylor, who was the intellectual partner of John Stuart Mill. The time has long since passed, however, when the true value of these women's contributions to the history of ideas needs to be acknowledged and celebrated.

Probably one of the most neglected aspects of Martineau's intellectual career is her pioneering work as an early methodologist. In her book *How to Observe Morals and Manners*, she set out in great detail general principles for the empirical study of social phenomena. Included in this work are discussions on a range of topics, such as scientific research, facts and theories, induction, objectivity, bias and many other issues that continue to preoccupy social scientists. She also offered general advice on how to collect data, how to prepare field notes and ethnographic reports, and how to study social facts. In all essential respects, Martineau compiled an early manual on the practice of social science research, which was all the more remarkable for the time of its appearance. Although her reputation is often overshadowed by that of Comte, she was in fact greatly ahead of him in her skill as a methodologist and as an empirical social scientist.

Another remarkable aspect of Harriet Martineau's life was the extent of her travels. She travelled on both sides of the Atlantic, spending two years in the U.S., and later visited the Middle East, as well as many places in England and Ireland. Her international travels provided her with a comparative perspective on other societies and their institutions, and a deeper understanding of her own . Her travels enriched and enhanced her sociological vision in much the same way that similar experiences helped to shape the sociological ideas of Montesquieu, Marx, Weber and many other classical social theorists.

Many of the observations of American life that she recorded in her book *Society in America* resemble similar impressions recorded by Tocqueville in his *Democracy in America*. Whereas Tocqueville spent only nine months in the U.S, Martineau spent almost two years. However, both writers commented on the relative fluidity and flexibility of the class divisions in the U.S. when compared to the far more entrenched class divisions in European societies. Both writers were impressed by the relative absence of extreme poverty in America and by the widespread ownership of land and private property — even among poorer citizens and subsistence farmers. However, Martineau and Tocqueville differed in some of their assessments of life in America. Whereas the aristocratic Tocqueville wrongly assumed that women in America were largely content with their purely domestic role in society, Martineau accurately foresaw the rise of a women's movement. And whereas Tocqueville interpreted high rates of church attendance as a sign of religiosity, Martineau more realistically saw these rates as a sign of conformity — and as fear of dissent.

Besides the greater economic independence of Americans when compared to their European counterparts, Martineau and Tocqueville were also impressed by the vitality of grassroots organizations and town-hall meetings — in other words, by the presence of local democracy. These characteristics of political life in America compared very favourably with the destitution and marginalization of the poorer classes in Britain and Europe. Martineau also praised the strong individualist beliefs of Americans, concluding that the prevalence of these beliefs was evidence that greater class mobility existed in the U.S. than could be found in any European nation. Most of all, Martineau was convinced that the experiment of self-government in the New World had been successful. The American case repudiated the traditional, self-serving argument advanced in England by the Tories that the colonies of the British Empire were unfit to govern themselves. America — with all its faults and excesses — had managed to disprove this central tenet of the ideology of imperialism.

At the same time, however, Martineau was not blind to the contradictions and inconsistencies that threatened the stability of the new American republic. More than anything else, Martineau recognized that the central contradiction in American society was rooted in the institution of slavery. Throughout her stay in the United States, Martineau confronted the issue of slavery and documented her encounters with enslaved Africans, slave-owners and others whose lives had been impacted by the institution. As an abolitionist, Martineau was strongly opposed to slavery, but in order to advance her own investigations, she tried to hide her strong feelings when interviewing those who supported and attempted to justify the practice. Several interesting points are mentioned in Martineau's observations regarding slavery. Among other things, Martineau stated that, unlike Europe, where most mob violence originated in the lowest classes of society and was often motivated by destitution and desperation, in the U.S., mob violence was often instigated by members of the wealthier classes in defence of their property rights and class privileges. She also observed that there was strong opposition to the abolitionist movement — even in the so-called "free states" of the North. She records numerous examples of public abolitionist meetings being violently broken up by pro-slavery mobs, and of abolitionist newspapers being forced to close down through force of public opinion. Martineau describes how women played a leading role in the abolitionist movement, and for this reason they bore the brunt of much of the violence directed against it. She also records the "conspiracy of silence" that characterized many newspapers — in both the North and South — which failed to report many of the lynchings and other atrocities and acts of terrorism committed against both enslaved Africans and African free men. Some of her observations about the craven nature of media coverage of controversial events in the U.S. may well remind us of the absence of critical commentary in the American media during the run-up to the invasion — and rush to war — of Iraq in 2003.

In her recorded observations of slavery in the U.S., Martineau has provided us with a vivid and memorable picture of plantation society in the nineteenth century. Martineau's impressions of the delicate subject of sexual and racial relations in the Old South were recorded with great honesty and insight. She concluded that the authoritarian system of slavery corrupted everyone — the caste of slaves, the class of owners and the class of free whites. She was particularly concerned with how the sexual exploitation of enslaved African women by their male owners destroyed the basis of family relations in the enslaved community and led to a culture of impunity, in which the owners were not accountable to anyone for the mistreatment or even the murder of their slaves.

Harriet Martineau's detailed historical accounts of nineteenth-century America also left us with a compelling portrait of a colonial society in which patriarchy, racial privilege and class domination were perpetuated through ideology and physical force. Martineau was quick to recognize the parallels between the total subordination and exploitation of enslaved people and the degraded status of women, who were similarly deprived of political, legal and property rights. She was also sensitive to the obvious hypocrisies of a system in which men like Thomas Jefferson and George Washington, who were celebrated as revolutionary democrats, continued to defend the institutions of slavery and patriarchy and the continued exclusion of enslaved Africans and women from full American citizenship. Martineau's collected impressions of life in nineteenth-century America clearly show that she was far more than simply an accomplished diarist of her age. She was a meticulous observer of social life who paid great attention to the methodology of empirical data collection. She had a sharp eye for contradiction, conflict and hypocrisy in social relations and a strong sense of social justice. Using her skills as a social researcher and her insights as a social theorist, she produced a classic study of American society which is as erudite and informed as that authored by de Tocqueville. She deserves to be remembered as one of the pioneers of empirical social research and as an early social scientist.

Harriet Taylor: Philosophical Feminist

Until fairly recently, the main claim to historical fame of Harriet Taylor was as the wife of the renowned philosopher John Stuart Mill. Her story may be seen, therefore, as another case of an unacknowledged woman scholar who deserves recognition for her contributions to social thought. Harriet Taylor was born Harriet Hardy, and after an early marriage to John Taylor, married John Stuart Mill in 1851, following the death of her first husband. Although there is some disagreement among scholars regarding the full extent of Taylor's contributions, the strongest testimony to her originality and intellectual rigour comes from John Stuart Mill. Indeed, Mill credited Taylor's influence and partnership on some of his most important works, including *The Enfranchisement of Women*, *Principles of Political Economy*, *On Liberty* and his most powerful essay, *The Subjection of Women*. A number of these works were described by Mill as a "joint production" — particularly those that dealt with the status of women. But while many commentators emphasize the profound influence of his wife on the works of John Stuart Mill, there are some dissenting opinions. Kinzer, for example, insists that Harriet Taylor's influence has been exaggerated: "Bruce Kinzer (2007) has recently demonstrated that Harriet's influence during the decade of the 1830s was restricted to the development of Mill's emotional side. Her intellectual influence grew, to be sure, during the following two decades but, as argued by Reeves, many of the revisions that Mill made to his seminal works owed much less to Harriet's thought than has commonly been perceived. Reeves indicates where there were clear differences of opinion between them. He concludes that, 'whatever Mill said [in the Autobiography], Harriet never directly dictated his views, but as two intelligent, passionate people, they certainly debated them'" (Donoghue 2010: 92). See also Reeves (2008) for more details on the lives of John Stuart Mill and Harriet Taylor.

However, passages from Mill's works, especially from his *Autobiography*, seem to confirm the close collaboration that existed between him and Harriet Taylor over the course of their twenty-eight years of intellectual partnership, especially in the areas of feminism and liberal democracy, in which her input appears to have been decisive.

There is no doubt that Taylor's strong commitment to the emancipation of women had a deeply radicalizing effect on Mill. For Taylor, Mill and other reformers of their generation, the emancipation of women meant several things. First and foremost, it meant female suffrage — granting women the right to vote in all elections. It also meant opening up the professions, such as medicine, law and politics, from which women had traditionally been excluded. The issue of women's rights also extended to the family. Mill and Taylor both argued in favour of marital equality. They supported laws that would enshrine a woman's right to independently own property, to divorce abusive husbands and to obtain legal protection and redress from domestic violence. Mill presented all of his arguments for the emancipation of women in his powerful essay *The Subjection of Women* and in the major parliamentary speeches he delivered over the course of his three year (1865–1868) political career as a member of Parliament. In his published work, he confronted all of the standard justifications for preserving male privilege, and he rebutted each of these arguments through a rational and logical demolition of their premises and conclusions. Given the entrenched prejudices he faced, Mill presented one of the strongest and most revolutionary arguments of his age in support of the emancipation of women (Reeves 2008). Not even Marx and Engels ever produced such a clear and unequivocal call for women's full equality. Without the influence of Harriet Taylor, it is doubtful that Mill would ever have achieved this extraordinary level of passion and insight into one of the most pressing social issues of his time.

Besides her passionate advocacy for the rights of women, Taylor was also concerned about the rights of minorities and individuals within the larger society. She had earlier published her own paper on toleration, and she remained throughout her life a strong defender of the rights of the individual in society and a proponent of the rights of dissent and diversity of opinion. Much of the emphasis placed by Mill and Taylor on individual rights was a response to the growth of collectivist ideologies and movements — such as Comtean positivism, chartism (and trade unionism), Marxism, Christian socialism, and more conservative movements for social order. While both Mill and Taylor supported and campaigned for democratic and popular social reforms, they continued to insist on safeguards for the rights of the individual in mass society. Taylor, in particular, emphasized the need to recognize freedom of expression and freedom of action. Indeed, she and Mill argued that not only should a society tolerate diverse opinions, but also diversity in lifestyles — a variety of "experiments in living." This insistence on toleration of lifestyle differences gives their work an up-to-date feel, which resonates with many postmodernist writers who call for a celebration of difference and diversity.

Though much of Mill's published work is highly regarded today for its eloquent defence of individual liberties, there is a discernible tension in some of his writing between the competing imperatives of "freedom" and "equality" in human affairs. Indeed, this was a tension between Mill and Taylor in their own partnership. While Mill emphasized the importance of free enterprise in the first draft of his book *Principles of Political Economy*, Taylor insisted that a chapter be included on the conditions of the working class in society and how to improve these conditions. In the intervening years, the tension between the imperatives of freedom and equality has become a significant divide, not only in political thought, but in the real politics of nation-states. In our own time, capitalist, communist, socialist and even some Islamic states have each described themselves as "democracies" — some as "liberal democracies" (capitalist), some as "peoples' democracies" (communist) and some as "social democracies" (socialist). But the central divide between freedom and equality has continued to differentiate politics of the right from politics of the left; the goal of reconciling these two imperatives has proven elusive and difficult to implement. Mill and Taylor, as their writings show, wrestled with this tension as honestly and as conscientiously as any who came after them.

Charlotte Perkins Gilman: Radical Feminist

Charlotte Perkins Gilman was one of the most original and radical women social thinkers of the nineteenth century. Gilman, more than any other feminist of this period, began to develop an independent social theory of what we today would call "gender oppression" and also introduced some important new terms and concepts into the study of society. Besides her contributions to feminist theory, Gilman was an influential social activist who, along with Jane Addams, founded the *Women's Peace Party* in 1915. Beyond her analysis and critique of the sexual subordination of women in patriarchal society, Gilman also proposed a number of radical social reforms which, she believed, could lay the foundations for a genuinely democratic and non-sexist society. Many of these proposals would still be considered revolutionary in their implications.

Gilman's social analysis introduced offered fresh insights into the subordination of women in nineteenth-century society. In her own way, she was able to advance the development of a uniquely feminist perspective in modern social theory. One of her earliest observations on the sexual division of labour concluded that it was only in human society that females have grown wholly dependent upon males for the provision of food, shelter, protection and other basic necessities of life. In other animal societies, females of the species are able to subsist independently of males.

On the basis of her observations, Gilman concluded that all known human societies are characterized by a "sexuo-economic arrangement" which privileges men as a "master-class" and which relegates women to the status of a servile underclass. Indeed, there are some striking similarities between Gilman's analysis of sexual stratification and that offered by Marx and especially by Engels in his book *Origins of the Family, Private Property and the State)*. Marx, Engels and Gilman each emphasized the importance of the economy in sexual stratification and the significance of work, or labour, as an activity of human self-development. However, whereas Marx and Engels defined the central concept of "class" in socio-economic terms, Gilman saw the concept of class as inextricably related to sexual status. For Gilman, the concept of "sex-class" was essential for any understanding of the system of sexual stratification in modern society. The enslavement of women and their forced economic dependency had led to the progressive development of a generalized dependency in all aspects of women's lives. Economic and physical dependency had also led to exaggerated cultural differences between men and women, which, in turn, were further reproduced through educational and psychological dependency — in other

---

Figure 7-4 The Female of the Species

We are the only animal species in which the female depends on the male for food, the only animal species in which the sex-relation is also an economic relation. With us an entire sex lives in a relation of economic dependence upon the other sex, and the economic relation is combined with the sex-relation. The economic status of the human female is relative to the sex-relation.

It is commonly assumed that this condition also obtains among other animals, but such is not the case. The female bee and ant are economically dependent, but not on the male ... And with the carnivora, if the young are to lose one parent, it might far better be the father: the mother is quite competent to take care of them herself. In no case is the female throughout her life supported by the male.

In the human species the condition is permanent and general, though there are exceptions, and though the present century is witnessing the beginnings of a great change in this respect. We have not been accustomed to face this fact beyond our loose generalization that it was "natural," and that other animals did so, too.

(Gilman 1966: 5–6).

---

words, through socialization. In this way, the cycle of sexual dependency was endlessly reproduced.

Unlike Marx and Engels, who focused on the need for revolutionary changes in the large-scale structures of society, Gilman drew attention to the need for changes in the "little household" — or what modern feminists call the "domestic sphere of production." Gilman suggested that much of the drudgery and toil associated with household labour could best be performed by well-paid professionals. She also envisaged that many routine household necessities — such as cooking, health care and recreation — could be reorganized around a communal lifestyle that would allow greater democratic access to these basic facilities and services. Through these and other social reforms,

Figure 7-5 Gillman — the Sexuo-Economic Arrangement

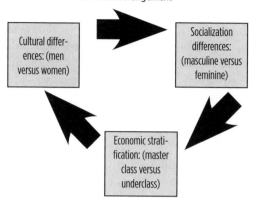

Gilman proposed a revolutionary reorganization of society as a necessary condition for the emancipation of women and as a way to end the patriarchal system of sexual stratification. Gilman was a prolific writer who contributed to most of the major sociological journals of her day. Moreover, in books such as *Women and Economics* (1898), she formulated a theory of society which sought to explain the oppression and exploitation of women as a sex-class more clearly and more eloquently than any of her male contemporaries. She was one of the most influential intellectuals and activists of the nineteenth century, and her theoretical contributions addressed many of the same social topics as those addressed by Marx, Durkheim, Weber, Spencer and others. However, Gilman chose to address these topics from the standpoint of a radical woman thinker, and for this reason her contributions were — until recently — largely expunged from the record of classical social theory.

Jane Addams: Social Researcher and Social Reformer

If most students taking this course were asked: which of the classical social thinkers included in this book was included on the FBI's list of dangerous radicals and was also awarded the Nobel Peace Prize, very few would know. The answer is, of course, Jane Addams. Besides her theoretical and method-ological work as a social thinker and as an early social scientist, Jane Addams was one of the most influential social reformers of her generation. She was an unacknowledged founder of the Chicago School of Sociology — along with more well-known male theorists John Dewey, George Herbert Mead and Robert E. Park. She was also a leading intellectual contributor to the nineteenth-century movement of progressivism. However, one of the most enduring legacies of Jane Addams was her settlement project at Hull House in Chicago. This project, established in a working-class neighbourhood, became a living laboratory for many different social experiments — social clubs, garbage collection, low-cost housing, consumer cooperatives, trade unions and evening classes, as well as many other progressive social reforms. The experiences of Hull House influenced the work of Addams in many different ways. She pioneered the methods of field observation and qualitative research that later became the hallmark of the Chicago School of Sociology. She also combined the scientific goal of sociological research with the ethical goal of social improvement.

The linking of social research to the need for progressive social change has become a defining characteristic not only of feminist social research but, more generally, of many other versions of "critical social science." In the case of Jane Addams, her contributions to the study of society are marked by the following distinct features:

- *All her sociological work was motivated by a strong democratic ethic.* She was always concerned that her work should contribute to the "welfare of the community." At the same time, Addams believed that much ordinary human behaviour was often driven by what we shall call an "ethical imperative." Unlike many of the liberal or utilitarian thinkers of her time, who believed that individuals were motivated primarily by selfishness, or rational egoism — that is, by the pursuit of rational self-interest — Addams concluded from her experiences at Hull House that much human interaction was motivated by more altruistic impulses. Although she was influenced by the Darwinian ideas of her day, her version of social Darwinism was tempered by the influences of progressivism and by the "social gospel" tradition of Christian activism. For Addams, evolutionism implied movement towards social progress and social reform.

- *Much of her sociological work was descriptive and empirical.* She used many case studies from the Hull House experiment as a basis for her empirical social research. Unlike most of the male theorists who constructed general theories of society, Addams produced vividly drawn portraits of social life. She also pioneered the methodological techniques of participant observation and urban ethnographic research.

- *She was influenced by the developing theory of symbolic interactionism at the University of Chicago* inasmuch as she conceived of society as a vast network of individuals rather than as a set of large-scale societal structures and processes. As a woman social thinker, she always thought of the "individual" not as an abstract entity — as did Mead, Cooley and other symbolic interactionists — but as a real living person with a distinct gender, racial and ethnic identity. However, as postmodernist writers such as Lemert (2005) suggest, the "abstract individual" of traditional social theory invariably turns out to be an (undeclared) white, middle-class heterosexual male, who functions as a universal cipher — or "zero signifier" — for all social actors. Because of her attention to differences of race, ethnicity and gender, Addams may be seen as an early pioneer of what later came to be called "standpoint theory" — a theoretical perspective understood from the vantage point of a particular social group, or individual.

- *She explained many of the social problems and social conflicts of her time by reference to a theory of what today would be called "cultural lag."* Unlike Marx and the socialist theorists who explained many of the problems of modern society in terms of "class conflict," Addams argued that social problems arose from what she called "belatedness" (see also Ogburn 1957). She believed that many of these problems would be solved when appropriate "democratic ethical systems" evolved to correspond with the new systems of industrial production. In other words, many social problems resulted from a failure of ethics to catch up with the new forms of production and enterprise.

Jane Addams was clearly a woman of unusual courage and clarity of vision. Her vocal opposition to American involvement in World War I exposed her to widespread criticism and condemnation. She was expelled from the Daughters of the American Revolution. The establishment of the settlement at Hull House provided her with the opportunity to experiment with projects of social improvement and social reform, and to utilize a living laboratory for social scientific research. She was one of the most distinguished intellectuals, public educators and social activists of her generation. Her proposals for the collective self-improvement of inner-city neighbourhoods, as well as for other types of democratic social reform, have as much relevance and urgency today as they did when she first advanced these ideas.

Marianne Weber: Politician and Women's Advocate

Marianne Weber was the wife of Max Weber, the world-renowned sociologist, but she never received from him the adulation and respect that Harriet Taylor received from her husband, John Stuart Mill. However, Marianne Weber became an increasingly public figure after her husband retired from public life following his nervous breakdown in 1897. As a European woman thinker, Marianne Weber showed a greater interest in purely theoretical issues than any of the Anglo-American women thinkers already discussed in this chapter. In this respect, she was caught up in the continental cultural divide whereby European social thinkers were more attracted to speculative theories of society, while Anglo-American social thinkers were more concerned with descriptive studies, methodology and measurement, and the practical applications of empirical research. This is not to suggest that Marianne Weber was disinterested in practical matters. She was the first female member of the

German Parliament from Baden and president of Germany's most powerful feminist organization.

The most interesting aspects of Marianne Weber's work centre on her criticisms of established social theories and her attempts to advance beyond criticism to develop a feminist perspective on social theory. An example of her critical encounters with social theory may be seen in her critique of Max Weber's typology of domination. Whereas the male Weber only distinguished between legitimate domination (i.e., authority) and non-legitimate domination (i.e., power), the female Weber suggested a more nuanced distinction. For Marianne Weber, both types of domination implied control over individuals in society and a denial of individual autonomy and freedom. The only difference was that non-legitimate domination was maintained through the use of "hard" power, whereas legitimate domination (or "authority") was maintained through the use of "soft" power. As a woman, Marianne Weber was very much aware that even the exercise of "soft" power in the patriarchal nuclear family restricted the autonomy and freedom of women. In place of Max Weber's typology, therefore, Marianne Weber suggested that the real distinction was that between "domination" and "autonomy."

Marianne Weber also critically examined existing empirical data on women in the workplace, although much of her published work — with the exception of her biography of her husband — is still only available in German She described and condemned the long hours, low wages and back-breaking work that characterized all forms of female employment — whether industrial, agricultural, domestic, clerical or professional. Although she recognized that modern industrial capitalism had loosened some of the traditional ties of patriarchy, she also acknowledged the continued link between capitalism and the modern patriarchal family. For Marianne Weber, the emancipation of women had to begin in the home — in the patriarchal household. Only after reforming the politics of the family would it be possible for women to press for greater reforms in society and in the workplace.

Beatrice Potter Webb: Public Intellectual

The last woman social thinker to be covered in this chapter is the English socialist, economist and social researcher Beatrice Potter Webb. Beatrice Webb should not be confused with Beatrix Potter, another well known woman of the nineteenth century, who became famous as an author and illustrator of children's books — the Peter Rabbit stories — as well as an environmentalist. Interestingly, both women died in the same year, 1943.

Among her many accomplishments, Beatrice Webb — along with her husband, Sydney Webb — founded a number of important institutions, including the London School of Economics (LSE), the Fabian socialist movement, the Cooperative Wholesale and Consumer movement and the weekly socialist magazine *The New Statesman*. In England, Beatrice Webb was probably the most influential woman thinker and activist of her generation, and the record of her accomplishments is still remembered and respected. For the sake of brevity and simplicity her main contributions may be summarized under the following headings:

- *Social research*: Beatrice Webb was one of the early pioneers of empirical social research in the U.K. Among other things, she helped to refine the methods of data collection used in social research, and her own empirical studies contributed a great deal to the evolution of public education and social policy in the U.K. Her earliest experience of social research was as an assistant to Charles Booth, the philanthropist (who was married to her cousin Mary). In 1889, Booth completed a huge seventeen volume statistical survey of poverty in London which was published as *The Life and Labour of the People of London*. One year later, another (unrelated) Booth, William Booth — founder of the Salvation Army — also published a study of poverty and crime, entitled *Darkest England and the Way Out*. There is no evidence, however, that these two Booths ever met each other, or exchanged ideas. Drawing on her experience as an investigator with Booth, Webb later undertook her own empirical studies, including a participant-observation study of the sweatshops in the garment industry, where she worked briefly as a seamstress. Her strong interest in empirical research led Webb to publish a number of papers dealing with such methodological issues as the use of statistics in research, the scientific method in social inquiry, methods of interviewing and note-taking, and the distinction between fact and value. Many of these papers appeared before the publication of the more well-known methodological works of Durkheim and Weber. During her intellectual career, Webb, often in collaboration with her husband, Sydney, conducted a wide range of quantitative and qualitative social research, which included the use of statistical surveys, case studies, questionnaires, interviews and participant observation studies. Many of these techniques were later taught in the London School of Economics. As a pioneer of empirical social research, Beatrice Webb was a prescient thinker whose ideas often anticipated the conclusions of later sociologists.

- *Social theory and social policy*: Although Beatrice Webb was influenced by the writings of Auguste Comte and Harriet Martineau, it was Herbert Spencer, a friend of the family, who first shaped her theoretical ideas. The young Beatrice Webb embraced the *laissez-faire* liberalism and radical individualism popularized by Spencer, although she later rejected these ideas in favour of her own version of socialism and state interventionism. An important turning point for Webb was her collaboration with Charles Booth on the statistical survey of London's poor. This experience exposed her to the full extent of poverty and social misery in London and convinced her of the need for social reform and state intervention — in contradiction to the teachings of Spencer. Over her lifetime, Webb campaigned for many social reforms, including those related to the Poor Laws, compulsory education, public health, trade unions, working conditions and, somewhat belatedly, female suffrage. Today, it is generally acknowledged that Webb's social thought and social activism directly contributed to the rise of the welfare state in Britain.

- *Socialism*: Beatrice and Sydney Webb are probably best known in Britain as the founders of the Fabian Society, a group of socialist intellectuals dedicated to public education and social reform. Unlike the Marxist socialists, the Fabians rejected revolutionary social change in favour of gradualism and reformism. They believed that social reforms could be implemented through public education and growing state intervention. In other words — their view of socialism was evolutionary rather than revolutionary in nature. Beatrice Webb was also involved in working-class movements and organizations such as the cooperative movement and the trade union movement. In 1932, after a visit to the USSR, the Webbs published a glowing, naive and wholly uncritical account of the Soviet Union entitled *Soviet Communism: A New Civilization?* Strangely, this book contradicted many of the methodological principles advocated so strongly by Beatrice Webb in her other works. Most notably, it accepted at face value the official accounts of Soviet society without any attempt to test their validity. In this respect, Beatrice Webb remained a genteel socialist — a product of her privileged upbringing and philanthropic background. Her upper-class socialism led her to campaign for the reform of the capitalist system rather than for its revolutionary overthrow and radical transformation.

- *Feminism:* At the start of her intellectual career, Beatrice Webb was opposed to giving women the right to vote. In her autobiographical book, *My Apprenticeship*, Webb admits to signing an anti-suffrage petition, and she maintained that position for over twenty years. When she finally decided to support the suffrage movement, she explained her earlier opposition as a rebellion against her father, who strongly supported the vote for women. In later life, Beatrice Webb campaigned not only for female suffrage but also for other women's causes, such as protective labour laws and equal pay legislation. But because of her earlier "false step" of opposing the vote for women, some feminists have remained ambivalent in their assessment of Webb's feminist legacy.

We have just begun the task of recovering the works of women social thinkers and of incorporating these works into the history of social thought. It has been through the efforts of feminist scholars — male and female — and the support from women's studies programs that the lost record of women's intellectual achievements is slowly being retrieved. In this respect, the present review is still a work in progress.

References

Amin Samir. 1976. *Unequal Development: An Essay on the Social Formations of Peripheral Capitalism*. New York: Monthly Review Press.

Askin, Kelly Dawn. 1997. *War Crimes Against Women: Prosecution in International War Crimes Tribunals*. Dordrecht, Netherlands: Martinus Nijhoff Publishers.

Baran, Paul. 1957. *The Political Economy of Growth*. New York: Monthly Review Press.

Biggs, Lesley C., Susan Gingell and Pamela J. Downe (eds). 2011 *Gendered Intersections: An Introduction to Women's & Gender Studies*, 2nd Edition. Halifax: Fernwood.

Booth, Charles. 1902–1903. *Life and Labour of the People in London*. 17 vols. London: Macmillan.

___. 1890. *In Darkest England and The Way Out*. London International Headquarters of the Salvation Army.

Burke, Edmund. 1959 [1790]. *Reflections of the Revolution in France*. Ed. William B. Todd. NY: Holt, Rinehart and Winston.

Cardoso, Fernando Henrique, and Enzo Faletto. 1979. *Dependency and Development in Latin América*. Berkeley, CA: University of California Press.

Clark, Lorenne M.G., and Lynda Lange. 1979. *The Sexism of Social and Political Theory*. Toronto: University of Toronto Press.

Comte, Auguste. 2000 [1896]. *The Positive Philosophy of Auguste Comte*. Translated by Harriet Martineau (3 Vols). London: George Bell & Sons; Kitchener: Batoche Books.

Coser, Lewis A. 1965. *Men of Ideas*. New York: Free Press.

___. 1967. *Masters of Sociological Thought: Ideas in Historical and Social Context*. New York: Harcourt Brace Jovanovich.

Crasnow, Sharon. 2009. "Is Standpoint Theory a Resource for Feminist Epistemology? An Introduction." *Hypatia* 24, 4: 209–18.

de Beauvoir, Simone. 1989 [1953]. *The Second Sex*. English translation. New York: Vintage Books.

Donoghue, Mark. 2010. "Review of J.S. Mill Revisited: Biographical and Political Explorations." *History of Economics Review* 49: 81–98.

Emmanuel, Arghiri. 1972. *Unequal Exchange: A Study of the Imperialism of Trade*. New York: Monthly Review Press.

Engels, Friedrich. 1942 [1884]. *The Origin of the Family, Private Property and the State*. NY: International Publishers.

Ferguson, Susan. 1999. "The Radical Ideas of Mary Wollstonecraft." *Canadian Journal of Political Science/Revue canadienne de science politique* 32, 3: 427–50.

Frank, Andre Gunder. 1969. *Capitalism and Underdevelopment in Latin America: Historical Studies of Chile and Brazil*. Rev. ed. New York: Monthly Review Press.

Gilman, Charlotte Perkins.1966 [1898]. *Women and Economics: A Study of the Economic Relation Between Men and Women as a Factor in Social Evolution.* New York: Harper Torchbooks.

Godwin, William. 1793. *Enquiry Concerning Political Justice, and its Influence on General Virtue and Happiness.* 2 vols. London: G.G.J. and J. Robinson.

Grovier, Kelly. 2005. *The Observer,* Sunday 2 January. <http://www.guardian.co.uk/books/2005/jan/02/biography.features>.

Harding, Sandra (ed.). 2004. *The Feminist Standpoint Theory Reader.* New York and London: Routledge.

Hemming, Heidi, and Julie Hemming Savage. 2009. *Women Making America.* Kansas City, KS: Clotho Press.

Kanda, Terry R. 1988. *The Woman Question in Classical Sociological Theory.* Gainesville, FL: University Press of Florida.

Kenney, Sally J., and Helen Kinsella (eds.). 1997. *Politics and Feminist Standpoint Theories.* New York and London: Haworth Press.

Kinzer, Bruce L. 2007. *J.S. Mill Revisited: Biographical and Political Explorations.* Basingstoke: Palgrave Macmillan.

Lange, Lynda. 1979. "Rousseau: Women and the General Will." In Lorenne M.G. Clark and Lynda Lange (ed.), *The Sexism of Social and Political Theory.* Toronto: University of Tornoto Press.

Lemert, Charles. 2005. *Postmodernism Is Not What You Think.* Second edition. Boulder, CO: Paradigm Publishers.

Martineau, Harriet. 1988 [1838]. *How to Observe Morals and Manners.* With an ntroduction and analytical index by Michael R. Hill. New Jersey: Transaction Publishers.

___. 2009 [1837]. *Society in America.* Three volumes. [London: Saunders and Otley]; Cambridge, UK: Cambridge University Press.

McDonald, Lynn. 1994. *Women Founders of the Social Sciences.* Ottawa: Carleton University Press.

Mill, John Stuart. 1848. *Principles of Political Economy.* London: Longmans, Green and Co.

___. 1955 [1859]. *On Liberty.* Chicago: Henry Regnery Company (A Gateway Edition).

___. 1997 [1869]. *The Subjection of Women.* New York: Dover Thrift Editions.

Mill, Mrs John Stuart (Harriet Hardy Taylor Mill). 1868. *The Enfranchisement of Women.* Reprinted from *The Westminster Review,* July 1851. London: Trüber & Co.

Mousset, Sophie. 2007. *Women's Rights and the French Revolution: A Biography of Olympe de Gouges.* New Brunswick (U.S.A.) & London (U.K.): Transaction Publishers.

Ogburn, William. F. 1957. "Cultural Lag as Theory." *Sociology and Social Research* January–February: 167–74.

Okin, Susan. 1978. *Women in Western Political Thought.* Princeton, NJ: Princeton University Press.

Purvis, Jane. 1995. "The Prison Experiences of the Suffrgattes in Edwardian Britain." *Women's History Review* 4, 1: 103–33.

Reeves, Richard. 2008. *John Stuart Mill: Victorian Firebrand.* London: Atlantic Books.

Rousseau, Jean-Jacques Rousseau. 1979 [1762]. *Émile, or On Education.* Translation by Allan Bloom. New York: Basic Books.

Sarkar, Mahua. 2004. "Looking for Feminism." *Gender & History* 16: 318–33.

Schwartz, Joel. 1984. *The Sexual Politics of Jean-Jacques Rousseau.* Chicago: University of Chicago Press.

Shelley, Mary. 1818. *Frankenstein; or, The Modern Prometheus.* London: Lackington, Hughes, Harding, Mavor and Jones.

Spender, Dale. 1983. *Feminist Theorists: Three Centuries of Key Women Thinkers.* New York: Pantheon Books.

Sydie, R.A. 1987. *Natural Women; Cultured Men: A Feminist Perspective on Sociological Theory.* Toronto: Methuen.

Tocqueville, Alexis de. 2000 [1835–1840]. *Democracy in America.* Chicago: University of Chicago Press.

Wallace, Ruth (ed.). 1989. *Feminism and Sociological Theory.* Newbury Park, CA: Sage Publications.

Webb, Beatrice. 1926. *My Apprenticeship.* London: Longmans, Green & Co.

Webb, Sidney, and Beatrice Webb. 1935. *Soviet Communism: A New Civilization?* London: Longmans.

Wollstonecraft, Mary. 2009 [1792]. *A Vindication of the Rights of Woman.* Third edition. Ed. Deidre Shauna Lynch. New York: W.W. Norton and Company.

Young, Iris Marion. 1989. "Polity and Group Difference: A Critique of the Ideal of Universal Citizenship." *Ethics* 99, 2 (Jan.): 250–74. University of Chicago Press.

Chapter 8

The Historical Materialism of Karl Marx

The Unquiet Ghost of Karl Marx

A spectre is haunting the office towers and boardrooms of the failed banks, mortgage companies and insurance companies of the past few years. It is the spectre of Karl Marx. More than any other theorist covered in this book, the ghost of Karl Marx refuses to rest in peace; his critique of capitalism has never seemed as relevant as it does today.

The past few years have seen a steadily deepening crisis in the global financial system — a crisis unprecedented in recent memory. The early symptoms of this downward spiral were first seen in 2007 with the start of "the sub-prime mortgage" crisis. After a decade, or more, of conspicuous consumption — often financed through the equity of their homes — American homeowners were suddenly faced with plummeting house values, soaring mortgage interest rates, an end to easy credit and crippling levels of personal debt. The results of this economic meltdown were catastrophic for many ordinary people: mortgage foreclosures,

Figure 8-1 Marx and the Current Economic Meltdown: Give Karl Marx a Chance to Save the World Economy

Policy makers struggling to understand the barrage of financial panics, protests and other ills afflicting the world would do well to study the works of a long-dead economist: Karl Marx. The sooner they recognize we're facing a once-in-a-lifetime crisis of capitalism, the better equipped they will be to manage a way out of it....

Consider, for example, Marx's prediction ... in "Das Kapital," companies' pursuit of profits and productivity would naturally lead them to need fewer and fewer workers, creating an "industrial reserve army" of the poor and unemployed.

The process he describes is visible throughout the developed world.... Companies' efforts to cut costs and avoid hiring have boosted U.S. corporate profits ... to the highest level in more than six decades, while the unemployment rate stands at 9.1 percent and real wages are stagnant.... U.S. income inequality, meanwhile, is by some measures close to its highest level since the 1920s.

Marx also pointed out... The more people are relegated to poverty, the less they will be able to consume all the goods and services companies produce. When one company cuts costs to boost earnings, it's smart, but when they all do, they undermine the income and demand on which they rely for revenues and profits.

As Marx put it in Kapital: "The ultimate reason for all real crises always remains the poverty and restricted consumption of the masses."

Source: George Magnus, Aug. 28, 2011, Bloomberg <bloomberg.com/news/print/2011-08-29/give-marx-a-chance-to-save-the-world-economy-commentary-by-george-magnus.html>.

personal bankruptcy, dispossession and eviction from their homes. And much more was to come. Like a toxic virus, the financial crisis spread from the banks and mortgage companies to other institutions in the economy — insurance companies, credit rating agencies and bond markets. And having infected the financial centres of the U.S., the contagion migrated to Europe, Asia and the rest of the planet. In just half a decade we witnessed a complete cycle of boom-bubble-bust: a crisis that originated in the housing market but which spread to every corner of the economy.

The roots of the present financial crisis extend back to the 1980s Republican administration of President Ronald Reagan in the U.S. and to the Conservative government of Prime Minister Margaret Thatcher in the U.K. (although Richard Duncan (2008) argues that the rot actually began with President Richard Nixon in the 1970s). It was during the 1980s that the neoliberal agenda was first unleashed on an unsuspecting public: de-regulation, privatization and full marketization; tax cuts for the rich and super rich, and cutbacks in social spending for middle and low income families; as well as increased militarization and bloated defence budgets. The deregulation of the financial sector allowed the banks and mortgage companies new and unprecedented opportunities for speculative trading in the financial markets. Mortgages were offered to unqualified applicants who had no collateral or down payments for them; mortgages were bundled to-gether and sold to overseas investors; and credit was marketed through hype and high pressure sales campaigns. But this bubble of infinite consumption was doomed to burst, and when it did — several decades later — the results were disastrous for almost everyone.

The crunch came in 2008. After the first wave of foreclosures and evictions in the housing market, the bank failures followed. Northern Rock collapsed in February 2008; Bear Stearns in March; Lehman Brothers in September, along with Fannie Mae, Freddie Mac and Washington Mutual. By October 2008, President George W. Bush had persuaded the U.S. Congress to establish a $700 billion bank rescue fund. In February 2009, President Barak Obama signed into law a $700 billion-plus stimulus package. In May 2009, Chrysler Corporation entered into bankruptcy protection. In the years that followed, the virus spread to the European Union, where Greece continues to face the prospect of a sovereign default on its national debt. Other European nations — including Portugal, Ireland, Iceland, Spain and Italy also find themselves in deep economic trouble.

For many working people, the financial collapses that led to the loss of their homes were further exacerbated by contractions in the energy, manu-facturing and retail sectors of the economy. In order to cut their production and distribution costs, many corporations — and public sector employers — resorted to various measures to shore up declining profit margins, including

Figure 8-2 Global Economic Crisis Timeline: Key Dates of the Global Economic Crisis

2008

February 17	British government announces that struggling Northern Rock bank is to be nationalised.
March 17	Wall Street's fifth-largest bank, Bear Stearns, is acquired by larger rival JP Morgan Chase.
September 7	U.S. Federal Reserve takeover of Fannie Mae and Freddie Mac.
September 14	Merrill Lynch is sold to Bank of America.
September 15	Lehman Brothers files for bankruptcy protection.
September 17	The U.S. Federal Reserve lends $85 billion to American International Group (AIG) to avoid bankruptcy.
September 25	Washington Mutual, the giant mortgage lender, which had assets valued at $307bn, is closed down by regulators and sold to JP Morgan Chase.
September 29	The Icelandic government takes control of the country's third-largest bank, Glitnir.
September 29	The British mortgage lender Bradford & Bingley is nationalised.
October 1	The financial crisis spreads to Europe.
October 3	President George W. Bush signs the Emergency Economic Stabilization Act, creating a $700 billion Troubled Assets Relief Program to purchase failing bank assets.
October 3	The U.S. House of Representatives passes a $700bn (£394bn) government plan to rescue the U.S. financial sector.
October 6–10	Worst week for the stock market in 75 years.
October 8	The U.K. government announces details of a rescue package for the banking system worth at least £50bn ($88bn).
November 12	Treasury Secretary Paulson abandons plan to buy toxic assets under the $700 billion Troubled Asset Relief Program (TARP).
November 14:	The Eurozone officially slips into recession after EU figures show that the economy shrank by 0.2% in the third quarter.

2009

January 15	The Irish government says it is to nationalise the Anglo Irish Bank
February 17	President Obama signs a $787 billion stimulus package into law.
April 2	G-20 Summit committed $1.1 trillion mostly to the IMF.
May 1	One of the "big three" U.S. carmakers, Chrysler, enters bankruptcy protection
June 24	The Organisation for Economic Co-operation and Development says the world economy is near the bottom of the worst recession in post-war history

Source: <wikipedia.org/wiki/2007%E2%80%932012_global_financial_crisis>

workforce cutbacks and wage rollbacks, layoffs, reduced benefits, outsourcing, downsizing and, of course, off-shore relocations. The consequences of these measures have been depressingly similar for a growing percentage of the workforce — unemployment, underemployment and declining real incomes. But perhaps the most shocking picture to emerge from the carnage of the present financial crisis is the ever widening gap in income and wealth between the super rich and the rest of society. In the U.S. and other affected economies, the middle class is disappearing into the ranks of the working class and lower income groups. While the top corporate elite has experienced an unprecedented gain in wealth and income over the past few decades, the disappearing middle class and lower income groups have seen their standards of living rapidly eroded — in many cases — into poverty and penury. Not since the Gilded Age of the late nineteenth century has the polarization between the rich and the rest of society been so sharp — in both the U.S. and Canada — and the potential for political protest and civil unrest has never been greater.

None of this would have surprised Karl Marx. Over 150 years ago he predicted that capitalist societies would remain vulnerable to recurrent crises of boom-bubble-bust. His critical analysis of capitalism convinced him that boom periods of production and accumulation would inevitably slump into recessions and even depressions. During these economic meltdowns, it was only the capitalist elite that would profit from its financial speculation while the majority of the working-class population would slide downwards into greater poverty and insecurity. Indeed, he believed that capitalism was an inherently unjust system of social and economic relations in which those who produced the wealth in society — whether in fields, factories, mines, drilling sites or offices — were doomed to have this wealth extracted from them as profit for the capitalist class, which owned the means of production.

Whatever we may think about Karl Marx, his diagnosis and prognosis of capitalism as an unjust and unstable economic system remains as relevant today as on the day that he completed the first volume of his famous three-volume work, *Das Kapital*, in 1867. Indeed, during 2011, we witnessed the rise of a grassroots movement, Occupy Wall Street, that protested against the excessive salaries, bonuses and profits pocketed by the financial elite, which has, through its ruinous policies of speculation and accumulation, put private greed far above any consideration of public need. Although the Occupy Movement resists demands to formulate a detailed political platform or program, there can be no doubt about its main concern: the growing gap between the super rich and the rest of the population — in the U.S. and beyond. Unsurprisingly, these concerns have been echoed in many other parts of the world. The movement identifies itself with what it calls the 99 percent of the population, in opposition to the 1 percent, who own and control an inordinate share of global wealth and income and who exercise disproportionate political influence over the rest of us. In other words, the Occupy Movement wants an end to the system in which a privileged elite is able to exploit and dominate the overwhelming majority of the population in contemporary capitalist society. The ghost of Karl Marx casts a long shadow.

Revisiting Marx

Of all the social thinkers covered in this book, Karl Marx has, without question, exerted the greatest impact on world history. No other thinker of the nineteenth century, with the possible exceptions of Charles Darwin and Sigmund Freud, achieved anywhere near the influence of Karl Marx. Marx's ideas inspired some of the most momentous events of the twentieth century: the Russian Revolution (1917), the Chinese Communist Revolution (1949), the Cuban Revolution (1959) and many of the anti-colonial and independence struggles around the globe since the end of World War II. Until the fall of communism in 1989, a doctrinaire version of orthodox Marxism was enshrined as the official ideology of the USSR and much of Eastern Europe. But as shall see, Marx would have rejected attempts to turn his critical ideas into a dogmatic doctrine, especially one that was designed to control and oppress entire societies. After all, Marx once proclaimed in a letter to Eduard Bernstein, "If anything is certain, it is that I myself am not a Marxist" (Marx-Engels 1924, Vol. 46: 353). Even though Marx's ideas have been used to legitimize oppressive governments, this fact has not prevented the growing influence of Marx's social theories. In the closing months of the twentieth century, for example, the British Broadcasting Corporation conducted an online poll to see who the general public would elect as the greatest thinker of the millennium. The winner was Karl Marx, who received more votes than any other intellectual celebrity — including Albert Einstein, Charles Darwin, Sigmund Freud and even Isaac Newton and Rene Descartes. And the *Financial Times* (of London), a mouthpiece for big business and high finance, published a leading article in August 1998 entitled "*Das Kapital Revisited.*" Although this article concerned the earlier Asian financial crisis, the reference to Marx was unmistakable. By the time the more recent global financial crisis erupted in the opening decade of the twenty-first century, references to Marx in the popular press and mass media had become almost commonplace (see, for example, Desai 2004; Wheen 2007; Wolff 2002). Today, we can count the number of Comteans, Spencerians or Durkeimians on the fingers of one hand, but there are still plenty of Marxists. Marx's ideas remain a vital force for mobilizing social and political action around the world.

In view of the resurgent interest in Marx and his ideas, we are certainly entitled to ask how it is that Marx has managed to outlast his critics, to be resurrected as a prophet who foresaw the gloomy economic times through which we are now passing. What is it about Marx that strikes such a resonant chord in the modern breast? When did he finally come in from the cold after enduring decades of hostility and derision from scholars, politicians and the general public? The truth is that every age reappraises the past through the eyes of the present. Social thinkers whose ideas were once dismissed as outmoded and disproved are often "rediscovered" and invested with a new contemporary relevance. Thus has it been with Marx. Today, more than ever, Marx's critical analysis of capitalism speaks to us with a renewed sense of urgency and realism. What aspects of Marx's work have caught the public imagination, and which of his ideas speaks most directly to us? Several major themes of Marx's work appear particularly relevant to our present economic and political predicament. In retrospect, it is clear that Marx anticipated some of the most troubling features of our present socio-economic landscape from an accurate reading of trends that were already evident in his day.

- *Marx would not have been surprised by the recent global economic recession:* He believed that recurrent economic crises were inevitable in capitalist societies. The periodic economic boom and bust cycles were, he concluded, endemic to the production and consumption processes of capitalism.
- *Marx anticipated the rise of corporate globalization:* He predicted the growing interconnectedness of national economies around the world. He also foresaw how even the remotest regions of the globe would someday be penetrated by capitalist businesses and drawn into the world capitalist system. He described how all natural resources would one day be converted into commodities that could be bought and sold. In this respect, Marx foresaw how global capitalism would eventually commodify the whole world, a trend which has been described by writers such as Naomi Klein, among others (see Klein 2002a, 2002b, 2007; Friedman 2005a, 2005b; Bhagwati 2004; Stiglitz 2002; Strange 1986; Beck 2000).
- *Marx predicted that the rich would continue to get richer at the expense of the majority of society, who would continue to get poorer:* This "Law of Immiseration," the tendency for capitalism to widen the gap between rich and poor, is particularly evident today. The wealth and income gap has widened between the Global North and the Global South, but it has also widened within many developed countries.
- *Marx predicted that, in the long term, the capitalist class would accumulate progressively more and more wealth:* This would happen while the working class would receive progressively less and less of the revenues of production. Marx also emphasized that this progressive polarization would not only intensify class divisions "within" capitalist societies, but also — on a global scale — divisions "between" the richer capitalist societies and those societies in the poorer, less developed parts of the world.

Over the past decade, a growing number of reports have documented the increasing income disparities within capitalist societies, and between the rich and poor nations of the world. In Canada, for example, the Canadian Centre for Policy Alternatives (Yalnizyan 2007) published *The Rich and the Rest of Us* (Yalnizyan 2010). According to this report, the top 10 percent of the population received eighty-two times the income of the lowest 10 percent. The top 10 percent received almost 30 percent of total earnings, while the bottom 20 percent received only 2.5 percent of total earnings. These inequalities have contributed to the greatest economic polarization in Canada for the last thirty years. This gap continues to widen even though most Canadians are working longer hours, are better educated than ever before and are living at a time of unprecedented growth and national prosperity. The total picture presents a classic case of what Marx would have described as a "general increase in the rate of exploitation." Similar reports may readily be found for the U.S., Great Britain and other Western capitalist societies. At the same time, the United Nations, through its various agencies, continues to document the ever-widening gap between rich and poor countries.

- *Marx anticipated the rise of the giant corporation and of the multinational and transnational enterprise*: He predicted the demise of the free and competitive marketplace and the rise of huge capitalist enterprises, some of which are now bigger than many nations. He would not have been surprised to see the disappearance of independent competitive firms and their replacement by giant conglomerate corporations. The structure and logic of capitalism means smaller business enterprises are swallowed up, through takeovers, mergers, consolidations, amalgamations, conglomerations and the like, by larger business competitors. According to Marx, this transformation involves two distinct but related processes: "concentration" and "centralization." "Concentration" refers to individual capitalist enterprises expanding their scope of ownership and control by increasing the size of their businesses. Examples of such concentration of capital may be seen in businesses such as Walmart and Tim Hortons expanding into an extensive cross-Canada network of franchised businesses.

"Centralization" refers to the incorporation of existing businesses through takeovers, mergers, consolidations, amalgamations and so on. Each of these processes results in the growth of larger and larger corporate units. Today, there are many industries in Canada and the U.S. which have seen the disappearance of competitive companies and their replacement by a few powerful gigantic corporations. Examples can be seen in the auto industry, the oil industry, the media industry, the retail trade industry, the brewery industry, the mining industry and many others. Who now remembers independent automobile companies with names like *Packard, Studebaker, Hudson, Nash, DeSoto, Imperial, Duesenberg, Buick, Oldsmobile, American Motors* and *Lincoln*? Who now remembers departmental stores with names like Kresge's, Woodward's, K-Mart,

Johnstone Walkers, Consumer Distributors, Woolco, Woolworths or even Eaton's?

Concentration and centralization, as Marx foresaw, have also gone global in a number of industries, including oil (BP, ExxonMobil, ChevronTexaco, Royal Dutch Shell, ConocoPhillips), computer software (IBM, Microsoft, Apple) and soft drinks (Pepsi, CocoCola, Cadbury-Schweppes), among others. The accelerated rate of globalization has given way to the age of transnational corporations (TNCs). None of this would have surprised Marx, who predicted that capitalism was destined to become a universal system of commodity production before it was finally overthrown and replaced by more democratic forms of production, distribution and exchange.

- *Marx concluded that in a capitalist economy, corporations would experience a long-term tendency for their rates of profit to decline:* This view was widely shared by many

---

Figure 8-3 The Silent Surrender of Canadian Companies

Here's a list of some of the big-name Canadian companies that have fallen under foreign control in the past two years — since February 2007 — (or are due to become foreign-owned):

- Falconbridge of Sudbury, Ont., is acquired by Swiss-based Xstrata for $18 billion.
- Houston-based Kinder Morgan Inc. buys Vancouver-based utility company Terasen Inc. for $6.9 billion.
- Hamilton steelmaker Dofasco is bought for $4.7 billion by Luxembourg-based Arcelor SA.
- Graphics chip-maker ATI Technologies of Markham, Ont., is sold to California-based Advanced Micro Devices Inc. for $5.34 billion US.
- The Fairmont Hotel chain (the Chateau Frontenac, the Banff Springs hotel among others) is bought for $3.24 billion by an investors group led by a Saudi prince.
- Intrawest, owner of B.C.'s famed Whistler resort, is sold to a New York firm for $1.8 billion US.
- Vincor, Canada's largest winemaker, sold to N.Y.-based Constellation Brands for $1.1 billion.
- The Hudson's Bay Co., owner of the Bay and Zellers, taken private by South Carolina investor Jerry Zucker for $860 million.
- Sleeman Breweries of Guelph, Ont., bought by Japan's Sapporo Breweries for $400 million.
- Four Seasons Hotels agrees to $3.7-billion U.S. takeover bid from Bill Gates's Cascade Investments and Kingdom Hotels International.
- Facing two competing foreign takeover bids, Inco finally agrees to $19.8-billion offer from Brazil's CVRD.

And Montreal-based paper-maker Domtar has agreed to a $3.3-billion merger with a unit of U.S. paper giant Weyerhaeuser.

Cross-border takeovers go the other way, too. Toronto-based Manulife Financial's $15-billion takeover of Boston-based John Hancock Financial in 2003 and TD Bank's $5-billion acquisition of New England's Banknorth are the biggest recent examples.

Source: CBC News, "The urge to merge," Feb. 26, 2007 <cbc.ca/news/background/mergers/>.

other political economists of his time, such as Ricardo and Malthus. However, unlike many of his contemporaries who assumed the "historical inevitability" of these tendencies, Marx recognized that capitalists could intervene to slow down, postpone or even reverse the falling rate of profit by increasing the exploitation of their workers. They could do this by reducing the cost of labour and/or increasing the productivity of labour. This could be done in several ways: by forcing "speed-ups" in production; by lengthening the work day; by importing cheaper migrant labour; by displacing workers with technology; and finally, by moving their operations (or threatening to move) to cheaper overseas labour markets. Thus, Marx would have recognized the current waves of lay-offs, cutbacks, rollbacks, downsizing and outsourcing for what they really are — attempts by corporations to reverse their declining rates of profit. He would also have understood the impact of these measures on working people. Naomi Klein (2002a: 353) reports a shocking but common example of how the labour of off-shore workers in the Global South is routinely super-exploited by Western transnational corporations:

Figure 8-4 Global Transnational Corporations Revealed: The Capitalist Network That Runs the World

As protests against financial power sweep the world this week, science may have confirmed the protesters' worst fears. An analysis of the relationships between 43,000 transnational corporations has identified a relatively small group of companies, mainly banks, with disproportionate power over the global economy.

The study's assumptions have attracted some criticism, but complex systems analysts contacted by *New Scientist* say it is a unique effort to untangle control in the global economy. Pushing the analysis further, they say, could help to identify ways of making global capitalism more stable.

The idea that a few bankers control a large chunk of the global economy might not seem like news to New York's Occupy Wall Street movement and protesters elsewhere. But the study, by a trio of complex systems theorists at the Swiss Federal Institute of Technology in Zurich, is the first to go beyond ideology to empirically identify such a network of power. It combines the mathematics long used to model natural systems with comprehensive corporate data to map ownership among the world's transnational corporations (TNCS).

When the team further untangled the web of ownership, it found much of it tracked back to a "super-entity" of 147 even more tightly knit companies — all of their ownership was held by other members of the super-entity — that controlled 40 per cent of the total wealth in the network. "In effect, less than 1 per cent of the companies were able to control 40 per cent of the entire network," says Glattfelder. Most were financial institutions. The top 20 included Barclays Bank, JP Morgan Chase & Co, and The Goldman Sachs Group.

Source: Andy Coghlan and Debora MacKenzie, October 24, 2011, *New Scientist* <newscientist.com/article/mg21228354.500-revealed--the-capitalist-network-that-runs-the-world.html#bx283545B1>.

> Prior to leaving for Haiti, I went to a Wal-Mart store on Long Island and purchased several Disney garments which had been made in Haiti. I showed these to the crowd of workers, who immediately recognized the clothing they had made ... all at once, in unison, the workers screamed with shock, disbelief, anger, and a mixture of pain and sadness, as their eyes remained fixed on the Pocahontas shirt.... In a single day, they worked on hundreds of Disney shirts. Yet the sales price of just one shirt in the U.S. amounted to nearly five days of their wages! (Ross, cited in Klein 2002a: 353)

Marx realized that the falling rate of profit could produce a crisis that, if uncorrected, would threaten the stability of the capitalist system. The tendency for falling rates of profit has led to long-term cycles of boom and bust, some of which have become recessions and depressions. During the most serious of these economic downturns, a falling demand for commodities can result in the collapse of the economy. In the past, such crises have often ended when capitalists have succeeded in driving the price of labour (i.e., wages) down or when wars have stimulated industrial production and increased employment. Marx was one of the earliest theorists to recognize that the falling rate of profit often results in the export of capital to cheaper overseas markets for raw materials and labour. Indeed, the international scramble for resources has often ignited a growing rivalry between competing capitalist nations, which sometimes resulted in conflict and war. Although he predicted the eventual collapse of capitalism, Marx did not regard the business cycles of boom and bust as signals of an impending fundamental breakdown. He recognized that most capitalist systems were flexible enough to recover from these periodic cycles.

In many ways, Marx reappears to us today as a thoroughly modern thinker, whose insights into the dynamics of global capitalism are still relevant. Many of the concerns he raised continue to preoccupy us, and many of the dilemmas he confronted still remain unresolved. Why is it that so many workers today are treated like other disposable commodities — as means to an end rather than as ends in themselves? Why are so many of the consumer products in our local supermarkets and departmental stores produced in low-wage off-shore economies rather than at home — especially when there is such a high rate of unemployment at home? How come ordinary working people in so many countries have paid the heaviest price for the recent economic recession — in lay-offs, cutbacks and roll-backs — while the investment bankers, mortgage brokers and financiers who caused the crisis continue to earn super profits and pocket large bonuses? Why is it that when all the indicators show that ordinary people are working harder and longer than ever, they are receiving proportionately less and less of the economic pie? In one way or another, Marx addressed many of these questions in his work, but his critical analysis of capitalism was always underscored by a strong sense of outrage over what he considered to be social injustice and exploitation. So let us take a closer look at some of the classical contributions Marx made to our understanding of modern capitalist society.

Settling Accounts

Like other great theorists, Marx was influenced by other social thinkers. Much as Isaac Newton had done before him, Marx stood on the shoulders of other scholars, past and in his own time, and he freely acknowledged their influence on his own work. He often suggested that his work could be read as an argument, or a "critique," of the ideas of other thinkers. He called this type of critique a "settling of accounts" with other thinkers and intellectual traditions. In fact, Marx observed in the preface to the *Critique of Political Economy* (1859), that in *The German Ideology*, he and Engels "resolved to work out in common the opposition of our view to the ideological view of German philosophy, in fact, to settle accounts with our erstwhile philosophical conscience" (Marx 1970: 22). However, Marx only ever settled his accounts with thinkers whose work he took seriously, even when he disagreed with them. His critiques, therefore, always involved an acceptance of some ideas as well as a rejection of others.

In the most general terms, Marx's social thought may be seen as a critique of three major intellectual traditions of the Enlightenment: French utopian socialism, British political economy and German historicism. Unlike conservative attacks on Enlightenment ideas, which sought to turn back the historical clock, Marx's critiques analyzed the limitations of the present and mapped the probable future course of history. In settling his accounts with these three traditions, Marx was acknowledging his indebtedness to them. In fact, he used each tradition as a springboard for launching his own theoretical ideas. Marx also recognized the limitations of each tradition, and he sought to transcend these limits by creating new theoretical models and causal explanations. In other words, he salvaged what he regarded as useful from each tradition, while jettisoning what he regarded as obsolete. The following describes how Marx settled accounts with each of the three major Enlightenment traditions:

- *French utopian socialism*: This tradition was represented in the works of such social thinkers as Henri de Saint-Simon, Pierre-Joseph Proudhon, Charles Fourier and Louis Blanc. Although Marx ridiculed these early socialists for what he considered their unrealistic goal of returning modern capitalist society to a pre-industrial state of harmony and for their attempts to rise above class conflict, he appropriated their ideas of "class conflict" and "class struggle," concepts that Marx incorporated into his own much broader and more radical theory of social and historical change.

- *British political economy*: This tradition was represented in the works of Adam Smith, David Ricardo and Thomas Malthus. Although Marx dismissed much of the classical tradition of political economy, he appropriated the "labour theory of value" into his own more critical "theory of surplus value." The labour theory of value, espoused by both Smith and Ricardo, states that the value of any commodity is determined by the amount of labour time required to produce it. In other words, all objects produced for sale on the market derive their value from the amount of work used to produce them. Marx's theory of surplus value states that all profit in capitalist enterprises is derived from the exploitation of labour. Marx believed that in this theory, he had uncovered the "hidden secret" of capitalist accumulation and provided a scientific justification for socialism.

- *German historical idealism*: This tradition was represented by a number of different thinkers, but most prominently by the German philosopher Georg Hegel. Hegel's theory of historical idealism maintained that all human history should be understood as the progressive development of reason. In other words, all historical development was driven by an evolution in human consciousness and knowledge. Hegel also insisted that historical development followed a "dialectical" rather than a "unilinear" pattern of progress. Historical changes were the result of internal oppositions, or "contradictions," which arose between conflicting elements in the historical process. These contradictions were finally resolved through a unification, or synthesis, of opposing elements into a new form. Over time, this new form (which Hegel called a "thesis") would generate its own opposing form (antithesis), and together these two opposing forms would ultimately unite into a third new form (synthesis). Inevitably, however, the synthesis would eventually generate a new antithesis, which meant that the dialectical process of historical change was endless.

Hegel's dialectical philosophy of history earned him a reputation as a revolutionary social thinker, at least during the early phase of his career. Among the monarchs and elite of the European societies of his day, any belief that the established social order was destined for future transformation was viewed as seditious. Indeed, the young Hegel was widely regarded as a revolutionary rationalist: a firebrand representative of the German Enlightenment. This young Hegel profoundly influenced the young Marx. It was only later in his career, when Hegel began to view the established Prussian state as the supreme embodiment of reason, that he passed from revolutionary rationalism to romantic conservatism. Similar to his intellectual encounters with French socialism and British political economy, Marx borrowed some aspects of Hegel's thought and revised other aspects. Marx adopted Hegel's dialectical method (with its emphasis on the emergence of internal contradictions), but adapted this method for the study of concrete historical societies.

The dialectical method of social and historical analysis was very different from the positivist method, popularized by such social thinkers as Auguste Comte and Emile Durkheim (in France) and Herbert Spencer (in England). Whereas for positivists, the search for "truth" is normally restricted to the collection of available "facts," or "data," for dialectical thinkers, the existing facts are always understood to be in a process of change. Thus, the facts available at any given time contain the "potentiality" for future development and transformation. The dialectical perspective, according to Hegel — and Marx — emphasizes the constantly changing forms of social phenomena. Nothing ever stays the same; everything is in a state of flux. For dialecticians, therefore, the search for "truth" always involves recognition of the future potentiality contained in the present order of facts (see Marcuse 1969).

Marx was greatly influenced by Hegel's theory of history. Indeed, as a student at the University of Berlin, he began his intellectual life as a "young Hegelian." In time, however, he came to reject Hegel's emphasis on reason as the driving force of human history. Instead, Marx insisted that "practical activity" in the world was the real motor of historical development, especially when such activity involved opposition and conflict, and resulted in social change. In other words, Marx retained Hegel's dialectical approach to history, but substituted a materialist theory of human activity for Hegel's idealist theory of reason. Marx replaced Hegel's theory of "historical idealism" with his own theory of "historical materialism" (sometimes called "dialectical materialism"). In a memorable phrase, Marx proclaimed that he had "turned Hegel on his head" and had "extracted the rational kernel from the mystical shell" of Hegel's dialectical theory of history (Marx 1961: 20).

Figure 8-5 Marx's Intellectual Influences

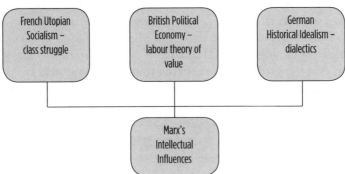

The Class Struggle

Marx saw the history of human society as the history of class conflict and class struggle. In this respect, Marx's ideas were very different from those of his contemporaries. Whereas Comte and Hegel and other theorists of the rationalist tradition saw history as driven by idealist factors such as knowledge, consciousness and reason, Marx saw history as driven by materialist factors — primarily class conflict.

It is important to understand that for Marx, "class" meant something rather different from what it means today. When Marx used the term "class," he was not referring to the division of society into different income groups — as in upper, middle or lower classes. Nor was he referring to different occupational groups — as in blue collar, white collar, black collar or pink collar. These are the ways in which the term is often used today, particularly by sociologists who study social inequality and social stratification. For Marx, the term "class" referred to something more basic and fundamental in society — the division between those who owned (and controlled) the means of production (the institutions that created wealth such as factories, banks, mines, oil wells, agri-businesses, construction companies, supermarkets and departmental stores, financial corporations, even sports teams) and those who owned nothing except their own ability to work for a living. Marx's definition of "class," therefore, was based upon the criterion of ownership or non-ownership of productive property — whether this property was land, capital or the labour of other human beings. In other words, the concept of "class" defined a "structural relationship" between those who owned and controlled the economic resources in society, and those who did not.

However, although he defined social classes in terms of their economic position in society, Marx also included an important dynamic element in his conceptualization of class. For Marx, a fully developed class was not only defined (objectively) in terms of its relation to the means of production, but also (subjectively) in terms of whether or not it had achieved a shared, or collective, identity. In other words, a class was defined not only in terms of its economic interests, but also in terms of its "class consciousness." This is an important point to understand in Marx's theory of classes. Although a class may be defined objectively — whether or not its members own the means of production — it only begins to play an active role when its members fully understand their collective position and common interests in society. In order to highlight his dynamic conception of social class, Marx outlined two progressive phases in the process of class formation. First of all, a class can be defined as a "class-in-itself" when all of its members share a common relationship to the means of production. This is a simple objective definition of class that refers only to the economic position of the class in society. However, for an economic class to begin to play an active role in society, it

Figure 8-6 Growth of Class Consciousness

Class-in-irself =
Objective
+ Passive

Class-for-irself =
Subjective
+ Active

has to transform itself into a "class-for-itself," in which all its members share a consciousness of their common interests. Without such "class consciousness," a class-in-itself is doomed to remain a passive aggregate of individuals with only the potential for class formation.

According to Marx, therefore, even though individuals may occupy a similar economic position in society, they cannot be said to constitute a class until they have developed some consciousness, or recognition, of their common class interests. For this reason, Marx did not view the peasantry in nineteenth-century France as a fully developed class, even though they occupied a similar economic position in society.

> The small holding peasants form a vast mass, the members of which live in similar conditions but without entering into manifold relations with one another. Their mode of production isolates them from one another instead of bringing them into mutual intercourse.... In so far as millions of families live under economic conditions of existence that separate their mode of life, their interests and their culture from those of other classes, and put them into hostile opposition to the latter, they form a class. In so far as there is merely a local interconnection among these small holding peasants, and the identity of their interests begets no community, no national bond and no political organization among them, they do not form a class. (Marx-Engels 1958, Vol. 1: 334)

Similarly, even the major historical classes that emerged with the rise of industrial capitalism — the bourgeoisie and the proletariat — only became fully developed classes, in Marx's view, once they had achieved class consciousness and were able to act in their own collective self-interests. Marx identified several different classes that emerged under capitalism, each with its own membership and its own historical agenda.

Marx's Conceptual Toolbox

According to Marx, in capitalist society, there are two main antagonistic classes:

- *The bourgeoisie:* The capitalist class, the owners of the means of production, distribution and exchange.

- *The proletariat:* The working class of wage-labourers, those who are forced to sell their labour-power as a commodity in order to survive.

Marx also distinguished other classes that remain marginal in capitalist society, but whose interests may overlap with one or other of the two main antagonistic classes. Marginal classes are the following:

- *The transitional class:* This includes the peasantry, the former aristocracy and the petit bourgeoisie — people who own and operate small businesses — as well as small farmers, artisans and other so-called "independent commodity producers." Marx believed that sooner than later, most elements of the transitional class would pass into extinction, crushed in the jaws of the huge nutcracker — the modern struggle between labour and capital. As pre-modern remnants of an earlier historical period, these elements of the transitional class were destined to perish in modern capitalist society. Some would be absorbed into the capitalist class, while others would swell ranks of the working class.
- *The dependent class:* These elements include government officials, bureaucrats, administrators and managers who remain dependent for their existence either upon the state or private capitalist corporations. According to Marx, members of the dependent class do not have an independent basis for their economic existence.
- *The underclass:* Marx refers to this class as the "lumpenproletariat"; it may be composed of unemployed workers, transients and homeless people, racial and ethnic minorities, the destitute and criminals. Members of the underclass are drawn from social groups that have been socially marginalized and socially excluded. Sometimes, members of the underclass may rise in incipient forms of protest and social unrest. The riots that erupted during the 1960s in the inner-city racial ghettos of the U.S. are examples of these events. At other times, members of the underclass have been recruited as shock-troops for the most reactionary elements of the ruling class — as in the Nazi Party during the 1930s, and in the Black and Tan military campaigns of the British Army in Ireland during the 1920s. In other words, the underclass is an inherently unstable class and may swing from revolutionary to reactionary forms of political action.

In his writings on class, Marx was primarily interested in the sociology of conflict, rather than the sociology of inequality or stratification. Marx believed that each historical society — with the exception of early "primitive communist" societies (i.e., hunting and gathering societies) — was characterized by a fundamental structural antagonism between the two major classes. In ancient civilizations, this antagonism was between free people and enslaved people. In feudal societies, it was between the landowners and the peasantry.

In capitalist societies, the fundamental conflict was between the bourgeoisie and the proletariat. Each historical society contained the seeds of its own downfall, and of its own transformation. Or, in Marx's terms, each society developed its own "contradictions," or irreconcilable antagonisms, between the major classes.

For Marx, the central contradiction in capitalist societies is between the social nature of the "forces of production" versus the private nature of the "relations of production." This contradiction refers to the fact that although the forces of production — tools, techniques and technology — had, under capitalism, developed the capacity to eliminate scarcity, poverty and public want, because these productive forces remained privately owned, they were used primarily to accumulate private wealth rather than to satisfy public need. In other words, to use Marx's own expression, the private nature of productive relations imposed "fetters" (or constraints) on the social character of the productive forces.

If Marx were alive today, he would find many examples of the ways in which the capacity of modern technology to satisfy human need is constrained, or fettered, by private ownership and profit-driven priorities. The following examples spring to mind:

- *Food:* One of the most obvious examples of how the private relations of production have prevented the satisfaction of basic human needs is seen in the commodification of food. When food is produced primarily for profit rather than as a human right — basic human needs remain unmet. According to the U.N., there are close to a billion people around the world who suffer from malnutrition and associated health problems and early death. Despite this, in many parts of the developing world, cash crops for the Western market are grown by the big land and plantation owners without regard for the food needs of the local population. Increasingly, arable land is being used for the cultivation of bio-fuels — again for Western markets. The results may be measured in high rates of malnutrition, disease and rural depopulation in the poorest parts of the planet. In the world of global food production, private greed has long ago supplanted public need:

    The commodity nature of food by itself limits access by the poor.... The "highest and best use" of any commodity is where it can get the best price, regardless of the social, ecological, or humanitarian consequences.... When food — a basic necessity for human health and survival that is currently produced in sufficient quantity to feed everyone in the world a basic nutritious diet — is a commodity, the results are routine hunger, malnutrition, premature deaths, and famines when tight supplies result in exceptionally high prices. (Magdoff 2012: 15)

- *Pharmaceuticals*: The availability and affordability of anti-retroviral drugs for fighting HIV infections has been greatly restricted in many developing countries by the refusal of the major pharmaceutical companies to allow the distribution of generic versions of these drugs. The company that first produces a drug is normally granted a patent or legal monopoly over the production and pricing of that drug for a certain period of time. Pharmaceutical companies claim that it is necessary to patent a new drug in order to recoup the research and development costs associated with its discovery and production. However, the high price of patented drugs has meant that they are unaffordable in many parts of the developing world where they are most needed to fight infection and disease. A growing number of countries have begun to challenge these patents by producing generic brands at more affordable prices.
- *New technology*: Another example of how property relations may impose "fetters" on technology may be seen in the documentary movie *Who Killed the Electric Car?* This movie follows the short history of the EV1, the first commercially available electric car, manufactured by General Motors in 1996. Although this car was environmentally friendly and required no fossil fuel, the electric car project was scrapped in 2002. The documentary claims that the electric car project was defeated by a combination of vested interests including the oil industry, the automobile industry and a disinterested U.S. government.
- *Alternative energy*: There is a growing research literature on the topic of "energy suppression," with some researchers arguing that the development of the renewal energy sector (solar, wind, tidal and hydroelectric generation, etc.) is being suppressed by the traditional energy sector (oil, petroleum, natural gas, coal, etc.) and associated industries (automobiles). Even the most sober observers conclude that the traditional energy sector is primarily concerned to preserve the existing carbon economy and to ensure the sustained increase in fossil fuel prices.

Marx's Theory of Society

Marx's method of studying societies is distinguished by of the following features:

- *Holistic*: Marx studied societies as total sets of social relations. Unlike theorists of the Enlightenment, who had emphasized particular factors in the study of society, such as reason, the division of labour or social solidarity, Marx insisted that all societies must be understood as social wholes, as totalities of socio-politico-economic relations.
- *Historically specific*: Marx studied particular historical societies. Often now called social formations, Marx was adamant about examining particular,

empirical societies rather than societies in the abstract, or societies in general. Unlike other social thinkers, who tried to codify universal laws to explain the historical development and social organization of all societies — such as Comte's law of the three stages, Spencer's theory of evolution or Hegel's theory of history, Marx believed that each society was historically specific and subject to its own particular laws of development. Marx was firmly opposed to what we might call today a "cookie cutter" or a "one size fits all" approach to the study of history and society. He did not believe that it was either possible, or desirable, to develop universal, positivistic, historical laws of the kind that Saint-Simon, Comte, Spencer, Hegel and others had in mind. Although, as we shall see in the next section, Marx did formulate several economic and social laws to explain the development of capitalist societies, these were not intended as universal laws. When Marx suggested that the rate of profit in advanced capitalist societies would begin to decline, or that the capitalist class would grow richer while the working class would grow proportionately poorer, he was formulating what he called, "a law of tendency." A law of tendency, according to Marx, was a law which predicted the development of a particular trend, or tendency — on the assumption that the conditions which produced this trend would remain unchanged. In other words, his laws had the caveat: "other things being equal," or *ceteris paribus*. Marx always acknowledged that if conditions changed, then the trend he had predicted could be negated, countered, reversed or otherwise invalidated. Marx proposed probabilistic, rather than deterministic, laws of political economy and society. In this respect, Marx was well ahead of his time as nearly all of his predecessors and most of his contemporaries formulated laws that were far more deterministic. A deterministic law is one that provides for no exceptions and which assumes the inevitability of its prediction. But Marx was neither a shallow nor a superficial thinker. Even in his own lifetime, he ridiculed attempts to reformulate his ideas as universal laws.

- *Materialist*: Marx claimed that every society is based upon a particular mode of production. In what is, perhaps his most well-known assertion, Marx argued that the mode of production formed the

> **Figure 8-7 Marx against Marxism**
>
> One example of Marx's resistance to the oversimplification of his ideas can be seen in his response to a Polish admirer, Mikhailovsky, which was published in the journal, *Otecestvennye Zapiski*. "He feels he absolutely must metamorphose my historical sketch of the genesis of capitalism in Western Europe into an historico-philosophic theory of the general path every people is fated to tread, whatever the historical circumstances in which it finds itself.... But I beg his pardon (He is both honouring and shaming me too much)."
>
> [*Marx/Engels, Selected Correspondence*, Foreign Languages Publishing House Moscow 1953: 313].

Figure 8-8 Superstructure

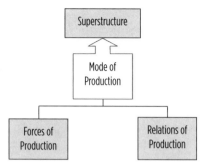

economic base of all other social relations. A mode of production refers to the ways in which members of society produce their livelihood, how they subsist, how they make their living. Marx argued that economic activities were primary activities in any society because they involved production of the means of subsistence. Subsistence, or survival, Marx reminds us, is the most fundamental challenge faced by all humanity. All other social relations follow from economic activity and are secondary to it. It seemed obvious to Marx that a society in which the mode of production was based upon, say, hunting and gathering, will have developed a set of social relations — kinship, religion, law, politics — very different from a society based upon another mode of production — for example, pastoral, horticultural, agricultural or industrial. In this sense, the mode of production is the engine that drives the rest of society. It is the base upon which all other social structures rest. For Marx, the mode of production was a complex concept which can be broken down into two parts: the "forces of production" and the "relations of production." The forces of production refer to the technology (the tools and techniques) of production, while the relations of production refer to the division of social classes, the technical division of labour and the property relations in society. Taken together, the mode of production constitutes the "real" or material economic base of

> ### Figure 8-9 Marx on the Primacy of Production
>
> Men enter into definite ... relations of production which correspond to a definite stage of development of their material productive forces. The sum total of these relations of production constitutes the economic structure of society, the real foundation.... The mode of production of material life conditions the social, political and intellectual life process in general.... In changing their mode of production ... men change all their social relations. The hand-mill gives you society with the Feudal lord, the steam-mill, society with the industrial capitalist.
>
> Source: K. Marx,1859, Preface to *A Contribution to the Critique of Political Economy*

society — the ways in which real individuals make their livelihood and produce their subsistence. On the other hand, Marx classified all other non-economic institutions, practices and beliefs as part of what he called the "superstructure of society." The superstructure refers to those social relations and forms of social consciousness that are involved in such institutions and practices as politics, law, ideology, religion, art, science, culture, and other non-economic activities.

There is no doubt that Marx ascribed a major role to economic activities in the social life of capitalist societies. He strongly suggested that the material base of capitalist society largely determines the superstructure of non-economic activities. But at the same time, Marx was careful not to say that the economic base always determines the superstructure in all societies. As we have already seen, Marx was not interested in formulating "universal" or trans-historical laws of social development. He acknowledged that every society is a product of its particular history and culture and is, therefore, governed by its own internal, historically specific, laws of development. Economics exerted a primary influence in capitalist societies only because under capitalism, everything — and everybody — had become a commodity. Capitalism was the era of universal commodity production.

> **Figure 8-10 Underlying Causal Mechanisms**
>
> Other writers have refused to take political and ideological rationalizations at face value, see, for example, Eric Williams's writings on slavery, and William Chambliss's writings on the vagrancy laws. In his book *Capitalism and Slavery*, Eric Williams (1944), the late prime minister of Trinidad, showed that slavery was finally abolished because it became an uneconomic form of production. During the late eighteenth century, slavery was unable to compete with the system of free labour that was gradually introduced into the plantation economy of the southern U.S. Contrary to popular belief, slavery was defeated not so much by the abolitionist movement, but by its own internal (economic) contradictions, although Solow (2012) reminds us that this is still a contested theory.
>
> And in a somewhat different context, William Chambliss (1964) showed how the twelfth-century vagrancy laws in England were legislated by the landed nobility in order to overcome the chronic labour shortages resulting from the Black Death.
>
> Each of these examples shows that legislation (to abolish slavery and to criminalize vagrancy) was often driven by underlying economic imperatives arising from crises in the mode of production. Critics of current U.S. foreign policy have questioned whether the politics and the legislation surrounding the so-called War on Terror may also be driven by partially concealed economic and geo-political motives.

Although Marx believed that the mode of production was the primary determinant of social relations, he acknowledged that in non-capitalist societies, other sectors could become dominant at any particular historical period. It was only in capitalist society that the economy was both dominant and determinant. Marx also believed that we cannot take at face value what societies say about themselves — especially with regard to their politics, ideology or religion. The explanations and justifications that social groups may give for their actions in society — especially when these groups represent ruling classes or governing elites — are often rationales for deeper material and economic interests. It is always necessary, in Marx's view, to dig beneath the surface of political, ideological or religious rationalizations in order to discover the real motives that drive human actions. And these motives are often related to the material conditions of production.

Consciousness and Ideology

In Marx's model of society, human consciousness in its different forms — expressed as religion, art, culture, ideology and so on — was often defined as epiphenomenal, or as dependent upon the material conditions of social life.

Time and time again, Marx states that the forms of consciousness present in any society are primarily determined by the existing mode of production. In the binary model of society that Marx often used to describe social relations, consciousness was usually relegated to the "superstructure," while practical and "sensuous" activities related to making a living were normally included in the material "base." Unfortunately, later followers of Marx transformed his schematic view of social relations — as base and superstructure — into a rigid mechanistic and deterministic theory of history and society. This dogmatic interpretation of Marx's ideas downplayed the importance of consciousness and saw the development of political consciousness (and political action) as entirely dependent upon so-called "objective historical conditions." According to this view, political actors were seen as little more than dry leaves blown around by material forces over which they had no control. This highly mechanistic interpretation of Marx was later challenged by humanistic Marxists — such as Georg Lukacs, Jean-Paul Sartre, Erik Fromm, Herbert Marcuse and Jurgen Habermas — who sought to recapture some of the original subtlety and dynamism of Marx's social analysis This dispute remains with us today, between those Marxists who emphasize the active and conscious role of the working class or other revolutionary groups in the process of class struggle, versus other Marxists who believe that it is the "objective historical conditions" which set the limits on all political and

Figure 8-11 Consciousness and Life

Morality, religion, metaphysics, and other ideologies, and their corresponding forms of consciousness, no longer retain therefore their appearance of autonomous existence. They have no history, no development: it is men, who in developing their material production and their material intercourse, change, along with their real existence, their thinking, and the products of their thinking. Life is not determined by consciousness, but consciousness by life.

Source: K. Marx, *The German Ideology* 1947 [1845-46]; 14-15).

revolutionary action. In the discourse of social theory, this debate has become known as that between "agency" and "structure."

An important part of Marx's consideration of the role of consciousness in social and historical change may be found in his discussion of ideology. For Marx, the term "ideology" refers to the dominant ideas and beliefs of any society, irrespective of whether these ideas are expressed as philosophical systems, political doctrines, economic theories or other well established forms of social thought. Much of Marx's interest in ideology was focused on the role of ideology in capitalist societies. Although his discussions of ideology are scattered between his different works, the following two basic assumptions underlie much of what Marx had to say on this topic:

- *The social conditions of existence determine, or at least condition, forms of social consciousness:* In other words, individuals and groups tend to see the world in terms of categories derived from their real (material) social relations.
- *The ruling ideas of any age are the ideas of the ruling class:* Marx argued that ideas were used by the ruling class of any society in at least two ways: to "legitimate" its interests and to advance its accumulation of wealth. Marx believed that a ruling class was able to legitimate its position in society by ensuring that its core values were well represented in the dominant beliefs and ideas of a society. Marx also believed that ideas played an important role in the production and accumulation of wealth. For example, scientific ideas have played a major role in modern technological advances in the forces of production. But, as Marx suggested, some of these ideas — such as the principles of machine production — had been known long before the eighteenth century. However, it was only with the expansion of modern capitalism that many of these scientific ideas were eventually disseminated and applied to industrial production.

For Marx, the role of ideology is very important in modern capitalist society. Indeed, it is through ideology that the ruling class legitimates and maintains its system of class domination. Marx concluded that every dominant class in history had claimed a universal ideology and had sought to extend its ideas to all other classes and groups in society.

The Distorted Mirror of False Consciousness

Marx used the term "false consciousness" to describe the situation of those social classes in society which accepted the ideology of the ruling class even

Figure 8-12 Ruling Ideas and Ruling Classes

The class which has the means of material production at its disposal has control at the same time over the means of intellectual production, so that thereby, generally speaking, the ideas of those who lack the means of intellectual production are subject to it.

Source: K. Marx, *The German Ideology* [1845–46], (1947: 39).

when their own material interests were structurally opposed to those of the ruling class. Although this term can be used to analyze the distorted beliefs of any class, Marx focused on the case of the working class, which had accepted and internalized the values and beliefs of capital. For Marx, "false consciousness" refers to the inability on the part of individuals and social groups to correctly identify their position in society and their relation to other social groups — especially to the dominant or ruling class. Indeed, there is often a disjuncture, or a break, between what individuals, or social classes, think about themselves, and what can be shown through a more dispassionate historical analysis. For example, even though the eighteenth-century French peasantry was severely exploited and oppressed by the land-owning nobility, many individual peasants saw themselves as independent and self-reliant farmers, and they distained to join with other peasants in any movement for social or political change. In much the same way, many poor white sharecroppers in the U.S. southern states saw themselves as superior to their Black counterparts and were therefore opposed any class-based movements for social, political or economic justice. Today, Marx would probably see the Tea Party in the U.S. — with its demand for corporate tax cuts, reduced government spending on health education and social services — as yet another example of a working-class party that has fully embraced the propaganda of the ruling class. Over the years, there have been many factors that have contributed to the internal division of the working class and which have prevented the growth of solidarity, unity and class consciousness. These factors have included differences of race, ethnicity, nationality, gender, religion, language and politics.

For the most part, Marx focused

Figure 8-13 False Consciousness in Popular Culture

For those television viewers who can remember the 1970s, the popular show *All In the Family* provided a vivid example of false consciousness. The main character in this show, Archie Bunker (played by Carroll O'Connor), was a blue-collar, white working-class male who remained hostile to any ideas of class consciousness or group action. Not only did Archie continually express racist, sexist, homophobic and other politically conservative opinions, but he also dismissed all welfare recipients as "lazy bums" and all trade unionists as "communists." Archie saw himself as a "rugged individualist" in the classic American mode, opposed to big government, big business and big labour. Marx would have seen Archie Bunker as a paradigm case of false consciousness: a blue-collar worker opposed to progressive taxation, income redistribution, anti-war, civil rights or social justice movements, or any other movements for social or political reform. *All In The Family* was originally inspired by an earlier British show, *Till Death Do Us Part*, which featured the character Alf Garnett (played by Warren Mitchell), a "working class Tory" whose opinions were even more bigoted than those of Archie Bunker. Today, some of these attitudes and opinions are expressed in characters such as Homer Simpson, of *The Simpsons*.

on the working class in his discussions of false consciousness. Indeed, in his polemical writings — such as *The Communist Manifesto* — Marx, with his colleague, Friedrich Engels, attempted to educate and mobilize the working class and to prepare it for the revolutionary seizure of state power. At the same time, Marx recognized that members of any social class could suffer from the distortions of false consciousness. The bourgeoisie, which owned and controlled the means of production, for example, tended to believe that capitalism was the only rational system of production, distribution and exchange. The logic of the market place was seen as the only rational principle which could guarantee economic efficiency and political freedom. Today, in the twenty-first century, we hear powerful echoes of this belief in the contemporary ideologies of neoliberalism and neoconservatism. Marx also noted that members of the petit-bourgeoisie — those who own small businesses, neighbourhood stores, family farms and so on — often believe that they stand above the class antagonism of labour and capital. Because of this false consciousness, the petit-bourgeoisie has always been unprepared for its own eventual fate, which has either been a merger with the bourgeoisie or absorption into the proletariat. Similarly, members of other transitional classes, such as the old aristocracy, have often been unable to understand their changed position in society and their changed relationship to newly emergent classes.

In contrast to false consciousness, Marx reserved the concept of "class consciousness" for those members of a social class who had become fully conscious of their own common class interests and of their conflict of interests with other social classes. For Marx, class consciousness could be developed by any class and was a necessary precondition for collective action. In the case of the working class, class consciousness was a necessary precondition for revolutionary political action. As we have already seen, the development of class consciousness was the essential dynamic factor that transformed a class-in-itself into a fully formed class-for-itself.

Marx's Theory of History

Marx's theory of history has remained controversial. Many critics insist that Marx's view of history was both unilinear and deterministic. These claims are based on the belief that Marx saw only one path of historical development for all societies, a path which led from primitive society to modern capitalism through the intervening stages (or "progressive epochs") of slavery and feudalism. These claims also imply that Marx believed in the historical inevitability of this path of development, that all societies are fated to follow this path without exception. Those who subscribe to this interpretation of Marx's theory of history have characterized Marx as a "social evolutionist" and have placed him in the same camp as Comte and Spencer.

On the other hand, there is plenty of evidence to suggest that Marx did not subscribe to a rigidly deterministic theory of history. Some of this evidence comes in the form of Marx's own disclaimers — "what is certain is that I myself am not a Marxist" (a remark cited by Engels in his letter to Bernstein of 2–3 November 1882: see Engels, (1882) 1967: 388) — and his own rejection of all universal, trans-historical social and historical laws. For Marx, all theories and explanations of society and history could only ever be historically specific in their spheres of application and probabilistic in their predictive outcomes. In these respects, Marx's understanding of the role of historical explanation differed greatly from the crude positivism of Comte and Spencer.

However, the greatest evidence of Marx's relatively flexible view of human history is to be found in his introduction of the concept "Asiatic mode of production." Marx concluded from his study of Asian civilizations that the different political-economic conditions in these societies represented a separate path of historical development from that of European societies. The most important factor distinguishing Asian from European modes of production, according to Marx, was the central importance of irrigation. Those who controlled the systems of irrigation in the Asian civilizations (of India and China) effectively controlled the populations, which were totally dependent for their survival upon these systems. The ability of Asian rulers to reduce their subjects to total dependency was often referred to in the European literature of the eighteenth and nineteenth centuries as "Oriental despotism," and the societies based upon irrigation agriculture were often referred to as "hydraulic civilizations" (see Wittfogel 1957, 1960, 1969).

Today, we are likely to reject such stereotypical descriptions as "oriental despotism" not only as racist, but as sadly misinformed Eurocentric images of the East constructed largely through Western colonial eyes. (For a penetrating criticism of Western accounts of the East, see the works of the late Palestinian scholar Edward Said, especially his book *Orientalism* 1978). However, the acknowledgement by Marx that Asian societies developed along a different historical path from that of European societies showed that Marx — unlike many of his contemporaries — did not subscribe to a single, universal theory of history based exclusively upon the European experience. For Marx, every society was a product of its own historical and social conditions. And while today, we may reproach Marx for his oversimplified and Westernized view of Asian civilizations, in the context of his times, Marx's theory of history was more subtle and more sophisticated than many of his detractors acknowledge.

Marx's Economic Theory
How Capitalism Commodifies Everything

It was in his later, mature works, most notably *Das Kapital*, that Marx laid out a detailed critique of capitalism as a universal system of commodity production. In order to explore Marx's later "scientific" analysis of capitalism, we need to familiarize ourselves with the language — including the key concepts — he uses to analyze the process of commodity production.

A "commodity" is any object which acquires value through the process of exchange. In capitalist societies, commodities are objects which are sold and purchased in the marketplace. And in capitalist societies, the labour-power of the worker is a commodity. Whether we sell our manual labour as blue-collar workers (in manufacturing plants, construction sites, the oil patch or other industries), or whether we sell our mental labour as white-, black- or pink-collar workers (in offices, classrooms, department stores and supermarkets, call-centres or in other service sectors), our labour is a commodity that we need to sell in order to make a living. "Money" is the universal commodity in a capitalist society. It is the commodity which is used to express the values of all other commodities. However, in times of economic crisis and financial upheaval, money — as the universal commodity — may be replaced by a more stable currency, notably by gold or other precious metals.

Over time, as more and more commodities are produced, the general public becomes increasingly dependent upon the marketplace for goods and services. Everything can be bought and sold, and everything — even intimate services such as sex and childcare — has its price. The penetration of the market into every sphere of public and private life signalled the advent of "consumerism" as a dominant cultural theme in contemporary life. Marx recognized the growing influence of consumerism in the culture of capitalism, and he referred to the power that commodities can exercise over the minds and lives of consumers as the "fetishism of commodities."

This term refers to the way in which most of us now take for granted the range of products available in our supermarkets and department stores. These products simply appear on the shelves as part of our consumer lifestyle. When purchasing them we rarely think about the human labour that went into their production or the conditions under which they were produced. Most of us have lost the connection between commodities and the human labour that is incorporated in them. Indeed, many commodities now appear to have their own independent identities. Instead of hamburgers, we may think Big Macs; instead of motor-cycles, we may think Harley-Davidson; instead of vacuum-cleaners, we may think Hoover; instead of pain-killers, we may think Aspirin or Tylenol, and so on. One critic who has examined our fixation on brand names is Canadian writer Naomi Klein, whose popular book *No Logo* explains how the marketing executives of large corporations go to great lengths to promote their products as brands that are not only instantly familiar, but which also have a strong emotional connection to the consumer. This branding strategy to create commodity fetishism is obvious in the following observation of a marketing executive who moved from *Nike* to *Starbucks*:

> Nike, for example, is leveraging the deep emotional connection that people have with sports and fitness. With Starbucks, we see how coffee has woven itself into the fabric of people's live, and that's our opportunity for emotional leverage.... A great brand raises the bar — it adds a greater sense of purpose to the experience, whether it's the challenge to do your best in sports and fitness or the affirmation that the cup of coffee you're drinking really matters."
> (Peters 1977: 96)

The long-term effect of thinking about commodities as though they were natural or ready-made objects is that we lose sight of the human connection to these products. We forget that all these objects are produced by workers for the market. They are all produced by human labour. Only in a few controversial and highly publicized cases — such as the violence associated with "blood" diamonds, or the exploitation of enslaved children and trafficked workers who produce such products as coffee, carpets and chocolate — are we reminded of the human connection to the commodities we buy and consume. Most of the time, however, we inhabit a consumer bubble where we are largely oblivious to the workers who produce our goods. The connection between commodities and labour has become invisible.

Our failure to recognize any human dimension to commodities means that most of us remain ignorant of the underlying "social relations" that connect us to the products and services we buy and consume. Every commodity involves a chain of labour that extends from the oil well, the mine, the plantation, the farm or the factory, through its refining and processing, through its transportation by road, rail, sea or air, to the retail outlet. Much of the industry associated with the production of commodities is organized through private companies — increasingly by huge transnational corporations which produce for the global market, and for most of the time, the web of owners and workers remains invisible to most consumers. However, some consumers are showing an increasing interest in the bio-economic dimension of certain commodities. This interest has resulted in concerns about "fair trade" for staple crops such as coffee. "Fair trade" implies that the revenues from the sale of a product should go directly to the local producers — many of whom are increasingly organized into cooperatives — rather than to transnational corporations such as *Nestle* or *Maxwell House*. Consumer interest has also resulted in a demand for more "organic" produce, grown without chemical pesticides, herbicides or fertilizers. And most recently, some consumers have begun to consider the environmental impact — or the ecological "footprint" — of the long distance transportation of produce. Concerns over the use of fossil fuels and emission of greenhouse gasses have persuaded some consumers to buy local rather than imported produce.

In a similar way, many institutional practices appear to have a life of their own, independent of the social actors who perform these activities. Thus, when we are shocked to discover that the price of gasoline has jumped ten cents a litre at the pumps, we may resign ourselves in the belief that price hikes are a result of the "economy" — the impersonal forces of supply and demand over which we have no direct control. We easily forget that these so-called "economic forces" originate in corporate boardrooms, with CEOs making decisions about pricing and marketing. Similarly, other problems — such as job losses, cutbacks and rollbacks, rising taxes, housing prices, etc — may be blamed on large, impersonal, anonymous forces such as the "economy," "city hall" or even "globalization." This tendency to objectify the consequences of human decisions and activities, and thereby surrender any responsibility for challenging these decisions, is referred to by some neo-Marxists as the problem of "reification." Reification is the social equivalent of the economic process of commodity fetishism. When people believe that their lives are controlled by large, impersonal forces, they do not think they can exercise any significant control or direction over their lives. Reification thus becomes

---

Figure 8-14 Privatizing Our Water

Corporate Campaign Briefing: Stealing our Water, Implications of GATS for Global Water Resources

Last year in Cochabamba in Bolivia, people were forced to take to the streets in protest when, after privatisation, they could no longer afford their own water. Under pressure from the World Bank, the Bolivian Government privatised Cochabamba's water resources, giving a monopoly to a subsidiary of International Water Ltd (a UK company owned by U.S. engineering company Betchel).

In addition to making people hand over (without compensation) autonomous water supplies and requiring them to buy permits to collect rainwater from their roofs, the company immediately introduced price increases of up to $20 per month – over a fifth of the minimum wage in the region. By making market demand the primary consideration in developing infrastructure for water delivery, most developing countries would be placed in an impossible situation: accept the investors' (i.e., the water companies') terms, or be denied development. In Bolivia only after months of, sometimes violent, protests, International Water left with their contract broken, the experiment in water privatisation having failed miserably with the community suffering as a consequence.

Source: Friends of the Earth, Press Release, November 20, 2001, Briefing – *Stealing Our Water: Implications of GATS for Global Water Resources* <foe.co.uk/resource/briefings/gats_stealing_water.pdf>.

another means whereby large numbers of people are rendered passive and quiescent and are subordinated to indirect and increasingly abstract forms of domination and social control (see Lukacs 1967).

The process of commodity production is central to any understanding of Marx's theory of society. In fact, Marx's critique of capitalism remains, first and foremost, a critical analysis of commodity production. Marx believed that under capitalism, especially in its later stages, everything could be converted into a commodity; fewer and fewer things would be freely available, more and more things would have to be purchased. In our own time we have even seen such things as rainwater converted into a commodity in some parts of the world.

All commodities, as products of human labour, embody a certain "value." For Marx, as for the classical political economists, such as Adam Smith and Ricardo, who preceded him, the value of any product could be measured according to objective as well as subjective criteria. Marx distinguished between three different types of value: use value, exchange value and surplus value. The "use value" refers to the value a product has for the consumer who uses and derives satisfaction from it. The "exchange value" refers to the value a product has for the seller when it is sold in the marketplace. To put it another way, exchange value is the value realized through the process of exchange. An object may have both a use value and an exchange value, depending upon the circumstances. If I build a house for myself to live in, that house has a use value — but only for me. However, if I later decide to sell the house, that house will acquire an exchange value for me as the vendor — once it has been sold to a purchaser. The house only becomes a commodity when it is listed for sale on the real-estate market. The "surplus value" refers to the value that is extracted from the worker during the process of commodity production and realized by the capitalist as profit. The process of extracting surplus value from the worker is referred to by Marx as "exploitation." Thus, for Marx, "exploitation" is much more than a term of moral condemnation. It refers to the hidden mechanism by which wealth is accumulated in capitalist society.

The Labour Theory of Value

The starting point for Marx's critical analysis of commodity production under capitalism begins with the labour theory of value. Marx, along with other political economists of his time, believed that the value of any commodity is determined by the amount of (average, or "socially necessary") labour time used to produce the commodity. What, we may ask, is the meaning and significance of the labour theory of value? First of all, it has to be understood that for Marx, "value" is a general standard which can be used to measure the relative worth of all socially produced or socially adapted products. Whether we are talking about a bushel of grain or a barrel of oil, tables and chairs, or iPhones and iPods, all commodities can be evaluated in terms of a standard unit of measurement. And this standard is based upon the amount of work (or labour time) required to produce the product for human consumption. Thus, oil only acquires its value from the work of exploration, refinement, transportation and marketing. Similarly, all other commodities have a standard value which is equal to the amount of work required to produce them. Marx eliminated any problems which could arise from differences between the labour time of industrious workers versus that of idle workers by specifying that the measure of value be based upon "socially necessary," or average labour time, as an industry standard. Marx also distinguished the concept of value from that of "price." Whereas value refers to the constant standard of labour time embodied in a commodity, price refers to the variable worth of a commodity when it is sold in the marketplace. Price is determined by supply and demand; value is determined by work — or labour time. Depending upon market conditions, a commodity may sometimes sell above its value and sometimes below its value. However, while prices may fluctuate, the value of a commodity remains constant. It is the only objective yardstick that we have to compare the relative social worth of different products in society.

The labour theory of value, according to Marx, can also be used to estimate the value of human labour power, because, under capitalism, labour — like everything else — has become a commodity. The value of human labour is determined by the amount of average labour time that is required to produce the living conditions, or subsistence, of the labourer. In other words, the value of labour is determined by the "reproduction and maintenance costs" of the worker; these include the costs of food, shelter, clothing, healthcare, childcare, transportation and other essentials. This interpretation of the value of labour (which is hotly contested by many non-Marxist economists) is known as the "subsistence theory of wages."

Why was the labour theory of value so important to Marx, and what was its significance for his critique of capitalism? More than anything else, the labour theory of value allowed Marx to argue that all wealth is produced by human labour and that without labour there can be no production or accumulation of wealth. Without labour, oil would remain in the ground, wheat would remain unplanted, uncultivated and unharvested, and nothing would ever be produced. For Marx, therefore, labour is the source of all wealth. From this assumption, he was able to conclude that the reason for the poverty and oppression of the working class in capitalist society (or of other "toiling" classes in earlier historical societies) was because it was "alienated" (that is, separated) from the wealth it had produced for the capitalist class. The producers were alienated from the social product of their labour. In a sense,

Marx had updated a sentiment earlier expressed by Rousseau in his famous opening sentence to *The Social Contract*: "Man is born free, but everywhere he is in chains." It was this conclusion that led Marx towards his most powerful theoretical critique of capitalism — the theory of surplus value.

The Theory of Surplus Value

The most important part of Marx's critique of commodity production in capitalist society is his analysis of surplus value. Marx believed that all commodities produced by labour contained what he called "surplus value." Surplus value was the value produced by workers in factories (or other industrial settings) after they had produced the value of their own wages — which is to say, their own subsistence. In other words, Marx calculated that only a part of the regular working day was necessary for the average worker to produce an amount of value that was equal to the wages they received for the working day. This part of the work day — when the worker was producing the value of their own wages — was defined by Marx as "necessary labour-time." The value produced by the worker above and beyond their wages was described by Marx as "surplus value." Surplus value was produced by workers during that part of the work day defined by Marx as "surplus labour time." Or, to put it in starker terms: surplus value is the value produced during that part of the working day for which the worker is not paid.

For Marx, the theory of surplus value provided an answer to the fundamental question he posed about capitalist society: "Where does profit come

Figure 8-15 Analysis of the Working Day

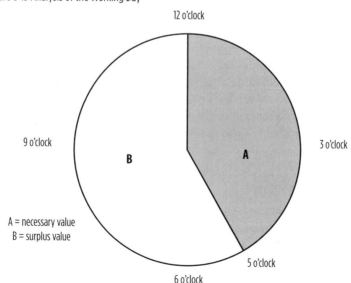

Figure 8-16 The Origin of Profit

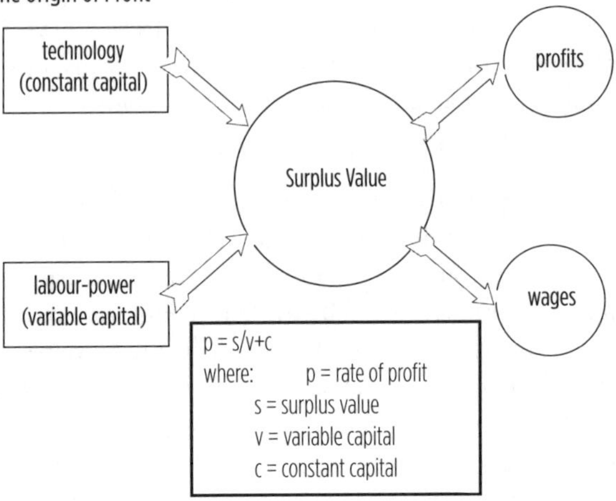

from?" His theory showed that, contrary to popular belief, workers were not paid "a fair day's wage for a fair day's work." For Marx, the theory of surplus value exposed the secret of capitalist accumulation — the generation of profit. It revealed the "hidden mechanism" underlying the amazing capacity of capitalist production to expand, to constantly revolutionize its tools and techniques of production, and to accumulate wealth at an unprecedented rate. The secret of capitalism, the hidden mechanism of its extraordinary productivity, was the extraction of surplus value through the exploitation of human labour-power. Herein lay the root of the irreconcilable antagonism — or contradiction — between labour and capital. And, for Marx, it was the exploitation of labour by capital that constituted the foundation of his critique of capitalism.

The critical analysis of surplus value remains an important landmark in Marx's social thought. It signals a progression in Marx's investigations from his earlier philosophical study of alienation to his later political-economical study of exploitation under commodity production. By uncovering what he believed to be the hidden mechanism of capitalist accumulation, Marx moved beyond the realm of speculative philosophy into the world of empirical social science.

Marx's Vision of the Future

Although Marx spent the best part of his adult life producing his critical analysis of commodity production under capitalism, he spent relatively little time outlining his view of a post-capitalist society. He was not given to crystal-ball gazing and did not attempt to provide any utopian blueprint for either a socialist or a communist society. Indeed, both Marx and Engels criticized the "utopian socialists" for constructing speculative philosophical models of socialism, which, according to Marx, were not based upon any concrete or materialist analyses of social life. The few references Marx made to future post-capitalist society are to be found scattered in such works as *The German Ideology*, *The Economic and Philosophical Manuscripts* and *The Critique of the Gotha Programme*. In the most general terms, Marx emphasized that any post-capitalist society that had evolved beyond the fundamental contradictions of capitalism would be characterized by at least three necessary conditions:

- *The socialization of the means of production, distribution and exchange:* According to Marx, this was a necessary condition for the working class to end the alienation and exploitation of its labour-power and to regain public ownership and democratic control over the social product of its labour.
- *The abolition of the state as an instrument of class domination, and its assimilation into civil society:* Although Marx used the expression "dictatorship of the proletariat" to describe the revolutionary seizure of state power by the working class, he certainly was not in favour of installing new autocratic or totalitarian governments based on police states. Indeed, he criticized Napoleon Bonaparte's seizure of state power as a betrayal of the French Revolution and as an example of a new form of "Caesarism." It is likely that he would have also criticized Stalin — and other communist dictators — in the same way.
- *The eventual abolition of the division of labour in society and the free development of individuals according to their interests and personal needs.* In a famous passage from *The German Ideology*, Marx describes, in admittedly idealized terms, the social potential for free individual development resulting from the abolition of the division of labour in society. (see Figure 8-17).

Marx also emphasized that socialism could only be constructed in a society once the preconditions had already evolved in the mature development of capitalism. Socialism required the centralization and concentration of capital, the internationalization of capital and the development of an educated and powerful working class. These were some of the objective

---

Figure 8-17 The Humanization of Work

As soon as the division of labour begins to come into being, each man has a particular, exclusive sphere of activity, which is forced upon him and from which he cannot escape. He is a hunter, a fisherman, a shepherd, or a critical critic, and must remain so if he does not want to lose his means of livelihood; while in communist society, where nobody has one exclusive sphere of activity but each can be accomplished in any branch he wishes, society regulates the general production and thus makes it possible for one to do one thing today and another tomorrow, to hunt in the morning, fish in the afternoon, rear cattle in the evening, criticize after dinner, just as I have a mind, without ever becoming hunter, fisherman, shepherd or critic.

Source: K. Marx, (1947) *The German Ideology*, (p. 22).

historical conditions that favoured the transformation of capitalism into a more humanized system of production, in which the public needs of the population would replace the private greed of the capitalist class for the accumulation of profit.

Criticisms of Marx

While Marx has remained the most influential of the classical social theorists, he has also remained the most controversial. His ideas have been challenged by many different critics — historians, politicians, economists, feminists and other social theorists. Some critics address what they see as the failed predictions of Marx's theories; others challenge his alleged historical and economic determinism; and others condemn Marx for his failure to recognize the role of women in social production. The following are some of the more common criticisms of Marx's theoretical ideas:

*   *Political*: the most popular criticism of Marx is that his ideas have not only failed in practice, but have led to some of the most repressive regimes of the twentieth century.
*   *Epistemological:* the most common academic criticism of Marx is that he was an "economic determinist" who believed that all major historical events and social structures could be explained by reference to economic, or material, causes.
*   *Feminist:* many feminists criticize Marx for failing to recognize the value of women's work in the home. For feminists, non-waged labour in the household (the "domestic sphere of production") produces significant social and economic values which contribute to the maintenance and reproduction of the labour force. Marx's failure to acknowledge that domestic labour is also "productive labour" has led many feminists to criticize his "androcentrism," a characteristic shared by most nineteenth century (white, Western, middle-class, heterosexual, male) social thinkers.
*   *Postmodernist:* postmodernist critics dismiss Marx's theory of society because it presumes to offer a universal and totalizing theory of history and society. According to Marx, the history of humanity is best understood as the history of class struggle. For postmodernists, however, any theory which presumes to offer a universal meta-narrative can only do so by excluding or suppressing other viewpoints or narratives — such as those of women, the colonized, the elderly, racial or sexual minorities, and so on. Postmodernists oppose all "grand narratives," including that of Marxism.
*   *Economic:* for many orthodox economists, the labour theory of value is a useless concept for all practical purposes. It has no use as a theory for predicting or explaining prices. Supply and demand is the basic indicator

for understanding market conditions. Indeed, the very term "value" is now regarded as an anachronism — a philosophical throwback to the pre-scientific discourse that existed before the rise of modern economic theory.

The subsistence theory of wages is also dismissed by many contemporary economists. Although Marx was careful not to formulate his law of immiseration in an overly simplistic way, some later critics argue that his conclusions have already been falsified by the facts of recent history. These facts include the evident rise in the real income of most workers throughout the immediate post-World War II period in Western Europe and North America. Indeed, this period of growth and prosperity led one British prime minister, Harold Macmillan, to famously declare to the British people in 1957, "Most of our people have never had it so good" (see Evans 2010). These facts, alone, persuaded many observers that Marx's prediction was hopelessly obsolete. But history seems to have nullified such criticisms.

- *Sociological*: many sociologists and social theorists criticize Marx's economic definition of "class" as oversimplified and reductionist. Today, social class is commonly defined in terms of multiple indicators such as occupation, income, education and lifestyle. It is often argued that Marx's definition of class overlooks the internal stratification, or segmentation, that exists within the working class — between blue-collar, white-collar, pink-collar, black-collar workers. Classes are not simple bipolar social groups (bourgeoisie versus proletariat). Class conflict is often pluralistic and complex.

Some critics of Marxism also insist that not all conflict is reducible to class conflict and that class conflict is not the most significant type of social conflict. Many present-day conflicts are based upon racial, ethnic, national, religious, linguistic or gender inequalities. Classical Marxism has very little to say about these social divisions and even less to say about conflicts over the environment, or around identity politics.

Although Marx remained severely critical of many of the manifestations of capitalism — its tendency to polarize social classes, to produce unemployment and poverty, to colonize and exploit overseas labour and to lead to war and inter-imperialist rivalry — he also acknowledged many of the historical strengths of capitalism. He understood that capitalism had become the most productive economic system yet known. It was a system that had the potential to satisfy human needs and to put an end to poverty and material want. The technology of capitalism promised to alleviate the suffering of humanity; only the private ownership of this technology prevented it from doing so. For Marx, capitalism laid the foundation for the possibility of a more equitable and humane world order. It was a system destined to outgrow itself. There would come a time when the progress of capitalist technology would necessitate more democratic forms of ownership and control. Capitalism created the conditions for its own transformation. It would, in time, said Marx, become its own grave digger.

At the same time, as we have already seen, Marx had relatively little to say about post-capitalist societies. He offered no blueprint for future societies and would probably have condemned what have passed for "communist" societies in the twentieth century. For Marx, communism was, at best, a transitional stage leading to a new period of human history. Marx remained a realist. He never believed that all the problems of human existence could be eradicated in a new social order. But he did believe that it was possible, through careful analysis and committed political action, to overcome the injustice and inhumanity of class society and to put an end to the exploitation of labour by capital.

References

Althusser, Louis. 1969. *For Marx*. Translated by Ben Brewster. London: Allen Lane: Penguin Press.

Althusser Louis, and Étienne Balibar. 1970. *Reading Capital*. Translated by Ben Brewster. London: New Left Books.

Beck, Ulrich. 2000. *What Is Globalization?* Cambridge, England: Polity Press.

Bhagwati, Jagdish. 2004. *In Defense of Globalization*. Oxford: Oxford University Press.

Braverman, Harry. 1974. *Labor and Monopoloy Capital: The Degradation of Work in the 20th Century*. New York, Monthly Review Press.

Chambliss, William. 1964. "A Sociological Analysis of the Law of Vagrancy." *Social Problems* 12, 1 (Summer): 67–77.

Desai, Meghnad. 2004. *Marx's Revenge: The Resurgence of Capitalism and the Death of Statist Socialism*. London: Verso.

Duncan, Richard. 2008. "Bring Back Link Between Gold and Dollar." *Financial Times* (London), Sunday, November 23. <ft.com/cms/s/0/ba673d22-b977-11dd-99dc-0000779fd18c.html?ncli>.

Engels, Friedrich. 1967 [1882]. "Letter to Eduard Bernstein, 2-3 November 1882." In volume 35 of Karl Marx and Friedrich Engels: *Werke*. Berlin: Dietz Verlag.

Evans, Martin. 2010. "Harold Macmillan's 'Never Had It so Good' Speech Followed the 1950s Boom." *The Telegraph*, 19 Nov. <telegraph.co.uk/news/politics/8145390/Harold-Macmillans-never-had-it-so-good-speech-followed-the-1950s-boom.html>.

Financial Times. 1998. "Das Kapital Revisited." August 31: 14.

Foster John Bellamy. 2000. *Marx's Ecology, Materialism and Nature*. New York: MRP.

Friedman, Thomas L. 2005a. *The Lexus and the Olive Tree: Understanding Globalization*. Reprint edition. New York: Anchor.

___. 2005b. *The World Is Flat: A Brief History of the 21st Century*. New York: Farrar, Straus and Giroux.

Galbraith, John Kenneth. 1977. *The Age of Uncertainty.* Boston: Houghton Mifflin Harcourt.

Giddens, Anthony. 1971. *Capitalism and Modern Social Theory: An Analysis of the Writings of Marx, Durkheim and Max Weber.* Cambridge, UK: Cambridge University Press.

Hitchens, Christopher. *The Revenge of Karl Marx.* <theatlantic.com/magazine/archive/2009/04/the-revenge-of-karl-marx/7317/>.

Klein, Naomi. 2002a. *No Logo: No Space, No Choice, No Jobs.* Toronto: Vintage Canada.

___. 2002b. *Fences and Windows: Dispatches from the Front Lines of the Globalization Debate.* Toronto: Vintage Canada.

___. 2007. *The Shock Doctrine: The Rise of Disaster Capitalism.* Toronto: Alfred A. Knopf Canada.

Lukacs, George. 1967. "Reification and the Consciousness of the Proletariat." *History and Class Consciousness.* Translated by Rodney Livingstone. London: Merlin Press.

Magdoff, Fred. 2012. "Food as a commodity." *Monthly Review* 63, 08: 15.

Marcuse, Herbert. 1969. *Reason and Revolution: Hegel and the Rise of Social Theory.* Boston: Beacon Press.

Marx, Karl. 1961. *Capital.* Vol. I, trans. S. Moore and E. Aveling. Moscow: Foreign Languages Publishing House.

___. 1964. *Selected Writings in Sociology and Social Philosophy.* Translated and edited by T.B. Bottomore. New York: McGraw-Hill.

___. 1964. [1844]. *The Economic and Philosophical Manuscripts.* Edited by Dirk J. Struik. New York: International Publishers.

___. 1970 [1859]. *A Contribution to the Critique of Political Economy.* Moscow: Progress Publishers.

___. 1977 [1859]. *Preface to A Contribution to the Critique of Political Economy.* Moscow: Progress Publishers.

Marx, Karl, and Friedrich Engels. 1947. [1845–46]. *The German Ideology.* New York: International Publishers.

___. 1953. *Selected Correspondence.* Moscow: Foreign Languages Publishing House.

___. 1958. *Selected Works.* Vols. 1–2. Moscow: Foreign Languages Publishing House.

___. 1970. [1875]. "Critique of the Gotha Program." *Selected Works.* Volume 3. Moscow: Progress Publishers.

___. 1976 [1845–46]. *The German Ideology.* Sct. 1; reprinted in *Collected Works.* Volume 5. Moscow: Foreign Languages Publishing House.

___. 1992. [1848]. *The Communist Manifesto.* Oxford: Oxford University Press (The World's Classics).

Marx-Engels Collected Works. 1924. *Marx Engels Archives.* Volume 46. Moscow: Foreign Languages Publishing House.

Mészáros, István. 1970. *Marx's Theory of Alienation.* London: Merlin Press.

Ollman, Bertell. 1971. *Alienation: Marx's Conception of Man in Capitalist Society.* Cambridge, UK: Cambridge University Press.

Peters, Tom. 1977. "What Great Brands Do." *Fast Company.* August-September.

Poulantzas, Nicos. 1968. *Political Power and Social Classes.* London: NLB.

___. 1975 [1973]. *Classes in Contemporary Capitalism.* London: New Left Books.

Ross, Andrew. 1997. *No Sweat: Fashion, Free Trade and the Rights of Workers.* New York: Verso.

Rousseau, Jean-Jacques. 2008 [1962]. *The Social Contract.* New York: Cosimo Inc.

Said, Edward. 1978. *Orientalism.* New York: Pantheon Books.

Schmidt, Alfred. 1971. *The Concept of Nature in Marx.* London: NLB.

Shaw, Martin. 1974. *Marxism versus Sociology: A Guide to Reading.* London: Pluto Press.

Solow, Barbara L. 2012. "The British and the Slave Trade." Letter to *The New York Review of Books* 59, 1 (January 12): 57.

Stiglitz, Joseph. 2002. *Globalization and Its Discontents.* New York: W.W. Norton.

Strange, Susan. 1986. *Casino Capitalism.* Oxford: Blackwell.

Szaki, Jerzy. 1979. *History of Sociological Thought.* London: Aldwych Press Wheen. Francis.

____. 2007. *Marx's "Das Kapital": A Biography.* Boston: Atlantic Monthly Press.

Who Killed the Electric Car? 2006. Distributor: Sony Pictures Classics.

Williams, Eric. 1944. *Capitalism and Slavery.* Richmond, VA: University of North Carolina Press.

Wittfogel, Karl August. 1956. *The Hydraulic Civilizations.* Chicago: University of Chicago Press.

Wittfogel,, Karl August. 1957. *Oriental Despotism; a Comparative Study of Total Power.* New Haven, CT: Yale University Press,

____. 1960. "Class Structure and Total Power in Oriental Despotism." In E. Stuart Kirby (Hrsg.), *Contemporary China 3.1958-59.* Hongkong: Hongkong University Press.

____. 1969. "Results and Problems of the Study of Oriental Despotism." *Journal of Asian Studies* 28, 2: 357–65.

Wolff, Jonathan. 2002. *Why Read Marx Today?* Oxford University Press.

Wood, Stephen. 1981. *Degradation of Work: Skill, Deskilling and the Braverman Debate.* London: HarperCollins.

Yalnizyan, Amine. 2007. *The Rich and the Rest of Us: The Changing Face of Canada's Growing Gap.* Toronto: Canadian Centre for Policy Alternatives.

____. 2010. *The Rise of Canada's Richest 1%.* Toronto: Canadian Centre for Policy Alternatives.

Zeitlin, Irving. 2000. *Ideology and the Development of Sociological Theory.* Seventh edition. NJ: Prentice Hall.

Chapter 9

The Skeptical Modernism of Max Weber

Modernity and Its Discontents

On October 21, 2009, as Figure 9-1 reminds us, Patrick Clayton walked into the Workers' Compensation Board (WCB) in Edmonton, Alberta, with a loaded shotgun and took nine people hostage. Clayton announced that he was trying to publicize his long standing and unresolved grievances against the WCB. Apparently, after his benefits had been cut off, he was forced to turn to street drugs as an alternative source of pain medication — resulting in his subsequent addiction. Later that day, he released all the hostages unharmed before he was arrested, charged and taken into custody. On November 2011, he finally went to trial, where he pleaded guilty to a number of criminal offences arising from this incident and was sentenced to eleven years' imprisonment. Besides the obvious drama of the hostage-taking spectacle, this event focused greater public scrutiny on the WCB in particular and, more generally, on how individuals are treated by large bureaucratic organizations in our society.

In the aftermath of the hostage-taking, plenty of opinions were expressed about this incident. Most editorials found it safest to simply condemn the hostage-taking as a serious criminal offence and to empathize with the hostages, who were traumatized — although physically unhurt — by their experience. At the same time, while no one condoned the kidnapping, there was also an outpouring of sympathy for the hostage-taker, especially from those who claimed to have been victimized by the WCB. Whatever the merits of Patrick Clayton's case against the WCB, it is clear from other testimonials that many individuals feel they have been poorly treated by the WCB. Stories abound of how many compensation claims for workplace injuries have been unjustifiably denied and how many claimants have been demeaned and degraded by WCB officials.

These horror stories exemplify some of the worst features of large bureaucracies. Many people perceive the treatment they've received at the hands of bureaucratic officials as unfair, unreasonable and unjust. Complaints about callous, dismissive and indifferent treament have also been made about officials from other Canadian government departments, such as Immigration, Customs and Excise and Revenue Canada, as well as from private health management (or health maintenance) organizations (HMOs) in the U.S., and private insurance companies. These stories share a similar profile: the impersonal application of rules and regulations without any concern for the individual case; a wooden obedience to an hierarchical chain of command; secrecy and unaccountability; ensuring that the operational requirements of the organization always trump the demonstrated needs of the individual; an overemphasis on 'red tape' and documentation; and the triumph of authority over humanity. Although most individuals who have been frustrated by harsh treatment from bureaucratic officials do not take the law into their own hands, instances of aggressive and even violent retaliations against bureaucracies are not unknown. Indeed, in 2002, a dramatic case of personal retaliation against a health maintenance organization was portrayed in the Hollywood movie *John Q*, starring Denzil Washington. Some commentators have even suggested that Patrick Clayton's actions may have been inspired by this movie.

The Skeptical Modernist

This brings us to the work of Max Weber, who was one of the earliest theorists to recognize the historical significance of the large, complex, formal organization — i.e., the modern bureaucracy. Weber saw beyond his own time into the future — which is our present — when bureaucracies, for better or worse, would become a definitive

---

Figure 9-1 Edmonton Hostage Taking Incident

On 21 October 2009, 38-year-old Patrick Clayton walked into the main Alberta Workers' Compensation Building in Edmonton with a rifle, fired a single shot, and took nine hostages. Clayton was an injured construction worker with a long-running claim dispute. He had been on and off benefits for the previous six years and was cut off again the week prior to the hostage taking. Unable to work or gain compensation and allegedly further injured during a workers' compensation board (WCB) medical exam, Clayton's life unravelled: bankruptcy, welfare, living in social housing, drug addiction, domestic violence, and a custody dispute. "I just got sick and tired of being treated like a piece of crap by WCB," Clayton told an interviewer from jail. "I never knew where I was going to stand with them from one day to the next, all that uncertainty was nerve racking and constantly wearing me down.... I thought that I had already lost everything including [his son] Brandon, and that I didn't have anything else to lose except my life.... I never had any intentions of hurting any of those people, I just wanted for someone to listen to my story and for someone to help me."

This incident is the most recent in a series of incidents over the years. In 1991, a brain-injured steel worker killed himself in a WCB parking lot. His death resulted in two inquires, program changes, and a government apology to his family. Protestors smashed WCB windows in 1991 and 1992. In 1993, a disabled construction worker used a shotgun to take hostages.... While it is tempting to dismiss these incidents as aberrant, the media coverage of the Clayton hostage taking caused many injured workers to speak out about their frustration. A recurring theme is that workers' compensation is coercive and unfair — that employers and the WCB appear to conspire against them. These claims deserve consideration.

Bob Barnetson, *The Political Economy of Workplace Injury in Canada* (Athabasca: AU Press 2010: 145–146) <http://www.aupress.ca/books/120178/ebook/07>.

feature of modernity. Weber saw both the promise as well as the threat that bureaucracies offered to the modern world and to the life of the individual in modern society. Even now, Weber's name is often invoked whenever the negative effects of bureaucratic rules and regulations hit the headlines. It doesn't take much for any of us to feel like victims when confronted with an implacable bureaucracy. He was the first major theorist to anticipate the rise of the modern bureaucracy and to foresee its impact upon our lives.

Feelings of powerlessness similar Patrick Clayton's are often felt by injured claimants battling with the Workers' Compensation Board; by jobless applicants for unemployment insurance; by motorists appealing parking tickets; by individuals awaiting payouts from insurance companies; by family members sponsoring relatives to come to Canada; or by customers seeking refunds for faulty products from large corporate franchises. Bureaucracies are big and strong, and fighting them is tantamount to climbing a very large legal mountain. It can take a lot of time and energy.

While Weber foretold the rise of large state and corporate bureaucracies as part of the trend towards increasing rationalization, he remained highly ambivalent about the impact of these changes on society. 'Rationalization', according to Weber, was an irreversible historical trend towards ever greater efficiency, standardization and uniformity. At the same time, rationalization also led to increasing impersonality, regimentation and conformity. It was like an historical tidal wave that swept everything before it; out with the old beliefs and practices based on tradition, faith and religion, and in with the new forces of secularization, science and modernization. It was a process that Weber famously described as the "disenchantment of the world": "The fate of our times is characterised by rationalisation and intellectualisation and above all by the 'disenchantment of the world'" (Weber 1946: 155; see also: Ritzer 1999; and Koshul 2005).

Later in this chapter, we shall see that Weber distinguished between several types of rationality. But it was "formal rationality" — the instrumental logic that emphasizes above all else the drive for greater efficiency — which has been responsible for the rationalization of our worldview and our institutions. It is formal rationality that has led to the disenchantment and modernization of our contemporary world. But although Weber anticipated many of the ways in which formal rationality has transformed our lives through scientific and technological innovation, he was also keenly aware that some of these rational innovations could result in negative or even irrational social consequences. Indeed, Weber sometimes darkly alluded to the potential "irrationality of rationality." Thus, while a bureaucracy may provide officials with an efficient means for mass processing a large number of cases — be they clients, patients, customers, citizens or inmates — the same bureaucracy may also deal with individual cases impersonally and insensitively.

Today, we can echo Weber's ambivalence towards the irrationality of rationality on a much larger scale. The formal rationality that has driven ever greater economic and technological development has also led to the irrationality of climate change, global warming and environmental degradation. Similarly, the rationality of nuclear physics has also produced the irrationality of the nuclear bomb. Bureaucratic rationality lay behind the founding and expansion of *McDonald's* and *Walmart*, and both have had negative consequences (bad food and destroying small communities). Bureaucratic rationality also assisted the deadly irrationality of the Nazi death camps at Auschwitz and Treblinka (see Ritzer 2008a; and Bauman 1989). There is a sense, therefore, in which Weber saw rationalization as a paradoxical process. On the one hand, it was a force for intellectual and material progress, while on the other it carried a potential for domination, dehumanization and even destruction. It could lead to innovation and modernization, but it could also result in atomization, alienation, depersonalization and tyranny. Indeed, for Weber, the world-historical process of rationalization conjured up the prospect of a new age in which the "iron cage" of bureaucracy would dominate and suppress the human spirit. Weber also described the rationalization of society (especially the process of bureaucratization) as "the polar night of icy darkness" (Weber 1994: xvi). Rationalization was a sword with a double edge: while it could enhance the struggle for liberty and eliminate scarcity and want, it could also — either intended or unintended — result in new forms of slavery and inhumanity. Once the genie escaped from the bottle, there was no way to recapture it.

Weber's gloomy apprehensions of the possibly counter-productive and dysfunctional consequences of formal rationality have led some commentators to describe him as a cultural pessimist. However, this is far from the truth. Cultural pessimism can best be seen in the works of historians such as Oswald Spengler and Arnold Toynbee, each of whom predicted the future decline of Western civilization. The theme of cultural pessimism normally included at least the following two specific components: a distinctly anti-modernist bias and nostalgia for a past golden age; and a cyclical interpretation of history in which the future decline and fall of Western civilization was somehow predestined and fated.

But the work of Max Weber assiduously avoided the philosophical assumptions or the historical conclusions of cultural pessimism. While Weber remained troubled by some of the possible future ramifications of rationalization, he was not an anti-modernist, and he certainly did not subscribe to any cyclical theory of historical decline. Above all, Weber was a skeptical modernist. He discerned what he believed to be the world-historical process of modernization, but he also remained alert to its possible negative implications for future societies. In this respect, he was a precursor, or forerunner, of the later twentieth-century postmodernists, who also refused to be seduced by the rationalist propaganda of the Enlightenment (see Seidman 1983: 44, 4: 267–78).

From Scholar to Social Scientist

Like all the social theorists covered in this book, Max Weber's reputation has ebbed and flowed with the changing intellectual fashions of successive generations. In the past, Weber was hailed as a prophet who foretold the rise of the giant bureaucracy and the coming age of the iron cage. His ideas have inspired countless studies of bureaucratic organizations, including, in our own time, studies of the fast food giant *McDonald's* — a bureaucracy which some writers have seen as a new paradigm of global rationalization (Ritzer 2008a). Consequently, Weber is now often celebrated as a pioneering student of globalization, and his ideas on rationalization and modernization are sometimes recycled into current discussions of modernity — and its discontents. But Weber's most enduring legacy remains his sponsorship of the nascent discipline of sociology. Among his most important methodological contributions to the development of sociology was his introduction of *verstehen* (or interpretative understanding) as a technique for analyzing the meaning of social action from the subjective perspective of the social actor. He also introduced the notion of the "ideal type" as a method of comparative and cross-cultural social and historical analysis. In these and other ways, Weber helped to transform the study of society from a traditional scholarly discipline into a modern social science. We shall examine some of these methodological innovations more fully later in this chapter.

Weber's methodology is clearly illustrated in his iconic studies of religion, culture, economy and society. His famous essay *The Protestant Ethic and Spirit of Capitalism* (Weber 1958) shows how he succeeded in converting an historical study of Calvinism into a powerful sociological argument for the causal influence of religious ideas

> **Figure 9-2 Max Weber's Centenary: The Calvinist Manifesto**
>
> This year is the 100th anniversary of the most famous sociological tract ever written, "The Protestant Ethic and the Spirit of Capitalism," by Max Weber. It was a book that stood Karl Marx on his head. Religion, according to Weber, was not an ideology produced by economic interests (the "opiate of the masses,"as Marx had put it); rather, it was what had made the modern capitalist world possible. In the present decade, when cultures seem to be clashing and religion is frequently blamed for the failures of modernization and democracy in the Muslim world, Weber's book and ideas deserve a fresh look.
>
> [Francis Fukuyama is a professor of international political economy at the Johns Hopkins School of Advanced International Studies]
>
> Francis Fukuyama, March 13, 2005, *New York Times* <http://query.nytimes.com/gst/fullpage.html?res=9406EEDE103DF930A25750C0A9639C8B63>.

on the rise of industrial capitalism. And while early American sponsors of Weber's work — most notably Talcott Parsons — tried to represent Weber as a counter-theorist to Karl Marx, the truth is that Weber saw himself engaged in an extension, or rounding out, of Marx's ideas rather than in a contradiction or repudiation of them (Zeitlin 2001). Most of Weber's later works — such as *The Religion of China*, *The Religion of India* and *Ancient Judaism* — were driven by a similar sociological animus. Whereas previous German historians had remained content to study ancient cultures and civilizations for their intrinsic antiquarian interest, Weber studied these cultures in order to highlight the uniqueness and originality of the West. He remained pre-occupied with the historical process of rationalization that had led to the modernization and secularization of the Western world. For Weber, the study of non-Western cultures was never undertaken for its own sake, but always in response to sociological questions that he posed and always using methods of sociological research that he, himself, pioneered and refined. Although many of Weber's classical studies — especially the *Protestant Ethic* — were later subject to criticism and controversy for their Eurocentric and Orientalist bias (see Turner 1974; Roth 1993: 148–62; Swedberg 2003: 283–306; Salvatore 1996: 412–33; Love 2000; Schluchter 1999), his work has stood the test of time as an example of how historical scholarship was transformed into social scientific — that is, sociological — research.

Weber's Politics

One of the more contested aspects of Weber's political legacy has been his politics and personal opinions. In the eyes of some commentators, Weber was a political liberal who countered the more extreme conservative ideas of his day with appeals to reason and realism. Other critics have drawn attention to the frankly nationalistic tone of some of Weber's political views and to his denunciation of the leading socialist and revolutionary figures of his day. But, as is usually the case when faced with contrasting arguments over past personalities, the truth invariably lies somewhere in between.

Weber's reputation as a man of liberal conscience was championed by the American sociologist Talcott Parsons, who introduced him to an English-speaking public. For Parsons — and for other American sociologists — Weber was a liberal scholar and politician who supported the modernization of Germany and who advocated a science of society based on professional norms of ethical neutrality and value freedom. Within the context of his life and times, Weber was seen in America as the prototypical German democrat: the "good German" — untainted by either Nazism or Marxism. Moreover, Weber was considered one of the constitutional architects of the earlier Weimar Republic, which, although overthrown by Adolph Hitler in the early 1930s, prefigured the later liberal-democratic Federal German

Republic, which arose from the ashes of World War II. Throughout most of the English-speaking world, therefore, Weber's democratic credentials have remained unquestioned and above suspicion. However, his reputation in Germany has been more controversial. As far back as 1959, the German historian Wolfgang Mommsen undertook "a meticulous reconstruction of Weber's 'unsentimental politics of power' [which] created a furore in Adenauer's Germany" (Thomas 2006, 41: 148).

For his critics on the left, Weber has long been a target of suspicion for his occasional nationalistic and militaristic sentiments. A recent biography records that, in his 1894 inaugural speech at Freiburg, Weber called for the recolonization of parts of Germany in order to resist the growing "polonization" — the increasing number of Polish migrant workers (Thomas 2006: 151). Weber's opposition to the Polish presence in Germany revealed a distinctly racist character. Other critics have cited Weber's rejection of the peace proposals contained in the Versailles treaty of 1919 and his support for German rearmament as further evidence of his militaristic sympathies. As Pfaff (2002: 88) suggests: "Given the irrationality, emotionalism, and political myopia of the masses, Weber ultimately concluded that Caesarist figures might provide effective political direction in a democratic age."

There is no doubt that throughout his intellectual career, Weber remained hostile to Marxism — both as a social theory and as a political ideology — although he retained a respect for the scholarly brilliance of Karl Marx. Indeed, as we have already suggested, Weber regarded his own work as an extension, and rounding out, of Marx's studies of history and political economy. But Weber dismissed Marxism as a one-sided, deterministic theory of society which overemphasized the role of economic factors in its explanations of historical and social change. Beyond this academic disagreement, Weber also ridiculed some of the leading socialists and revolutionary figures of his time. For example, Thomas (2006: 154) records: "He polemicized furiously against the Sparticists declaring in January 1919 that 'Liebknecht belongs in the madhouse and Rosa Luxemburg in the zoo'."

Like most great thinkers and theorists, Weber's ideas echoed many of the paradoxes, contradictions and inconsistencies of his age. But there can be no doubt about the overall value of his scholarly legacy. Although he never formally occupied a chair in sociology (his appointment was in political economy), he is now remembered as one of the foremost pioneers of the discipline. His contributions to the methodological, theoretical and professional development of sociology have secured his reputation as one of the founding figures of the discipline.

Settling Accounts

What were the major intellectual influences on Weber and how did they help to shape his work in social theory and sociology? In much the same way as Marx (and many other social thinkers covered in this book), Weber succeeded in "settling his accounts" with several different intellectual traditions. From his criticism of these traditions and his attempts to reconcile some of their differences, Weber developed his own distinctive approach to the study of society. Today, this approach is sometimes called the "social action perspective." Although Weber acquired an encyclopedic range of knowledge and interests throughout his lifetime, much of his early work grew out of his encounters with three important intellectual traditions of his age — Marxism, historicism and positivism. The story of Weber's sociology is the story of how he adapted each of these different traditions for his own use and incorporated them into his own theoretical and methodological approach to the study of society.

- *Marxism:* In a memorable phrase, Irving Zeitlin describes Weber's social theory as an extended debate with Marx's ghost (Zeitlin 2001). And, in many ways, this is an apt description of the relationship that Weber had with Marx's work. While Weber remained a harsh critic of Marxism especially the dogmatic form of "vulgar" Marxism (or historical materialism) favoured by some of Marx's later followers — Weber never lost his respect for Marx's own scholarly work.
- *German historicism:* Weber was deeply influenced by historicism an intellectual tradition that emerged in Germany as a response to the doctrines of the Enlightenment. More specifically, German historicism arose in opposition to the ideas of positivism, which had spread from France to many of the intellectual centres of Europe and North America.
- *Positivism:* Weber was also influenced by the tradition of positivism, which had migrated from France to Germany — and to other European coun-

Figure 9-3 Weber's Intellectual Influences

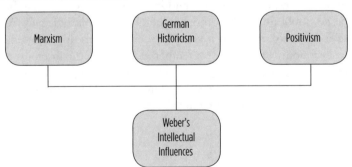

tries. For this reason, Weber was faced with two contrasting intellectual traditions: positivism, which proposed a unified methodology for all the sciences, and historicism, which insisted that the historical and cultural disciplines required different methods of inquiry from those used in the natural sciences. Weber took from each tradition what he thought was valuable and abandoned those aspects that he thought were problematic. By combining the best ideas from both the positivists and the historicists, Weber crafted his own methodological toolbox. This toolbox helped to define his distinctive approach to the study of society and included the following precepts:

- *Sociology should be seen as the study of subjectively meaningful social action.* Weber agreed with the historicists that the social/cultural sciences should be concerned with the subjective meanings and motives of human actions. In other words, it was necessary to discover the point of view of the social actor. Weber rejected the positivist view (of Durkheim and others) that sociology should only study the externally observable and measurable (objective) social facts. Unlike the positivists, Weber believed that the method of sociology should interpret these facts and render them intelligible from the perspective of the social actors themselves.

- *Sociology should use the method of* verstehen, *or interpretative understanding, to study social action.* Weber agreed with the historicists that in order to under-

Figure 9-4 Weber's Sociological Synthesis

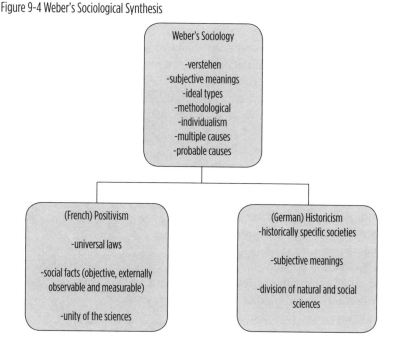

stand the meanings of unique and unrepeatable historical events, it was necessary for the social theorist to re-experience these events in the imagination through the process of interpretative understanding. For this reason, Weber concluded that the historical methods of interpretation and understanding were absolutely necessary for the proper study of society.

- *The study of society begins with the study of individual social actors.* On this point, we encounter something of an inconsistency in Weber's ideas — an example of where he said one thing, but did another. In his methodological statements, Weber pronounced himself a "methodological individualist." In other words, he stated that the study of society should always be reduced to the study of individuals. It was only individuals who could perform (subjectively meaningful) social actions. Organizations, institutions and other large-scale social structures were only collections, or aggregates, of individuals. All social action was only understandable at the level of the individual. For this reason, Weber was opposed to what is sometimes called "sociologism" — or to the "reification" of social relations. (Reification means attributing to abstractions — like society, the state, globalization, the international community etc. — the properties of real individuals. Only real individuals can have purposes or goals, or can experience fear, hope etc). However, the problem for us, his readers, is that in his actual research and scholarship, Weber frequently violated his own rule of methodological individualism. In many of his studies, he examined large-scale social structures and processes without reducing them to the level of individual social actors. Thus he studied comparative religions, Protestantism and capitalism, bureaucracies and rationalization as

> **Figure 9-5 Weber on Understanding from the Actor's Viewpoint**
>
> Sociology ... is a science concerning itself with the interpretative understanding of social action and thereby with a causal explanation of its course and consequences. We shall speak of "action" insofar as the acting individual attaches a subjective meaning to his behavior — be it overt or covert, omission or acquiescence. Action is "social" insofar as its subjective meaning takes account of the behavior of others and is thereby oriented in its course.
>
> Max Weber, Economy and Society 1968: 4.

> **Figure 9-6 Weber on Methodological Individualism**
>
> Interpretative sociology considers the individual and his action as the basic unit, as its "atom."... The individual is the upper limit and the sole carrier of meaningful conduct.... Such concepts as "state," "association," "feudalism," and the like, designate certain categories of human interaction. Hence it is the task of sociology to reduce these concepts to "understandable" action, that is, without exception, to the actions of participating men.
>
> Weber, cited in Gerth and Mills 1946: 55.

large-scale social phenomena in their own right. He did not always try to reduce these societal units to their constituent social actors. We can only conclude from these examples that, as with most great intellectual figures, Weber was sometimes inconsistent and contradictory; his broad, sweeping comparative and historical approach did not easily fit with his methodological norm of individualism. He did not always practise what he preached.

- *The basic tool for studying social action from an historical and comparative perspective is the ideal-type.* The ideal-type was a method of social research that was popularized and refined by Weber, although some previous social thinkers — such as Montesquieu — had already made use of this method in their own studies. An ideal-type is an abstract description of some aspect of society (such as a structure, a process or an event) which is constructed from observations made from a number of real cases. An ideal-type has the following characteristics: (a) it is an abstraction from reality; (b) it never completely corresponds to any real case; and (c) it is typical of most cases. For example, an ideal-type of a university would include — faculty members, graduate and undergraduate students, a board of governors, classrooms, etc. However, although this abstract description may correspond to most cases, it does not correspond to all cases. Some universities do not include graduate students. Other universities — such as distance learning universities — may not have classrooms. Weber used the ideal-type as a way of comparing and contrasting an abstract, hypothetical case to an actual case under study. In this sense, the ideal-type may be thought of as a control case, while the actual case under study is the experimental case. By comparing any real university with an ideal-typical university, it becomes easier to identify some of the distinctive features of the real university which depart from the ideal-type. For Weber, the ideal-type was used as a thought experiment.

There are several important things to remember about Weber's use of ideal-types.

The ideal-type is not intended to portray the average features of a social phenomenon but rather the typical characteristics. Whereas the average Protestant may (contrary to the teachings of his church) drink himself stupid every Friday night, the typical Protestant is hard-working, self-denying and thrifty. The ideal type is not intended to portray the morally desirable features of a social phenomenon but rather the typical

Figure 9-7 Ideal Types

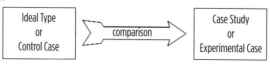

characteristics. We can construct an ideal-type of a brothel or of a concentration camp as easily as we can for a church or a university. The ideal type is *not* intended to portray a classification or taxonomy of a social phenomenon, only its most typical characteristics. These are some of the ways in which Weber's use of the ideal-type have been misunderstood. For Weber, it was used primarily as a means of cross-cultural and historical comparison and contrast. It was meant to provide an objective basis for the study of subjectively meaningful social action. It was Weber's way of combining the best of positivism and historicism.

> ### Figure 9-8 Weber Against Historical Materialism
>
> I would like to protest the statement by one of the speakers that some one factor, be it technology or economy, can be the "ultimate" or "true" cause of another. If we look at the causal lines, we see them run, at one time, from technical to economic and political matters, at another from political to religious and economic ones etc. There is no resting point. In my opinion, the view of historical materialism, frequently espoused, that the economic is in some sense the ultimate point in the chain of causes is completely finished as a scientific proposition.
>
> Max Weber, *Verhandlungen der Ersten Deutschen Soziologengages*, cited in Bendix and Roth 1971: 70.

- *Sociology is the science which studies the causes of particular historical, social and cultural facts.* Unlike the historicists, who rejected any notion of causal analysis of historical events, Weber believed that it was possible to isolate the causes of particular events. On the other hand, unlike the positivists, Weber did not believe that historical explanations could or should be formulated as universal laws, but only as "historically specific explanations" (limited to specific historical events). Weber also pioneered the concept of "multiple causality" — or what is sometimes known today as "multivariate causal analysis" — the idea that any historical event may have a number of different causes. He strongly opposed the idea of single-factor, or mono-causal, explanations of historical events — especially those of Marxism.

The Popular Max Weber

Without a doubt, Weber's most famous work, *The Protestant Ethic and the Spirit of Capitalism*, has become a classic of historical sociology. His study of the rise of capitalism helped Weber to pose the more fundamental question: Why was it that the modern world first emerged in the West? This question preoccupied Weber for the remainder of his life. It became the driving interest behind much of his comparative, cross-cultural and historical research and scholarship. And although the Protestant Ethic has been subject to much criticism and controversy for its Eurocentric and Orientalist bias and for its historical inaccuracies (see Fischoff 1944; Grossman 2006; Green 1973; Blum and Dudley 2001: 207–30; Delacroix 2001: 509–53; and Samuelsson [1957], 1993), it remains an example of how historical scholarship was transformed into social scientific — that is, sociological — research. This is his enduring gift to our times.

Weber's study was completed during the years 1904 and 1905. He became interested in the relationship between Protestantism and capitalism as a result of his visit to the United States in 1904. His book opens with the following observation: "Business leaders and owners of capital, as well as higher grades of skilled labor, and even more the higher technically and commercially trained personnel of modern enterprises, are overwhelmingly Protestant" (Weber 1958: 3). Coming from Europe, a continent in which large numbers of Protestants and Catholics were distributed across different nations and regions, Weber became interested in discovering the connection between Protestantism and capitalism. The underlying question his book tries to answer is: Why is it that the development of industrial capitalism was brought about mainly by Protestants?

Unlike some earlier historical explanations for the agricultural and industrial revolutions that swept through European societies in the seventeenth and eighteenth centuries, Weber did not subscribe to the belief that Protestantism had somehow relaxed the regulations of mediaeval economies. On the contrary, Weber was quick to point out that Protestant societies — especially the early Puritan societies — were more tightly regulated than were Catholic societies of the same period. Many of these early Protestant societies enforced strict prohibitions on dancing, singing, music, popular festivals and other forms of entertainment and enjoyment. After reviewing the available historical evidence, Weber concluded that the link between Protestantism and capitalism was to be found in the specific beliefs of Protestants. He believed that the strong influence of these beliefs on the social and economic practices of Protestant communities led directly to the modern spirit of capitalism. What, then, according to Weber, were these beliefs and how did they lead to new forms of economic conduct? Or, to put the question in another way: "What were the characteristics of the new spirit of capitalism?"

- *Work is valued as an end in itself.* The early Protestants emphasized the importance of hard work as a moral duty, that is, as a calling or vocation. This Protestant view of work may be contrasted to the view of other major world religions, many of which saw work as a distraction from spiritual activity. Compared with Protestantism, Weber characterized Catholicism as otherworldly in its social orientation. He also noted that many Eastern religions — especially Hinduism and Buddhism — emphasized detachment and renunciation of the material world as a necessary condition for spiritual growth and personal enlightenment.

- *Accumulation of wealth is an indication of personal virtue as well as of economic success*: As Weber wrote, "The earning of money within the modern economic order is, so long as it is done legally, the result and expression of virtue and proficiency in a calling" (Weber 1958: 53–54). Unlike other major religions, the accumulation of wealth was seen by the early Protestants as the just reward of hard work and industriousness.

- *The methodical life governed by reason is valued as a state of righteousness, as well as for economic efficiency:* For the early Protestants, the methodical life meant the planning of all activities, often down to the smallest details. Only deliberate and conscientious planning could prevent the individual from wasting time through idleness and slothfulness. It was a commonly observed truth of the times that the Devil finds work for idle hands to do. (This sentiment is illustrated in the poem by Isaac Watts, in Figure 9-9). The importance of planning and calculation entered into many aspects of social life. Rational accounting practices became part of the everyday running of business enterprises. Timetables, production schedules, deadlines and other planning and time-management devices were used in factories, farms and stores as well as schools, orphanages, poor houses and other institutions. The great emphasis was on using all time constructively and productively — "time is money." The Protestant obsession with the constructive use of time led to a general concern for increased economic productivity, increased financial profitability and increased technical efficiency — in other words, a concern for ever-increasing rationalization. Weber's finding from looking for a link between Protestantism and capitalism was that this religious movement gave birth to the process of rationalization — a process which had begun to transform traditional into modern societies, a process that gave birth to the modern world.

Figure: 9-9 Puritan Hymn

Isaac Watts (July 17, 1674 – November 25, 1748) is recognised as the "Father of English Hymnody," as he was the first prolific and popular English hymn writer, credited with some 750 hymns.

How doth the little busy bee
Improve each shining hour,
And gather honey all the day
From every opening flower!

How skillfully she builds her cell!
How neat she spreads the wax!
And labours hard to store it well
With the sweet food she makes.

In works of labour or of skill,
I would be busy too;
For Satan finds some mischief still
For idle hands to do.

In books, or work, or healthful play,
Let my first years be passed,
That I may give for every day
Some good account at last.

- *Economic success should not be used for personal enjoyment*: The wealth created through productive labour should not be consumed for personal gratification. Pursuit of wealth for its own sake was regarded by the early Protestants as sinful. Such personal gratification could lead to idleness, gluttony and the enjoyment of the temptations of the flesh. There was a great premium placed on the responsible use of wealth for good works. The significance of these injunctions limiting personal gratification and consumption was that they encouraged the re-investment of profit back into the business enterprise. The result of this practice can be seen in the cycle: production plus reinvestment equals accumulation. These strictures against consumption led directly to the accumulation of wealth and to the transformation of wealth into capital. In this way, the ethical practices of the early Protestants helped to prepare the way for the rise of industrial capitalism. These practices were driven by certain strongly held doctrinal beliefs associated with the early Puritan sects — especially the Calvinists, followers of John Calvin. Weber recognized the significance of these religious beliefs and referred to them collectively as the "Protestant ethic." The following were some of the main characteristics of the Protestant ethic:

- *The doctrine of predestination*: The early Puritans did not believe in the contemporary idea of a free will. Instead, they believed that the fate of each individual was fixed at birth. Humanity was divisible into two groups: those destined for salvation (known as "the elect") and those destined for damnation. According to this doctrine, there was no way to learn one's fate and no way to alter it. In this respect, the doctrine of predestination was similar to the concept of "kismet" (or fate), which figures prominently

> **Figure 9-10 John Bunyan's Hymn**
>
> **He Who Would Valiant Be**
>
> He who would valiant be
> 'Gainst all disaster,
> Let him in constancy
> Follow the Master.
> There's no discouragement
> Shall make him once relent
> His first avowed intent
> To be a pilgrim.
>
> Who so beset him round
> With dismal stories,
> Do but themselves confound,
> His strength the more is.
> No foes shall stay his might
> Though he with giants fight;
> He will make good his right
> To be a pilgrim.
>
> Since, Lord, Thou dost defend
> Us with Thy Spirit,
> We know we at the end
> Shall life inherit.
> Then fancies flee away!
> I'll fear not what men say,
> I'll labor night and day
> To be a pilgrim.
>
> Words by John Bunyan, 1684, modified by Percy Dearmer, *The English Hymnal* (London: Oxford University Press, 1906).

in some Middle-Eastern and South Asian cultures.

- *Inner loneliness and anxiety*: Many of those who fully internalized the doctrine of predestination spent much of their lives in a state of perpetual uncertainty and anxiety. The inability to learn one's fate, or to avert it, led many to experience intense inner loneliness — a state that existential philosophers of the twentieth century would call angst. Unlike the Catholic Church, the Puritans had no priests to administer sacraments or to absolve them from the guilt of their sins. Without the priesthood and without the sacraments of the church, Puritan believers stood alone before their God. For Weber, this sense of spiritual isolation signalled the birth of a new individualism, which was to become the hallmark of modernity.

- *The search for signs of salvation*: In many ways, the doctrine of predestination was a harsh and pitiless doctrine which led to the torment and torture of those who were judged to be impious. Lest we forget, the Puritan communities in Great Britain and the American colonies were zealous in their hunting and burning of those unfortunates labelled as witches. The new efficiencies of the Protestant ethic were employed for brutal as well as for productive purposes. But for many Puritans, the uncertainty of their fate led them to search for signs of their own personal salvation, and many individuals sought for signs, or clues of their salvation, the most important of which was faith. The elect were recognized by their unquestioned belief in their own salvation and by their ability to resist doubt and to overcome uncertainty. (This spirit is illustrated in Figure 9-10, a hymn taken from the novel *The Pilgrim's Progress*, written by John Bunyan in 1684).

The other strong sign of salvation was the record of good works performed by an individual for their community. In practice, good works frequently meant the accumulation of wealth for the good of the community. Thus, wealthy business owners who produced goods for the local market and employed local workers could confidently assume their

---

Figure 9-11 Puritan Names

Puritans like good, Christian names, which include:

Zeal-of-the-Land
Praisegod
Wrestle
Celerity
Strength
Morality
Arise
Faith-my-joy
More-fruit
Kill-sin
Fight-the-good-faith-of-faith
If-Christ-had-not-died-for-thee-thou-hadst-been-damned
The-Lord-is-near
Reformation
Lamentation

Albion Wiki (Puritanism) <albion.chaosdeathfish.com/other_christians>.

own probable salvation. Good works, and philanthropy, therefore, were seen to be the result of productive labour, measured by the standards of worldly success.

- *Reason and asceticism*: The early Protestants stressed the importance of living a methodical life combined with self-denial. This was a life of psychological repression and harsh physical discipline. There were to be no irrational emotions or superstitions, and all desires of the flesh were rigorously suppressed. The Christian virtues were cultivated and celebrated. Indeed, many Puritans were given personal names such as Punctuality, Frugality, Probity, Chastity and, more colourfully, Flee-from-Fornication. (See Figure 9-11 for other Puritan names you may wish to give your children.)

The ethic of self-denial was particularly apparent in the strongly Protestant cities Belfast, Glasgow and Toronto, where it was customary to close playgrounds and recreation areas on the Sabbath and even to pad-lock the swings and roundabouts. In reviewing these and other aspects of the Protestant ethic, Weber based his understanding of the doctrines of Puritanical Protestantism (Calvinism) on the writings of Richard Baxter and Benjamin Franklin, whose writings he had encountered during his visit to the United States in 1904.

Weber's Conceptual Toolbox

Although Weber's work on the Protestant ethic and spirit of capitalism is now recognized as a classic historical study in its own right, it can also be seen as a stepping stone to Weber's broader interests in the advent of modernity. It was part of his wider interest in the transition of traditional societies into mod-ern societies. In this sense, Weber was preoccupied with the same problem that engaged most of the nineteenth-century classical social theorists — the transition crisis. For Marx, this transition was the passage from feudalism to capitalism. Durkheim saw the transition as the passage from mechanical to organic forms of social solidarity. Other theorists devised their own criteria for defining and classifying these historical differences. Weber, like most of his contemporaries, was also fascinated by how the modern world had come into existence and how it had left the old world behind. The most eloquent testimony to Weber's abiding interest in this topic is provided by his wife, Marianne Weber (see Figure 9-12).

Above and beyond its importance as an historical study, Weber's exami-nation of the link between Protestantism and capitalism led him to develop the methodological tools to study the different aspects of modernization. It is in his study of modernization that we first encounter the concept of "rationalization," a concept that acquired a central place in Weber's theory of society. According to Weber, it was the historical process of rationalization that best described and explained the transition from traditional to modern societies. What exactly did Weber mean by the term rationalization?

In the most general terms, the process of rationalization was described by Weber as the progressive "disenchantment of the world" (Jenkins 2000). This process involves a movement away from traditional beliefs about the world (religious, magical, mystical and mythical) towards a modern scientific worldview. The process of rationalization, Weber believed, affected all aspects of modern life. Rationalization could be observed in the following different ways.

- *As an intellectual process*: Rationalization involves the development of systematic and empirical knowledge best exemplified in the rise of modern science and its applied technologies.

> **Figure 9-12 The Big Question**
>
> This recognition of the particular character of Western rationalism and the role it played in Western culture constituted for Weber one of his most important discoveries. As a result, his original question of the relation of religion to economics became the wider more general question of the particular character of the entire Western culture. Why does rational science which produces verifiable truths exist only in the West? Why only here rational harmonic music, or architecture and plastic art which employ rational constructions? Why only here a rational state, a trained bureaucracy of experts, parliaments, political parties — in a word, the state as a political institution with a rational constitution, and rational law? Why only here the fateful power of modern life — namely modern capitalism? Why all this only in the West?
>
> Marianne Weber (cited in Szaki 1979: 365)

- *As a social process*: Rationalization involves the development of methodical and efficient forms of social and economic organization best exemplified in the specialized division of labour, modern business planning and accounting systems, and the growth of private (corporate) and public (government) bureaucracies. The elements of the social process of rationalization include calculability, predictability, quantification, standardization and uniformity, which combine to produce greater efficiency, productivity and profitability. Examples of rationalization in our modern world include fast-food franchises, precision-guided weapons systems, big box retail stores and so on.
- *As a cultural process*: Rationalization involves the unification and generalization of cultural themes in the area of religion (where monotheism superseded polytheism and animism), music and literature.

Rationalization can be broadly understood as the process of modernization which has affected all institutions in society, not simply business enterprises but also hospitals, the armed forces, churches, non-governmental organizations, universities, prisons and even the nuclear family. Weber's "ra-

Figure 9-13 Weber — Rationalization

tionalization" has nothing in common with Freud's later concept of the same name, and it is important not to confuse the terms. Freud's "rationalization" refers to the process of trying to find a rational (or logical) explanation for an apparently irrational (or emotionally motivated) action, speech or thought process. In psychoanalytic terms, the process of rationalization is a psychological defence mechanism. Thus, the convicted shoplifter may rationalize their offence by arguing that stores are exploiting the public by over-pricing their merchandise in order to make a fast profit. As we have seen, however, Weber's "rationalization" refers to social actions and practices that are driven by a need for greater efficiency and that hasten the growth of modernity and the decline of traditionalism.

Although Weber recognized that the process of rationalization brought about revolutionary changes in the structures and functions of many institutions in society, he remained ambivalent and skeptical in his assessment of these changes. While the rationalization of industry and commerce had led to greater efficiency, productivity and profitability, Weber acknowledged that not all the effects of rationalization were necessarily so positive. In fact, he suggested that the rationalization of the modern world also entailed some very negative and dysfunctional consequences. He sometimes referred to these negative consequences as the "irrationality of rationalization." In Weber's view, the following were some of the more obvious sources of irrationality associated with the process of rationalization:

- *Loss of meaning*: according to Weber, the erosion of religion and tradition has often resulted in a loss of meaning and purpose in our lives. When the German philosopher, Nietzsche, proclaimed "God is dead" the world became a lonelier and more chaotic place. Science is not able to fully replace the lost values associated with these earlier traditions of thought.
- *Loss of freedom*: Weber also felt that the increased efficiency of many institutions in society may sometimes result in a loss of individual freedom. This has most obviously been the case in the growth of totalitarian societies. But it is also true for our own society in regard to the growth of public and private bureaucracies and the way in which many individual

activities are now regulated in the interests of public order, national security or the common good. Recent examples of this loss of individual freedom in our society range from anti-smoking by-laws to the security regulations governing air and cross-border travel. In the U.S., since 9-11, a huge new public bureaucracy, the Department of Homeland Security, curtails many individual rights and freedoms in the name of national security. In Canada, the new Ministry of Public Safety exists as an echo of its U.S. counterpart.

Throughout his life, Weber remained ambivalent and apprehensive about the process of rationalization, which he saw as an irreversible world historical tendency in all modern societies. Towards the end of his life, he grew increasingly pessimistic about the fate of modern humanity. In passages which strike us today as alarmingly prescient, Weber ruminated darkly on the growth of bureaucracy in modern societies. He referred to the expanded scale of bureaucracy as "an iron cage" which could easily begin to imprison humanity. It was almost as though he saw the future nightmares of Nazism and Stalinism and later variations of these totalitarian societies.

> **Figure 9-14 The Irrationality of Rationalization**
>
> There are many other examples that could be cited of the irrationality of rationalization. The rational organization of science and technology that led to the construction of the atomic (and then the nuclear) bomb has resulted in the irrational capacity of humanity to annihilate itself. Similarly, the rational planning and bureaucratization of industrialized genocide at Auschwitz (and other death camps) resulted in the irrationality of the Holocaust. In our own time, the rationalization of heavy industry, the dominance of the carbon economy, and the mass production (and distribution) of such consumer goods as the automobile, domestic appliances and other commodities which contribute to the emission of greenhouse gasses have resulted in the irrationality of climate change and global warming.

Analyzing Social Action

Based on his theory of rationalization, Weber distinguished between several different types of social action. The most important distinction he made was between rational and non-rational social action.

- *Rational-purposive (or goal-oriented) rational action:* This first type of rational action is, according to Weber, based upon "formal rationality." Individuals are motivated by formal rationality when their actions are directed towards an instrumental goal — that is, to the successful completion of a particular task. This type of rational action is based upon the need to select the most efficient means in order to accomplish a specific end.

Figure 9-15 Weber's Typology of Social Action

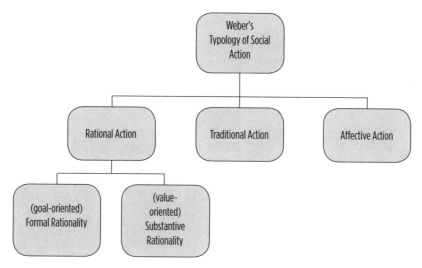

Weber believed that modern science was one of the highest expressions of formal rationality — the most efficient means for discovering valid knowledge of the material world. But the danger of formal rationality is that the end may be used to justify the most efficient means without regard for the morality of these means or the end that they serve. In an extreme example, if the maximization of personal income is an individual's goal, then such means as embezzlement, fraud (or armed robbery) may be more efficient means than simple gainful employment — as we have seen in the corporate scandals associated with Enron, WorldCom and others. Action is never undertaken for its own sake, but always in the service of some instrumental (usually material) end.

- *Value-oriented rational action:* This type of rational action is based upon "substantive rationality." Individuals are motivated by substantive rationality when their actions are oriented, not towards an instrumental goal, but to the realization of certain expressive values. These values may be religious, political, ideological or personal in nature. Thus, individuals may be motivated to act in the name of patriotism or revolutionary ideals or to uphold or advance basic civil or human rights. The French Revolutionary ideals of liberty, fraternity and equality are examples of expressive values that have motivated actions based upon substantive rationality. Similarly, the values of hard work and self-denial associated with the early Puritans provided grounds for value-oriented rational action. Action is always carried out for its own sake rather than as a means to an end. What is important to understand is that social action based upon formal rationality may, on occasion, come into conflict with or contradict action based upon substantive rationality. Thus, as the French sociologist Georges Friedmann once observed, "While Auschwitz was a rational place, it certainly was not a reasonable place" (cited in Ritzer 2008b: 146–47). Or, to express the matter in a different way: although Auschwitz may provide an example of formal rationality, it contradicted any notion of substantive rationality. In his later writings, Weber grew increasingly fearful that the pressures for greater formal rationality in modern society would eventually displace the need for substantive rationality.

- *Traditional action:* This is a type of non-rational action mentioned by Weber. Individuals performing various forms of traditional action are oriented towards customary and habitual types of action. The goals and purposes of this action are not always as precisely defined as they are in more rational types of action. Actions are often justified in terms of maintaining a continuity of tradition, or a preservation of customary ways. Examples of traditional social action could include the coronation ceremonies of the kings and queens of England or of the popes at the Vatican; traditional public festivals such as Carnival (in Rio and in parts of the Caribbean); traditional parades such as the Fourth of July parades in the U.S.; the traditional throne speech in the British and Canadian Houses of Commons; and age-grading ceremonies or rites of passage in indigenous and aboriginal societies.

- *Affective action*: This is another type of non-rational action. Individuals performing various types of affective social action are motivated to

---

Figure 9-16 Michael Moore's Movie Sicko

A dramatic example of the conflict which can arise between the competing demands of formal and substantive rationality in modern society is shown in the movie *Sicko,* by Michael Moore. This film documents how the need for an adequate system of health care in the U.S. has been severely compromised by the power and greed of private health care "providers" who have consistently placed the drive for profit above the need for patient care. The movie recounts many examples of how the poor and the catastrophically sick are denied access to adequate or affordable health care either because they are uninsured, or because they are denied coverage under existing insurance policies. The conclusions of the movie are stark and sober: while private insurance companies, pharmaceutical companies and health management organizations (HMOs) reap spectacular profits from the health care "industry," large numbers of average Americans are either unable to access adequate healthcare, or are bankrupted in their efforts to do so. For Max Weber, this movie would provide a striking example of how the need for substantive rationality (universal health care) has been largely eclipsed by the demands of formal rationality (profitability, and a leaner and meaner organizational "efficiency"). For us, the movie helps to pose the critical question of rationalization: *rational for whom?*

act largely from emotional needs. Unlike rational actions, there are no specific instrumental or expressive goals which motivate affective social action. Examples of affective action may include collective euphoria at rock concerts or raves (such as the Beatlemania of the 1960s); collective expressions of religious sentiment; crowd or audience behaviour — including riots and disturbances in hockey or soccer games; and other forms of collective sentiment (or hysteria).

Weber uses his typology of social action in order to show how some types of social action have contributed to the process of rationalization in modern societies while other types of social action have obstructed or actively resisted this process. The process of rationalization was advanced by the value-oriented rational action of the Protestant ethic and by the goal-oriented rational action of the spirit of capitalism. However, rationalization has often been resisted (and sometimes prevented) by different types of traditional or affective social action.

Finally, as we have already noted, Weber became fearful that the world of formal rationality would eventually come to dominate the world of substantive rationality. This is a theme that was later explored by other social theorists, such as the Frankfurt School of critical theorists in the twentieth century.

Power and Authority

During the middle period of his intellectual career, Weber became interested in how societies were governed and how organizations were administered. This interest in "domination" arose from Weber's cross-cultural studies of ancient civilizations such as China and India, and from his historical studies of European societies. These studies led Weber to distinguish between two (analytically) distinct types of domination in society — "power" (or "Macht" in German), and "authority" (or "Herrschaft" in German).

Power refers to the probability that a social actor can achieve their goals even when opposed by others. According to Weber's definition, the exercise of power may require coercion or the use of force, at least as a last resort. Weber believed that in all centralized societies, social order was ultimately insured only through the threat, or through the actual use, of force. In his famous definition of the state, Weber declared: "A state is that political organization which is successfully able to exercise a legitimate monopoly over the organized use of force within a given territory" (Gerth and Mills 1946: 78). In the contemporary world of the twenty-first century, some political scientists distinguish between a number of different types of state — including a failed state and a rogue state. Failed states — such as Afghanistan, Sudan and Somalia — have been unable to exercise a monopoly

Figure 9-17 Power versus Authority

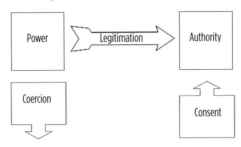

over the use of "legitimate" force, while rogue states — such as Rwanda (during the genocide), Yugoslavia (during the ethnic cleansing of Bosnia and Kosovo) and Cambodia (during the genocide) — have, according to the international community, attempted to exercise a monopoly over the use of "illegitimate" force.

Authority, on the other hand, refers to those cases of the exercise of power in which a social actor is able to secure the voluntary consent and compliance of others in the achievement of their goals. In other words, authority is based upon the belief of those who are dominated in the right of others to dominate them. The motives for compliance may include cultural values, custom and tradition, self-interest or even love. The process involving the acknowledgement of the right of others to dominate is referred to by Weber as the process of "legitimation." Authority can best be understood as "legitimated power" — inasmuch as authority rests upon the consent and compliance of the governed in the conditions of their governance.

In reality, of course, most states depend upon their authority over citizens for the routine processes of government. Only during periods of crisis, when the legitimacy of authority is brought into question, will most states resort to the use of naked power as a last resort. In Canada, the federal government resorted to the use of the armed forces during the October Crisis in 1970. In Ontario, the provincial government requested to the use of Canadian Armed Forces during the Oka Crisis of 1990. At these times of crisis, the state reveals the iron fist that is normally concealed within the velvet glove — in other words, the gloves come off.

Authority Figures

Weber's interest in the study of power and authority in societies led him to develop a classification or typology of the types of authority that could be found both within particular societies and between different societies. Weber's classification is an example of his use of an ideal-type, in this case for the purpose of comparing and contrasting different historical examples of authority.

Weber suggests that there are three types of authority, or legitimate sources of power: traditional authority, rational-legal authority and charismatic authority. How does Weber distinguish these different types of authority?

- *Traditional authority*, according to Weber, is based upon a long-lasting system of beliefs and traditions. Leadership is often based upon hereditary privileges passed down through generations, clans or families. In indigenous societies, leadership may be conferred upon the elders (a gerontocracy is a society ruled by the aged). In European societies, traditional authority was often based upon patriarchal domination (of the immediate household), patrimonial domination (of the extended retinue) or feudal domination (based upon reciprocal obligations between the lord and his tenants). The most obvious form of traditional state authority is the monarchy. The hereditary right of the monarch to pass on the crown from one generation to the next was originally enshrined in the doctrine of the Divine Right of Kings.
- *Rational-legal authority* is based upon impersonal norms which have been officially established to realize explicit goals. Compliance with this type of authority implies acceptance of these impersonal norms. Authority is not based upon personal obligations or customary obligations but on the status of the office-holder. The best examples of rational-legal state or corporate authority figures are those leaders who have been elected, appointed or recruited to their positions through a set of formalized and rationalized procedures, for example prime ministers, presidents and CEOs. Rational-legal leaders are usually associated with bureaucratic organizations, which are based upon impersonal and universalistic rules and regulations. One of the most common examples of a rational-legal authority figure is the police officer. Police officers, irrespective of their race, ethnicity, gender or physical appearance, exercise their authority over the general public. Their authority comes from the office they hold in society and from the formal rights and privileges associated with that office. Rational-legal authority, therefore, is based upon generally ac-

Figure 9-18 Weber's Typology of Authority

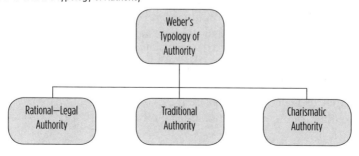

cepted and explicit rules and procedures of appointment, election or recruitment.

- *Charismatic authority*, in some ways the most intriguing of Weber's types, is authority based upon extraordinary abilities or personal qualities of an individual leader. (Indeed, the very term "charisma" from the Greek means magic or grace). Charismatic leaders may be regarded as supernatural or superhuman or as having exceptional, exemplary or outstanding personal qualities. The personal power of charismatic leaders has often influenced and mobilized large numbers of followers. Charismatic leaders may be religious, moral or spiritual leaders (the Prophet Muhammad, Moses, Buddha, Jesus, Gandhi, Ayatollah Khomeini, Socrates), political demagogues (Joan of Arc, Napoleon, Hitler, Stalin, Churchill, Lenin, Mao, Che Guevara) or other heroic or iconic figures (Elvis Presley, the Beatles). In our own time, both Martin Luther King Jr. and Osama Bin Laden have, in their own very different ways, risen to the status of charismatic leaders. Unlike other sources of authority, which develop a fixed organizational membership, charismatic leaders typically depend upon social movements made up of followers, disciples, believers, the faithful, supporters or fans. Charismatic leaders often renounce the past and have a revolutionary impact on society and its institutions. Weber regarded charismatic authority as unpredictable and incalculable in its consequences. It was potentially disruptive. Charismatic leaders may appear without warning and change everything overnight — including rational-legal forms of authority. They are the wild cards in the pack.

- *The routinization of charisma* summarizes Weber's suggestion that the type of authority founded by a charismatic leader will eventually develop into a system based either on traditional authority (if authority is passed on through the leader's relatives, descendants or followers) or into a system based upon rational-legal authority (if authority is passed on through a system of formalized rules and procedures). Thus, the authority of the Pope in the Roman Catholic Church is based upon tradition inasmuch as this authority is believed to have descended from the first pope, the apostle St. Peter. Similarly, the authority of the Imamate in Shia Islam is presumed to have descended from the blood line of the Prophet Muhammad through his son-in-law and cousin Ali. On the other hand, the legacy of other charismatic leaders, such as Lenin, Mao and Che, was passed on through revolutionary political organizations which established rational-legal systems of authority and domination. Charismatic authority, therefore, is always relatively short-term and transitory in nature. Sooner or later, the routinization of charismatic authority is followed by either traditional or rational-legal forms of authority.

The Iron Cage of Bureaucracy

Weber's most famous example of the use of rational-legal authority is the modern bureaucracy. For many of us, the term "bureaucracy" carries a pejorative connotation. More often than not, in popular discourse, bureaucracy has come to refer to "red tape" and time-wasting procedures. The term implies inefficient government departments which make excessive and unreasonable demands upon our time and energy. The popular view is that bureaucracies frustrate rather than expedite our requests. And as we saw at the beginning of this chapter — with the example of the WCB — the frustrations that people experience with bureaucracies can sometimes turn ugly.

Modern bureaucracies often receive bad press from novelists, journalists and other social critics. In the world of literature, bureaucracy was portrayed by novelists Franz Kafka, George Orwell and Aldous Huxley as a totalitarian institution, and by Nikolai Gogol as "a rigid and impersonal state machine producing meaninglessness, absurdity, and tragedy" (Samier and Lumby 2008). George Orwell, in particular, was apprehensive about the growing power of governments to regulate and monitor our lives — even as far back as 1949, when he published his famous novel *Nineteen Eighty-Four.* It was in this dystopian portrayal of the future that we first heard the expression, "Big Brother is watching you."

In addition to being considered time-wasting and inefficient, in the public mind, bureaucracies are sometimes regarded as shadowy and sinister unelected centres of power and secret information. Recent events have conspired to fuel popular concerns over the growing power and global reach of large government bureaucracies. Since 9/11, for example, there have been many stories of individuals apprehended at airports, or other public places, and relocated — through the extra-judicial practice of "extraordinary rendition" — to secret sites for "enhanced interrogation." Individuals caught up in this shadowy web of the secret state — such as the Canadian Maher Arar, — have found themselves transported into a Kafkaesque world without any due process, constitutional or legal protections, and stripped of their human rights (see such movies as *Rendition* [2007], *Extraordinary Rendition* [2007] and *Taxi to the Dark Side* [2007]).

At the same time, the growing power and secrecy of public and private sector bureaucracies has generated counter-movements of resistance and revelation. The age of the giant bureaucracy has also become the age of the whistleblower. Perhaps the most famous of all whistleblowers today is the web-based organization *WikiLeaks* and its founder Julian Assange. But other whistleblowers — such as Daniel Ellsberg (during the Vietnam War in the U.S.) and Richard Colvin (during the Afghan detainee controversy in Canada) — have also tried to hold powerful government bureaucracies accountable for their concealment, or distortion, of the truth.

Today, in the post-9/11 world, most of us have become sensitive to the fact that large government and private corporate bureaucracies collect and share information about us as never before. The recently concluded Beyond the Border agreement between Canada and the U.S. (Public Works and Government Services Canada 2011) gives the Canadian government unparalleled powers to share information on Canadian citizens, permanent residents and others, with U.S. national security and law enforcement agencies. Within Canada, the privacy commissioner and civil liberties organizations have expressed grave reservations concerning these greatly enhanced powers of surveillance and information-sharing. And even while working on our computers in the privacy of our own homes, most of us realize that every keystroke is tracked by private marketing companies, which use this information to send us pop-up advertisements based on our recorded interests and purchases. The age of Big Brother has finally arrived.

But, of course, this is not the whole story; bureaucracies also play a vital and indispensable role in our everyday lives. Without bureaucracies, even the most routine tasks — such as registering a motor vehicle, renewing a driver's licence, submitting a health care expense claim or paying taxes — would be infinitely more complicated and drawn out. Indeed, without bureaucracies, these community-wide certifications would likely not happen at all. Notwithstanding their popular reputations as time-waster, bureaucracies actually save most of us a lot of time and effort. It should come as no surprise that the strongest denunciations of bureaucracy come from political conservatives — especially the neoconservatives of the past three decades. For those on the political right, "bureaucracy" has become a negative buzzword for all that is wrong with contemporary society. Conservatives are particularly opposed to any further expansion of the public sector and are likely to decry many government services — whether unemployment insurance, social welfare, childcare or even health care — as evidence of a growing "nanny state." They are equally opposed to most forms of government intervention and regulation — whether of the economy, the environment or civil society. In Canada, for example, the Harper government abolished the "long gun" firearms registry because it allegedly constituted an unnecessary bureaucracy. In the U.S., Republican Party candidates oppose the health care reforms of President Obama, which are disparaged as Obamacare, because these reforms supposedly create an unnecessary bureaucracy which hinders individual freedom of choice and opens the door to "creeping socialism" or even "totalitarianism." The very term "bureaucracy" has become an ideological weapon in a partisan war of words.

Whatever our own feelings about bureaucracies, they are a quintessential part of modern life. Most of us work in bureaucracies, study in bureaucracies, consume in bureaucracies and are entertained and amused in bureaucracies.

Bureaucracies have become an inescapable part of our urban landscape. Love them or loathe them, we just can't live without them. As one journalist observed some time ago:

> Bureaucracy is like a sin — we all know something about it, but only those who practice it enjoy it. Ordinary people tend to be against both, and experts on the subject tend to become obsessed, so that some see bureaucracy everywhere as fanatical clerics see sin up every back alley. If you hold that all sex is sin, you simply mean you wish you had never been born; if you believe all bureaucracies are degenerate you are simply registering a protest against modern society. (Chapman 1961)

Weber used the term "bureaucracy" in a far more neutral and analytical way. It simply referred to an organization largely administered by rational and impersonal rules, and oriented to maximum efficiency. Weber saw the modern bureaucracy as a striking example of the process of rationalization. Even though he lived at the beginning of the twentieth century, Weber realized that the process of bureaucratization was transforming many different organizations and institutions in society. Not only were government departments becoming bureaucratized, but so also were business enterprises and private companies, universities, the military, political parties, trade unions and many other organizations. The early twentieth century gave birth to the age of the modern bureaucracy. The very term means "government by officials," or, more precisely, "administration of government through departments and subdivisions managed by a set of appointed officials following an inflexible routine" (*Webster's New World Dictionary of American English* 1988: 186).

History has proven Weber correct in his assumption that bureaucracies are here to stay. Today, the organizational landscape is filled with bureaucracies — both public and private. Living as we do in an age of transnational corporations, global non-government organizations and a growing number of international organizations (the United Nations, World Bank, World Trade

---

Figure 9-19 Bureaucracy as Bad News

When people hear the term "bureaucracy," they are likely to think of all the bad experiences they have had with large organizations, especially with government agencies. Trying to collect an unemployment cheque from a Canada Employment and Immigration Centre; filling in tax returns for Revenue Canada; nominating relatives for immigration to Canada: most of us have had some frustrating and time-wasting experiences with government bureaucracies. It's hardly surprising then, that for many people the term "bureaucracy" conjures up images of "red tape," lost files, unanswered letters, forms in triplicate, unsympathetic officials, and general hassles with authority. More than anything else, the term "bureaucracy" has come to mean "inefficiency."

Mills, Simmons and Mills 2005: 50.

Organization and International Monetary Fund, for example), bureaucracies have become an inescapable part of our lives. And although the term may still be used more as a curse than as a blessing, the truth is we could not live our present lives without bureaucracies. We have all become dependent on the bureaucratic delivery of goods and services, and the bureaucratic organization of tasks ensures that most of these transactions are completed efficiently. Without large bureaucracies, none of us could expect to receive these services in the style to which we have all grown accustomed.

What are the typical characteristics of a bureaucracy? Most sociologists would define the concept of bureaucracy in the following terms: "a large, formal complex organization which is organized around an elaborate division of labour, under a hierarchical structure of authority, and which operates according to explicit rules and procedures" (Mills, Simmons and Mills 2005: 50). However, as we have already noted, no ideal-type, not even that of the modern bureaucracy, ever fully corresponds to any actual organization or institution. When we compare any real organization to the ideal-type, there will always be some differences and discrepancies. Recognizing this fact, Weber outlined the following typical characteristics of the modern bureaucracy:

- *A highly specialized division of labour*: Each office in a bureaucracy has a clearly defined job description, and office-holders are only responsible for their official obligations. The work of a modern organization is divided among all its members so that each member performs a highly specialized task. Canada Post, for example, divides its work among letter carriers, mail sorters, counter clerks, supervisors and so on. Everyone becomes a cog in the organizational machine.
- *An hierarchical authority structure*: Bureaucracies have a system of authority which flows downward from the top of the organization. This is the official chain of command, in which the highest officials in the organization have most of the authority. All officials in the organization give orders to those immediately below them, and accept orders from those immediately above them. In other words, all bureaucracies are arranged in an elaborate pecking-order; each position has a clearly defined jurisdiction and span of control.
- *Use of written rules*: All bureaucracies are run according to an elaborate set of written rules and regulations. These may be manuals of technical instruction which have to be followed to the letter, as in the case when auto mechanics or computer technicians service and repair equipment. Or there may be procedural or policy manuals used by government officials to process applications for unemployment benefits, health-care claims, accident compensation claims, child allowances, immigrant visas and so on. Bureaucracies are notorious for their paperwork and for

following written rules and regulations to the letter. But it should be understood that written rules are designed for efficiency (everyone can learn to administer the same sets of rules) and for fairness and equity (everyone is treated according to the same sets of rules). There are supposed to be no favourites in bureaucracies: everyone is treated the same.

- *Impersonal relationships*: People who work for bureaucracies relate to each other primarily as office-holders and only secondarily as individuals. This means that people are defined first and foremost in terms of the jobs they do rather than who they are as people. People may come and people may go in a bureaucracy, but the jobs remain to be done if the organization is to survive. As a result people usually treat each other in an impersonal manner because it is their jobs which bring them together rather than friendship, or common interests. Similarly, people who work in bureaucracies usually try to treat their clients, members of the public, in a formal manner — as "cases" rather than as unique individuals. If everyone is treated the same, then everyone will be treated impersonally.

> **Figure 9-20 Weber's Fear of Bureaucracy**
>
> Imagine the consequences of that comprehensive bureaucratization and rationalization which already today we see approaching. Already now ... in all economic enterprises run on modern lines, rational calculation is manifest at every stage. By it, the performance of each individual worker is mathematically measured, each man becomes a little cog in the machine and, aware of this, his one preoccupation is whether he can become a bigger cog ... It is apparent that today we are proceeding towards an evolution which resembles [the ancient kingdom of Egypt] in every detail, except that it is built on other foundations, on technically more perfect, more rationalized, and therefore much more mechanized foundations. The problem which besets us now is not: how can this evolution be changed? — for that is impossible, but: what will come of it?
>
> Max Weber, cited in Mayer 1956: 126–27.

- *Appointment on the basis of technical competence*: People who work for bureaucracies are normally hired because of their training, qualifications and experience for the job. Most bureaucracies will claim to hire people on the basis of their knowledge and skills, not on their personal qualities. Similarly, promotions are supposedly made on the basis of individual merit rather than on family or social connections, gender, race or ethnicity, patronage or bribes.

- *Professional careers*: Bureaucracies usually offer their employees the opportunity for long-term careers. With the proper training and experience, it is usually possible to move up the rungs of the organizational ladder. Workers in a bureaucracy are heavily dependent upon the organization for their long-term employment. The bureaucracy may protect job

Figure 9-21 The Dysfunctions of Bureaucracy

Rigid: Bureaucracies can sometimes appear inflexible and inefficient when dealing with unusual, exceptional or atypical cases. Example: a passport applicant without a birth certificate or an applicant for a city building permit without a detailed building plan.

Impersonal: Many people who work for bureaucracies, or who are clients of bureaucracies, have found them to be impersonal, insensitive and uncaring institutions. Example: victims of sexual assault interviewed by police, negotiating a tax dispute with city authorities.

Goal displacement (and bureaucratic ritualism): In some bureaucracies, the goals of individual bureaucrats (or the departments they work for) may become more important than the official goals of the organization. In other words, the tail may begin to wag the (bureaucratic) dog. Example: when cost-cutting measures in the prison system begin to make it very difficult for inmates to complete educational courses, these measures may defeat the broader correctional goal of rehabilitation.

Empire building (and self-perpetuation): One of the most famous critics of bureaucracy was the popular author C. Northcote Parkinson, who concluded that bureaucrats have a vested interest in making work for themselves in order to justify hiring assistants and thereby increase their own status. Bureaucracies will often continue to stay in business long after their original goals have been achieved. Many will redefine their original goals. Example: NATO continues to expand even after the fall of communism in Europe.

Resistance to change: Bureaucracies often develop an institutional inertia which makes them unsympathetic, resistant or even hostile to change. This is often seen in the case of senior government bureaucrats — in the civil or public service sectors — who may try to obstruct the programs, policies and legislation of newly elected governments. Example: the problems encountered by the first CCF provincial government in Saskatchewan, or the post-war Labour government in the U.K.

Secrecy: Government bureaucracies may also attempt to conceal information from the public domain, justifying such concealment in the name of "national security." Corporate bureaucracies may also conceal information which may jeopardize their profit margins. Example: The administration of Richard Nixon in the U.S. withheld information about its unauthorized bombing of Cambodia during the Vietnam War; the Bush administration has withheld information regarding detainees and other aspects of the Iraq war.

Anti-democratic: Ever since the time of Max Weber, bureaucracy has been seen as incompatible with the ideals of democracy. This is because hierarchy remains the cornerstone of bureaucracy and stands opposed to the basic assumptions of democracy. Example: The writer Robert Michels concluded that all large bureaucratic organizations would eventually succumb to the iron law of oligarchy. He meant by this that all large organizations would sooner or later fall under the domination of "oligarchies" — small ruling elites.

Sexist: Feminist critics argue that the values of rationalization, impersonality, hierarchy, etc. represent patriarchal and masculinized values and interests. Feminists propose that other, more humane forms of organization are possible and desirable.

security through seniority rules, pensions and benefits, and may even open up new career paths within the organization.

For Weber, the bureaucracy represented the supreme triumph of the process of rationalization and the clearest example of rational-legal authority. The modern bureaucracy had become the material expression of the process of rationalization. However, Weber remained ambivalent and even apprehensive towards the growth of large bureaucracies in the modern world. While he recognized that bureaucracies could improve efficiency in the production of goods and in the delivery of services, he also feared that they could begin to exercise a dark influence on the fate of humanity. In several passages, Weber expressed great concern that large bureaucratic organizations could easily reduce individuals to the status of human cogs in vast organizational machines — depriving them of their individual freedom and their sense of personal meaning. These concerns led Weber to propose his famous description of the bureaucracy as an "iron cage" — an organizational machine into which increasing numbers of human cogs would become trapped and dominated. Some later writers have interpreted Weber's gloomy predictions as proof that he foresaw the rise of totalitarianism in the twentieth century. Whether or not this conclusion is warranted, there is no doubt that Weber harboured serious doubts about the role of large bureaucracies in modern societies.

Today, many sociologists recognize that bureaucracies do not always live up to their textbook descriptions as models of rationality and efficiency. Figure 9-21 lists some of the more commons problems of bureaucracies.

Weber's Study of Social Inequality

Through his writings on social classes and social structure, Weber laid the groundwork for the sociological study of social stratification in modern societies. In some respects, Weber agreed with Marx's analysis of social class. But in at least one very important respect, Weber departed from Marx's analysis or — more precisely — from the analysis advanced by the Marx's followers, the historical materialists. Weber did not believe that all social divisions were ultimately rooted in economic causes. On the contrary, he insisted that different kinds of social divisions arose from quite different causes. In his discussion of what he regarded as the main social divisions in modern societies, Weber distinguished between three dimensions of social stratification — economic, cultural and political.

Weber agreed with Marx in a general sense that social classes were primarily economic divisions in society. And like Marx, Weber believed that classes could be defined by the ownership or non-ownership of the means of production. Weber also distinguished ownership classes from what he called commercial classes. He distinguished between the two main ownership classes in the following way:

- *The positively privileged ownership classes* — which includes those classes with property and skills to sell in the market, such as entrepreneurs, financiers,

Figure 9-22 Weber's Dimensions of Social Stratification

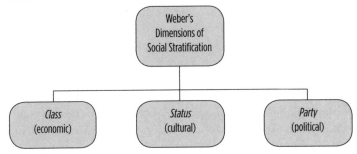

bankers etc. These were the classes whose income was derived from ownership and from rents, profits, interest, etc.

- *The negatively privileged ownership classes* — which includes the property-less working class without property or skills to sell in the market. These were the classes whose income was derived from labour — from the sale of their labour-power in exchange for wages.

Among the middle classes, Weber included the petty bourgeoisie (small business owners) and officials and managers in public and private organizations. These classes derived their income from the sale of their marketable skills and services.

Based upon these distinctions of class membership, Weber's analysis of the class structure of early industrial society included the following social classes:

- *Manual working class,* which was partly divided between different skill levels (such as skilled, semi-skilled and unskilled workers);
- *Petty bourgeoisie,* which was composed of those who owned and operated their own small businesses, farms and other means of production and distribution;
- *White collar middle classes,* which were composed of professional groups of employees such as officials, managers, technocrats, bureaucrats, scientists, intellectuals and others who worked for a salary; and
- *dominant propertied groups,* composed of those who owned big businesses as well as those who had acquired or inherited large-scale landed property.

Several points need to be emphasized regarding Weber's picture of social classes in modern society. Some of these points suggest that Weber's view of social class was, in some ways, more refined than that of Marx. In other ways, there were striking similarities between the views of Marx and Weber on social class.

First, Weber's concept of class was based not only on criteria of production (as in relationship to the means of production) but also on criteria of consumption. In other words, class membership was partly based upon individuals' disposable incomes — how much they had to spend and how much they could save. Thus, Weber opened the door for later sociologists who would further define class membership in terms of income, education, occupation and lifestyle, as well as other factors not directly linked to the means of production.

Second, for Weber, class conflict only occurred at those times when class inequality was no longer seen as natural, but rather as social in origin, in other words, when class inequality was no longer seen as inevitable. During these times — when earlier legitimations of inequality are under attack — subordinate classes no longer accept their position in society as legitimate. This view is very similar to Rousseau's critique of inequality in such works as *The Social Contract*, and *The Origins of Inequality*.

Third, for Weber, class consciousness only occurs when classes become aware of their common interests and thereby develop into a community, that is, a collective actor capable of collective action. Weber suggested that such class communities only develop when the following conditions are present:

- when the class enemy is a social group which is highly visible and is also in direct competition with one's own class;
- when large numbers of individuals are included in one's own class;
- when communication, organization and mobilization is relatively easy to achieve between members of a social class. These conditions are typically found wherever there is a centralized labour force (as in a factory, or other industrial workplace); and
- when the social class has developed an effective leadership as well as a set of clearly defined and articulated goals.

In many ways, Weber's understanding of how a social class develops into a community has much in common with how Marx saw the development of a class-in-itself into a class-for-itself. The main difference between these two accounts is that Weber specified the necessary conditions for this transformation more precisely than did Marx.

The second major dimension of the social divisions in society, according to Weber, is what he called "status." Status groups are determined by cultural factors rather than simply by economic factors, as is the case with social classes. Weber suggested that the status of an individual "refers to the evaluations which others make of him, or his social position, thus attributing to him some form of (positive or negative) social prestige, or esteem" (Weber, cited in Giddens 1970: 166). The status of a social group is measured by the amount of social honour or prestige shown to that group relative to other groups in society. The concept of "status," therefore, is related to tradition, lifestyle and the subjective differences between social groups. Weber provides some historical examples of status divisions in society that were not necessarily dependent upon class differences. In this respect, status divisions have a life of their own which is not fully reducible to economic criteria or causes. Weber's historical examples include the caste system of India, the segregation of the Jews as a pariah group and the "estates" of mediaeval European societies — the monarchy, gentry and commoners. Today, status divisions are more likely to be based upon lifestyle differences (such as occupation, education, consumption, etc) than upon inherited divisions. Surgeons, lawyers and architects are likely to occupy higher positions in the prestige hierarchy of modern societies than, for example, construction workers, garbage collectors and janitors. However, some status differences in our society may still be maintained on the basis of traditional or inherited criteria — such as race, ethnicity, nationality and gender. Other status divisions may be based upon similarly entrenched social criteria such as religion, language and political beliefs.

Weber's concept of status — as a measure of the social divisions in society (social stratification) — is significant for a number of reasons. Status divisions may sometimes determine the power of different parties in an economic relationship. Thus, in some societies, women may be seen as property rather than as legal persons. In other historical societies different groups — whether Jews, Catholics, African-Americans or Indigenous peoples — have sometimes been restricted, or even excluded, from engaging in certain types of economic relations or transactions.

Status divisions may not be wholly dependent upon class position. Thus the *nouveau riche* (those who have recently acquired wealth) have often been patronized by more traditional elites in society because of their perceived vulgarity, brashness, ostentation etc. Notwithstanding their self-made fortunes, many members of the *nouveau riche* have never been fully accepted into, or accorded equal status with, the traditional ruling classes.

Status divisions may also override class relations. Thus a low-class Brahmin in India may still be accorded greater social prestige than a high-class Dalit (or Untouchable). Until the advent of the civil rights movement in the U.S., even distinguished and relatively wealthy African-Americans were routinely denied the most basic human and civil rights. In other words, race, ethnicity and gender have often trumped social class when it comes to assigning social status to groups and individuals in society.

Weber's third dimension of the social divisions in society refers to any voluntary association, or party, that aims to secure control over an organization or institution and to implement a program of political or social change. For Weber, "party" refers primarily to political parties which are designed to enable their members to secure control over the state and its institutions.

Weber believed that political power — in its own right — should be recognized as another dimension of social stratification in modern society. In this respect, party may relate to both class and status as a basis for power, but may also be viewed as analytically separate. In the modern world, party has become an important source of power and prestige. Before the fall of communism in the USSR and in Eastern Europe, elite members of the Communist Party were often referred to as the *Nomenklatura*. Because of their party connections, these communist officials managed to secure privileges that were unobtainable for the mass of ordinary citizens, including vacation homes (or *dachas*), high salaries and long term job security, access to hard currency stores, privileged education for their children, jobs for their relatives and so on. Even in our own society, membership in a ruling political party sometimes confers unauthorized privileges such as patronage appointments, sponsorship, financial kick-backs, travel junkets and other aspects of what has been called in Canada "the culture of entitlement." In many other societies, membership in a ruling political party has automatically conferred high social status and economic privilege. In the U.S., for example, the politics of the Tammany Society played a major role in the early settlement and employment of immigrants, even though it became notorious for its graft, corruption and patronage. "It was the Democratic Party political machine that played a major role in controlling New York City politics and helping immigrants, most notably the Irish, rise up in American politics from the 1790s to the 1960s" (Wikipedia, n.d.). These examples suggest that Weber's recognition of the power of parties in social stratification was extraordinarily accurate and prescient.

Weber and Marx on Social Stratification

Although Weber broadly agreed with Marx's general description of social classes, he remained critical of some aspects of what he perceived as the Marxist analysis of social inequality in modern society, although some of these deterministic interpretations of Marx's ideas were advanced by his more zealous followers. The following are the ways that Weber distanced himself from the Marxist theory of social stratification:

- *Weber was not a reductionist in his analysis of social stratification*: He did not believe that some primary social divisions (i.e., class) necessarily determined all other divisions in society. He did not believe that everything was dependent upon class membership. He concluded that cultural and political divisions were also significant factors in their own right.
- *Weber introduced an expanded definition of class:* Although he agreed with Marx's association of class with ownership or non-ownership of the means of production, Weber also believed that consumption (the ability

to purchase goods and services in the marketplace) was also an important indicator of economic class differences.

- *Weber recognized a subjective, socio-cultural dimension to social stratification.* He considered that such factors as social honour and prestige could be important determinants of social structure and social stratification. These subjective divisions could only be understood in terms of the meanings that were culturally associated with these status differences.
- *Weber pioneered a pluralistic conception of social division and social conflict.* He believed that there were many potential sources of division and conflict in modern society beyond the antagonism of labour and capital. His work laid the foundation for later sociological studies of power and domination based not simply on economic class, but also on nationalism, race, ethnicity and gender, as well as forms of inequality associated with religion, language and other cultural factors.
- *Weber saw that power was often distributed between dominant elites and class fractions.* Although he conceded that economic wealth and political power often went hand in hand, he recognized that there were several dominant elites rather than one, single, uniform ruling class, as the Marxists often proclaimed. In his own way, Weber prefigured such concepts as the military-industrial-congressional complex, first introduced by President Dwight Eisenhower in an effort to warn Americans of the powerful alliances that had been forged between private corporate interests and parts of the American state (the Department of Defense). In many ways, Weber's views were ahead of their times.

Max Weber: Yesterday, Today and Tomorrow

Much has changed in the world since Max Weber first published his most popular book, *The Protestant Ethic and Spirit of Capitalism* (1904–5). During his lifetime, Weber not only witnessed the terrible events of World War I, he also observed the Russian Revolution and gloomily anticipated the rise of the totalitarianisms that led to the outbreak of World War II. Although never a pessimist, Weber was more of a realist — a skeptical modernist — in his assessment of the human condition. What, we may wonder, would he have thought of the world today? In all likelihood, very few of the global changes that have taken place since his death would really have surprised Weber. His astute historical vision allowed him to spot some of the major social and economic trends of his own time that were already beginning to define the contours of the future global economic and political order.

Over the past several decades — and especially since the 2008 financial crisis — we have seen the rise of what some commentators term "casino capitalism" (Strange 1986), or what others even label "zombie capitalism" (Harman 2009). Unlike the early entrepreneurs described by Weber, who generated profit through producing real goods, the casino capitalists of today generate their profits, bonuses and fees through trading financial assets — whether these are international currencies, securitized mortgages, derivatives, credit default swaps, hedge funds or other forms of paper or digital wealth. Whereas the early industrial capitalists accumulated their wealth through production and reinvestment, the finance capitalists of today accumulate their wealth through speculation and trading. Weber would quickly have grasped the significance of these different forms of capitalism. And, as at least one perceptive commentator has suggested (Dahrendorf 2010), Weber would undoubtedly have recognized an essential difference between the worldview of the early entrepreneurs and that of the later casino capitalists — namely, their time-span perspective. For the entrepreneurial capitalists of the past, the investment of capital — the building of factories, shipyards, iron and steel or textile mills; the digging of mineshafts; the hiring of workers; and the production of commodities — was the work of a lifetime. The founding of an industry — whether coal, pottery, confectionary, automobiles, ships, armaments or textiles — often defined the growth of towns and cities. The impact of industrialization was felt by everyone. In this respect, the early capitalist was always an important corporate member of the local community — as an employer, as a supplier of goods and services, and sometimes as a philanthropist. The time span of the industrial tycoon, or even of the retail giant, was usually long term — often over several generations of a family business.

The difference between this long-term perspective and the short-term perspective of our current casino capitalists could hardly be greater. The financier of today is essentially a gambler, trading in paper assets for short term gain while spreading the risks of each venture as widely as possible — to overseas investors, to employees, to pension fund contributors, to bank customers, to mortgage holders and, ultimately, to the public treasury. Whereas the earlier entrepreneurs mostly assumed personal or family responsibility for the enterprise as a private risk, today's casino capitalists have managed to nationalize their risks — often, as we have recently seen, at huge public expense. Weber may have been disappointed, or even appalled, at this turn of events, but he probably would not have been surprised. He had already begun to recognize that the growth of modern capitalism had rendered obsolete many of the earlier values of the Protestant ethic. Most of these ethical values had already been eclipsed by the more self-serving values of the ledger book, the profit margin and what we would today call the bottom line. Indeed, in a passage that could easily have been written by Karl Marx, Weber expressed his growing disenchantment with the new ethos of modern capitalism. It had become a system, he concluded, characterized by "specialists without spirit, sensualists without heart; this nullity imagines that it has attained a level of civilization never before achieved" (Weber 1958: 123–24). For Weber, the driving force behind the modernization of all societies was that of rationalization. And although, in his estimation, the processes of rationalization had originally sprung from the Protestant ethic, they were destined to develop far beyond their Puritanical origins. As we already seen, Weber anticipated that the forces of rationalization could eventual breed irrational forms of consciousness and conduct: the irrationality of rationalization. For this reason, he would not have been surprised to see the rise of casino capitalism — accumulation through speculation; profit-making without production; rationalization without a public purpose: the capitalist no longer a prudent and frugal Puritan but now an improvident gambler.

Although Weber has been much criticized for his alleged ethnocentrism and Orientalism — especially in his depiction of the Eastern civilizations — he probably would not have been surprised by the rise of China, Japan and India as the economic powerhouses of the twenty-first century. Nor would he have been unduly fazed by the Arab Spring — or by similar developments in other parts of the world. In this respect, Weber would likely have shown more prescience than others who have misappropriated his work to advance a "clash of civilizations" thesis (Huntington 1998; Lewis 2003), or to argue for the inherent stagnation of non-Western cultures and societies (Kuran 2010). For Weber, rationalization remained the overwhelming world historical trend that was fated to spread around the globe and to transform everything in its path. Rationalization was spread beyond the West through the influences of colonialism, immigration and settlement and through the impact of modern forms of transportation and communication. However, as an acute scholar of comparative religions and cultures, Weber would also have realized that the process of rationalization is never fully standardized or homogenous; every society achieves rationalization through its own cultural and religious resources.

Although the traditional religious beliefs and worldviews of India, China and Japan may have impeded the early modernization of these countries — at least according to Weber — he probably would have foreseen how each society would eventually succumb to the forces of rationalization as these forces radiated out from the West. But he would also have expected each society to undergo modernization using its own historical and cultural resources. In this respect, he would have agreed with Marx: "Men make their own history, but they do not make it as they please; they do not make it under self-selected circumstances, but under circumstances existing already, given and transmitted from the past" (Marx 1969 [1852]: 15). Hence, the modernization of Japan was led by the traditional samurai caste, which emphasized corporatism and national solidarity. In India, the modernization process appears, in some ways, to have incorporated rather than eliminated the caste system of social inequality. Similarly, modernization in Turkey has occurred within a secularized structure of Islamic cultural and religious values. And although traditional Islamic values — especially the strict interpretations of Sharia law — may have prevented the emergence of the Western capitalist values of "possessive individualism" (Kuran 2010), some of these traditional values may now offer an alternative for many Muslim societies to the exclusively Western model of modernization. Thus, while rationalization may be universally defined by the methodical practices of efficiency, calculability, predictability and control (Ritzer 2008a: 13–15), the ways in which these practices are adopted by any particular society are always filtered through a pre-existing set of cultural beliefs and values. In this sense, there are many different cultural paths to modernization. Weber would have understood this.

References

Barnetson, Bob. 2010. *The Political Economy of Workplace Injury in Canada.* Athabasca: AU Press. <http://www.aupress.ca/books/120178/ebook/07>.

Bauman, Zygmunt. 1989. *Modernity and the Holocaust.* Ithaca, NY: Cornell University Press.

Bendix, Reinhard, and Guenther Roth. 1971. *Scholarship and Partisanship: Essays on Max Weber.* Berkley: University of California Press.

Birnbaum, Norman. 1969. *The Crisis of Industrial Society.* Oxford: Oxford University Press.

Blum, Ulrich, and Leonard Dudley. 2001. "Religion and Economic Growth: Was Weber Right?" *Journal of Evolutionary Economics* 11, 2: 207–30.

Bunyan, John. 1997. "John Bunyan and the Pilgrim's Progress." *Christian History* 11, (Carol Stream, IL: Christianity Today, Inc.).

Chapman, B. 1961. "Facts of Organized Life." *Manchester Guardian Weekly*, January 26.

Coser, Lewis. 1977. *Masters of Sociological Thought.* Second edition. New York: Harcourt.

Dahrendorf, Ralf. 2010. "After the Crisis: Back to the Protestant Ethic? Six Critical Observations." *Max Weber Studies* 10, 1: 11–21.

Delacroix, Jacques Francois Nielsen. 2001. "The Beloved Myth: Protestantism and the Rise of Industrial Capitalism in Nineteenth-Century Europe." *Social Forces* 80, 2: 509–53.

Fischoff, Ephraim. 1944. "The Protestant Ethic and the Spirit of Capitalism: The History of a Controversy." *Social Research* 11: 53–77.

Fukuyama, Francis. 2005. "The Calvinist Manifesto." *New York Times Book Review* March 13. <http://query.nytimes.com/gst/fullpage.html?res=9406EEDE10 3DF930A25750C0A9639C8B63>.

Gerth, H.H., and C.W. Mills. 1946. *Max Weber: Essays in Sociology* (trans). New York: Oxford University Press.

Giddens, Anthony. 1970. *Capitalism & Modern Social Theory: An Analysis of The Writings of Marx, Durkheim and Max Weber.* Cambridge: Cambridge University Press.

Green, Robert (ed.). 1959. *Protestantism and Capitalism: The Weber Thesis and Its Critics*. Boston: D.C. Heath.

___. 1973. *The Weber Thesis Controversy*. Boston: D.C. Heath.

Grossman, Henryk. 2006. "The Beginnings of Capitalism and the New Mass Morality." *Journal of Classical Sociology* 6, 2: 201–13.

Harman, Chris. 2009. *Zombie Capitalism: Global Crisis and the Relevance of Marx*. London: Haymarket Books.

Huff, Toby E., and Wolfgang Schluchter (eds.). 1999. *Max Weber and Islam*. New Brunswick and London: Transaction Publishers.

Huntington, Samuel. 1998. *The Clash of Civilizations and the Remaking of the World Order*. First edition. New York: Simon & Schuster.

Jenkins, Richard. 2000. "Disenchantment, Enchantment and Re-Enchantment: Max Weber at the Millennium." *Max Weber Studies* 1: 11–32.

John Q. 2002. Starring Denzel Washington, James Woods, Robert Duvall; Director — Nick Cassavetes. DVD:Infinifilm

Koshul, Basit Bilal. 2005. *The Postmodern Significance of Max Weber's Legacy: Disenchanting Disenchantment*. New York (and Basingstoke, UK): Palgrave Macmillan.

Kuran, Timur. 2010. *The Long Divergence: How Islamic Law Held Back the Middle East*. New Jersey: Princeton University Press

Laslett, Peter. 1965. *The World We Have Lost: England Before the Industrial Age*. New York: Charles Scribner's.

___. 1983. *The World We Have Lost: Further Explored*. London and New York: Charles Scribner's.

Lewis, Bernard. 2003. *What Went Wrong? The Clash Between Islam and Modernity in the Middle East*. New York: Harper Perennial.

Love, John. 2000. "Max Weber's Orient." In S. Turner (ed.), *The Cambridge Companion to Max Weber*. Cambridge: Cambridge University Press.

Marx, Karl. 1969 [1852]. *The 18th Brumaire of Louis Napoleon*. New York: International Publishers.

Mayer, Jacob Peter. 1956. *Max Weber and German Politics*. Second edition. London: Faber & Faber.

Mills, Albert, Tony Simmons and Jean Helms Mills. 2005. *Reading Organizational Theory: A Critical Approach to the Study of Organizational Behaviour and Structure*. Toronto: Garamond Press.

Moore, Michael (Dir., writer). 2007. *Sicko*. Dog Eat Dog Films, Weinstein Company.

Pfaff, Steven. 2002. "Nationalism, Charisma and Plebiscitary Leadership: The Problem of Democratization in Max Weber's Political Sociology." *Sociological Inquiry* 72: 81–107.

Public Works and Government Services Canada. 2011. *Beyond The Border: A Shared Vision For Perimeter Security and Economic Competitiveness*. Government of Canada: Ottawa @ <www.borderactionplan.gc.ca>.

Ritzer, George. 1999. *Enchanting a Disenchanted World: Revolutionizing the Means of Consumption*. Thousand Oaks, CA: Pine Forge Press.

___. 2008. *Classical Sociological Theory*. Fifth edition. New York: McGraw-Hill.

___. 2008a. *The McDonaldization of Society*. Fifth edition. Thousand Oaks, CA: Pine Forge Press.

____. 2008b. *Modern Sociological Theory.* Seventh edition. Boston and New York: McGraw-Hill.

Roth, Guenther. 1993. "Between Cosmopolitanism and Ethnocentrism: Max Weber in the Nineties." *Telos* 96: 148–62.

Salvatore, Armando. 1996. "Beyond Orientalism? Max Weber and the Displacement of 'Essentialism' in the Study of Islam." *Arabica* 43: 412–33.

Samier, Eugenie, and Lumby, Jacky. 2008. "Corruption, Futility and Madness: Relating Gogol's Portrayal of Bureaupathology to an Accountability Era." *Biennial Conference of the Commonwealth Council for Education Administration, Durban, South Africa*, 08–11 Sep. 2008.

Samuelsson, Kurt. 1993 [1957]. *Religion and Economic Action: The Protestant Ethic, the Rise of Capitalism, and the Abuses of Scholarship.* Toronto: University of Toronto Press.

Seidman, Steven. 1983. "Meaning, Modernity and Cultural Pessimism in Max Weber." *Sociological Analysis* 44, 4: 267–78.

Story, Jack Trevor. 1963. *Live Now, Pay Later.* London: Secker & Warburg. *Live Now — Pay later* (1962) was also released as a film directed by Jay Lewis.

Strange, Susan. 1986. *Casino Capitalism.* Oxford: Blackwell.

Swedberg, Richard. 2003. "The Changing Picture of Max Weber's Sociology." *Annual Review of Sociology* 29: 283–306.

Szaki, Jerzy. 1979. *History of Sociological Thought.* Westport, CT: Greenwood Press.

Thomas, Peter. 2006. "Being Max Weber." *New Left Review* 41: 147–58.

Turner, Bryan S. 1974. *Weber and Islam: A Critical Study.* London: Routledge & Kegan Paul.

Turner, Jonathan. 2006. *The Emergence of Sociological Theory.* Sixth edition. Belmont, CA, Wadsworth Publishing.

Watts, Isaac. 1866. *Divine and Moral Songs for Children.* New York: Hurd & Houghton.

Weber, Max. 1946. "Science as a Vocation." In H.H. Gerth and C. Wright Mills *From Max Weber: Essays in Sociology.* New York: Oxford University Press.

____. 1951. *The Religion of China.* Translated and edited by Hans H. Gerth. Glencoe, I: Free Press.

____. 1952 *Ancient Judaism.* Edited by Hans H. Gerth and Don Martindale. (Glencoe, IL: Free Press.

____. 1958. *The Religion of India.* Translated and edited by Hans H. Gerth and Don Martindale. Glencoe, IL: Free Press.

____. 1958. *The Protestant Ethic and Spirit of Capitalism.* Translated by Talcott Parsons. New York: Charles Scribner.

____. 1968. *Economy and Society.* Translated and edited by Guenther Roth and Claus Wittich. Berkeley CA: University of California Press.

____. 1994. *Political Writings.* Translated by Ronald Speirs, edited by Peter Lassman. Cambridge: Cambridge University Press. (Cambridge Texts in the History of Political Thought.)

Webster's New World Dictionary of American English. 1984. 2nd College Edition. New York: Simon and Schuster.

Wikipedia. <http://en.wikipedia.org/wiki/Tammany_Hall>.

Zeitlin, Irving. 2001. *Ideology and the Development of Sociological Theory.* Seventh edition. New Jersey: Prentice Hall.

Chapter 10

The Sociologism of Emile Durkheim

A Summer of Discontent

In Vancouver, London and in many other cities, the summer of 2011 will be remembered for many years to come as a summer of discontent. It was a summer marked by some of the worst riots seen in Canada and Britain for many years. The riot in Vancouver on June 15, which began in the downtown core, was apparently started by disgruntled hockey fans angered over the defeat of their team, the Vancouver Canucks, by the Boston Bruins during the seventh game in the National Hockey League's Stanley Cup play-offs. Television viewers across Canada were astounded to see young people smashing store windows, looting stores, burning buildings and setting fire to automobiles — including police cars. Perhaps the eeriest aspect of these disturbances was the fact that many rioters and vandals made no effort to conceal their identities. Indeed, they appeared to pose for the camera, assuming heroic and defiant postures on top of burning vehicles, or in front of police lines. Many rioters recorded their exploits on smart phones and posted these video clips later — via Facebook — onto the internet. For the crowds of spectators on the streets, these events appeared to unfold like a wild and uninhibited reality show, and — via TV — into the living rooms of the nation.

> **Fig 10-1 Things Fall Apart**
>
> One of the problems that Emile Durkheim took most seriously — the problem of "anomie," or how many individuals may feel a sense of rootlessness and personal detachment from modern society — was given a clear expression by the Dr. Rowan Williams, the Archbishop of Canterbury, in his Christmas Day sermon in 2011. Speaking about the urban riots that had erupted in London and in other British cities during August 2011 — after the police shooting of a young black man, Mark Duggan — Dr. Williams moved beyond a condemnation of the individual rioters to a more serious reflection on the state of British society. In his sermon, he described a state of disintegration and demoralization that he saw as modern-day England. "The most pressing question we now face, we might well say, is who and where we are as a society. Bonds have been broken, trust abused and lost. Whether it is an urban rioter mindlessly burning down a small shop that serves his community, or a speculator turning his back on the question of who bears the ultimate cost for his acquisitive adventures in the virtual reality of today's financial world, the picture is of atoms spinning apart in the dark" (Archbishop of Canterbury website, Dec. 25, 2011 <http://www.archbishopofcanterbury.org/articles.php/2292/>).
>
> Durkheim, himself, could not have stated the problem more eloquently.

Although the destruction in downtown Vancouver horrified most Canadians, this vandalism was minor in comparison to the widespread urban violence that broke out two months later in many English cities — on August 7, 2011. These disturbances began in the London borough of Tottenham and were precipitated by the police shooting of an unarmed Afro-Caribbean man — a motorist named Mark Duggan. Within hours, the riot had spread to other London boroughs and to other cities — including Manchester, Salford, Liverpool, Nottingham and Birmingham. Some observers concluded that London had not seen devastation on this scale since the Blitz in World War II.

The aftermath of these riots was accompanied by a predictable flurry of soul-searching, hand-wringing and recrimination — among media pundits, politicians, clergy and the general public. Everyone, it seemed wanted to offer an instant explanation for these disturbances, as well as an instant fix. In Vancouver, both Mayor Gregor Robertson and Police Chief Jim Chu initially blamed the violence on "anarchists," until it became clear that no real anarchists had taken part in these disturbances. In the U.K., Secretary for Justice Kenneth Clarke blamed the riots on "a feral underclass" — a description that demonized the rioters as wild animals, devoid of any humanity, and caused acting commissioner of the Metropolitan police, Tim Godwin, to disassociate himself from these comments. Meanwhile, the mayor of London, Boris Johnson, impatiently dismissed what he labelled "economic and sociological justifications" for the riots. Even before the dust had settled and the fires extinguished, the war of words had already begun: in the newspapers, on TV and radio talk shows, and on internet blog sites. The orgy of violence and destruction had left in its wake a host of competing explanations, as well as proposals designed to prevent the reoccurrence of these events. Predictably, these attempts to make sense of all the chaos ranged widely across the political spectrum — from the far right to the far left and everywhere in-between.

For leading conservative commentators, the riots were explained quite simply in terms of the "pure criminality" of the rioters. Images of looters hauling away stolen merchandise, often in branded store bags, only served to reinforce the conviction of many observers that these were opportunistic crimes. The looters wanted the same things as the rest of us, except that they were unwilling, or unable, to pay for them. There were even some published reports of looters who tried on store clothes to check their fit, before stealing them. There appeared to be no political motive for these actions, only hyper-consumerism.

Besides emphasizing the wanton criminality of the rioters, conservatives also speculated on other factors that may have contributed to the disturbances, including the alleged failure of the penal system to adequately punish or deter juvenile crime; the high incidence of family breakdown and single parent households — especially among low income groups; and a perceived decline in public morality and traditional values. Needless to say, these explanations were often followed by equally tough-minded proposals for dealing with these or any future disturbances. Some British tabloids — the *Daily Mail* for example — advocated the use of plastic bullets and water canons, as well as the deployment of the army, to contain the violence on the streets. Previously, these measures had only ever been used within the U.K. in Northern Ireland. Almost everyone insisted on tougher sentences for law breakers and far less leniency for juvenile offenders. Many Facebook and Twitter feeds went even further, some calling for "shoot to kill" crowd control policies, others for the return of such Victorian remedies as compulsory sterilization of those convicted of civil disorders.

On the other hand, liberal and left-wing commentators were more willing to ascribe the causes of the riots to underlying social and economic conditions. Many blamed government cutbacks and other neoliberal policies that have led to increasing economic inequality and social polarization. In his analysis of the Vancouver riot, Murray Dobbin (2011) had this to say:

> It seems to me that one of the broad reasons is the systematic attack on government and indirectly on community. The pillars of neo-liberalism and globalization all attack community: privatization, starving government through tax cuts, deregulation — another term for capitalist free-for-all, the slashing of social programs and the commercialization of everything.

Socially marginalized inner city neighbourhoods and toxic housing estates are seen as breeding grounds for crime, substance abuse and family breakdown. In some ethnic communities, racist police attitudes and practices have been cited as reasons for a general distrust and disrespect of the law. Others believe that the sense of entitlement and impunity displayed by many rioters is a direct result of the recently exposed corruption at the very top of society — at least in the U.K. The scandals that have plagued the financial, media and political elites has created a pervasive climate of cynicism and disrespect for law and order, and a widespread contempt for the authority of the state. For some observers, the rot in British society began at the top and has simply worked its way down to the bottom. Whereas the conservatives argue for a stronger law-and-order agenda and a return to more traditional family and civic values, the liberal/left calls for greater income redistribution, youth employment programs, more educational and training opportunities, and greater social inclusion. Each side of the political spectrum believes that while it has pin-pointed the underlying causes of the social crisis, the opposition has only addressed the symptoms.

The polarization of the left and the right over how to interpret and deal with social unrest is an old story. The French Revolution gave us both radicals and reactionaries; and all subsequent revolutions and movements for social change have had their apologists and their critics. The question of what causes social unrest and political upheaval has preoccupied generations of social thinkers. It was certainly a question that French social theorist Emile Durkheim took seriously. Indeed, had Durkheim witnessed the riots in London or Vancouver he undoubtedly would have seen these events as examples of a pathological social condition he called "anomie."

Anomie, for Durkheim, was a state in which individuals no longer feel any real connection to each other, nor any sense of responsibility to a community. More than anything else, anomie is experienced as a state of social detachment in which the individual no longer feels any strong bonds of group membership — whether to the family, the local community, the church or the nation. In the modern world, the demands of group membership have become increasing remote and abstract. Few social ties last for a lifetime, and few loyalties or codes of conduct are fixed. We are, once we become adults, pretty much alone out there to blaze our own trail and determine our own destiny. This is the individualism that has come to define the modern world. But as Durkheim suggested, if all social ties are eventually dissolved and traditional moral restraints are dismissed as irrelevant, we have reached a pathological state of hyper-individualism, of anomie. And this is a state when bad things are more likely to happen — suicide, homicide, crime, alcoholism, drug addition and civil disorder. Or, in the words of the Archbishop of Canterbury: "The picture is of atoms spinning apart in the dark."

Durkheim in the Digital Age

When Durkheim first announced that one of the most serious problems of modern society was anomie, he really hit the jackpot. While Marx may have foreseen the growth of global capitalism and Weber may have anticipated the perils of totalitarianism, it was Durkheim who first diagnosed the social malaise that would eventually spread in so many directions. As we shall see, there has long been academic disagreement over the best way to translate the concept of "anomie." However, most social theorists recognize that the term signifies a fundamental problem in the way individuals fit into society. Durkheim realized that during periods of rapid social change, especially when individuals were being uprooted from traditional communities, many found great difficulty in adjusting to the impersonal and anonymous conditions of modern life. To Durkheim's trained eye, traditional communities provided most individuals with a well-defined social identity, as well as a strong sense of meaning and purpose. People who lived and worked in small communities normally knew who they were, accepted their place in society and understood their purpose in life. Small communities were normally tightly integrated through local institutions such as the family, the church, the school, village council, volunteer fire department, baseball team, Masonic lodge, women's institute and so on. These institutions not only reinforced the identities of members of the community but also helped to socialize individuals into a common set of norms and values. Most people were well integrated into their local community and were guided and regulated by its customary rules and beliefs. This is not to idealize or mythologize small town life — whether in a Newfoundland outport, a First Nations reserve, a Quebec village or a small town on the Prairies, which has always been more complex than nostalgic images acknowledge. Traditional communities are often integrated through strong informal social controls and rigid conformity, and outward appearances sometimes conceal a dark side of prejudice, hypocrisy and even of violence. One of the more astute observers of small town life in Canada who quickly discerned the gap between appearance and reality was Stephen Leacock, in books such as *Sunshine Sketches of a Little Town*.

All this began to change with the growth of towns and cities and with the inevitable migration of people from rural areas to urban centres. In the big city, individuals truly became individuals for the first time in history — alone and often unattached to traditional networks of kinship, religion or community. Life in the big city or the boom town seemed to offer unlimited new experiences and opportunities, while many of the old community-based norms and values no longer served as a practical guide for modern living. But without their traditional standards of right and wrong, many individuals succumbed to a state of moral confusion and social isolation — a state of excessive individualism. One Durkheim expert suggested:

> Durkheim called anomie 'the malady of infinite aspiration.' His central idea was that human beings need regulation — a framework of informal and formal rules that set limits to what they are entitled to expect, for instance, in the form of economic rewards. It is an idea that contrasts sharply with the culture of capitalism, not least its U.S. version. Could there be any more striking contrast with his idea than the culture of Wall Street and the City of London in the last three decades? (Lukes 1972: x, 2008)

For Durkheim then, the problem of anomie reflected a state of "excessive individualism," which involved large numbers of people who were uprooted from their traditional livelihoods and thrown into new urban environments, where they were left to sink or swim on their own. Today, some of the worst problems of anomie — those caused by uprooted populations moving from traditional into modern social environments — are experienced by rural migrants and refugees from the Global South who are pushed or pulled into sprawling metropolises around the world. In many ways, this process may be seen as a repeat of the history of eighteenth- and nineteenth-century European urbanization on a larger and more brutal scale. Indeed, the global explosion of immigrant shanty towns and squatter settlements has led one writer to refer to the present era of urbanization as a *Planet of the Slums* (Davis 2006). But even for those of us who live in the relatively settled and affluent states of the Global North, problems of anomie plague our lives in a number of ways that Durkheim would have both understood and expected.

One of the central problems of contemporary societies, social isolation is variously described by social commentators and cultural critics as "civil privatism" (Habermas 1975: 75), "loneliness" (Reisman 1950) and "alienation" (Fromm 1942; 1941). If Durkheim recoiled from what he considered to be the excessive individualism of post-revolutionary France, he would have been profoundly disturbed by the rampant "hyper-individualism" of our contemporary digital age.

The problem of anomie appears to be increasing rather than diminishing in the general population. In a recent study conducted in the U.K., and published in 2008, researchers discovered that 97 percent of communities studied have become more socially fragmented over the past three decades. The primary cause of this social fragmentation remains linked — as it was for Durkheim — to mobility. Today, people are on the move for many reasons. Rising income levels have made it easier to move for work, education, retirement or — simply for a new life. Marital breakdowns, divorces, overseas migration and growing student populations have also contributed to rising rates of mobility. Increased mobility has resulted in less rooted communities, lower levels of social integration and participation, and a deepening sense of "not belonging."

The irony of today's information society is that the present culture of hyper-individualism is accompanied by the ever more frenetic efforts of individuals to stay "fully networked" and "connected" to each other, through computers, smart phones and tablets and the ubiquitous social media. Nowadays, many individuals try to stay

> **Figure 10-2 The Loneliness of Contemporary Life**
>
> Community life in Britain has weakened substantially over the past 30 years, according to research commissioned by the BBC. Analysis of census data reveals how neighbourhoods in every part of the U.K. have become more socially fragmented. The study assesses the health of a community by looking at how rooted people are in their neighbourhood. Academics created "loneliness indices," to identify where people had a "feeling of not belonging." The study ranks places using a formula based on the proportion of people in an area who are single, those who live alone, the numbers in private rented accommodation and those who have lived there for less than a year. The higher the proportion of people in those categories, the less rooted the community, according to social scientists. They refer to it as the level of "anomie" or the "feeling of not belonging."
>
> Easton 2008.

connected wherever they happen to be — at home, at work, in their cars, in busses, airports, restaurants, on the street. It almost seems as though we are fearful of losing our connection to each other, however momentary and contrived these connections may be. The popularity of social networking sites such as Facebook, MySpace and Twitter further indicates this search for friendship, companionship or simple social contact. The larger profile of this digital wasteland was partially revealed in an article in the *Times* of London:

> Digital technology has advanced human communication to an extent that was barely imaginable even a decade ago. But its ubiquity conceals a paradox.... Even among young people, the availability of social networking may disguise a lack of personal contact and rootlessness. A recent Samaritans survey found that young people worried still more than the elderly about loneliness.... In a digital age, it is possible to buy the names of Facebook 'friends' as a status symbol and sometimes, dispiritingly, as a substitute for 'real' virtual friends." (Dec. 31, 2009: 2)

If, as is suggested by credible sources, our contemporary culture is afflicted by an endemic state of anomie, this would help to explain the remarkable displays of collective sentiment that followed public events such as the death of Princess Diana in 1997 and the royal wedding in 2011 in the U.K., and in Canada, the Vancouver Olympic Games in 2010 and the Stanley Cup riot in Vancouver, not to mention the riots in cities in the U.K. in 2011. Each of these occasions, in its own way, provided an excuse for a collective sharing of emotion and an (albeit temporary) opportunity for group inclusion and heightened social solidarity. Many New Yorkers testified to the surprisingly close sense of community that emerged in their city during the aftermath of 9/11. A state of anomie, which normally suppresses the need for intimate social contact, becomes most transparent when it is breached. The deeper the general sense of anonymity and impersonality, the more intense will be those infrequent expressions of collective sentiment which, however briefly, overcompensate for a culture of hyper-individualism.

Anomie and the Culture of Selfishness

The thread that runs throughout much of Durkheim's work is his concern with the problem of how the individual fits into modern society. Modernity, says Durkheim, is a mixed blessing. While it has opened the door to new and seemingly unlimited opportunity, it can also precipitate a freefall into moral confusion and social isolation. According to Durkheim, the problem of anomie is especially acute during periods of rapid economic change — whether downward cycles of recession or depression, or upward cycles of rapid growth and sudden prosperity. Both economic boom and bust cycles contribute to a weakening of collective norms and values and to a loosening of social ties.

Besides the endemic symptoms of loneliness and estrangement already mentioned, anomie may also be expressed in other social problems. The age of hyper-individualism is an age of unlimited appetites and overblown ambitions. It is an age in which anything seems possible and everything appears available. Old moral restraints that once regulated desire are abandoned, and individuals pursue their particular "dreams" without much thought or concern for each other, or for the larger community. Durkheim (1951: 253) vividly describes the moral chaos of anomie:

> One no longer knows what is possible and what is not, what is just and what is unjust, which claims and expectations are legitimate and which are immoderate. As a result there is no limit to men's aspirations ... appetites, no longer restrained by a disoriented public opinion, no longer know where to stop.... From top to bottom of the scale, greed is aroused unable to find ultimate foothold. Nothing could calm it, since its goal is infinitely beyond all it can attain.... A thirst arises for novelties, unfamiliar pleasures, nameless sensations, all of which lose their savor once known.

Durkheim's description of anomic social relations could easily be applied to the run-up to the financial crisis that broke in 2008 (Novak 2004). Indeed, the vast accumulation of super-profits by the banks, mortgage companies and investment houses, and the gigantic bonuses and fees paid out to investment bankers, hedge fund managers and other financiers before the bubble finally burst, provides a spectacle of unrestrained greed and avarice not seen since the Gilded Age of the late nineteenth century. Even the politically conservative *Telegraph* newspaper recognized the tell-tale signs of public anomie: "The credit crunch will generate a wave of anomie" (Taylor 2008). Today, the symptoms of public anomie are manifested in a number of different ways — some more pathological than others. At the lower end of the anomic scale is the desperate search for self-affirmation and recognition that preoccupies so many individuals in our society. The rise of the celebrity culture, the popularity of reality TV shows and the relentless tide of self-promotion through social media and networking sites testify to a widespread need for self-celebration and self-celebritization (see Lasch 1979 for a detailed discussion of narcissism in society).

The culture of anomie has also produced more destructive social side-effects, more aggressive forms of behaviour. Some social observers (Reich 1933; Poulantzas 1974; Hoffer 1951) suggested a link between the widespread social fragmentation and demoralization that follows war and revolution and the rise of demagogues and populist political leaders. An obvious example is the rise of Adolph Hitler in the aftermath of the defeat and postwar humiliation of Germany in 1914. A similar case could be made for the rise of Napoleon in post-revolutionary France, Mussolini in Italy and many other "strongmen," "caudillos" and dictators. Profound disenchantment with political institutions has always been fertile ground for the rise of demagogues who offer simplistic and appealing "solutions" to the complex social problems of their day. Robert Nisbet recognized this many years ago in *The Quest for Community*, when he observed: "The greatest appeal of the totalitarian party, Marxist or other, lies in its capacity to provide a sense of moral coherence and communal membership to those who have become, to one degree or another, victims of the sense of exclusion from the ordinary channels of belonging in society" (1990: 32). Today, in the second decade of the second millennium, the Tea Party in the U.S. appears to be thriving on a state of anomie that has gripped some sections of the American public in the aftermath of the financial crisis and two costly overseas wars — in Afghanistan and Iraq. In Europe, there has been a resurgence of radical right-wing political parties — the Front National in France, the Northern League in Italy, the Freedom Party in Austria, the Lijst Pim Fortuyn in the Netherlands and the British Nationalist Party and English Defence League in the U.K. — which have capitalized on growing concerns over immigration, perceived threats to national sovereignty and, of course, the financial crisis.

Anomie has also been used to explain other manifestations of social violence, including, for example, soccer hooliganism in France and Britain (see Bodin, Héas and Robène 2004; Taylor 1971, 1982), as well as violent political protests among young people in the townships of South Africa (Marks 1992). Other writers have suggested that anomie can also been seen in the relentless search for new and ever more bizarre experiences and spectacles. Extreme sports, dark (or death) tourism (see Tarlow, n.d.), extreme pornography, as well as passing fads such as "happy slapping," body piercing, tattooing, bungee jumping, parkour (or free running) and "planking" all testify, in their own ways, to the insatiable need in a culture of hyper-individualism to push beyond the limits of "convention."

At the other end of the continuum of social attachment, Durkheim identified the problem of "altruism": the willingness of individuals to sacrifice themselves for the greater good of the collectivity — whether a national, racial or ethnic, religious or tribal or other social group. Whereas the pathology of anomie was explained as the under-attachment of the individual to the collectivity, the pathology of altruism was explained as the over-attachment of the individual to the collectivity. The major social indicator that Durkheim used to illustrate the social pathologies of anomie (egoism) and altruism was the rate of suicide. In his study of suicide Durkheim expanded upon his concepts of anomie and altruism, and integrated them into his evolutionary theory of society.

Studying Suicide

Durkheim's book *Suicide* (1897) remains an important landmark in the history of sociology for a number of reasons. First, it is one of earliest examples of empirical research. Whereas most other social theorists of his age remained locked in theoretical discussions and debates, Durkheim was among the first to break out of social philosophy into the brave new world of social research. He was, in this sense, a pioneer in the use of empirical research methods. Second, *Suicide* also provides us with an example of how to integrate theory and research. Durkheim never conducted research simply to collect, count or classify social facts for their own sake. Research for Durkheim was always driven by strong theoretical interests, and even though many of his methods and conclusions may now be questioned (or even rejected), he still provides us with a model for integrating theory and research.

The study of suicide provided Durkheim with an opportunity to demonstrate the importance of "social facts," that is, facts that have an independent social existence which cannot be fully reduced to psychological or biological explanations. Suicide or, more precisely, "the rate of suicide" in society, is a powerful example of a social fact. Durkheim made it clear that he was not interested in the individual causes of suicide. He did not attempt to collect or analyze individual suicide notes, nor did he propose any study of the family or psychological backgrounds of suicide victims. He was primarily interested in comparing the suicide rates between different societies, as well as between different social groups within the same society. Durkheim believed that the rate of suicide could be used as an empirical indicator of a breakdown in the social mechanisms that normally function to integrate individuals into society, and regulate their actions. Suicide was an indicator of a social (rather than a psychological or biological) pathology.

After examining the suicide rates for a number of European countries, Durkheim concluded that populations with certain sociological characteristics showed a higher frequency of suicide than populations with different characteristics. These statistical data showed that the incidence of suicide was related to the following sociological factors:

- the suicide rate for men was higher than the rate for women;
- the suicide rate for Protestants was higher than the rate for Catholics;
- the suicide rate for Catholics was higher than the rate for Jews;
- the suicide rate for single males was higher than the rate for married males;
- the suicide rate for married women was higher than the rate for single women; and

- the suicide rate for a parent with several children was higher than the rate for a parent with few children.

Durkheim insisted that the causes of these statistical differences could best be explained in terms of sociological factors. Take for instance that the rate of suicide for Protestants was higher than that of Catholics. Dukheim rejected any notion that the differential rates of suicide could be explained by doctrinal differences in the beliefs of Catholics and Protestants — both religions strongly proscribe suicide. Instead, Durkheim concluded that Protestants had a different relationship to their religious community than Catholics. He argued that Protestantism is founded on the spirit of free inquiry. Protestants are individually free to question the meaning of the "Holy Scriptures," unlike Catholics, who traditionally have had to accept the doctrines of the Church as set out by the ecclesiastical authority of the pope and his officials. Protestantism is also a relatively unstructured religious community. In Protestant churches, there is no priesthood, no confessional, no liturgy and very few ritualized forms of collective devotion. In contrast to Catholics, Protestants "stand alone before their God" — without the support of priests, or the intercession of other symbolic figures such as the Virgin Mary. In other words, Protestants, rather than Catholics, exemplify the individualism of contemporary society — with all the personal responsibility and anxiety that this condition entails.

In contrast to Protestants, Durkheim suggested that Catholics still inhabited a relatively structured religious culture and were part of a more cohesive religious community. Unlike Protestantism, Catholicism still included many elements of a shared set of beliefs and practices. Together, these elements — such as the priesthood, the sacraments, the doctrinal orthodoxy — provided Catholics with a strong sense of collective identity.

Durkheim's great achievement was to interpret the statistical data of different suicide rates in terms of his general evolutionary theory of society. He concluded that Catholics had a lower frequency of suicide than Protestants because they were more socially integrated into their religious community and were subject to greater moral regulation than were their Protestant counterparts. In other words, the religious world of Catholicism exhibited a stronger "conscience collective" than that of Protestantism.

There are, of course, some interesting parallels between the ways in which both Durkheim and Weber theorized the historical significance of Protestants. Durkheim saw Protestants as a prototype of the new modern individual — alone in the world, without the support of a strong traditional conscience collective. Weber also saw Protestants as alone in the world, gripped with doctrinal uncertainties and anxieties regarding their predestined fates and afterlives. For Durkheim, this new social isolation and anxiety was a primary cause of rising suicide rates. For Weber, it was a major factor in the rise of industrial capitalism. However, whereas Durkheim studied suicide as an objective social fact, Weber studied the Protestant ethic as a rationalized type of subjectively meaningful social action. While both theorists arrived at a similar conclusion regarding the social and spiritual isolation of Protestants, each reached his conclusion through a different method of empirical social analysis — one which examined the objective social facts of collective behaviour, and the other which examined

> **Figure 10-3 Egoism and the Individual**
>
> The more weakened the groups to which he belongs, the less he depends on them, the more he consequently depends only on himself and recognizes no other rules of conduct than what are founded on private interest. If we agree to call this state egoism, in which the individual ego asserts itself to excess in the face of the social ego and at its expense, we may call egoistic the special type of suicide springing from excessive individualism.
>
> (Durkheim 1951 [1897]: 209)

the subjective meaning of individual action. But when all is said and done, Durkheim was one of the earliest modern social thinkers to integrate his social theory so closely with his social research.

Types of Suicide

Durkheim's theory of suicide is closely related to his evolutionary theory of society. His central thesis maintains that, as societies evolve from simple to more complex forms of social organization, there is a corresponding weakening of the conscience collective. In simple societies, there is typically a very strong and well defined conscience collective. However, in more complex societies, the conscience collective grows weaker, more diffuse, more abstract and less commanding. Whereas the conscience collective in simple society expresses a strong sense of collective identity, in a more complex society this sense of shared identity is progressively eroded and fragmented into many different group and individual identities. Durkheim saw the erosion of the conscience collective in modern society as an increasingly serious social problem. In traditional society, the conscience collective had served to integrate the individual into society and to morally regulate the individual according to the established norms and values. Without a strong mechanism for the social integration of members of society, Durkheim feared that individuals would lose their sense of shared identity and abandon any commonly held rules and regulations for socially acceptable behaviour. In the complex, urban, industrial setting, modern people were rootless, isolated and morally adrift. Durkheim offered his study of suicide as an example of his evolutionary theory of society. Data on comparative suicide rates within and between European states suggested four different types of suicide in nineteenth-century Europe.

Egoistic Suicide

The first type of suicide occurs in situations where the social bonds linking individuals to social groups (such as the family, the church and the community) are weak. As a result, the individual may face a world in which any sense of personal meaning and purpose is loose, or even absent. Empty lives are often vulnerable to alcoholism, drug abuse or other addictions — such as gambling or compulsive sex. And, as Durkheim concluded, they are also vulnerable to suicide. Above all, the problem of egoistic suicide is a problem of excessive individualism caused by a lack of social integration into any supportive social structures. In this respect, egoistic suicide differs from anomic suicide inasmuch as the latter is caused by a lack of moral regulation — as outlined below.

Anomic Suicide

The second type of suicide occurs in situations where individuals are exposed to countless and unlimited new opportunities for personal gratification of their desires — the "malady of infinite aspirations" — without any clear moral rules to guide their conduct. The problem of anomie is essentially a problem of "normlessness." Durkheim saw the problem of anomie as a transitional state. It was precipitated by the very rapid transformation of simple into complex societies

In more recent times, some critics (Pope 1976; Pickering and Walford 2000: 1–10; Phillips, Ruth and MacNamara 1994: 90–100; Lehmann 1995: 904–30) suggest that Durkheim's categories of egoistic and anomic suicide overlap with each other. Indeed, they are merely opposite sides of the same coin. Both categories are related to the problem of modernity. Durkheim's own examples of egoistic and anomic types of suicide include those cases associated with business crises when the personal fortunes of individuals may be lost in financial disasters. These types of suicide are often associated with rapid downward social mobility brought about through economic depressions. However, Durkheim also recognized that rapid upward social mobility can be just as disintegrative. This is often the case for migrants and other transient individuals who travel to "boom towns" or other areas of expanding economic opportunity. These areas of rapid economic growth may also experience relatively high rates of egoistic and anomic suicide.

Altruistic Suicide

The third type of suicide is more likely in simple societies. This type of suicide occurs in situations where the individual is strongly integrated, or even over-integrated, into the social order. As a result, the collective interest of the society is placed above the private interest of the individual. Altruistic suicide is thus a case of individuals willing to sacrifice themselves for the benefit of the larger community or society.

Most examples of altruistic suicide come from traditional cultures — such as the long discontinued practice of "senicide" (killing the elderly) during times of famine, when the elderly members of the community would some-times voluntarily sacrifice themselves in order to reduce the pressure on food and other resources. Another example is the ritual military suicides ("*seppuku*," more vulgarly known as "*hara-kiri*") of Japanese samurai warriors; or the Japanese (*kamikaze*) suicide pilots during World War II. The self-immolation of Buddhist monks during the Vietnam War is another example. Altruistic suicide was often driven by concerns over honour, respect and duty. The individual was deeply conscious of their community obligations and respon-sibilities. As Durkheim observed,

> When a person kills himself … it is not because he assumes the right to do so but, on the contrary, because it is his duty. If he fails in this obligation, he is dishonoured and also punished, usually, by religious sanctions…. Now, we have seen that if such a person insists on living he loses public respect; in one case the usual funeral honours are denied, in another a life of horror is supposed to await him beyond the grave. The weight of society is thus brought to bear on him to lead him to destroy himself. (1979: 219)

In Western societies, examples of altruistic suicide are few and far between. Recent examples might include ten Irish Republican hunger strik-ers in Northern Ireland (1981) who were members of closely knit political organizations — although each of these organizations tried unsuccessfully to dissuade its members from undertaking these strikes. Earlier in the twentieth century, a number of suffragette hunger strikers also lost their lives through being force-fed when imprisoned for their campaign for women's franchise (Purvis 1996). Many cases of altruistic suicide in the West are linked to politi-cal struggles for social justice. In all of these cases, the individuals involved were highly motivated by a strong set of beliefs and united within a tightly integrated community or organization.

Today, the most dramatic and troubling examples of altruistic suicide are the suicide bombers, who have killed themselves, and many others, in such places as Sri Lanka, Chechnya, Palestine and Israel, Lebanon, Afghanistan, Iraq, Pakistan and Kashmir — as well as in several European capitals. The most famous are the 9/11 suicide attacks — when nineteen men hijacked three commercial jets and crashed two of them into the World Trade Towers in New York City, killing themselves and over 3,000 other people. The sacrificial meaning of these attacks can be seen in the many martyr-dom videos made by the *shaheeds* (martyrs) who sacrificed their own lives in order to attack these "enemy targets." For obvious reasons, many writers have been reluctant to classify these suicide bombings as "altruistic." Such a designation could appear to confer a false legitimacy on what are unarguably acts of appalling violence. Nevertheless, notwithstanding the horrific nature of these acts, suicide bombings may still be "altruistic" suicide. First, many of the bombers are members of closed and tightly knit political, military or religious organizations — such as Hamas (Palestine), Hezbollah (Lebanon), the Taliban (Afghanistan-Pakistan), the Tamil Tigers (Sri Lanka) and Al-Qaeda (global). As Durkheim suggested, such individuals have a strong attachment to and integration into their particular group. Second, as several researchers (Atran 2004; 2006) have discovered, many suicide bombers are drawn from the wealthier and more educated sections of their communities; they are not normally driven by poverty, ignorance or privation. Finally, these attacks are often justified by those involved as resistance to foreign invasion and occupation, or as retribution for the killing of family, tribal, ethnic or religious compatriots. In all these senses, the suicide attack is undertaken on behalf of a larger collectivity and is, therefore, "sacrificial" in its intent.

At the same time, the issue of how best to classify and explain suicide attacks remains controversial. Research (Holdredge, no date; Zevallos 2006) has shown the futility of generalizing

Figure 10-4 Terrorists or Martyrs?

Suicide as a Weapon of Mass Destruction: Emile Durkheim Revisited

[Altruistic suicide can be] associated with ... [some] socio-religious system [that] stress "insufficient individuation." That is, a premium is placed on rigid doctrinal conformity and the propensity to dissolve one's individual identity in larger wholes. Transcendence of the individual Self and its dissolution into an all-encompassing Cosmic Being is the ultimate form of salvation.... This tendency is at the heart of the mystical traditions [such as] ... Hinduism and Buddhism ... [and] is a key doctrinal aspect of Islam.... It enjoins complete submission to the will of Almighty God, Allah ... [finding] its maximal expression in ... the doctrine of Jihad — the obligation to wage holy war against unbelievers without regard to personal comfort or even survival. Today's Muslim radicals, Osama bin Laden in particular, have harnessed this concept ... of absolute subordination of self to the greater cause, as perhaps never before in all of Islamic history.... It is this realization that compels the U.S. and the other secular states ... to stop dismissing jihadis as mindless killers who take perverse joy in killing and maiming innocents. They are in fact "true believers."

Harold A. Gould, *Counterpunch*, 2003, Weekend Edition November 28–30, <http://www.counterpunch.org/2003/11/28/suicide-as-wmd/>.

about these events: the motive and execution of each attack differs depending upon its origin and context. Thus, while many Palestinian suicide attacks are freely undertaken by "martyrs" (or *shaheeds*) who volunteer for these "operations," this is not always the case in other conflict zones. Suicide missions undertaken by the Black Widows in Chechnya, for example, may be the last resort of women whose lives have been irrevocably ruined by rape and humiliation at the hands of Russian troops. Similarly, many Tamil Tiger suicide bombers have been coerced by threats against their families. Such attacks are more fittingly described as "fatalistic" rather then "altruistic." Even supposed volunteer attackers can be described and explained in other than "altruistic" terms. Most volunteer suicide attacks are carried out by single men, who have neither wives nor children. According to Durkheim, single men have the highest probability of anomic suicide because of their weak attachments to family and community. Many of these attacks, therefore, may more accurately be classified as "anomic" rather than as "altruistic." In view of the nuances surrounding the diverse motives of suicide attacks, some researchers have refined their definition of altruism in order to distinguish "anomic," "fatalistic" and "altruistic" suicide terrorists (Bates 2010) — bearing in mind that Durkheim, himself, differentiated between three types of altruistic suicide — obligatory, optional and acute.

Fatalistic Suicide

The last type of suicide mentioned by Durkheim is relegated to a brief footnote in his work. This type of suicide occurs in situations where individuals are oppressed by excessive constraint, or over-regulation. In Durkheim's own words, these are situations, "of persons with futures piteously blocked and passions violently choked by excessive discipline" (1951: 276, footnote). Fatalistic suicide is typically found in simple societies with very strong consciences collectives and harsh, repressive codes of morality and justice. In such societies, individuals may have little or no personal freedom or autonomy. Durkheim's examples include the cases of slaves and prisoners, married women without children, and others whose hopeless situations lead them into desperation and despair. More recently, fatalistic suicide may be found in those societies where women are deprived of their most basic human rights. Highly patriarchal societies in which young girls are forced into "arranged" marriages with much older men, or trafficked into sexual slavery, or threatened with "honour killings" by family members, may experience

Figure 10-5 Suicide and Social Structure

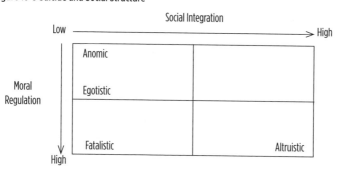

high rates of female fatalistic suicide. But in comparison to the three other types of suicide, fatalistic suicide is the least common.

Settling Accounts

In much the same way as Marx, Weber and other social thinkers covered in this book, Durkheim "settled accounts" with a number of intellectual and ideological traditions. Durkheim developed his own distinctive approach to the study of society from his critical responses to several earlier traditions. Durkheim's perspective on the study of society is sometimes referred to as the "sociologistic" perspective, which means that Durkheim focused on the large-scale objective structures and processes of society rather than on the day-to-day subjective experiences of individuals.

Durkheim's theory of society was shaped by his attitude towards the major emergent political ideologies of his day. He was particularly opposed to three powerful political ideologies that exercised considerable influence in nineteenth-century France and that continue to influence politics today.

Durkheim and Liberalism

Durkheim rejected the utilitarian philosophy, which formed the intellectual backbone of the British tradition of liberalism. Often known as the principle of *laissez-faire* (or non-intervention) this philosophy proposed that society (especially the economy) works best when individuals are left alone to pursue their own (rational) self-interests. Or, stated more formally, the greatest good for the largest number of people is best secured through the unregulated pursuit of individual, rational self-interest. This doctrine was espoused by many English and Scottish social theorists, including Adam Smith, John Stuart Mill, Jeremy Bentham and, notably, Herbert Spencer.

Durkheim, however, disagreed with the fundamental premise of *laissez-faire*. For him, selfishness and excessive individualism were problems to be overcome rather than principles to be embraced. In common with most French social theorists (including Rousseau, Saint-Simon, Comte and de Tocqueville), Durkheim was convinced that any society was ultimately held together by a common set of moral beliefs — a moral order. Without a moral order, any society was in danger of disintegrating into a mass of competing individuals. In the case of France, Durkheim concluded that such a state of normlessness and anarchy had already led to the development of serious social problems and dysfunctional behaviour. Durkheim's critique of liberalism, therefore, sprang from his disbelief that any moral order could arise spontaneously from the selfish actions of individuals. He did not believe that a stable moral order could emerge from the economic market. On the contrary, he felt that a moral order was needed to regulate the natural selfishness of individuals and to integrate them into a harmonious set of social relations.

Durkheim rejected liberalism because, in his view, it was unable to address the fundamental questions of political stability and moral order in society.

But in one sense, Durkheim — along with Montesquieu and De Tocqueville — represented the tradition of French liberalism. Each of these thinkers championed basic human freedoms — of speech, thought and assembly — as well as the separation of government powers (executive, legislative and judicial). They were also political pluralists inasmuch as they supported the growth of non-governmental institutions such as the family, community, church, schools and colleges, and other voluntary organizations. In other words, they recognized the importance of what we today would call civil society — as buffers, or checks and balances, against the totalitarian power of the state. In this respect, they differed from many of the radicals of the French Revolution for whom the state was the ultimate expression of the popular will.

Durkheim and Socialism/Communism

Durkheim rejected the ideas of the socialists and communists and their programs for social reconstruction. He did, however, understand the social forces that had led to the deep class divisions in capitalist society, condemn the exploitation of the working class and sympathize with the misery of the destitute. Indeed, Durkheim identified the exploitation of the working class as a major social problem, one which he saw as an unhealthy, or pathological, distortion of a normal division of labour. He referred to this distortion as the "anomic division of labour." Durkheim criticized the socialist/Marxist theory of society because, in his view, it overemphasized economics and grossly underemphasized moral order. In fact, Durkheim concluded that Marxism shared with liberalism an overemphasis on economics. While liberalism recommended a return to the forces of the marketplace, Marxism recommended the collective ownership of production as a remedy for all major forms of social injustice. Durkheim opposed what he perceived as economic reductionism or determinism. Throughout his entire career, he insisted on the autonomy of social, or moral, facts. Consequently, although he remained sympathetic to the problems addressed by the socialists (he was a friend of French socialist Jean Jaurès), Durkheim concluded that socialism/Marxism should be seen as a symptom of the pathology of modern industrial society rather than as a cure.

Durkheim and Conservatism

Durkheim rejected the conservatism of many social thinkers of his time, especially the romantic-conservatives (such as Louis de Bonald and Joseph de Maistre). However, his own theory was influenced more by conservative ideas than by the other two major ideologies. Yet, Durkheim did not believe that it was either possible, or desirable, to turn back the historical clock. He had no desire to see a return of the *ancien régime* in France, and he had little sympathy for the downfall of the traditional French elites. In fact, Durkheim was a political and social progressive in regards to many of the pressing issues of his day. He supported the principles of the French Revolution as outlined in the Declaration of the Rights of Man and the Citizen. He also supported Captain Alfred Dreyfus, a French, Jewish military officer who was subjected to anti-Semitic persecution. Durkheim was an agnostic in his personal beliefs and supported the secularization of the French school system. At the same time, Durkheim was influenced by some conservative ideas, the most important of which were the idea of a moral community as a basis for social order and the idea of a society as a social organism made up of mutually interrelated parts. The idea of society as an organic unity composed of functionally interrelated institutions was a powerful and compelling image. It was almost inevitable that Durkheim, as a product of the French intellectual tradition, would incorporate some of these images and presuppositions into his own theory.

Durkheim thus stood between two distinct and opposing ideological traditions. On the one hand, he did not believe that it was either possible or desirable to turn back the historical clock and so rejected most of the romantic conservative ideas. But on the other hand, Durkheim did not share the unbounded optimism of the Enlightenment thinkers and their belief in the inevitable march of reason and progress. Nor did he put much faith in Marx's predictions of the imminent collapse of capitalism. Instead, Durkheim tried to keep his distance from strong ideological convictions. He remained a realistic theorist who saw the need to develop a systematic study of society based upon a careful observation of social facts.

Each of the three intellectual giants of nineteenth-century European social thought — Marx, Weber and Durkheim — was preoccupied with the issue of modernity. Each was concerned with the causes and the consequences of the break-up of traditional society and the birth of modern, urban, industrial capitalist society. The evidence of this transition crisis was all around them: the eviction of the peasantry from the countryside; the exploitation of the factory workers; the misery of the destitute in the cities; rising crime rates; and a host of other social problems. The agricultural and industrial revolutions across Europe had resulted in massive social upheavals. These changes sometimes led to outright political revolution (as in France), anti-colonial revolution (as in America) or to more gradual constitutional reforms (as in Great Britain). In the face of these changes, the leading social thinkers of the age attempted to analyze and explain the modernization of their societies and to propose ways of restoring social order. In this respect, Durkheim was no exception, and he devoted much of his work to the search for social order in a time of rapid social change.

Durkheim's first major work, *The Division of Labour in Society* (1893), was originally completed as his doctoral thesis. In it, Durkheim outlines his theoretical framework and key theoretical concepts for studying the historical transition from traditional to modern societies. At the same time, the book is also a polemic — an attack on the ideas of the British liberals/utilitarians, especially those of Herbert Spencer. Durkheim argues that unregulated individualism will never lead to the spontaneous emergence of social order. The utilitarians argued that just as economic order (in the marketplace) spontaneously emerges from the unregulated interaction of sellers and buyers (through supply and demand), social and moral order also emerges spontaneously from the unregulated interaction between free individuals in society. These beliefs have formed the core of classical liberalism from the time of Adam Smith to the present age of neoliberalism. Durkheim, however, remained unconvinced by this doctrine and offered a simple refutation. The utilitarians argued that any contract is honoured through mutual self-interest — the employer agrees to pay the worker at $20 per day, and the worker agrees to work for $20 per day. Durkheim countered that honouring any contract is based upon a pre-existing moral code. Otherwise, the self-interest of the employer would be to trick the worker into working without providing any pay. And the self-interest of the worker would be to trick the employer into payment without performing any work. Therefore, self-interest cannot be used to explain why contracts are honoured between parties.

The Division of Labour in Society also contains a critique of Augusts Comte, who assumed that the breakdown of traditional moral beliefs inevitably led to a state of anarchy and social disintegration. Comte believed that only his new scientific religion of humanity could save humans from the perils of modernity. Durkheim rejected this view of modernity much as he rejected utilitarianism. Neither tradition offered what Durkheim regarded as indispensable for any credible social analysis — the systematic study of empirical social facts. For Durkheim, the study of traditional and modern societies posed a fundamental question, sometimes referred to by sociologists as the "problem of social order": How are individuals integrated into modern societies when the moral beliefs that formerly integrated them into traditional societies have broken down and are no longer relevant to their lives? Durkheim's way of addressing this problem is to ask: How are patterns of social organization created, maintained and transformed over time?

Durkheim's Conceptual Toolbox

In addressing the problem of order in *The Division of Labour in Society*, Durkheim introduced the following key concepts, which have since become standard terms in the lexicon of sociology.

Division of Labour

This term was popularized by Adam Smith in *The Wealth of Nations* (1776). Durkheim observed in his own study that in the transition from traditional societies, the division of labour became progressively more complex and segmented. As Herbert Spencer had also concluded, the complex division of labour in societies is characterized by greater structural differentiation and greater functional specialization. The classic example of the complex, industrial division of labour is found in Adam Smith's discussion of the pin factory:

> One man draws out the wire, another straights it, a third cuts it, a fourth points it, a fifth grinds it at the top for receiving, the head; to make the head requires two or three distinct operations; to put it on is a peculiar business, to whiten the pins is another; it is even a trade by itself to put them into the paper; and the important business of making a pin is, in this manner, divided into about eighteen distinct operations, which, in some manufactories, are all performed by distinct hands, though in others the same man will sometimes perform two or three of them. I have seen a small manufactory of this kind where ten men only were employed, and where some of them consequently performed two or three distinct operations. But though they were very poor, and therefore but indifferently accommodated with the necessary machinery, they could, when they exerted themselves, make among them about twelve pounds of pins in a day. (Smith 1843 [1776]: Book 1, Chapter 1: 3)

Smith concluded that the greater division of labour led directly to more efficiency in the process of production. By emphasizing such characteristics as structural differentiation and functional specialization, Durkheim reveals his indebtedness to the doctrines of evolutionism and organicism. Another example of a complex division of labour is in the realm of science. Back in the sixteenth century, all aspects of scientific inquiry were contained in the discipline of "natural philosophy." By the nineteenth century, most of the established scientific disciplines had already evolved and were represented in institutions of higher learning. Today, the fragmentation of natural science continues unabated, including such specialties as cytogenetics, pharmacogenomics, astrobiochemistry, cryobiology and nanophysics, to mention only a few.

There are obvious differences between the division of labour in traditional and in modern societies. In hunting and gathering societies, for example, the division of labour was organized primarily by age and sex. Prestigious activities such as big game hunting, warrior training, magic and other shamanistic practices were largely performed by males. Females were left with the responsibilities for childcare, homemaking and the harvesting of edible wild foods. Similarly, the male band elders were likely to occupy a special status as counsellors and shaman-sorcerers.

Even in Canada and other industrial countries, there are significant differences in the division of labour between traditional and modern social settings. Those who come from small towns or villages, from outports or from First Nations reserves will have noticed some of these differences for themselves. In the small town or village, it is common for one individual to perform several different roles — whether as post office manager, mayor, volunteer fire fighter and sheriff, among others. However, in the city, each of these roles is normally performed by a specially trained individual.

Conscience Collective

Traditional societies are held together by a common set of moral beliefs, norms and values which Durkheim referred to as the "conscience collective" — (the collective consciousness or collective conscience). In his later work, Durkheim used the term "collective representations" to designate the prevailing belief system of any society. Durkheim defined conscience collective as follows: "The totality of beliefs and sentiments common to average citizens of the same society forms a determinate system which has its own life; one may call it the collective or common conscience" (Durkheim 1933: 79).

The conscience collective of any society refers primarily to the cultural and symbolic aspects of social reality. Everyone is born into a community of some kind, which shares a common set of cultural symbols. These symbols may be expressed in many forms — through language, ethnicity, nationality, law and even the money used as currency. These cultural symbols may be represented in tangible ways — through flags, anthems and costumes, for example. Durkheim argues in *The Division of Labour in Society* that traditional societies with a simple division of labour typically have very strong conscience collectives. Individuals in these societies share a common moral code which serves to integrate them into a uniform culture. However, with the increasing division of labour, the conscience collective is greatly weakened. In traditional societies, the conscience collective provides all individuals with a common set of moral standards, a common set of customs and traditions and a common sense of identity and shared history. These help to define the limits of acceptable behaviour and to provide the individual with a sense of belonging. In Durkheim's own words, the conscience collective serves both as a source of social integration and moral regulation.

Social Solidarity

Throughout his discussion of the division of labour in society and of the conscience collective, Durkheim focuses on the problem of social order: What enables a society to keep its members together, how are individuals integrated into social structures? Durkheim identifies what he believes to be the basis of social order in all societies: the condition he calls "social solidarity." This condition binds individuals together into social groups and makes social life possible. In many ways, this idea of social solidarity is similar to that of *"abbasiya"* — introduced centuries earlier by Ibn Khaldun. Durkheim concluded that although the moral bases of traditional societies had broken down, modern societies were evolving their own new forms of social solidarity. However, the social solidarity of modern societies was markedly different from that in traditional societies. Whereas traditional societies had been united on the basis of shared beliefs and customary practices, modern societies were held together by a network of interrelationships and interdependencies derived from a complex, highly specialized division of labour. If the members of traditional societies were viewed as homogenous peas in a pod, then the members of modern societies could be viewed as heterogeneous but interdependent parts of a living organism. This distinction led Durkheim to introduce his most famous typology — that of "mechanical" versus "organic" solidarity. This distinction is both a description of traditional and modern societies and a theory of societal evolution.

Mechanical versus Organic Solidarity

Durkheim explained that societies based upon mechanical solidarity are characterized by a relatively simple division of labour. The best example would be a hunting and gathering society, in which work is assigned on the basis of age and sex. These societies also have a very strong conscience collective, and the sanctions invoked against those who violate their norms may appear harsh and even cruel to outsiders. Durkheim refers to the penal codes of these societies as "repressive" inasmuch as punishments are motivated by the desire for retribution and vengeance on behalf of the whole society against the individual offender. These punishments may include the stoning of adulterers, the crucifixion or beheading of unbelievers, the amputation of the limbs of thieves and so-called "honour killings." During mediaeval times, European societies resorted to such punitive practices as the burning of witches, the use of the stocks and the pillory for thieves, "vagabonds," and "rogues" and the ducking stool for gossips and "scolds" (see, for example, Mays 2004: 366).

In general, societies based on mechanical solidarity achieve their unity through the sameness and similarity of their members. Examples in Canada today of societies based on mechanical solidarity may be seen in some religious colonies and communes, some First Nations reserves and other closed communities. It is important, however, not to romanticize these communities simply for the strength of their social bonds. Tightly knit communities can also have their downsides which may take the forms of malicious gossip and rumour, as well as the ostracism and shunning of deviant or unpopular individuals (for a revealing glimpse of the frustrations of growing up in a Canadian Mennonite community, see Toews 2004).

Durkheim characterized modern societies as based upon organic solidarity. These societies are characterized by a relatively weak conscience collective and a highly specialized division of labour. Whereas the mechanical solidarity of a traditional society is derived from the sameness and similarity of its members, the organic solidarity of a modern society is derived from the interdependence of its members within a complex division of labour. Similarly, whereas the strong conscience collective of traditional society is based upon a set of uniform and long held beliefs and practices, the weaker conscience collective of a modern society is expressed in more abstract terms. Instead of the traditional commandments of Mosaic, Christian or Sharia law, modern societies have evolved secular constitutions, charters, conventions and bills of rights designed to express the consensus — or social contract — of differentiated, and often multicultural, populations. In place of the "repressive law" of traditional societies, modern societies have evolved systems of "restitutive law," designed not only to punish and deter transgressors but also to compensate victims for their losses. In our own society, this distinction between repressive and restitutive law can be seen most clearly in the differences between prosecutions undertaken in a criminal court and actions initiated in a civil court.

According to Durkheim, even modern, highly differentiated societies based on organic solidarity and a weaker conscience collective must have some kind of common moral code . But in these societies, the conscience collective is likely to be relatively abstract and to emphasize rules and regulations, and rights and responsibilities, rather than an appeal to traditionally held beliefs.

Figure 10-6 Mechanical and Organic Solidarity

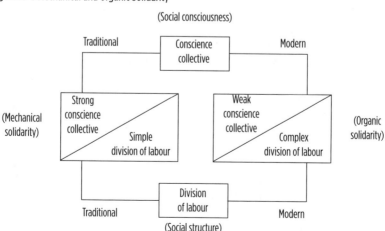

Examples of the more abstract expressions of the conscience collective in modern societies include the Constitution of the United States of America and the Canadian Charter of Rights and Fundamental Freedoms. Similarly, Canadian policies such as bilingualism, biculturalism and multiculturalism express the diversity of our conscience collective.

Durkheim's Methods of Social Analysis

To really appreciate the originality of Durkheim's work, we need to understand some of his basic methodological ideas and see how they were incorporated into his most famous piece of empirical research — his study of suicide. Durkheim's claim to fame rests not only on his reputation as a social theorist but equally on his accomplishments as a social researcher. Unlike Weber, who believed that the study of society began with the study of "subjectively meaningful social action," Durkheim believed that the study of society began with the study of "social facts" — although Durkheim originally called them "moral facts."

Social Facts

Durkheim believed that if ever sociology was to evolve from a speculative philosophical discipline into a mature social science, it had to begin with the study of social facts — social phenomena that had an independent, autonomous reality. For Durkheim, social facts were real things (social structures, social processes and social events) which existed or occurred in society due to social causes. They were, by definition, not reducible to non-social, biological or psychological causes. When Durkheim uses the term "social fact" he is referring to things in society that are the product of collective rather than of individual behaviour. Some facts are only ever produced by social groups. They are, in this sense, more "real" than the individuals who make up these groups. Indeed, individuals may exercise little or no control over many of the social facts in their societies. None of us can choose which language we speak at birth, and none of us can choose which currency we use to buy products in our local supermarkets. These facts existed before we were born, and they will continue to exist long after we have gone. For Durkheim "a social fact is every way of acting, fixed or not, capable of exercising on the individual an external constraint; or again, every way of acting which is general throughout a given society, while at the same time, existing in its own right independent of its individual manifestations" (Durkheim 1938: 13).

In emphasizing the irreducibility of social facts, Durkheim was arguing for the legitimacy of sociology as an academic discipline. He believed that sociology was the only discipline that was specifically oriented to the study of social reality. Durkheim likens the emergence of social reality from the actions of individuals to the emergence of living organisms from the elementary particles that compose these organisms. Although these particles can be studied in isolation from each other, when studied in combination as a living entity, they constitute a different order of reality. Similarly, although hydrogen and oxygen may be studied as individual chemical elements, when combined in the ratio of H_2O, they comprise a different and higher order of reality — i.e., water. In the same way, Durkheim argues that society, and social facts, constitute a different order of reality from that of the individuals whose interactions produce these social phenomena. Durkheim suggests that all social facts may be defined according to the following criteria:

- *Social facts are external to the individual:* Social facts are not produced by individuals but by the multiple interactions of many individuals. All social institutions — such as the church, the stock exchange and the government — both predate and outlive most individuals. Individuals are born into a set of social relations and remain dependent upon these relations for their identities, their beliefs, their practical activities and their sense of meaning and purpose.

- *Social facts constrain, or regulate, the individual:* Social facts exert a moral force over the individual; they have real consequences for individual behaviour. They constrain the behaviour of the individual even when these constraints can be resisted or overcome. Failing to stop at a red traffic light, for example, or burping loudly at a formal supper event are behaviours that are likely to be sanctioned in different ways. Social norms are examples of social facts, and any violation of these norms is likely to be sanctioned. Most of the time, we remain unaware of the extent to which social facts as moral forces constrain and regulate our behaviour. This is because we tend to fully internalize the rules and regulations of society and act in accordance. Only when we resist these rules, or contravene them, do they become visible and tangible to us in different ways — ranging from mild social disapproval to criminal prosecution. Even when we successfully overcome the constraints imposed upon us by social facts, they still have the power to influence us. As Durkheim observed, "Even when I free myself from these rules and violate them successfully, I am always compelled to struggle with them. Even when finally overcome, they mark their constraining power which is sufficiently felt by the resistance they offer" (1938: 3).

- *Social facts are objective phenomena:* Social facts are not the products of individual consciousness, they have an objective existence in the world, and are part of everyone's social reality. They are, in Durkheim's own words — *sui generis*. They have an independent reality which is not dependent upon the subjective consciousness of individuals. They exist, whether we like it or not.

Social Indicators

Once he had established that the study of society began with the study of social facts, Durkheim turned his attention to how these facts could best be studied. He was particularly concerned to show how these facts could be scientifically observed and measured. Durkheim acknowledged that the study of social facts was not always a simple or straightforward task. Although he insisted that social facts were objective phenomena, he also conceded that, unlike physical or biological facts, social facts were not always easily observable. Sometimes, their presence could only be detected indirectly. For this reason, Durkheim recognized that it was often necessary to identify "social indicators" to observe and to measure social facts. Durkheim's discussion of social indicators is important to his work and helped develop some standard methods of empirical social research. It should also be noted that Durkheim's discussions of research methods were invariably linked to his theoretical interests. For example, Durkheim concluded that one of the social indicators that could be used to measure the degree of social solidarity in a traditional society was the existence of a repressive penal code. Traditional societies were more likely to preserve strict customary laws and harsh penalties for their transgression. For Durkheim, the repressive penal code was an indicator of the presence of a strong conscience collective. In a somewhat different context, the relatively high rate of suicide in modern industrial societies was seen by Durkheim as a social indicator of individualism and anomie in these societies. Suicide rates were, for Durkheim, an important indicator of social disorganization. Durkheim used social indicators as a way to quantify and test his own social theories. He was, in this sense, a pioneer in the use of empirical methods in the practice of social research.

Causal Explanation

Durkheim suggested an important distinction between "causal" explanation and "functional" explanations of social facts. For Durkheim, casual explanation involves a search for the antecedent conditions that produced the social fact. In simple terms, a causal explanation is an "if — then, cause — effect" statement. If certain specified conditions are present, then the following event will occur. For example, if water is heated to a temperature of 100°C at standard pressure, then it will begin to boil. In a nutshell — a causal explanation is an explanation in which a social fact (effect) is explained by some antecedent social fact, or social facts (cause). Durkheim's causal explanation for the rise of organic social solidarity is an example.

Functional Explanation

Durkheim explains the functional explanation of a social fact differently. Functional explanation involves a search for the consequences that any social fact may have (regardless of its cause) for the larger social structure of which it is a part. In practice, this often means examining how a particular social fact contributes to the survival of the larger society, showing the function performed by a particular social fact within the larger structure of society. Functional consequences of a social fact may be either positive or negative. A functional explanation of religion is likely to show the positive consequences of religion for the mechanical social solidarity in a traditional society (pioneered by Durkheim, *The Elementary Forms of Religious Life* 1902). It is also possible, however, to produce a functional explanation of religion which may show its negative consequences — in divided societies such as Northern Ireland, Iraq, the former Yugoslavia and Sri Lanka, for example. Later, so-called, structural functionalist theorists showed that even an undesirable state such as poverty may have positive, beneficial consequences for some groups in society — such as social workers, counsellors, employers in search of cheap labour (Coser 1956; Gans 1972: 275–89).

This distinction between causal and functional explanation has proven to be an important one in sociology, although later sociologists often failed to properly distinguish between these types of explanation. In this respect, as in many others, Durkheim's discussion of these matters shows a greater clarity of thought than many of those who came after him.

Crime May Not Pay, But It's Here to Stay

Besides his interest in suicide, Durkheim was also more broadly interested in the general distribution of crime and deviance in modern society. Unlike many other social theorists, Durkheim did not regard deviant or criminal behaviour as either abnormal or as pathological. Durkheim defined the "normal" in statistical terms as "those conditions that are most generally distributed." In other words, Durkheim suggested that what is frequent in its occurrence may be defined as "normal," and what is infrequent in its occurrence may be defined as "abnormal," or "pathological." As such, Durkheim pointed out — not without some irony — crime should be regarded as normal because it is a frequent occurrence in all known societies. Moreover, Durkheim also insisted that definitions of criminal behaviour are always relative. Definitions of crime are dependent upon a particular social context. A "crime," therefore, is whatever a society decides to criminalize, and this may vary from one society to the next. In some countries today, witchcraft, heresy, apostasy, blasphemy, homosexuality and adultery are criminalized and punishable by death. But in our own society, none of these actions are any longer legal offences under the *Criminal Code of Canada*. On the other hand, certain new categories of crime have been created for actions which were not previously defined as crimes less than fifty years ago. Recently defined crimes include stalking, hate speech, possession of child pornography, failure to report a case of child abuse, squatting and financial support of terrorist groups, among many others. From these examples, it would seem that Durkheim's relativistic definition of crime has a strong ring of truth to it. His conception of crime accurately describes the evolution of the criminal codes in many countries over the past half century. Although the cultural relativity of "crime" may seem self-evident today, in Durkheim's day, such a claim was highly controversial —even scandalous. Many criminologists — such as Cesare Lombroso — were convinced that crime was an inherent and absolute evil and that criminals were best regarded as genetic degenerates, as evolutionary or atavistic "throwbacks" (Horn 2003; Gibson 2002). Whereas most criminologists of his time treated crime as a pathology rooted in an individual's psychological or biological make-up, Durkheim insisted that crime was a normal occurrence in all known societies. Indeed, in a famous observation, Durkheim suggested that even in a perfect society, there would still be actions defined as criminal:

> Imagine a society of saints, a perfect cloister of exemplary individuals. Crimes, properly so called, will there be unknown; but faults which appear venial to the layman will create there the same scandal that the ordinary offense does in ordinary consciousness. If, then, this society has the power to judge and punish, it will define these acts as criminal and will treat them as such. For the same reason, the perfect and upright man judges his smallest failings with a severity that the majority reserves for acts more truly in the nature of an offense." (Durkheim 1938: 69)

Not only did Durkheim regard crime as a normal social occurrence, but he also suggested that crime performed a positive function in society. This conclusion was greatly at odds with what most social theorists at the time thought about crime. But Durkheim's functionalist explanation of crime came to the following conclusions:

- *Crime helps to clarify the norms and values of society:* When criminals violate the norms and break the laws of society, they strengthen the commitment of other members of society to uphold these values and abide by these laws.
- *Crime helps to unify society:* Unacceptable criminal acts separate criminals from non-criminals and serve to increase the sense of integration and social solidarity among the general population.
- *Crime can sometimes bring about social change:* This is particularly true for political offences. When Rosa Parks refused in 1955 to obey the segregationist law that required her to sit at the back of the bus in Montgomery, Alabama, she started a civil rights campaign in the U.S. southern states. Similarly, when civil rights activists violated laws governing segregated

lunch counters, public washrooms and drinking fountains, their "criminal actions" resulted in the passage of the *Civil Rights Act* in 1964.

In these respects, Durkheim's theory of crime can be considered a precursor of modern criminology. He studied crime in the same way that he studied suicide — as an epidemiological phenomenon. He was not really interested in individual causes of crime but rather the frequency of crime and its distribution within a society.

Religion as Collective Self-Worship

Durkheim's theory of religion, elucidated in *Elementary Forms of Religious Life*, may be his most important and enduring contribution to sociology. Indeed, much of Durkheim's study of religion has influenced not only the sociology of religion but, more broadly, the sociology of knowledge. In common with many of the social theorists who studied and analyzed religion — such as Marx, Weber, Nietzsche and Freud — Durkheim was not a believer. His interest in religion was as a source of social solidarity. Although Durkheim never undertook his own empirical research into the religions of other cultures, he was well versed in the anthropology of his day. It was on the basis of existing anthropological accounts of the Australian aboriginal tribe, the Arunta, that Durkheim developed his functional explanation of religion in traditional society.

In common with many other social theorists of his day, Durkheim attempted to define religion through a process of elimination. After considering and rejecting any definition which entailed a belief in spiritual beings (because some religions — such as Buddhism — do not worship supernatural entities), Durkheim searched for a more universal definition. He concluded that all known religions distinguish between two essential categories — the sacred and the profane. The sacred are aspects of social life which are set apart as objects of ritualized veneration, and the profane are aspects of social life which are part of the practical everyday world For Durkheim, a religion was, first and foremost, a "moral community" whose members share a common set of beliefs and practices: "A religion is a unified system of beliefs and practices relative to sacred things, that is to say, things set apart and forbidden — beliefs and practices which unite into one single moral community called a Church, all those who adhere to them" (Durkheim 1965: 62).

Durkheim proceeded through a similar process to examine and reject previous theories of religion. Durkheim rejected the theory of "animism," which proposed that religious ideas sprang from deep psychological processes such as dreams and visions, because it was unable to explain how particular ideas were classified as either sacred or profane. He further rejected the theory of "naturism," which proposed that religious ideas were reflections of spectacular and fearful natural events — such as storms, hurricanes, tornados — because it was unable to explain how or why these events were classified as sacred rather than as profane. Durkheim then undertook his own study of "totemism," a set of religious beliefs and practices that is common to many traditional and "primitive" societies. The central religious symbol in totemic cults is the totem — an emblem which is used to represent the clan or the lineage group. A totemic emblem may portray an animal, a bird or even a plant or other natural object — such the sun, moon or stars. As one practitioner has noted:

> Many totem animals are top predators, like Bear, Wolf, Lion, or Eagle. Other totem animals are generous givers of bounty, prey animals we eat, like Buffalo, Wild Turkey or Deer. Sea mammals, Dolphins or Whales, are totem animals, but rarely fish, except Salmon. Snakes are totem animals, and sometimes Lizards, but other reptiles are rare. I know Frog shamans, and Turtle shamans. Butterfly and Spider are the only insects I have known to sponsor shamans.
>
> Plant spirits adopt shamans, just like animal spirits. Shamans often work with tree spirits, which may be the species of the tree they journey through or may be another species entirely. Medicinal herbs and culinary plants also adopt shamans. Totemic plants are extremely powerful, just as powerful as animals.
>
> Of all the totem animals, the most frequent one to sponsor shamans is Bear. Bear is very close to humans, so loving, kind and compassionate that Bear is like an ancestor. Spirit helpers are the oversouls of entire species, so for each shaman adopted by Bear, there is a particular sponsoring Bear species. Some people work with Grizzly, others with Black Bear, Panda, Koala or Polar Bear.
>
> I believe Bear was humanity's first totem animal. Archaeologists have found arrangements of Cave Bear skulls (an extinct species from the Ice Age) made by humans in caves, dating back hundreds of thousands of years. Cave Bear skulls have even been discovered arranged on a cave altar, the skulls stained with red ochre, a pigment used by the Neanderthalers to tint the bodies of their dead family members in funeral ritual. No other animal species was worshiped as long ago as Bear. Even before the end of human evolution, Bear had adopted us. (Kenner 2002)

But as Durkheim astutely observed, the totemic sign was far more sacred than the thing it portrayed. The power of the sign came not from what it portrayed, but from what it represented. In other words, the totemic sign is more sacred than the totemic species it portrays because it represents something more than simply an animal, a bird, a plant. The emblem, and the relationship that it represents, are all classified as sacred. From these observations, Durkheim concluded that although the totemic cult may appear to outsiders to be addressed to particular animals, birds, plants or other natural objects, it is actually directed to a supernatural power that gives life and meaning to all these creatures and entities. In a twist of logic, totemic emblems may best be understood as metaphors for a relationship rather than as literal representations of actual things. According to Durkheim, totems are metaphors for the supernatural power that has created all living things within its domain. The totemic emblem functions as a compact or covenant, linking the human and the supernatural. It is a relational metaphor. For Durkheim, religious categories such as sacred and profane illustrate a universal principle of social organization — that of "membership classification."

Durkheim offered his most original contribution to the sociological theory of religion in explaining how characteristics of this supernatural power are conceived and understood. He proposed that the source of all religious symbols, beliefs and practices is rooted in the reverence and awe that individuals feel towards society. From the perspective of the individual, society is all-powerful (omnipotent), all-present (omnipresent), all-knowing (omniscient), and sometimes vengeful and sometimes merciful. Society exists long before the birth of any particular individual, and will continue to exist long after the death of any individual. From the perspective of the individual, therefore, society is eternal. In other words, all of the characteristics normally attributed to gods and goddesses are first to be found in society. Although religious ideas may appear to address the relationship of the individual to a supernatural presence, they are really metaphors for the relationship of the individual to the society. This was especially true for both "primitive" religions and the major world religions. Religion, in other words, represented a "divinization" of society. On this basis, Durkheim proceeded to analyze the essential sociological components of religion.

In modern industrial and post-industrial societies, totemic cults are often popularly viewed as examples of a less enlightened and more "primitive" stage in the socio-cultural evolution. Before we deny any similarity between our own religions and those of our distant ancestors, however, we should learn to examine our own beliefs and practices more critically and more analytically. In many ways, totemic emblems still play a part in contemporary world religions. The Christian emblem of the cross, the Jewish emblem of the star of David and the Muslim emblem of the crescent moon (even though Islam officially rejects religious icons), the *aum* (or *om*) emblem of Hinduism, and the wheel of life (*samsara*) of Buddhism all function as totemic religious signs. Similarly, the swastika, the hammer and sickle and other political signs have functioned as modern-day totems. Even the insignia for sports teams function in this way. Each of these emblems signifies membership in a well-defined community, as well as a relationship between the community and the object of its reverence and veneration.

Durkheim's originality lay in the fact that he was able to find a social basis for religious beliefs and practices. Other theorists had attempted to explain religion in terms of economic factors (Marx), psychological factors (Nietzsche and Freud) and even environmental factors (Feuerbach). But Durkheim was the first theorist to argue that the symbols, rituals and moral categories of religion were representations drawn from social life. Durkheim also tried to show that even the fundamental categories of human understanding — causality, space and time — (categories that philosopher Immanuel Kant had defined as inherent in humans) were representations of particular human (social) activity. Yet, whatever criticism and correction it has received over the years, Durkheim's study of religion is still regarded as a classic.

Durkheim's Politics

Although Durkheim never proclaimed a strong political agenda or manifesto in the same way as Karl Marx, he did develop his own political vision. Besides examining the causes of many social problems, Durkheim proposed some solutions to these problems. Together, his analysis of the causes of social problems and his recommendations for their solution make up the substance of Durkheim's political vision for society.

Durkheim believed that the fundamental problem of modern society was rooted in the "pathological division of labour." This pathological division of labour led to excessive individualism, a condition which resulted in both egoism and anomie. Durkheim concluded that these pathological states, although serious, were essentially transitional problems brought on by the rapid process of modernization.

Having diagnosed the main cause of many social problems, Durkheim concluded that the solution to these problems lay in the reconstruction of the moral order of society. Although he shared with socialists a concern with the poverty, exploitation and class conflict of industrial capitalism, he believed that these problems could be solved by constructing a new moral order based upon a modernized conscience collective. Unlike the socialists, Durkheim was not convinced that economic transformation alone would solve the moral problems of industrial capitalism.

Along with Montesquieu and De Tocqueville, Durkheim represents the tradition of French liberalism. And like these theorists, Durkheim was a strong believer in political pluralism — that it was necessary to cultivate many different groups and organizations in society in order to protect the individual citizen from the tyranny of the state. Durkheim remained suspicious of mass democracy and populist forms of government as he feared that these forms could easily be usurped by political demagogues and dictators — much as Napoleon had come to power in post-Revolutionary France. Today, we might say that Durkheim encouraged the development of a civil society made up of a variety of voluntary groups, NGOs, occupational corporations, political parties, religious communities and other associations. Durkheim hoped that a rich and complex civil society, brought about through social differentiation and the increasing division of labour, would form the basis of organic solidarity.

For Durkheim, the most important element in the new form of organic solidarity was the "occupational corporation." Durkheim likened the occupational corporation to the mediaeval guild, which had regulated not only economic activity but also community life. (For contemporary examples of how occupational groups and associations, as well as other kinds of solidarity groups, have been created though the new technologies of communication and transportation in a globalized environment, see Hirsch et al. 2009).

Although Durkheim did not advocate the complete abolition of all private property — as did socialists and anarchists — he did favour basic socio-economic reforms. He supported the abolition of all inherited private property and also the idea of "sponsored mobility" — the requirement that all social positions be filled by suitably qualified candidates. He felt that the creation of this type of "meritocracy" would reduce the problem of class conflict in society.

Finally, Durkheim believed strongly in the power of education to bring about social change and moral reconstruction. For Durkheim, the role of education was to indoctrinate the young into a new conscience collective for modern industrial societies. Durkheim proposed that education be used as moral propaganda: "Education is the influence exercised by adult generations on those ... not yet ready for social life. Its object is to arouse and to develop in each child a certain number of physical, intellectual, and moral states which are demanded of him by both the political society as a whole and the specific milieu for which he is specifically destined" (Durkheim 1956: 71).

Criticizing Durkheim

Notwithstanding his historic contributions to social theory and social research, some aspects of Durkheim's work attract criticism from a number of quarters.

- *Durkheim is criticized for his conceptual confusion:* Modern reviewers of Durkheim's study of suicide treat this classic work with a mixture of criticism and respect. Some critics complain that Durkheim's typology of suicide was driven more by his social theory than by an objective examination of the statistical data. According to these critics, Durkheim's categories of suicide were designed to fit his theory of societal evolution, even at the cost of oversimplifying a complex set of empirical data. Other critics point out that Durkheim's typology is composed of overlapping and poorly defined categories. The categories of egoistic and anomic suicide, for example, appear to be different ways of saying the same thing. Durkheim's own examples of each type of suicide are confusing and often Eurocentric and culturally biased. In many cultures, there is often a fine line drawn between suicide and homicide, and Durkheim sometimes seems to cross this line with impunity. In a highly patriarchal society, it is debatable whether the now unlawful practice of *suttee* — the self-immolation of the Hindu widow on her husband's funeral pyre — should be defined as suicide or as homicide. However, most reviewers acknowledge the historical significance of Durkheim's classic study. It stands as a landmark in the history of social thought, and many of its observations and insights continue to motivate contemporary research into the aetiology and epidemiology of suicide.

- *Durkheim is criticized for his "sociologism":* Sociologism refers to the idea that society has a reality above and beyond the existence of the individuals who compose it. In more contemporary terms, Durkheim is criticized for committing the sin of "reification," the logical fallacy of attributing to abstract concepts the properties of real concrete things (Berger and Pullberg 1966; Dubeski 2001). Thus, while it is acceptable to say that real individuals have needs, goals or motives, it is unacceptable to suggest that an abstract concept — such as "society" — can experience any of these personal sensations or ideas. Throughout much of his work, Durkheim was inclined to invest the concept of "society," or other "social facts," with a kind of super-reality and to downplay the significance of the individual social actor. At times, Durkheim came close to advocating the use of such reified concepts as "group mind," as in this explanation of the conscience collective: "Individual minds, forming groups by mingling and fusing, give birth to a being, psychological if you will, but constituting a psychic individuality of its own" (Durkheim 1938: 103).

Contemporary critics reproach Durkheim for his portrayal of the individual as an essentially passive actor, wholly determined by large-scale social forces over which they have little or no control. In contemporary terms, Durkheim's theoretical perspective is criticized for subordinating human agency to social structure. These critics maintain that Durkheim did not recognize the meaningful, active role performed by goal-oriented individuals. In Durkheim's work, social actors are mostly portrayed as passive automatons swept along by social forces. As Ritzer (2004: 193) suggests: "Durkheim failed to give consciousness an active role in the social process. He treated the actor and the actor's mental processes as secondary factors or, more commonly, as dependent variables to be explained by the independent and decisive variables — social facts. Individuals are, in general, controlled by social forces in his theories; they do not actively control those forces."

- *Durkheim is criticized for his authoritarian and elitist conception of the role of sociology and education in society:* Thus, Pickering (2000: 103) suggests that Durkheim's "elitist view of knowledge" also applies "in other areas, for example morals, where the 'professional' has a clearer idea of the issues and problems ... than the 'lay' man or woman. This position he upheld as early as 1893 ... and repeated to his dying day." Similarly, Goldberg (2008: 307) reminds us that "Durkheim's political sociology has sometimes been taken to reflect an elitist distrust of mass politics."

  Durkheim emphasized the importance of moral education as a means of reconstructing the conscience collective in modern societies. His critics, on the other hand, believe that education should serve the public need for free and critical inquiry rather than the administrative need for moral propaganda. The implementation of Durkheim's ideas would greatly expand the power and authority of the state. Those who controlled the state would be empowered to define what was in the public interest and to supervise the social integration and moral regulation of the individual. While Durkheim never lost sight of the need for checks and balances and for pluralism in civil society, his moralistic agenda would encourage the empowerment of self-appointed and self-righteous governing elites.

- *Durkheim is criticized for his alleged conservatism:* While Durkheim seems willing to acknowledge the existence of social inequality and social injustice, he is more concerned with establishing social order and social control. Much of his work emphasizes the need for self-discipline and self-control rather than self-actualization or human emancipation. As one commentator observed: "He favored a 'moral liberalism' that also emphasized self-discipline and the individual's duty to others. He feared that the call of conscience was losing effectiveness in moderating behavior and that people increasingly lacked a moral compass" (*New World Encyclopedia*). In this respect, Durkheim offered us a conservative political agenda.

Durkheim Today

Although many contemporary social theorists dismiss Durkheim's views on moral reform as an example of his outdated conservative idealism, not everyone agrees with this assessment. Frank Pearce, in his book *Radical Durkheim*, offers this perspective on Durkheim's ideas:

> Why should we turn to Durkheim's work yet again? First, because, contrary to almost universal consensus amongst sociologists, in

> Durkheim's texts neither the dominant discourses, nor those present only as partially suppressed fragments can be construed as inherently conservative or positivistic. His *oeuvre* is complex, multi-faceted, often characterised by a ruthlessly anti-Utopian logic, and with an extraordinary potential fruitfulness…. To put it simply, it is because as a committed socialist and social scientist I believe that whilst Marxism is the most fruitful of all sociological discourses it needs the aid of Durkheim's concepts to rid itself of … its Utopianism." (Pearce 1989: xiv)

We should, perhaps, hesitate before consigning all Durkheim's ideas about morality to the garbage can of history. In our own time, we have witnessed an upsurge of corporate crime responsible for the collapse of world-size companies such as Enron and WorldCom, and the prosecution and conviction for fraud, corruption and the obstruction of justice of such powerful corporate figures as Bernie Ebbers, Kenneth Lay and Jeffrey Skilling, as well as Martha Stewart and Conrad Black. Nor has the issue of public dishonesty been limited to corporate CEOs. The disease seems to have spread in many directions. Major political figures (such as Scooter Libby, Jack Abramoff, Tom Delay — in the U.S., as well as those involved in the 2004 sponsorship scandal in Canada), and even sporting stars (such Ben Johnson, Floyd Landis, Marion Jones, Barry Bonds and maybe Lance Armstrong, among many others) have all been caught up in scandals (see McQuaig and Brooks 2011, for examples in the 2008–09 financial crash).

None of this would have surprised Durkheim. He would have seen in all these scandals evidence of the need for moral education and moral reconstruction. Furthermore, in Durkheim's view, the problem of public morality transcended differences of politics and ideology. The breakdown of the moral order could happen as easily in socialist as in capitalist societies, as easily in theocratic as in secular societies. In these respects, Durkheim was a non-partisan social critic of his times. We can still learn much from him.

References

Atran, Scott. 2004. "Mishandling Suicide Terrorism." *The Washington Quarterly* 27, 3.
___. 2006. "The Moral Logic and Growth of Suicide Terrorism." *The Washington Quarterly* 29, 2: 127–47.
Bates, Rodger A. 2010. "Terrorism Within the Community Context." *Journal of Public and Professional Sociology* 3, 1, Article 3. <http://digitalcommons.kennesaw.edu/jpps/vol3/iss1/3>.
___. 2012. "Dancing With Wolves: Today''s Lone Wolf Terrorists." *Journal of Public and Professional Sociology* 4, 1, Article 1. <http://digitalcommons.kennesaw.edu/jpps/vol4/iss1/1>.
Berger, Peter, and Stanley Pullberg. 1966. "Reification and the Sociological Critique

of Consciousness." *New Left Review* 35 (January–February): 56–71.

Bodin, Dominique, Stéphane Héas et Luc Robène. 2004. "Hooliganism: On Social Anomie and Determinism." (March) ; *Champ pénal/Penal field, nouvelle revue internationale de criminologie* [En ligne], Vol. I, mis en ligne le 01 mars, Consulté le 17 mai 2011. <http://champpenal.revues.org/71>.

Coser, Lewis. 1956. *The Functions of Social Conflict.* New York: Free Press.

Davis, Mike. 2006. *Planet of Slums: Urban Involution and the Informal Working Class.* London and New York: Verso.

Dobbin, Murray. 2011. "Preston Manning and the Vancouver Riots." *Canadian Dimension* June 16. <http://canadiandimension.com/blog/4010/>.

Dubeski, Norman. 2001. "Durkheim's Altruism as the Source of His Social Holism: A Discussion of the Viability of a Social Basis for Moral Principles." *Electronic Journal of Sociology.* <http://www.sociology.org/content/vol005.003/dubeski.html>.

Durkheim, Emile. 1933. *The Division of Labor in Society.* New York: Free Press.

____. 1938 [1895]. *The Rules of Sociological Method.* New York: Free Press.

____. 1951 [1897]. *Suicide.* New York: Free Press.

____. 1956. *Education and Sociology.* New York: Free Press.

____. 1964 [1893]. *The Division of Labour in Society.* New York: Free Press.

____. 1965 [1912]. *The Elementary Forms of the Religious Life.* New York: Free Press.

____. 1979. *Suicide: A Study in Sociology.* New York: Free Press.

Easton, Mark. 2008. "Life in the UK 'Has Become Lonelier'." <news.bbc.co.uk/go/pr/fr/-/2/hi/uk_news/7755641.stm>.

Fromm, Erich. 1941. *Escape from Freedom.* New York: Henry Holt and Company.

____. 1942. *The Fear of Freedom.* London: Routledge and Kegan Paul.

Gans, Herbert J. 1972. "The Positive Functions of Poverty." *American Journal of Sociology* 78, 2 (Sep): 275–89.

Gibson, Mary. 2002. *Born to Crime: Cesare Lombroso and the Origins of Biological Criminology.* Westport, CT: Praeger.

Goldberg, Chad Alan. 2008. "Introduction to Emile Durkheim's "Anti-Semitism and Social Crisis." *Sociological Theory* 26, 4: 299–321.

Gould, Harold A. 2003. "Suicide as WMD? Suicide as Weapon of Mass Destruction? Emile Durkheim Revisited." *Counterpunch* Weekend Edition, November 28–30. <http://www.counterpunch.org/2003/11/28/suicide-as-wmd/>.

Habermas, Jurgen. 1975. *Legitimation Crisis.* Translated by Thomas McCarthy. Boston: Beacon Press.

Hirsch, Paul, Peer C. Fiss and Amanda Hoel-Green. 2009. "A Durkheimian Approach to Globalization." In Paul S. Adler (ed.), *The Oxford Handbook of Sociology and Organization Studies.* New York: Oxford University Press.

Hoffer, Eic. 1951. *The True Believer: Thoughts on the Nature of Mass Movements.* New York: Harper and Row.

Holdredge, Philip Thomas. n.d. *A Durkheimian Explanation for Suicide Terrorism.* <http://www.hamilton.edu/documents//levitt-center/Durkheim-Suicide%20Terrorism%20paper.pdf>.

Horn, David. 2003. *The Criminal Body: Lombroso and the Anatomy of Deviance.* New York: Routledge.

Caroline Kenner. 2002. "MythKenner: 'Shamanic Spirituality and Spirit Helpers'."

<http://www.mythkenner.com/helpers.html>.

Lasch, Christopher. 1979. *The Culture of Narcissism: American Life in an Age of Diminishing Expectations.* New York: W.W. Norton.

Lehmann, Jennifer M. 1995. "Durkheim's Theories of Deviance and Suicide: A Feminist Reconsideration." *American Journal of Sociology* 100, 4: 904–30.

Lukes, Steven. 1972. *Emile Durkheim: His Life and Work. A Historical and Critical Study.* Harmondsworth, Middlesex: Penguin Books.

___. 2008. "Zero Confidence." *New Humanist* 123, 6 (November-December). <http://newhumanist.org.uk/1888>.

Marks, Monique. 1992. "Youth and Political Violence: The Problem of Anomie and the Role of Youth Organisations." Paper presented at the Centre for the Study of Violence and Reconciliation, Seminar No. 5, 30 July. <http://www.csvr.org.za/index.php?option=com_content&view=article&id=1543:youth-and-political-violence-the-problem-of-anomie-and-the-role-of-youth-organisations&catid=138:publications&Itemid=2>.

Mays, Dorothy A. 2004. *Women In Early America: Struggle, Survival, and Freedom in a New World.* Santa Barbara, CA: ABC-CLIO.

McQuaig, Linda, and and Neil Brooks. 2011. *The Trouble with Billionaires.* Toronto: Penguin Canada.

Merton, Robert K. 1938-10. "Social Structure and Anomie." *American Sociological Review* 3, 5: 672–82.

___. 1968. *Social Theory and Social Structure.* New York: Free Press

Mills, C Wright. 1959. *The Sociological Imagination.* London: Oxford University Press.

Nesbit, Robert. 1990 [1953]. *The Quest for Community: A Study in the Ethics of Order and Freedom.* San Francisco: Institute for Contemporary Studies Press,

New World Encyclopedia. <http://www.newworldencyclopedia.org/entry/Emile_Durkheim>.

Novak Tim. 2004. "The American Paradox: Applying Durkheim"s Critique of Modern Society to the Current "Moral Values" Debate." New School for Social Research, December 9. <timnovak.org/uploads/American_Paradox_proofed.pdf>.

Pearce, Frank. 1989. *The Radical Durkheim.* London: Unwin Hyman.

Phillips, David P., Todd E Ruth and Sean MacNamara. 1994. "There Are More Things in Heaven and Earth: Missing Features in Durkheim's Theory of Suicide." In David Lester (ed.), *Durkheim: 100 Years Later.* Philadelphia: Charles Press.

Pickering, W.S.F. 2000. *Durkheim and Representations.* British Centre for Durkheimian Studies. London: Routledge.

Pickering, W.S.F., and Geoffery Walford (eds.). 2000. *Durkheim's Suicide: A Century of Research and Debate.* New York: Routledge.

Pope, Whitney. 1976. *Durkheim's Suicide: A Classic Analyzed.* Chicago: University of Chicago Press.

Poulantzas, Nicos. 1974. *Fascism and Dictatorship: The Third International and the Problem of Fascism.* London: New Left Books.

Puffer, Phyllis. 2009. "Durkheim Did Not Say "Normleslness": The Concept of Anomic Suicide for Introductory Sociology Courses." *Southern Rural Sociology* 24 (1): 200–22.

Purvis, Jane. 1996. "Force-Feeding of Hunger-Striking Suffragettes." *Times Higher Educational Supplement* April 26. <http://www.timeshighereducation.co.uk/story.asp?storyCode=93438&sectioncode=26>.

Reich, Wilhelm. 1980 [1933]. *The Mass Psychology of Fascism*. Third edition. Translated by Theodore P. Wolfe. New York: Farrar, Straus and Giroux.

Reisman, David. 1950. *The Lonely Crowd: A Study of the Changing American Character.* With Reuel Denney and Nathan Glazer. New Haven: Yale University Press.

Ritzer, George. 2004. *Classical Sociological Theory*. Fourth edition. Boston: McGraw Hill.

Smith, Adam. 1843 [1776]. *An Inquiry into the Nature and Cause of the Wealth of Nations.* Book I, Chapter 1: "Of the Division of Labour." Edinburgh: Thomas Leeson.

Szaki, Jerzy. 1979. *History of Sociological Thought*. Westport, CT: Greenwood Press.

Tarlow, Peter. n.d. *"Dark Tourism" Tourism.* <http://tourismtalk4you.blogspot.ca/p/dark-tourism.html>.

Taylor, Ian. 1971. "'Football Mad' — A Speculative Sociology of Soccer Hooliganism." In E. Dunning (ed.), *The Sociology of Sport: A Selection of Readings*. London: Frank Cass.

___. 1982. "Class, Violence and Sport: The Case of Soccer Hooliganism in Britain." In H. Cantelon and R. Gruneau (dir.), *Sport, Culture and the Modern State*. Toronto: University of Toronto Press.

Taylor, Matthew. 2008. "The Credit Crunch Will Generate a Wave of Anomie." *The Telegraph* October 14. <blogs.telegraph.co.uk/news/matthewtaylor/5449617/>.

The Times (of London). 2009. "The Solitary Self." December 31: 2.

Toews, Miriam. 2004. *A Complicated Kindness*. Toronto: Knopf Canada.

Turner, Jonathan H., and Leonard Beeghley. 1981. *The Emergence of Sociological Theory*. Homewood, IL: Dorsey Press.

Zeitlin, Irving. 2000. *Ideology and the Development of Sociological Theory.* Seventh edition. New Jersey: Prentice Hall.

Zevallos, Zuleyka. 2006. *What Would Durkheim Say? Altruistic Suicide in Analyses of Suicide Terrorism.* TASA Conference, University of Western Australia & Murdoch University, December 4–7.

Chapter 11

The Interactionism of Georg Simmel

Life in the Fast Lane

Many of us often feel that we are living our lives at breakneck speed, trying to accomplish a host of different things, frequently at the same time, with no sense of fulfilment or completion. We hop like frogs from one lily pad to the next, from one set of tasks to another, and even from one relationship to another, without any sense of finality or consummation. Life in the twenty-first century can sometimes feel "provisional" — as though we never have enough time to fully complete our various projects, as though we can never quite discover our overriding goal or purpose. Instead, we move from one activity to the next without any strong sense of direction, or any obvious end in sight. Most of the time, we are simply trying to keep up with the pack, trying not to fall behind in the accelerating rat-race of life. For many of us today, life can be uncertain, unpredictable and unstable, and always in a process of change. Above all, it is about speed; we are all living in the fast lane. (For an amusing account of the rapid pace of contemporary life, see Gleick 1999.)

The elements of rapid social and technological change combined with the uncertainty, insecurity and anxiety of our times signal the fact that we have entered an age that is very different

Figure 11-1 Life in the Fast Lane

Reflections on Speed

I was rushing the other morning to get to my laptop to complete this essay. As I was driving my car, I was also talking to my wife on my cell phone, while eating my lunch and listening (was I?) to my favorite classical music radio station. In the midst of all this, my palm pilot [a handheld computer device similar to a BlackBerry] beeped, which meant it was protesting being ignored. The irony of rushing to write an article on the impact of speed on daily life did not escape me. Multitasking on my way to describing the importance of "standing still" truly seemed ludicrous.

Today, the sad fact is that we live in a hurried society in which people feel rushed, overscheduled, stressed and unable to keep up. We fill our lives with computers, cell phones, wireless laptops, palm pilots and other time saving gadgets, only to find ourselves deprived of time. We read books and take seminars on time management, we hire consultants to help us manage our businesses and personal lives more efficiently only to find ourselves frantic, impatient, short tempered and frustrated. We cram our children's lives full of music lessons, soccer practices, and tutoring and end up raising a new generation of hurried children.... "Being rich is having money; being wealthy is having time."

Zur (2010).

from those which preceded it. Sometimes labelled "late modern," or "post-modern," our present age is distinguished by its restless search for the novel and new, and its distain for — indeed, condescension towards — the old or the durable. The unprecedented speed, change, fragmentation, instability and flux that characterize the pace of contemporary life have led social theorist Zygmunt Bauman to describe our age as one of "liquid modernity," in which nothing is constant except change itself. For Bauman (2005: 1), we live in an age "in which the conditions under which its members act change faster than it takes the ways of acting to consolidate into habits and routines. Liquidity of life and that of society feed and reinvigorate each other. Liquid life, just like liquid modern society, cannot keep its shape or stay on course for long."

Although the frenetic pace and ad hoc quality of contemporary life may be troubling and disorienting for those baby boomers brought up in the more stable days of the post–World War II era, for generations born into liquid modernity — Generation Y (the Millennial Generation, the Net Generation, or Echo Boomers) and Generation Z (the Internet Generation and the Digital Natives) — nothing could seem more natural. After all, everything is relative and always a matter of perspective. More than anything else, "liquid modernity" is marked by the inescapable transience of everything. Many jobs today are casual and short-term; many relationships are fleeting; the things we buy — especially consumer electronics but also cars, appliances, etc. — are quickly outdated, planned for obsolescence; many businesses use "just in time" lean production and ordering strategies; even our entertainments and amusements shift abruptly from one fad to the next. Our attention span is short, even if its scope is broad and ever-changing. We live in a social world that breeds uncertainty, insecurity and anxiety — especially for those who were not born into this liquid modernity. In Bauman's words:

> The liquid life is a precarious life, lived under conditions of constant uncertainty. The most acute and stubborn worries that haunt such a life are the fears of being caught napping, of failing to catch up with fast-moving events, of being left behind, of overlooking "use by" dates, of being saddled with possessions that are no longer desirable, of missing the moment that calls for a change of tack before crossing the point of no return. Liquid life is a succession of new beginnings — yet precisely for that reason it is the swift and painless endings, without which new beginnings would be unthinkable, that tend to be its most challenging moments and most upsetting headaches. (Bauman 2005: 2)

For those growing up in this brave new world — especially in the world of work — there is a tremendous pressure to be adaptable, flexible, changeable and mobile. Lifetime careers and long-term employment are distant memories for many in the labour market. Today's jobs require short-term commitments for casual, part-time, temporary, shift and limited contract work, and an ability to move rapidly from one job to the next. Job security has become a thing of the past. We live in an age that is characterized by what one writer calls "workplace flexibility" (Sennett 1998) and another terms the "portfolio worklife" (Handy 1989: 183ff). "In the portfolio lifestyle, careers are a sequence of stepping stones through life, where workers as individuals and organizations as collectives do not commit to each other for much more than the short-term goal, the project at hand, the talent needed now" (Deuze 2006: 2).

The larger truth is that the insecurity of the workplace is simply an example of the impermanence that has penetrated all other aspects of liquid society. This transience is also to be found in our private lives — in the incessant search for the next and best that the marketplace has to offer. Most products are out of date soon after we purchase them. The production cycles of manufacturing plants, the revision cycles of textbook publishers, the upgrades to computer software programs, successive generations of smart phones, tablets and other consumer electronics — all encourage us to enter a race that few can keep up with and that none of us can win. We live in a disposable society in which we can move from person to person much as we move from product to product. On-line dating services, computerized chat rooms, Facebook pages, instant messaging, Skype and Twitter all provide us with an infinite network of potential contacts with whom we can "hook up" for casual encounters and trial friendships, only to later "unfriend" and move on if things don't work out.

> We are not just on the move from part-time job to flexible contract, nor just from one city to the next country; in the particular urban settings of flexible capitalism we also move from "pink-slip party" to yet another social networking event, from rented apartment to leased living space, from fling to affair, and from single-size servings to disposable everything. Our only shared condition increasingly seems to be the lived experience of being "permanently imperma-nent" in the context of constant change. (Deuze 2006: 6)

Although the advent of liquid modernity may threaten generations who were accustomed to job security, lifelong friendships, stable marriages and a sense of certainty and meaning at the core of their lives, for the younger generations the liquid age provides opportunities for freedom, autonomy and change. Whether it is hooking up with a virtual "soul mate" on an online dating service or in a chat room; buying and selling products on eBay; hanging out with Facebook friends; or finding a cheap flight on the web and hopping a plane to some remote resort, the internet has become a defining aspect of our liquid lives. And, if further proof were needed, the protest movements in Egypt, Tunisia and Libya in the 2011 Arab Spring — and their aftermath — have shown us how mobile communication devices can play a crucial role in helping to bring about social change. The liquid world presents both challenges and opportunities. Even without our realizing it, our world has become increasingly de-territorialized and de-materialized. Transnational corporations continue to shift their manufacturing and assembly plants from North America and Europe to offshore locations in the Global South in order to benefit from lower labour costs and cheaper raw materials. As far as Big Business is concerned, we now inhabit a world without borders. Even wealth has become less material, less real and increasingly liquid. As we saw during the 2008 financial crisis, the boom in the housing market that allowed so many consumers to purchase homes with sub-prime mortgages was based not on real material values, but on the speculative values of a debt-fuelled, artificially inflated economy. Similarly, in the world of high finance, investment bankers, hedge fund managers and other "masters of the universe" made their millions by converting real wealth into liquid assets that could be traded and gambled on the global money markets and international stock exchanges. But as we have also seen, when the fiscal bubble finally bursts, the speculative wealth of the liquid economy can disappear without a trace (see Ho 2009; Preda 2009; Stiglitz 2009). In this respect, the recent financial crisis provided an eerie echo of Marx and Engels' prophetic statement made in the *Communist Manifesto* back in 1848: "All that is solid melts into air, all that is holy is profaned" (6).

Although the liquid society of the twenty-first century contains some novel and unique features — especially those related to the revolution in telecommunications — many of its other characteristics had already begun to emerge much earlier, towards the

---

Figure 11-2 Simmel Is Fun

Of the ... Grand Men of classic sociology ... Georg Simmel (1858–1918) was clearly the most fun. No rigid positivism, and virtually no brooding focus on depressing topics like suicide or modes of domination, alienation, and exploitation — Simmel instead used his sharp eye and a playful, philosophical mind ... to telescope between microsociological encounters and world-historical backdrops. Where Marx would begin with modern capitalism's economic class structure, Simmel might start by studying the on-the-street *pas de deux* between a passer-by on his way to work and a beggar asking for money. His great subject was the *Großstadt* — Metropolis, or literally, Big City — especially his own rapidly transforming Berlin. The foundation of Simmel's work was individual human experience, beginning with the city's bombardment of the senses. From there, he tried to explain both new modes of being and new social structures. [In] his literary, phenomenological style and powerful interpretations of phenomena as wide-ranging as money, urbanization, and modern art ... [he] pulled off the impossible balancing act between critic, writer, philosopher, and social scientist.

Carmody 2010.

end of the nineteenth century. The speed, changeability and transience of metropolitan life, as well as its growing impersonality, anonymity and moral confusion, had already been noted by some of the major social thinkers of the past two centuries. But it was the German social theorist Georg Simmel who most clearly anticipated many of the social trends that later combined to form the liquid society of today. An astute observer of everyday life, Simmel was one of the earliest theorists to write about the culture of modern capitalism and to examine its impact on individuals. He drew attention to the power of money over people and how money converted everything — products and people — into commodities that could be bought and sold on the open market. In his own way, Simmel pioneered the study of everyday life, and his work on money, consumption, objectification, the metropolis and interpersonal conflict forms the backbone of our present understanding of everyday life today — irrespective of whether we define contemporary society as late modern, postmodern or liquid.

The Metropolis and Everyday Life

For many years, Georg Simmel fell between the cracks of classical social theory. Surrounded on all sides by such intellectual titans as Marx, Durkheim and Weber, it is hardly surprising that Simmel was largely overlooked in his own time and in his own intellectual milieu. The nineteenth century was an age of heroic social theory — social theory that was holistic and systematic in its scale and scope of analysis. All of the major social theorists addressed themselves to the "transition crisis" in their respective societies: to the social upheavals that accompanied the transition from traditional to modern forms of economic production and social organization. This was the age of "grand theory" and "meta-narratives" — of Marx's theory of class struggle; Weber's theory of rationalization; and Durkheim's evolutionary theory of social solidarity. In the midst of these trail blazing projects, it is easy to see how Simmel's more modest accounts of everyday life were largely overlooked. But in an important way, Simmel blazed a trail of his own. His careful vignettes of ordinary social characters — such as "The Stranger," "The Flirt, and "The Miser," as well as his artful studies of "The Metropolis and Mental Life," "Dyads and Triads," "The Sociology of Space," "Fashion,," "Secrecy" and his magnum opus, *The Philosophy of Money* — breathed new life into the study of social relations. The immediacy and directness of Simmel's urban portraits continue to intrigue us almost a century after his death. He was a conscientious and thoughtful observer of social interaction with a close attention to detail. But more than anything else, he was a pioneer of the sociological study of everyday life.

Like Marx, Durkheim and Weber, Simmel wrote at a time of rapid change and social upheaval. The shift of population from the rural countryside into the towns and cities was transforming workplaces and households throughout Europe and North America. Small towns expanded into big cities, and dispossessed farmers and displaced agricultural labourers swarmed from their villages into these swelling urban centres, drawn to the factories where they became the new working class — the industrial proletariat. Many of the classical social theorists reflected upon the dramatic societal changes that occurred during the course of the nineteenth century. Marx analyzed the revolutionary mode of commodity production introduced by industrial capitalism. Engels described the pitiful conditions of the working class in the big cities. Durkheim studied the changes in social solidarity that resulted from the increasingly specialized division of labour. And Weber warned of the sinister rise of bureaucratic rationalization and its consequences for freedom and human dignity. But it was Simmel who first examined the new culture that arose from the combined forces of industrialization, urbanization and commodification — the culture of the metropolis.

The Rootless Cosmopolitan

If there is a single underlying thread that joins together the dispersed and fragmented writings of Georg Simmel, it is the theme of rootlessness. More than anything else, this theme is central to Simmel's sociological vision and personal focus. In part, this theme reflected the circumstances of Simmel's own life and career. As a Jew in the mid- nineteenth century, Simmel experienced the anti-Semitism that was endemic throughout Europe at this time and that prevented him from obtaining a full-time university appointment in Germany.

> Although Simmel suffered the rebuff of academic selection committees, he enjoyed the support and friendship of many eminent academic men. Max Weber, Heinrich Rickert, Edmund Husserl, and Adolf von Harnack attempted repeatedly to provide for him the academic recognition he so amply deserved. Simmel undoubtedly was gratified that these renowned academicians for whom he had the highest regard recognized his eminence. (Coser 1977: 195–96)

And, as a Jew, Simmel was also racially stereotyped as a "rootless cosmopolitan," an anti-Semitic slur traditionally used by European governments to persecute Jews in the racist campaigns — or *pogroms* — and, most lethally, used by Hitler during the Holocaust and by Stalin during his anti-Semitic purges and show trials. However, while Simmel was victimized by the popular prejudices of his time, he was also sensitized to the experiences of other "outsiders" and to the sense of rootlessness than many individuals felt during this period of early modernity. Nowhere was this more the case than in the big city — the modern metropolis. (One of the seminal books to examine some literary and philosophical themes of being an "outsider" in the modern city is Colin Wilson's (1956) *The Outsider*. While Wilson wrote this book during the day in the British Museum library, he slept at night in a sleeping bag on Hampstead Heath, in London).

Indeed, one of the central characteristics of the metropolis that caught Simmel's imagination was the strong sense of detachment from traditional ties and obligations. The individual in the city became a symbol for a new type of personal freedom, but also for a new form of isolation and loneliness — an "outsider." The city provided a new landscape of anonymity and impersonality. This urban environment became a point of convergence for the new market forces of capital, commodities and people. It was a social space increasingly defined by objectification and quantification in which the old traditional values were transformed — in Marx's words — into the "cash nexus." Whereas the old order had been defined by inherited rank and ruled by custom and tradition, the city became an urban jungle in which only the financially fittest could prevail in the competitive struggle for existence. Unlike the old class divisions, which had often been integrated through a common set of values and sometimes softened by aristocratic *noblesse oblige*, the modern social divisions of the city were unrestrained by any norm of public welfare. Indeed, the sharp contrast between the squalid misery of the lower classes and the vulgar ostentation of the *nouveaux riches* was soon immortalized in the novels of such astute observers of the urban condition as Victor Hugo, Emile Zola, Honore Balzac, Charles Dickens, Elizabeth Gaskell and Upton Sinclair.

Although many other social theorists — including Marx and Engels, Durkheim, Weber and Jane Addams — also wrote about the city, Simmel was the first to appreciate the unique and unprecedented culture of the modern metropolis, and the implications of this culture for the transformation of everyday life. In his impressionistic essays on the different social types that emerged in the urban setting, and in his ability to capture the anonymity and impersonality of city life, Simmel set a course that would be followed by many later urbanologists — especially those of the Chicago School of Human Ecology and the Frankfurt School of Critical Theory. The strange new power that the metropolitan culture seemed to exert over the individual derived in large part, according to Simmel, from the apparent "objectivity" of this culture. The money economy reduces everything and everyone to a monetarized exchange value. Everything is for sale, and the value of anything is displayed in its price. Earlier subjective, or even spiritual, values that were once attached to things and to people in a more natural environment are translated into purely material values. (Oscar Wilde (1854–1900), in his play *Lady Windermere's Fan* [Lord Darlington, Act III], expressed his disdain towards the monetarized values of the modern urban economy by defining a cynic as "a man who knows the price of everything and the value of nothing.") Urban culture, therefore, is characterized by the mass production and mass consumption of commodities. However, Simmel also recognized that although the urban market of mass consumption offers unparalleled opportunities for the satisfaction of individual wants, it also creates an objectified culture in which commodities begin to displace human relations as a primary source of meaning and personal identity. As many modern writers observe, we increasingly come to identify ourselves with particular brands or "logos" (Klein 2000) in a lifestyle based on "conspicuous consumption" (Veblen 1899). In other words, Simmel describes for us in his own observations of urban life, the everyday experience of what Marx called "alienation" and "commodity fetishism" and what Durkheim called "anomie": the pathology of unlimited wants (or "infinite aspiration").

Today, it is difficult for us to recreate in our minds the sense of novelty and originality that Simmel communicated in his descriptions of nineteenth-century metropolitan culture. But for his readers, the contrasts between the traditional village lifestyle and the new metropolitan culture would have appeared sharp and unprecedented. The big city had begun to change forever the lives of those who had migrated from rural to urban settings — whether these migrants were "pushed" and displaced from the countryside, or "pulled" by the lure of employment in the new manufacturing industries. According to Simmel, much of the distinctiveness of the new metropolitan culture derives from the power of money. The dominance of the money economy transforms the everyday lives of ordinary people — especially their social interactions with each other — in a number of remarkable ways. Above all, as we have already noted, the money economy produces an objectified culture — a culture in which just about everything can be converted into cold hard cash. For the first time in history, all social relationships can now be evaluated according to a common criterion — money. Commodities that were once produced by individual craft are now mass produced and somehow appear to acquire a life of their own:

> The process of objectification of culture that, based on specialization, brings about a growing estrangement between the subject and its products ultimately invades even the more intimate aspects of our daily life…. The … sheer quantity of very specifically formed objects makes a close and, as it were, personal relationship to each of them more difficult: a few and simple utensils are more easily assimilated by the individual, while an abundance of different kinds almost form an antagonistic object to the individual self…. What is distressing is that we are basically indifferent to those numer-

ous objects that swarm around us…: their impersonal origin and easy replaceability…. Cultural objects increasingly evolve into an interconnected enclosed world that has increasingly fewer points at which the subjective soul can interpose its will and feelings. (Simmel 1974: 459–60)

Besides the objectification of popular culture, Simmel also saw how the money economy had accelerated the pace of everyday life in the city. The rapid circulation of capital and commodities, the increasing momentum of rural-urban migration and the exponential growth and density of city populations all contributed to the peculiarly frenetic quality of city life. Whereas the countryside always emphasized the natural rhythms of life — whether diurnal, seasonal or annual — the city was all about speed, change and constant innovation. Everything was always on the move; nothing ever stayed the same. For Simmel, modern metropolitan life was characterized by a "restless flux," which was at the same time both stimulating and stressful. Indeed, it would be true to say that the modern conditions of existence transformed the mental life and consciousness of the individual. The speed of modern life produces an ever-changing symbolic landscape, a succession of images which are often so fleeting and transient that they are soon forgotten and overtaken by new images. The novels of James Joyce, Marcel Proust and Virginia Woolf, among others, illustrated the "stream of consciousness" typical of high modernism (Humphrey 1968). Simmel, himself, explored this restless and ephemeral quality of modern life in a number of different studies — most notably in his study of fashion. In these respects, he was not only a pioneer in the study of consumerism, but his work was also a precursor of the mid-twentieth-century perspective of postmodernism.

Today, of course, the tempo of contemporary life has dramatically increased beyond anything experienced by Simmel's generation. The emergence of social media and messaging sites as well as the proliferation of mobile telecommunication devices have signalled the advent of a new "fully networked" social environment in which the speed and multitude of social interactions have increased exponentially for many individuals. But, as we have also learned, the attention span of the new information and communication media is short, highly selective and forgetful. Indeed, the liquid age has often been critiqued for its "cultural amnesia." The philosopher Herbert Marcuse, for example, regarded cultural amnesia as a characteristic of the "one-dimensional" consciousness of late capitalism. The short attention span of contemporary culture is especially apparent in the news media. Yesterday's news is soon forgotten; today's news has only a momentary and passing interest. Life sometimes seems to be reduced to a series of "sound bites" or "photo ops." Any historical sense of the past — in public or private life — has been largely supplanted by a succession of disjointed and disconnected fragments, without continuity or long-term meaning. "These fragments I have shored against my ruins," wrote T.S. Eliot in *The Wasteland* (line 430, page 67).

For Simmel, the objectification and commodification of human relations in modern metropolitan culture has definite implications for the quality of social life. Interpersonal relations in the city are often characterized by a brevity and superficiality that would have been unthinkable to those living in more traditional rural settings. Simmel suggests that many social interactions in urban settings are distinguished by a "cool reserve" and avoidance of intimacy. He referred to this sense of detachment as the "blasé attitude":

> The essence of the blasé attitude consists in the blunting of discrimination. This does not mean that the objects are not perceived, as is the case with the half-wit, but rather that the meaning and differing values of things, and thereby the things themselves, are experienced as insubstantial. They appear to the blasé person in an evenly flat and gray tone; no one object deserves preference over any other. This mood is the faithful subjective reflection of the completely internalized money economy. By being the equivalent to all the manifold things in one and the same way, money becomes the most frightful leveler. (Simmel 1903: 414)

Since Simmel's early identification of the blasé attitude, however, the typical reserve shown in many urban encounters has now acquired the status of a celebrated cultural style. In contemporary parlance, the term "cool" now signifies a sense of ironic detachment and composure and a strategy for deliberately maintaining social distance. Although the term may have originated in marginalized urban communities — among African Americans, jazz musicians, bohemians, beatniks, hippies and other counter-cultural urban rebels who needed to defy authority without open confrontation — it has now passed into public discourse. To be cool today is to exhibit self-control in the face of provocation or confusion. To be cool also implies an ability to manage complex, culturally diverse urban interactions with low-key self-assurance, personal competence and aplomb. Over the years, the term "cool" has also overlapped with other expressions — such as "hip," "hep," or "chill" — which share similar meanings of self-control. Earlier expressions such as *sang froid* and "stiff upper lip" also attest to the cultural significance of emotional restraint — especially in urban settings where frequent contact with strangers requires social competence and discretion (see Danesi 1994; Frank 1997 and Stearns 1994).

The Sociology of Everyday Life

Georg Simmel was the first sociologist of everyday life. Before Simmel developed his own approach to the study of sociation, most social thinkers focused on large-scale societal structures and process — such as the social contract (Rousseau), the social organism (the romantic conservatives), the mode of production (Marx), rationalization (Weber), social solidarity (Durkheim) and so on. Simmel was the first theorist to focus on the small-scale local settings of interpersonal relations — the everyday social contexts in which individuals interact with each other. Whereas earlier social theorists focused their theoretical gaze through a sociological telescope at the large-scale landscape of social structures and processes, Simmel used his sociological microscope to examine the transient and often fleeting encounters between individual social actors. He was, we may say, an early pioneer of the nascent tradition of micro-sociology.

For many years, Simmel's reputation as a social theorist failed to receive the recognition accorded some of his more celebrated contemporaries — such as Marx, Weber and Durkheim. Simmel was largely overshadowed by the towering presence of these other theorists, and it has taken several generations for his work to gain recognition and respectability. Today, as we look back at these nineteenth-century social thinkers, in many ways it is Simmel who seems closest to us in spirit and in his sociological vision. Marx and Durkheim were very much nineteenth-century figures in their ideals and in their hopes for the future. Each remained under the spell of Enlightenment optimism; each believed in his own version of historical progress and evolutionary development. They faced the future with a confidence fuelled by their strong convictions and by their moral and political ideals. Weber, on the other hand, was far more skeptical about the inevitability of "progress" and more fearful of the historical fate of humanity. He seems closer to us in his ambivalence, anxiety and lack of historical certainty than many of the other classical theorists. His sociological vision seems to us less clouded by false hopes and doctrinaire convictions than those of his contemporaries. But Marx, Durkheim and Weber were all systematic, or grand, theorists. Marx attempted to develop a general theory of history and society that would later become the doctrine of historical materialism. Durkheim developed his own version of a general theory of societal evolution. Even Weber's historical, comparative and cross-cultural studies were driven by a number of broad and over-arching themes related to the rationalization and modernization of society. Each of these social theorists tried, in his own way, to integrate his key concepts, his theoretical vision and his research observations into an all-encompassing theory of society.

Simmel was also fascinated by the social experience of modernity but in a way rather different from his contemporaries. The scale of his work and the scope of his sociological vision were quite distinct. Although there are important overlaps in their ideas, Simmel left his own theoretical legacy. Comparing Simmel with Marx, Weber and Durkheim, there are two main differences. First, Simmel was not a grand theorist. He constructed no general theory of society in the manner of Marx, Weber, Durkheim or even Spencer. Rather, Simmel's writings appear fragmentary and piecemeal. Much of his work was in the form of essays and occasional monographs rather than as lengthy tomes. With one singular exception, *The Philosophy of Money*, Simmel's writings are an assortment on a wide variety of topics. Some of his better-known essays bear such titles as "Fashion," "The Stranger," "The Flirt," "The Metropolis and Mental Life," "The Poor," "The Secret" and "The Secret Society," among others. If the works of Marx, Weber and Durkheim are viewed as the sociological equivalents of the great historical novels of the nineteenth century, then Simmel's works appear, by contrast, more akin to a collection of short stories.

The other way in which Simmel's work departed from that of his contemporaries was in the scope and scale of his theoretical analysis. Almost alone among the classical theorists of his time, Simmel was the first to focus his attention on the small scale, the mundane, the day-to-day. Unlike the grand theorists, who were typically concerned with large-scale societal structures and processes, Simmel focused on the everyday interactions between individuals, and the patterns and forms that these interactions exhibited in small, local social relations. In this respect, Simmel appeals to our contemporary sensibilities in a way that the grand theorists do not. He was an observer of casual encounters and fleeting interactions — a student of the minutiae of our social existences. Almost single-handedly, he introduced a new perspective into the study of society — the tradition of "micro-sociology." Although Simmel's fragmentary studies of everyday social life were not, at first, taken as seriously as the works of the grand theorists, over time his influence has grown. The seeds he sowed at the end of the nineteenth century germinated and grew into a legacy of many different micro-sociological traditions of today.

Settling Accounts

Like other social theorists, Simmel's originality lay in his ability to extract ideas from a number of leading thinkers of his time and to recombine these ideas in novel and innovative ways. Simmel was influenced by several traditions of social thought although he was selective in what he accepted and what he incorporated into his own perspective.

Figure 11-3 Simmel's Intellectual Influences

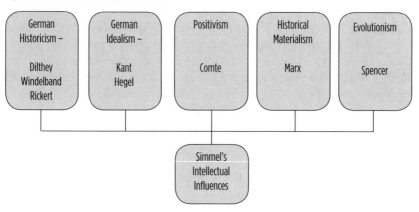

German Idealism

Growing up in Germany, it is hardly surprising that Simmel was deeply influenced by the prevailing German philosophy and historiography. One of the most important influences was the philosophy of Immanuel Kant, who became famous for his critique of empiricism: the doctrine which asserted that our knowledge of reality is based wholly upon our sense impressions from the natural world, that all knowledge is based upon experience. In his critique, Kant argued that our capacity to understand reality comes not from our direct experience of the world, but from innate mental categories which enable us to organize and classify our experiences. Our most fundamental mental categories — those which define "space," "time" and "causality" — cannot be derived from sensory experience, but only from inborn faculties of the human mind. Kant introduced an important distinction between the "form" and the "content" of knowledge. The form of all knowledge, according to Kant, is "framed" around the mental categories we impose upon our observations of the world. These categories function as "the spectacles we wear behind our eyes." They organize our sensory impressions of the world, and they process the sense data of our raw "experience." In other words, our perception of the world is always mediated by the deep categorical structures of the mind. Simmel borrowed these concepts , but instead of viewing forms as intellectual categories, Simmel saw them as patterns, or configurations, of social relations derived from the deep structures of social interaction, or what he called "sociation." Simmel's belief that the study of society begins with the study of the elementary forms of social interaction is one of the distinguishing characteristics of his social theory.

Simmel was also influenced by Georg Hegel. Although Simmel did not subscribe to Hegel's universal theory of history, he incorporated some other aspects of Hegel's philosophy into his own work. Hegel's "dialectics" influenced Simmel's study of society — especially the dialectical relationship between the subjects and objects of human activity. Hegel taught that the products of human thought and action — the objects and creations of human culture — invariably become objectified, which estranges those who produce these objects, from the objects themselves. This idea of "objectification" also formed the basis of Marx's concept of "alienation." The paradoxical relationship between the subjectively meaningful actions of individual actors versus the objectified cultural structures produced by these actors was a central preoccupation of Simmel's social theory. "The deepest problems of modern life flow from the attempt of the individual to maintain the independence and individuality of his existence against the sovereign powers of society, against the weight of the historical heritage and the external culture and technique of life" (Simmel 1950: 409)

Simmel's dialectical perspective is apparent in his conception of society. Although Simmel maintained a micro-sociological focus in much of his work, he was not a doctrinaire micro-sociologist. Unlike later micro-sociological theorists who insisted that "society" was nothing more than an abstraction, wholly reducible to the individuals who composed it, Simmel acknowledged the independent reality of larger social structures and relationships. In his work, Simmel never fully resolved the dialectical relation between individuals and society.

Simmel's sensitivity to the paradoxical, contradictory, dualistic, conflictual and dialectical nature of social reality is apparent in all of his published work. His study "The Stranger" (Simmel 1950: 402–408), for example, reveals the paradoxical truth that many of us are more likely to share intimate secrets with those we hardly know than with those we know well. His study "The Poor" (Simmel and Jacobson 1965) reveals the ties of reciprocity that bind those in need to those who can provide aid. His study "The Secret" (Simmel 1950) paradoxically suggests that secrets are an essential part of all social relationships, even marriage or close friendships. In these and similar studies, Simmel shows himself to be an accomplished sociologist of the inner life of the individual, those aspects of social life that were overlooked or ignored by the major classical social theorists. For this reason, Simmel has a strong appeal to modern readers, who often exhibit a fascination with the sociology of everyday life.

Besides Kant and Hegel, Simmel's social thought was influenced by two other German philosophers of his generation — Schopenhauer and Nietzsche. Schopenhauer's deeply pessimistic philosophy of the individual and Nietzsche's ironic and skeptical critique of rationalism each influenced Simmel's sociological outlook. The lesson that Simmel learned from these two philosophers was that the rationalist belief in the inevitability of progress in human history was illusory and unsustainable. Simmel also concluded that many of the dramas of social life were likely to have tragic rather than positive, or optimistic, outcomes. Schopenhauer and Nietzsche helped to ensure that Simmel remained grounded in what he regarded as a philosophy of realism, rather than in the heady optimism and idealism associated with the Enlightenment.

German Historicism

Simmel's social thought was also influenced by the tradition of German historicism represented in the works of such leading figures as Wilhelm Dilthey, Wilhelm Windelband and Heinrich Rickert. Unlike the French positivists, who advocated a unified method of scientific inquiry for all branches of knowledge, the German historicists insisted on a clear distinction between the natural sciences and the social (or cultural) sciences. They believed that the social sciences were distinct from the natural sciences in an important respect — both the subjects and the objects of social scientific inquiry were human actors. According to the historicists, this distinction meant that any study of history, or society, had to understand the viewpoints of those who were being studied. In other words, the historical, and sociological, method had to address not only the externally observable causes of historical events, but also the internally meaningful understandings that these events held for the people who initiated or participated in them. The need to understand the viewpoints of social actors led many German historians to reject the positivist method of scientific inquiry in favour of a more humanistic approach. Whereas positivists called for general explanations and universal laws — so-called "nomothetic" laws — historicists believed that the study of history needed to focus on what was unique and particular to any given period of history — so-called "idiographic" descriptions. Whereas the positivists studied the objective behaviour of objects and organisms, the historicists studied the subjectively meaningful actions of the social actor (see Adorno et al. 1976). Max Weber was strongly influenced by the historicist perspective, as seen in some of his key concepts, such as *verstehen*. Simmel was similarly influenced by the historicists and his approach to the study of society overlaps with that of Weber.

Other Intellectual Influences

Simmel's distinctive intellectual approach to the study of society was also informed by some of the other leading intellectual currents of his day. Although he shared Weber's aversion to historical materialism, Simmel was influenced by Marx's writings. He was particularly drawn to the centrality of conflict in Marx's studies of history and society, and made the study of conflict an important part of his own study of social relations. Unlike Marx, however, who believed that class conflict — as the major source of human conflict — could be overcome by a revolutionary transformation of society,

Simmel saw conflict as a perpetual aspect of all social relations. Indeed, Simmel was one of the earliest theorists to conclude that social conflict was essential to human relationships and that it could sometimes produce positive outcomes. Whereas for Marx, the study of conflict was always historically specific, for Simmel the study of conflict was more analytical and formal. He was interested in the study of "conflict in general" rather than its particular historical manifestations.

His interest in the formal and analytical approach to the study of social relations betrays a further intellectual influence on Simmel's social thought — that of positivism. While Simmel rejected some parts of positivism, other aspects fitted in with his own theoretical perspective. The positivist influences on Simmel's work can best be seen in his studies of "sociation." Simmel believed that a close analysis of interpersonal social relations would reveal a number of basic forms of social interaction. For Simmel, these forms constituted the building blocks of higher and more complex configurations of social relations. The simplest and most elementary forms of sociation, according to Simmel, were the dyad and the triad — groups composed of two and of three individuals. Each of these forms revealed a number of possible social relations between individuals, ranging from cooperation through competition and conflict to mediation. Simmel concluded that the study of society began with the study of the elementary forms of sociation and with a logical (and mathematical) analysis of the possible permutations and combinations of individuals within these different social forms. It is in his search for the timeless and universal forms of human interaction that the positivist influences on Simmel's thought can be seen most clearly.

Finally, Simmel's earliest works — including his very first sociological treatise, *Social Differentiation* (1890) — show the influence of Herbert Spencer's theory of societal evolutionism. Although Simmel's later works make little or no direct reference to Spencer, he retained an interest in the process of social differentiation and in how individuals form relationships within complex social systems. Unlike Spencer, however, who sometimes seemed to exhibit a callous disregard for the weakest and most vulnerable sections of society, Simmel's essays on the poor, on women and on the working class reveal a compassion and empathy for their difficulties and challenges. Perhaps because of his own firsthand experience of anti-Semitism in Germany, Simmel never lost his sympathy for those whom he regarded as the "underdogs" in society.

Simmel's Conceptual Toolbox

The goal of Simmel's social theory was to analyze the ever-changing flux of thoughts, feelings, actions and interactions which make up the lived experiences of all individuals in society in terms of the sociological form and content

Figure 11-4 The Main Divisions of Simmel's Sociology

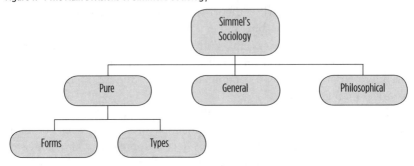

of these experiences. Simmel's wanted to reduce the overwhelming complexity of everyday social life to a set of underlying abstract forms. By identifying the elementary forms of social interaction, or sociation, Simmel believed that he had uncovered the basic building blocks of higher, more complex structures and networks of social relations. Simmel's preoccupation with the micro-sociological elements of social life was similar in some ways to that of the mathematician who is searching for a way to reduce the complexity of experience to a series of logical abstractions. Indeed, that parallel led Simmel to refer to his own study of forms as "social geometry." Because Simmel never constructed a general theory of society in the manner of the grand social theorists and because most of his contributions were published as specific studies of particular topics, it is difficult to provide a general overview of his ideas. Perhaps the best way to summarize the overall significance of Simmel's work is to identify the concepts and major themes in his studies and show how he used these intellectual tools to focus on particular sociological issues.

Pure Sociology

In the most general terms, Simmel divided his conception of sociology into three broad categories, or "problem areas," which he called "pure sociology," "general sociology" and "philosophical aociology." Under "pure sociology," Simmel included his studies of social interaction between individuals — the most elementary units of social relations. Simmel also included in "pure sociology" his studies of the forms and the types of "sociation." As mentioned, the most important of Simmel's forms were the dyad and triad. But Simmel also studied the range of possible patterns or configurations of social relations that could exist between interacting individuals — including those of subordination/superordination, exchange, conflict and sociability. It is probable that Simmel's concept of "pure sociology" was inspired by the parallel concept of "pure mathematics," which implies an intellectual discipline using reason for its own sake, rather than for its applied, or practical, use, as in disciplines such as engineering.

Pure mathematics also involves a search for universals — universal formulae, proofs and solutions — which are generally transferable to all other branches of mathematics. Similarly, Simmel saw his own pure sociology as a study of the elementary forms of sociation, the universal units to which more complex structures of social relations are ultimately reducible. Another way of understanding Simmel's study of the forms of sociation is to compare it to the study of grammar. When we study the grammatical structure of language, we are not really interested in the content, or the meaning or words, but in the rules that govern their use. In a similar way, Simmel's study of forms may be seen as a study of the universal principles that underlie all possible cases of social interaction.

General Sociology

Simmel never elaborated his conception of general sociology in any great detail. It appears as though he wanted to include the study of large-scale social phenomena such as politics, religion, economics, law, culture, language and other aspects of collective social behaviour. In other words, general sociology was the study of institutions, organizations and other macro-sociological topics.

Philosophical Sociology

Philosophical sociology, for Simmel, covered the nature of social and sociological knowledge. In some of his studies, Simmel questioned and examined the philosophical preconceptions and presuppositions of social knowledge. He concluded that the ways in which individuals saw their social worlds, or the ways in which they defined their relations to society, were always based upon particular philosophical assumptions, which could change from one historical period to the next. Simmel was fascinated by the ways in which social knowledge was constructed by ordinary individuals as well as by social theorists. For Simmel, the study of society began with the forms of reciprocal interaction that took place between individuals, for these interactions, or associations, were the building blocks of large-scale social structures and institutions. Thus, although "society" is made up of interacting individuals — much like an ant colony is made up of interacting ants — it is not fully reducible to these individuals. Out of all this interaction emerged a new collective, or social entity. Simmel expresses this dialectical relationship between the individual and society in the following way:

> What is society as such? Society exists where several individuals (for one another, with one another or against one another) enter into interaction…. On every day, at every hour, such threads are spun, are allowed to fall, are taken up again, replaced by others, intertwined with others. Here lie the interactions … between the

atoms of society which bear the whole tenacity and elasticity, the whole colourfulness and unity of this so evident and so puzzling life of society.... [But] if society is to be an autonomous object of an independent discipline then it can only be so by virtue of the fact that, out of the total sum of individual elements which constitute it, a new entity emerges; otherwise, all problems of social science would only be those of individual psychology. (Simmel, cited in Kaern et al. 1990: 45–48)

Sociation

The concept of "sociation" is basic to Simmel's study of society. For Simmel, the study of society begins with the study of sociation — its forms, types and underlying principles. "Sociation" in English may be understood as a contraction of "social association." Although sociation refers to the process of social interaction, it is meant to emphasize the subjectively meaningful aspects of social interaction. Simmel, much like Weber, believed that the defining property of human interaction lay in the fact that humans, unlike other animals, possess consciousness and self-awareness. Their actions and interactions are motivated by goals and intentions and above all by self-consciousness.

Forms

Forms are the elementary units of interaction, or sociation, to which all higher and more complex social structures can be reduced. The most basic forms are the dyad and the triad — combinations of two, and of three, individuals in a pattern of sociation. Each form contains a number of logically possible social relations, including, for example, dominance and subordination, exchange, conflict, cooperation and mediation, among others. One obvious example of the ways in which the social relations within a dyad are transformed by the addition of an extra individual is when a baby is born to parents in a nuclear family, now a triad. The arrival of a new individual may subtly, or even dramatically, change the relations between the two parents. Social interaction between three individuals is of a necessarily higher order of complexity than social interaction between two individuals. According to Simmel, the addition of an extra individual to a dyad opens up a range of new logical and empirical possibilities, including relations of mediation, arbitration and conflict resolution. Although the dyad often appears to be the most intimate and intense form of association in our lives — marriages, close friendships and partnerships — it is an inherently unstable relationship. All it requires is for one person to leave, and the relationship collapses. When there is a third person — a triad — the association is able to survive the departure of a single individual.

> The social structure here [the dyad] rests immediately on the one and on the other of the two, and the secession of either would destroy the whole. The dyad, therefore, does not attain that super-personal life which the individual feels to be independent of himself. As soon, however, as there is a sociation of three, a group continues to exist even in the case one of the members drops out. (Simmel 1950: 123)

However, as individuals with two siblings will recall, although the addition of a third person may allow for third-party mediation, it also makes possible alliances between two people against a third. Thus, while more stable, triads may also increase rather than reduce the potential for conflict.

In his discussion of the dialectical relationship between the individual and the larger society, Simmel acknowledges the two contrasting faces of modern individualism. On the one hand, the size and complexity of modern society frees the individual from the moral, social and political constraints of more traditional societies. But, on the other hand, the individual often feels compelled to resist the isolation experienced in modern society. This is what Simmel means when he suggests that while modern individuals are thoroughly incorporated into society, they are also, at the same time, compelled to differentiate themselves from the anonymous mass of other members of society. This dialectical theme of the individual who participates in, yet also resists, society runs throughout much of Simmel's work. It is expressed in the juxtaposition of individual culture to objective culture and in the commodification of society, which he discussed in *The Philosophy of Money*.

Social Types

The most intriguing part of Simmel's work is his study of social types. Unlike his study of forms, which is, for the most part, abstract and analytical, Simmel's study of types is concrete and descriptive. Simmel's essays portraying different social types describe how each of these stereotypical social roles and social identities — such as the miser, the spendthrift, the flirt, the stranger, the adventurer etc. — can only be fully understood when viewed in their social context. The stranger, for example, while unfamiliar to the group is, at the same time, a participating, although marginal, member of the group. If the stranger remained completely outside of the group, they would be unable to interact with any of its members. On the other hand, if the stranger is integrated into the group, they would no longer remain a stranger. The status and role of a stranger, according to Simmel, allows a unique form of social interaction between the stranger and other members of the group. In many ways, the stranger remains a remote and unfamiliar figure. However, this very quality of remoteness leads some group members to confide more intimately in the stranger than in more familiar members of the group. In his essay "The Stranger," Simmel demonstrates the originality of his sociological insight, for example, his challenge of the popular misconception that strangers always remain outside of the group and its influences. He shows that there are sociological possibilities open to the stranger not available to more established members of the group — such as the privilege of intimate confidences, or the mediation of disputes.

In this and other essays, Simmel confronts our taken-for-granted assumptions about particular social types and shows us that the web of human interaction is always more subtle and complex than we first imagined. In some ways, Simmel's social types may be compared to Max Weber's ideal types. Both theorists used these methodological tools to shed more light on the world of interpersonal interactions which underlies the larger, more impersonal structures and processes of society.

Objectification

One of Simmel's most pressing sociological concerns was the problem of "objectification" in society. By objectification he meant the process whereby the localized activities of individuals are collectively transformed into larger more objective societal structures and processes, which often come to dominate and control individual members of society. In other words, Simmel was preoccupied with how the practices of individual culture were inevitably transformed into the material and ideological products of "objective culture."

A present-day example of this trend can be seen in the changes which have taken place in home entertainment. Until the mid-twentieth century, much home entertainment was home-made. Families would sometimes entertain themselves by playing so-called "parlour games" — which could include card games, board games and party games such as tic-tac-toe, charades and pin-the-tail-on-the-donkey. Family gatherings and other social occasions might also encourage individuals to entertain by playing the piano, singing songs or performing recitations. Many of these traditional forms of home entertainment declined as television became the central focus of family attention (Gray 2011; Williams 2011). Today, even the television has been superseded by video games, personal music and movie players and other technologies that have further eroded any sense of common family entertainment. The new entertainment forms are not only more expensive, they are also relatively exclusive: they focus on the individual, and they further the trend towards greater privatization and social isolation. In these respects, the new information/communication technologies have come to dominate our lives and have transformed even our most intimate social relations.

Simmel would undoubtedly have seen this trend as further evidence of what he called "the tragedy of culture": the eclipse of individual culture by the growing influence of objective culture. Whereas the individual culture of traditional home entertainment was largely made by the families themselves, the new technologies of home entertainment are mass produced and controlled by large corporations. These concerns are closely related to Marx's analysis of alienation and to Weber's analysis of rationalization in modern society.

Philosophy of Money

Simmel's concerns over the progressive objectification of the modern world are strongly articulated in his longest and most extensive sociological study — *The Philosophy of Money*. In it, Simmel explored the ways in which money has influenced and transformed the lives of individuals. Simmel concluded that money has an enormous influence on most peoples' lives in ways that are not often fully recognized and understood.

Because money represents the most abstract and universal measure of value, it can be accumulated, transferred, converted, exchanged, quantified, consumed, multiplied, speculated, gambled and lost. In modern society, Simmel suggests, all commodities —goods and services — are eventually converted into money. Thus, money is the "super commodity": the universal medium of exchange. Simmel also suggests that in our society, money acquires a power that no other economic value has ever had. Because of its mobility and convertibility, money can be accumulated and moved around, often across national frontiers, in a way that was impossible for earlier forms of value — especially land. As we have recently seen, because of its speculative value and its easy convertibility into other forms of wealth, fortunes can be made or lost in minutes on the stock exchange and the money markets. Never before has it been possible to accumulate wealth on such a scale or with such speed as it is today in the money economy.

Simmel also observed that money has invaded the private and most intimate aspects of our lives. We live in a world in which each of us is judged in terms of money. We evaluate our friends, neighbours, relatives and strangers in terms of their income and their levels of conspicuous consumption. Today, an individual's personal worth is often seen as inseparable from their personal money wealth. Money has the power to dictate how service workers — in supermarkets, department stores and fast food restaurants — present themselves to us in their work places, with regulation smiles and exhortations to "Have a nice day!" Money has become an important link between us and our children. Our kids not only expect to receive a steady income (pocket-money or allowance), they may also expect to be paid for completing household chores, for obtaining good grades and for other activities. Slowly and surely, the money economy has seeped into our family relationships and has, to some extent, begun to subtly redefine these relationships.

The power of money in modern society provided Simmel with his most compelling and dramatic example of the rise of objective culture and of its tendency to dominate and transform all types of human relations. Simmel observed that the invasion of money into our private lives has brought about the growth of cynicism, superficiality, manipulation and impersonality in our relations with others, even in our closest and most personal social relationships. In other words, money has the power to transform our public and our private lives, and even our identities. In the words of folk singer Bob Dylan: "Money doesn't talk, it swears" (from, "It's Alright Ma, I'm Only Bleeding").

Today, the power of money opens up many possibilities for individuals. Money makes possible an expanded range of anonymous and casual sexual relations with partners who expect no commitment and no emotional involvement, only payment for their services. Money has made the world smaller and more accessible by bringing distant places within reach for more people than in the past. Tourism has become a mass consumer industry. Increasing numbers of people are able to pay for African safari adventure tours, Himalayan treks and trips to many other exotic locations that once were the sole preserve of intrepid travellers and seasoned adventurers. Mass tourism has also meant that more individuals can travel all over the globe to spend their vacations in high security gated communities — without ever venturing out into the world of real people. But Simmel also suggested that there is a price to pay for all these new possibilities, a price that is not always immediately recognized or understood. The age of infinite possibility is also the age of shallowness and superficiality. Access to the formerly exotic and unfamiliar does not necessarily lead to greater knowledge and understanding.

The Tragedy of Culture

The Philosophy of Money provides many examples of the objectification of culture and also illustrates what Simmel regarded as a central problem of the modern age: the tension between individual culture and objective culture. Simmel tried hard to avoid any simplistic or over-generalized discussion of these issues. Throughout his study of money, Simmel was at pains to point out that money produces both positive and negative outcomes for individual members of society. Money helps to free many individuals from the constraints of traditional society, opening up life opportunities in the areas of work, travel, entertainment, consumption and personal relations. At the same time, the penetration of money into our lives and the objectification and depersonalization of social relations that have followed in its wake introduces new social problems. The dark side of individual freedom includes the isolation, atomization and privatization that many of us feel today the gradual eclipse of a sense of community. The dominance of the money economy has also brought about a "relativization" of personal and cultural values and superficiality in our personal relations. The money economy and the objectification of culture are responsible — in Simmel's view — for the growing impersonality of human relations in modern society. In a famous passage in which he describes money as a "frightful leveller," Simmel sounds very much like Karl Marx:

> By being the equivalent to all the manifold things in one and the same way, money becomes the most frightful leveller. For money expresses all qualitative differences of things in terms of "how much?" Money, with all its colorlessness and indifference, becomes the common denominator of all values; irreparably it hollows out the core of things, their individuality, their specific value, and their incomparability. All things float with equal specific gravity in the constantly moving stream of money. All things lie on the same level and differ from one another only in the size of the area which they cover. (Simmel 1950: 414)

Simmel remained ambivalent about many of the social changes he observed. In this respect, his analysis of modernity overlaps with those of Marx, Weber and Durkheim. Each drew attention to the social problems of modernity and to the human costs of the transition from traditional to modern society. Much of Simmel's discussion of the effects of the money economy is strongly reminiscent of Marx's discussion of commodification and commodity fetishism in capitalist society. In other words, people have lost control over how they produce and what they produce in modern capitalist societies:

> Just as, on the one hand, we have become slaves of the production process, so, on the other, we have become the slaves of the products. That is, what nature offers us by means of technology is now a mastery over the self-reliance and the spiritual centre of life through endless habits, endless distractions and endless superficial needs.... Man has thereby become estranged from himself; an insuperable barrier of media, technical inventions, abilities and enjoyments has been erected between him and his most distinctive and essential being. (Simmel 1990: 483–84)

Similarly, much of Simmel's discussion of the objectification of culture overlaps with Weber's notion of "rationalization" and with Durkheim's observations on the progressive division of labour in modern (organic) societies. In summary, the tragedy of culture for Simmel lay in the fact that, notwithstanding the spectacular technological advances of modern culture, the human costs of cultural objectification are often disturbing and profound.

The objectification of culture has left many of us isolated and disconnected from any real sense of community. The new freedoms of modern society have come at a heavy price. The growing centralization and bureaucratization of power, wealth and information have left many of us relatively powerless, uninformed and alone as individual members of society. The objectification of culture — and the new individualism that it brings — has proven to be both a blessing and a curse for the individual in modern society.

Agency and Structure

For contemporary readers, the relevance of Simmel's work lies in the fact that he tried to link the private, subjective aspects of the individual to the network of social relations that define the objective location of all individuals in society. Sociologists refer to this difference between the subjective experiences of the social actor and the objective structures of society as the distinction between "agency" and "structure" In other words, Simmel related the inner life of the individual to the set of statuses and roles which define the outer life of the individual in society. This focus on the inner and outer life of the individual in society gives Simmel's work currency, connecting it to a number of contemporary micro-sociological traditions.

Simmel's attempts to link the inner thoughts and feelings of the individual to the network of social relations that define the outer public life of the individual in society are best seen in his studies of social types. In his descriptions of the stranger, the flirt, the spendthrift and the miser, Simmel examined how the presentation of the social self is influenced and constrained by the reality of social structures. Although Simmel is normally classified as a micro-sociologist — because of his preoccupation with the sociology of everyday life — he never lost sight of how larger social structures may shape and influence the form and content of interpersonal relations. This recognition of the dialectical relationship between the individual and society is evident in Simmel's observations on the "metropolitan individual." He suggested that the way people adjust to the conditions of big city life is through cultivating an attitude of indifference and social distance towards people they routinely encounter. This attitude is a defence mechanism against being emotionally overwhelmed by the stresses and strains of living in a crowed metropolis.

> The jostling crowdedness and the motley disorder of metropolitan communication would … be unbearable without … psychological distance. Since contemporary urban culture … forces us to be physically close to an enormous number of people … people would sink into despair if the objectification of social relationships did not bring with it an inner boundary and reserve. The pecuniary character of relationships, either openly or concealed in a thousand forms, places

> [a] … functional distance between people that is an inner protection … against the overcrowded proximity. (Simmel 1997: 178)

Conflict

Another field of social theory to which Simmel made a lasting contribution was the study of social conflict. However, unlike other social theorists, such as Marx, who viewed conflict in a largely negative light, Simmel believed that social conflict could also have positive outcomes. He observed that conflict is nearly always combined with cooperation in certain ways; individuals, or groups, may come to agreement on the rules which govern conflict — whether in marriage, business, sports or even war. Simmel concluded: "There probably exists no social unit in which convergent and divergent currents among its members are not inseparably interwoven. An absolutely centripetal and harmonious group … not only is empirically unreal, it could show no real life process" (Simmel 1955: 15).

Besides viewing conflict as a process which could have some positive outcomes, Simmel also believed that conflict is unavoidable and can never be fully eradicated from human relationships. In this respect, he differed from those social theorists, again, such as Marx, who maintained an optimistic Enlightenment belief in the possibility that a society free of conflict could be reconstructed through social revolution. Simmel regarded such beliefs as hopelessly naive. In contrast to many of the Enlightenment thinkers, he concluded that all individuals have an *"a priori* fighting instinct" — an inborn capacity for competition and conflict. Although this capacity can sometimes be civilized and tamed, Simmel believed that the instinct for conflict can never be fully eliminated from human relations.

Simmel suggested that the most intense conflicts occur between individuals, or groups, which share many common characteristics. This has been the case in warfare, where civil wars (such as those in the United States, (former) Yugoslavia, Ireland, Sri Lanka, Rwanda and Sierra Leone have often been fought with a brutality that has exceeded that found in international warfare. Even on an interpersonal level, conflicts between estranged spouses, relatives or former close associates may be pursued more ruthlessly than those between strangers, or more distantly related parties. Indeed, much criminological research confirms that most murders are committed by someone who was already known to the victim (Correctional Service Canada 1995; Mann 2005).

Simmel also suggested that conflict between groups is likely to lead to greater unity and solidarity within groups. Thus, a conflict between two nations, for example, may serve, at least temporarily, to override political and ideological conflicts within each nation. Thus, when Great Britain was at war with Germany during World War II, political differences between conservatives and socialists (and even communists) were suspended in order to present a united front against a common enemy. At the same time, however, the growth of in-group unity may lead to greater intolerance of diversity within the group. Thus, several minority groups in Canada, such as Japanese, Ukrainian, Italian and German Canadians, were subject to punitive measures in wartime, including incarceration.

Simmel further suggested that inter-group conflicts may lead to a centralization of authority within each group. During World War II, Adolph Hitler became the authoritarian dictator of Nazi Germany, while Winston Churchill emerged as the undisputed, and also authoritarian, leader of Great Britain. Similarly, in intense industrial conflicts between labour and management, the centralized authority of the corporate CEO is often matched by the centralized authority of the union leader.

Besides these observations, Simmel formulated many other propositions regarding the form and content of social conflict. Most of these were formulated as highly generalized and abstract statements which could be applied equally to large-scale conflicts between organized social groups and to small-scale interpersonal conflicts. Simmel's goal was to develop a set of theoretical hypotheses and observations which could be used to study all forms of human conflict — irrespective of where or when such conflicts occurred. His pioneering writings on this topic laid the groundwork for the later emergence of conflict theory as a distinct sociological perspective, represented in the works of such prominent conflict theorists as Lewis Coser, C. Wright Mills, Ralf Dahrendorf, Gerhart Lenski, John Rex, Michael Mann and Randall Collins, among many others.

Criticizing Simmel

Although Simmel has emerged from relative obscurity to become a popular social theorist among contemporary sociologists, his work has not escaped criticism over the years.

- *Simmel is criticized for the "cultural pessimism" of his sociological conclusions and for his reluctance to endorse political action as a solution to social problems*: His cultural pessimism has been inferred from his view on the "tragedy of culture," which emphasized the apparent dualism between the individual to society. Simmel believed that the increasing growth of "objective culture" through rationalization and the division of labour would eventually result in the subjugation and enslavement of the individual. Unlike Marx, or even Durkheim, he never presented any political, moral or education program designed to overcome this long-term erosion of the dignity and freedom of the individual. Whereas for Marx, alienation could be resolved in a future post-capitalist society, for Simmel the contradiction flowing from the antinomy of subjective personal life and objective culture is eternal. This apparent defeatism led at least one critic to observe that Simmel sometimes "displayed a characteristically German apathy towards contemporary politics" (Lawrence 1976c: 6); and Hungarian Marxist Georg Lukacs to accuse Simmel of surrendering to the status quo by interpreting as eternal a condition of the individual that is characteristic only of imperialism (Lukacs 1971).

- *Simmel is criticized for his unsystematic contributions to social theory and social analysis*: With the exception of his *Philosophy of Money*, his writings are scattered over a number of topical areas. Unlike Marx, Weber and Durkheim, he never developed a comprehensive theory of society. The fragmented and often impressionistic tone of much of Simmel's work led Max Weber to critique Simmel for his failure to develop a coherent and logical "sociological method." Among Weber's chief concerns was that Simmel had failed to properly distinguish the "motives" of individual social actors from the objective "meanings" and consequences of their social actions (Lichtblau 1991: 41–45).

- *Simmel is criticized for his micro-sociological focus*: Some critics have charged Simmel with a failure to take account of the larger macro-sociological structures and processes that influence the actions of individuals in society. In some of his writings, Simmel appears to offer a reductionist view of the study of society:

> On every day, at every hour, such threads are spun, allowed to fall, are taken up again, replaced by others, intertwined with others. Here lie the interactions *only accessible through psychological microscopy* [emphasis supplied] between the atoms of society which bear the whole tenacity and elasticity, the whole colourfulness and unity of this so evident and so puzzling life of society. (Simmel 1997: 109)

This view of society was criticized by more conservative theorists, such as Othmar Spann, who opposed any breaking down of the social organism into its constituent elements and charged Simmel with psychologizing sociology, referring to his theoretical perspective as "speculative atomism" (Frisby 1992: 28–29).

- *Simmel attracts criticism from some Marxists for his failure to acknowledge the primacy not only of the economic, but of any other sphere, of society*. Thus, Lukacs (1971) charged that this "struggle against law and causality" was a defence of imperialistic philosophy against dialectical materialism, a position which resulted in Simmel undermining objective scientific knowledge (Frisby 1992: 28–29).

- *Simmel is criticized for his alleged positivism*: For many critics, Simmel's search for the underlying universal principles of social conflict, or for the universal forms of sociation, represents a failure to examine the specific historical and socio-cultural contexts of these aspects of social life.

Needless to say, none of these criticisms represents the final verdict on Simmel's sociological legacy. Perhaps the verdict of history is best expressed in Simmel's own epilogue to himself: "I know that I shall die without spiritual heirs (and that is good). The estate I leave is like cash distributed among many heirs, each of whom puts their share to use in some trade that is compatible with their nature but which can no longer be recognised as coming from that estate" (Simmel 2004: lvi).

References

Adorno, Theodor, Hans Albert, Ralf Dahrendorf, Jurgen Habermas, Harald Pilot and Karl Popper. 1976. *The Positivist Dispute in German Sociology*. London: Heinemann Educational Books.

Bauman, Zygmunt. 2000. *Liquid Modernity*. Cambridge, UK: Polity Press.

___. 2003. *Liquid Love: On the Frailty of Human Bonds*. Cambridge: Polity Press.

___. 2005. *Liquid Life*. Cambridge, UK: Polity Press.

___. 2007. *Liquid Times: Living in an Age of Uncertainty*. Cambridge, UK: Polity Press.

___. 2010. *Living on Borrowed Times*. Cambridge, UK: Polity Press.

Carmody, Tim. 2010. "Georg Simmel." <hilobrow.com/2011/03/01/georg-simmel/>.

Correctional Service Canada. 1995. *A Profile of Homicide Offenders in Canada*. < ttp://www.csc-scc.gc.ca/text/rsrch/briefs/b12/b12e-eng.shtml>.

Coser, Lewis. *1977. Masters of Sociological Thought; Ideas in the Historical and Sociological Context*. Second edition. San Diego, CA: Harcourt Brace Jonanovich.

Danesi, Marcel. 1994. *Cool: The Signs and Meanings of Adolescence*. Toronto: University of Toronto Press.

Deuze, Mark. 2006. *Liquid Life, Convergence Culture, and Media Work*. (Working paper). <https://doc-10-94-docsviewer.googleusercontent.com/viewer/securedownload/dsn1aovipa7l846lsfcf94nedj8q2p4u/e0lc5>.

___. 2009. "Convergence Culture and Media Work." In Jennifer Holt and Alisa Perren (eds,), *Media Industries: History, Theory, and Method*. New York: Wiley Blackwell.

Dylan, Bob. 1965. "It's Alright, Ma (I'm Only Bleeding)." *Bringing It All Back Home*. Label: Columbia.

Eliot, Thomas Stearns. 1961. "The Waste Land." *Selected Poems*. London: Faber and Faber.

Frank, Thomas. 1998. *The Conquest of Cool: Business Culture, Counterculture, and the Rise of Hip Consumerism*. Chicago: University of Chicago Press.

Frisby, David. 1992. *Simmel and Since: Essays on Georg Simmel's Social Theory*. London: Routledge.

Fuller, Steven. 1988. *Social Epistemology*. Bloomington: Indiana University Press.

Gleick, James. 1999. *Faster: The Acceleration of Just About Everything*. New York: Pantheon Books.

Gray, Peter. 2011. "The Decline of Play and the Rise of Psychopathology in Children and Adolescents." *American Journal of Play* 3, 4: 443–63.

Handy, Charles. 1989. *The Age of Unreason.* Boston: Harvard Business School Press.

Ho, Karen. 2009. *Liquidated: An Ethnography of Wall Street.* Durham and London: Duke University Press.

Humphrey, Robert. 1968. *Stream of Consciousness in the Modern Novel.* Berkeley, CA: University of California Press.

Kaern, Michael, Bernard S. Phillips, and Georg Simmel. 1990. *Georg Simmel and Contemporary Sociology.* Dordrecht, Netherlands: Kluwer Academic Publishers.

Klein, Noami. 2000. *No Logo: Taking Aim at the Brand Bullies.* Toronto: Knopf Canada.

Lawrence, P.A. 1976. *Georg Simmel: Sociologist and European.* Sunbury Middlesex: Nelson.

Lichtblau, Klaus. 1991. "Causality or Interaction? Simmel, Weber and Interpretative Sociology." *Theory, Culture and Society* 8: 33–62.

Lukacs, Georg. 1971 [1923]. "Reification and the Consciousness of the Proletariat." In *History and Class Consciousness.* Translated by Rodney Livingstone. London: Merlin Press.

Mann, Ruth M. 2005. *Power and Resistance.* Fourth edition. Halifax, NS: Fernwood Publishing.

Marx, Karl, and Friedrich Engels. 1992 [1848]. *The Communist Manifesto.* Oxford: Oxford University Press (The World's Classics).

Preda, Alex. 2009. *Framing Finance: The Boundaries of Markets and Modern Capitalism.* Chicago: University of Chicago Press.

Sennett, Richard. 1998. *The Corrosion of Character.* New York: W.W. Norton.

Simmel, Georg. 1890. *Über sociale Differenzierung.* [*On Social Differentiation.*] Leipzig: Duncker & Humblot.

____. 1906. "The Sociology of Secrecy and of Secret Societies." *American Journal of Sociology* 11, 4 (Jan.): 441–98.

____. 1950 [1903]. "The Metropolis and Mental Life?" *The Sociology of Georg Simmel.* Translated by Kurt Wolff. New York: Free Press.

____. 1950 [1903]. "The Secret and Secret Society." *The Sociology of Georg Simmel.* Translated by Kurt Wolff. New York: Free Press.

____. 1950 [1908]. "Stranger." *The Sociology of Georg Simmel.* Translated by Kurt Wolff. New York: Free Press.

____. 1955. *Conflict/The Web Of Group Affiliations.* Translated by Kurt Wolff and Reinhard Bendix. New York: Free Press.

____. 1974 [1900]. *The Philosophy of Money.* London: Routledge and Kegan Paul.

____. 1976b [1908]. "The Stranger." *The Sociology of Georg Simmel.* New York: Free Press.

____. 1997. *Simmel on Culture.* Edited by David Frisby and Mike Featherstone. London: Sage.

____. 1984. "The Flirt/Coquette." *On Women, Sexuality, and Love.* Edited and translated by Guy Oakes. New Haven & London: Yale University Press.

____. 1990 [1900]. *The Philosophy of Money.* London: Routledge.

____. 2004. *The Philosophy of Money.* Third edition. Edited by David Frisby and translated by Tom Bottomore and David Frisby. London: Routledge.

Simmel, Georg, and Claire Jacobson. 1965. "The Poor." *Social Problems* 13, 2 (Autumn): 118–40.

Stearns, Peter. 1994. *American Cool: Constructing a Twentieth-Century Emotional Style*. NY: New York University Books.

Stiglitz, Joseph E. 2009. *Freefall: America, Free Markets, and the Sinking of the World Economy*. New York & London: W.W. Norton.

Turner, Jonathan H., and Leonard Beeghley. 1981. *The Emergence of Sociological Theory*. Homewood, IL: Dorsey Press.

Veblen, Thorstein. 1899. *Theory of the Leisure Class: An Economic Study in the Evolution of Institutions*. New York: Macmillan.

Wilde, Oscar. 2005 [1892]. *Lady Windermere's Fan*. Act 3. London: Nick Hern Books.

Williams, Alex. 2011. "Quality Time, Redefined." *New York Times*, Fashion and Style April 29. <.nytimes.com/2011/05/01/fashion/01FAMILY.html?_r=3&hp>.

Wilson, Colin. 1956. *The Outsider*. London: Victor Gollanz.

Zur, O. 2010. "From Speed.com to Soul.com: Reflections on a Hurried Culture and Psychotherapy." <http://www.zurinstitute.com/techspeed.html>.

Chapter 12

The Elitism of Vilfredo Pareto

The Street Versus the Elite

In the closing month of 2010, a poor vegetable seller named Mohamed Bouazizi set himself alight as a political act of protest against the arrogance and brutality of the police state in his homeland of Tunisia. This single act of self-immolation ignited a spontaneous uprising that has become known as the Arab Spring. Today, despite Bouazizi's martyrdom and the political firestorm that swept through the Middle East and around the globe, the future of the Arab Spring is anything but certain. Almost no one could have predicted that within months of the passing of Bouazizi we would see the former president of Tunis (Zine el Abidine Ben Ali) find refuge in Saudi Arabia; the former president of Egypt (*Hosni Mubarak*) face prosecution while lying on a stretcher in a Cairo courtroom; and the former leader of Libya (Muammar Gaddafi) slaughtered in front of the cameras following his capture in Misrata. For a while it almost seemed as though anything were possible. But the outlook for the Arab Spring no longer looks so rosy, at least to Western eyes. The much-vaunted hopes for freedom and democracy are starting to fade in the cold, harsh light of religious rivalries and tribal animosities. The dreams of another Age of Enlightenment may once again be shipwrecked on the rocks of human perversity.

> ### Figure 12-1 The Arab Spring
>
> **Who Will Replace Today's Middle Eastern Rulers?**
>
> Will the almost spontaneous, largely leaderless, Middle East uprisings now overtaking entrenched autocracies lead to democracy? Or will one group of autocrats simply replace another, once the smoke has cleared and the protesters return to their homes?
>
> The jury is still out on this. But past revolutions in these countries don't provide us with much hope. With a few exceptions, such as traditionalist Saudi Arabia, almost all of these states have previously experienced revolts and coups in the name of democracy....
>
> In the two countries where rulers have already been evicted this year, politics remains in flux. Tunisia's Ben Ali and Egypt's Mubarak may be gone, but no one knows yet what political system will emerge. In both states, the army, Islamists, and remnants of the old nomenklatura, along with pro-democracy groups, are vying for control....
>
> Kings were sent packing in Egypt, Iran, Iraq, Libya, and Tunisia between the 1950s and 1970s, replaced by rulers promising economic and political reforms. Revolutionaries gained control in Algeria and Syria. Slowly but surely, though, the new governments became as autocratic and despotic as their predecessors. Indeed, in places like Iran and Iraq, they proved to be worse.
>
> Henry Srebrnik 2011.

At first, it seemed as though the Arab "street" — the majority of ordinary citizens — had finally found a way to confront and overthrow the political elites that had oppressed and exploited them for so long. In Yemen, for example, the opposition movement even extracted a promise from President Ali Abdullah Saleh to cede power to his vice president in exchange for immunity from prosecution. This promise remains unfulfilled at the time of writing. Whereas it once looked as though 2011 could be the year in which the peoples of the Arab world would replace their dictatorships with Western style democracies, by 2012 storm clouds had already begun to gather in the wake of these popular revolts. As events continue to unfold, it is clear that the impetus for grassroots democratic reform throughout the region has been slowed in some countries and effectively halted in others. The record of political developments does not inspire confidence.

Tunisia, since the 2011 uprising, has seen the emergence of a powerful religious bloc headed by Ennahda, an Islamist party that won 90 out of 217 seats in the new National Constituent Assembly. Although the leadership of Ennahda has tried to reassure liberal opinion that it has no intention of introducing *sharia* law, the evidence suggests otherwise (Thornton 2012). Already there have been major confrontations between the secular authorities and the religious fundamentalists over such issues as the contentious religious expectation that women wear the *niqab* (the full veil), the need to ban allegedly "blasphemous" movies and campaigns to convert churches into mosques. The influence of the religious lobby is growing in Tunisia, especially in the more conservative rural areas. Najib Chebbi, leader of the Progressive Democratic Party, has called Ennahda "a non-democratic force" with "an ideological project they haven't acknowledged yet" (Thornton 2012: 1). The evidence suggests that a new Islamist elite is ready to replace the former dictator and his entourage.

In Egypt, since the fall of Mubarak, the picture is no more encouraging. The democracy movement that began in Tahrir Square appears to be in full retreat as the forces of law and order tighten their grip on the country. In the first rounds of the 2011 elections, the Muslim Brotherhood and other Islamist parties won 70 percent of the popular vote. At the same time, the army has consolidated its hold over the population by shooting democracy activists and Coptic Christian protestors, outlawing foreign pro-democracy NGOs and suppressing popular dissent. Political power has remained with the military elite, while the condition of the majority of the population remains largely unaltered. As one Middle East expert suggests:

> This latest adaptation of autocracy in the Arab world is more honest than its previous incarnations. Before the uprising in Egypt began, the military ruled from behind the curtain while elites, represented

by public relations firms and buoyed by snappy slogans, initiated neoliberal economic policies throughout Egypt. In this latest rendering ... the state's objective of restoring a structure of rule by military managers is not even concealed. This sort of "orderly transition" in post-Mubarak Egypt is more likely to usher in a return to the repressive status quo than an era of widening popular participation. (Stacher 2011: 4)

In Libya, where Gaddafi was overthrown with the help of NATO air support and a no-fly zone, the political situation remains in dangerous flux. Eastern Libya (Cyrenaica), the centre of resistance to the Gaddafi regime, is presently controlled by a strong Islamist presence with direct links to Al Qaeda through its local affiliate, the Libyan Islamic Fighting Group (LIFG). Besides its conquest of Benghazi and Darnah, and take-over of Tripoli, the LIFG has provided numerous fighters to the insurgencies in Afghanistan and Iraq. The Islamists are likely to play a major role in any future government in Libya; indeed, the flag of Al Qaeda has already been seen flying over the courthouse in Benghazi (Greenhill 2011). Even the leaders of the National Transitional Council, the interim government, have made it clear that in the new Libya there will be no separation of religion from the state. One of their first pledges was to repeal the old regime's ban on polygamy — as contrary to *sharia* law.

In Syria, the picture has been even grimmer. The repression of the early reform movement has escalated into a full-blown civil war. Peaceful protests against the authoritarian regime of Bashar al-Assad developed into an armed resistance, while the casualties multiply at an appalling rate. By the summer of 2012, it was estimated that over 19,000 people had died in the Syrian civil war over the previous six months (*Guardian* U.K., July 22, 2012). Meanwhile, in other nations of the region, Bahrain, Saudi Arabia and the Gulf States, a brutal counter-revolution is underway against the pro-democracy movements. The lesson for grassroots activists has been that regime change does not necessarily lead to social revolution, or even to democratic reform. While popular agitation can sometimes topple a dictator, the resulting political vacuum may quickly be filled by a regime that is even worse. A dramatic example of how a popular uprising can remove one dictator only to fall under the shadow of another is the case of Iran in 1979, when the secular regime of the Shah was replaced by the theocratic regime of the Ayatollah Khomeini. Regime change may result in the displacement of one elite and its replacement by another — while the interests of the majority remain unaddressed. From the time that the French Revolution was hijacked by Napoleon Bonaparte, many attempts at radical social change have met with a similar fate.

To further complicate the process of democratic reform, many of the oil-rich monarchies in the Middle East are sponsored and supported by outside interests — notably American. Ever mindful of its long-term energy needs and its close alliance with Israel, the U.S. has always favoured geo-political security over democracy in the region. Many of the political elites that have dominated Arab societies for so long have consistently relied on U.S. military and economic aid to buttress their regimes and provide them with international legitimacy. This begins to explain the longevity of some Arab dictatorships, or what one contemporary observer has termed the "Adaptable Autocrats" (Stacher 2012). The history of many of these societies could have been written by the early Muslim scholar Ibn Khaldun, who foretold the regular rise and fall of Arab dynasties. In more recent times, republican elites in the region have sometimes replaced royalist elites, and theocratic elites have sometimes replaced secular elites. During the Cold War period, pro-Western elites were sometimes replaced by pro-Soviet elites. But it was the Italian social thinker Vilfredo Pareto who first described what he called "the circulation of elites" in societies, a cycle of domination which has resulted in the permanent exclusion of the masses from any real participation in the political process.

The Impossible Dream of Democracy

None of this would have surprised Pareto. He believed that — notwithstanding the stirring rhetorical flourishes of "Liberty, Equality, Fraternity" from the French Revolution, "Life, Liberty and the Pursuit of Happiness" from the American Revolution and "Workers of the World Unite" from the international communist movement —revolutions simply replace one political elite with another. For the large majority of ordinary citizens, the "masses," as far as the exercise of power is concerned, nothing ever really changes. While new regimes may sometimes introduce other kinds of change — token political reforms, economic opportunities for foreign investors; cutbacks and austerity programs at home — the elites still remain at the top and the masses still languish at the bottom of society. Revolutions always maintain the ascendancy of the "top dogs" and the "fat cats" over the "underdogs." Thus has it been throughout the ages; thus will it always be. Because of these views, Pareto is often regarded as a pessimistic social theorist. Unlike most of the Enlightenment thinkers, who believed that historical change was driven by the imperatives of reason, liberty and progress (see Chapter 3), Pareto had a more cynical view of history. Instead of interpreting past liberal-democratic revolutions as progressive steps in the expansion of popular participation, the extension of human rights and majority rule, Pareto concluded that revolutions merely signal the swing of the political pendulum away from one displaced elite towards the installation of another. Although the composition of elites may change, life for the masses at the bottom of the social pyramid remains pretty much the same. Pareto's philosophy of history contends that the majority of the population of any society can never hope to equitably share power with the political elite or share wealth with the economic elite. For Pareto, democracy in any meaningful sense is an impossible dream.

In place of the linear and progressive narrative of the Enlightenment, Pareto offers us a cyclical narrative whereby the history of social and political change can best be understood as the displacement of one elite by another — a recurrent process he calls the "circulation of elites." According to Pareto, any elite will continue to exercise power until it is successfully challenged by a more robust counter-elite. In other words, any elite will continue to govern the masses until its power base begins to decay and its authority wanes. Only when the rot sets in will the incumbent elite be challenged and eventually overthrown by a counter-elite. Pareto distinguished between two types of elite: a tough-minded conservative elite committed to traditional values, honour and morality, which rules through coercion when necessary; and a more pragmatic elite motivated by profit, speculation and innovation, which rules through manipulation, deception and cooptation when necessary. Pareto referred to the repressive elite as the "lions" and the more opportunistic elite as the "foxes." According to Pareto, the circulation of elites is the story of an endless succession of coups and counter-coups; revolutions and counter-revolutions; and electoral reforms and counter-reforms. As we shall see, many power shifts in the contemporary world of politics can be interpreted through Pareto's theory of elites.

Like all powerful metanarratives, Pareto's theory of elites offers us a view of current and future social events based upon a generalization from past events. From this perspective, the future of the Arab Spring looks disappointingly bleak. Indeed, if we are to believe Pareto, the overthrow of the Tunisian, Egyptian and Libyan dictatorships will result in the installation of new elites that will exercise their power in less repressive ways. Although the replacement of old elites with new elites may serve to restrain the most brutal aspects of a regime, for the masses at the bottom of society, very little is likely to change — either in their economic standards of living or in their political freedoms. While life at the top may have changed with the circulation of elites, life at the bottom — on the Arab street — is likely to remain essentially the same. Thus spake Pareto.

Rotating Elites in the World Today

In many ways, Pareto's theory of political and social change makes a lot of sense. Indeed, the recent history of some of the most famous revolutions of our time can be easily understood using Pareto's theoretical perspective. Although to some, his conception of the circulation of elites may seem overly cynical, for others, it appears eminently realistic. Several examples may be used to illustrate the relevance of Pareto's argument.

The revolution that ended apartheid and introduced majority rule into South Africa, between 1990 and 1994, can be explained using Pareto's theory of the circulation of elites. In a nutshell: Pareto would probably have argued that the old hardboiled white, Dutch-speaking, Afrikaner political elite (the lions), which had always exercised raw power through state repression, was challenged by a rising white, English-speaking, Anglo economic elite (the foxes). This corporate elite concluded that, because of internal civil unrest, neighbouring wars and external sanctions, apartheid had become unsustainable. Whereas the traditional Afrikaner elite had maintained rigid control over the political system, the rising corporate elite realized that political reforms had now become necessary in order to avoid a major economic recession and social collapse. The growing antagonism between the intransigent Afrikaner political elite and the reform-minded Anglo corporate elite was already evident in the 1960s, as reported by van den Berghe (1967: 206):

> The English business class perceives the Nationalist government as threatening in several ways. In the strictly political sense, big businessmen notice with alarm the gradual erosion of the civil liberties and privileges which they have so far enjoyed as members of the dominant White group.... Economically, they view government policies as interfering with free enterprise, and with almost every rational principle of industrial development, as well as endangering export markets through increasing isolationism and unpopularity abroad.

Further evidence for this shift in elites can be deduced from several significant events — including a number of clandestine meetings that took place between top corporate executives and senior members of the African National Congress (ANC) — the Black African liberation movement — which was in exile. Most of these meetings were held in secret, behind the backs of the apartheid government. As van Wyk points out:

> By the mid-1980s some segments of white capital began to distance themselves from the regime as elites began increasingly to realise that "the centre cannot hold." In September 1986, Gavin O'Reilly, chairman of the South African mining conglomerate Anglo-American Corporation met with ANC elites in Zambia.... These initiatives, which paved the way for subsequent greater elite interactions, clearly illustrate the crucial role of elites and leaders in initiating change.... [By October 1987], ANC stalwart Oliver Tambo requested Michael Young, an English mining magnate, to facilitate what resulted in a series of twelve secret meetings between Afrikaner and ANC elites.

Subsequently known as the Mells Park talks, these were led on the ANC's side by Thabo Mbeki. (van Wyk 2009)

The interpenetration of the Anglo corporate capitalist elite with the Black ANC political elite produced a coalition that was able to supplant the old political system based on apartheid. The fusion of these two elites was made possible, in part, through guarantees given to big business — especially to the mining sector — by the ANC. These guarantees included pledges not to undertake the nationalization of big business and not to engage in land reform or in the wholesale redistribution of wealth.

As a liberation movement, the ANC advocated nationalisation, but once the political transition commenced, it discarded nationalisation. Instead of nationalisation and the redistribution of wealth as a framework to undo the socio-economic legacies of apartheid, ANC elites opted for pro-business/market policies, which stabilised the economy and attracted much needed foreign direct investment but produced mixed developmental results. (van Wyk 2009)

While the implementation of neoliberal policies — full marketization, privatization and de-regulation — secured the alliance between the ANC elite and the corporate elite, these policies have done little or nothing to raise the living standards of the African majority. Indeed, many observers note that the poverty and destitution in the Black townships and squatter camps remains largely unchanged. Much as Pareto would have predicted, the transfer of power from the lions of apartheid to the foxes of the ANC has left the conditions of the urban and rural masses in South Africa pretty much as they were under apartheid.

Many of the so-called "colour revolutions" in post-communist Eastern Europe and Central Asia were not the democratic revolutions they first appeared to be. It has become increasingly evident that the "rose revolution" in Georgia (November 2003–January 2004), the "orange revolution" in Ukraine (January 2005) and the "tulip revolution" Kyrgyzstan in (April 2005) were spearheaded by NGOs which were closely aligned with United States foreign-policy interests (strategic expansion, energy security and the war on terrorism). While evidence of this type of geo-political manipulation cannot be used to discredit all popular uprisings — many of which began as authentic grassroots struggles for democracy and social justice —the extent of superpower manipulation makes it imperative to evaluate each case on its own merits.

Observers continue to express skepticism regarding the fate of these revolutions. In many cases, it appears that the earlier autocratic communist elites (the lions) have simply been replaced by more astute and media-savvy political leaders backed by powerful financial oligarchs (the foxes). This realization led at least one writer (Furman 2008: 29–47) to critique what he calls the "imitation democracies" of the post-Soviet zone. Other commentators also describe the pattern of elite politics in this region as former communist dictatorships give way to new forms of elite governance.

> The Orange Revolution in Ukraine, the Rose Revolution in Georgia, and the Tulip Revolution in Kyrgyzstan have been widely interpreted as democratic breakthroughs. This largely misses the most important point. In fact, these revolutions reflect the continuity of the old system more than they reflect change. This old system, one of patronal presidentialism, is marked by regular and reasonably predictable oscillations between what appears to be autocracy and what appears to be democracy ... since the mid-1990s, the presidents of Belarus, Kazakhstan, Tajikistan, Turkmenistan, and Uzbekistan have all subverted constitutional term limits and remained healthy enough so that few expect them to willingly depart the political scene anytime soon. (Hale 2005)

At the same time, observers have seen further evidence of the circulation of elites, not only in South Africa and the post-Soviet states, but also in the stable western liberal democracies. Higley (2001, 2003, 2011; Higley and Pakulski 2007, 2011) suggests that there has been a transition from the fox-like diplomatic elites that governed most liberal democracies during the first half of the twentieth century to the more lion-like militaristic elites that came to power in the 1980s — and whose legacies continue to this day. Whereas the post-war Western diplomatic elites were led by wily politicians — such as Dwight Eisenhower, John F. Kennedy, Lyndon Johnson and Jimmy Carter in the U.S., and Harold Macmillan, Harold Wilson and James Callaghan in the U.K. — things changed abruptly in the last two decades of the twentieth century. The 1980s saw the rise of militaristic elites led by a new breed of lion-like politicians such as Ronald Reagan (in the U.S.), Margaret Thatcher (in the U.K.) and Helmut Kohl (in Germany). This generation of political leaders was far more combative and aggressive in both domestic and foreign policies than that which preceded it. Reagan authorized several aggressive foreign policy adventures, including the invasions of Grenada (to overthrow the revolutionary New Jewel government) and Panama (to overthrow Manuel Noriega), the bombing of Libya (in a failed assassination of Muammar Gaddafi), the funding of the "contras" in Nicaragua (to overthrow the Sandinista government of Daniel Ortega) and of the Mujahideen in Afghanistan, and the domestic political battle against the air traffic controllers' union. For her part, Thatcher launched the war in the Falklands (against Argentina), imposed neoliberal policies at home and broke the back of the national mineworkers' union.

Within the past decade, even more dramatic shifts have occurred in the nature of governing elites and their leaders. As Higley (2003: 25) suggests: "Concatenating world trends and international pressures, grievously punctuated by the 9/11 attacks on New York and Washington, are altering the character of elite rule in the United States in rough accord with Pareto's sketch. With the presidency of George W. Bush an exceptionally cohesive and leonine elite has gained ascendancy." Indeed, there appears to have been a wholesale shift to lion-like elites, and "Caesarist" leaders have come to power in many Western countries — ranging from George W. Bush (U.S.), Tony Blair (U.K.), Silvio Berlusconi (Italy), Angela Merkel (Germany), Nicolas Sarkozy (France), and last, but not least, Stephen Harper (Canada). At the time of writing, the lions continue to hold sway over the foxes in some nations, while in others — with the re-election of Barak Obama in the US, and of Francois Hollande in France, for example — the foxes appear to have regained their power.

Manipulated Masses

The corollary to Pareto's theory of elites is his theory of the masses. For Pareto, the majority population, or mass, of any society is forever destined to be ruled by elites — either through force or manipulation. He believed that the masses are incapable of governing themselves, and for this reason he concluded that the ideal of a popular or mass democracy was an impossible dream. Pareto's view of governance is summarized in his contemptuous observations on what he considered to be the sham institutions of democracy:

> We need not linger on the fiction of "popular representation" — poppycock grinds no flour…. one finds everywhere a governing class of relatively few individuals that keeps itself in power partly by force and partly by the consent of the subject class, which is much more populous…. A governing class is present everywhere, even where there is a despot, but the forms under which it appears are widely variable. In absolute governments a sovereign occupies the stage alone. In so called democratic governments it is the parliament. But behind the scenes in both cases there are always people who play a very important role in actual government. To be sure they must now and again bend the knee to the whims of ignorant and domineering sovereigns or parliaments, but they are soon back at their tenacious, patient, never-ending work, which is of much the greater consequence. (Pareto 1935: 1569, 1573)

These and similar sentiments led one commentator on Pareto to conclude: "The inevitability of elite rule makes democracy an imaginary dream. Elites can never be accountable to 'the people.' There is an inverse relationship between elites and democracy so that institutions proclaimed to be 'democratic' are in reality exercises in futility" (Higley 2001).

According to Pareto, as well as other elite theorists, like Gaetano Mosca and Robert Michels, there is no such thing as a truly democratic society in which government is "of the people, by the people, for the people" — to quote Abraham Lincoln. True social equality is unattainable, and all supposedly "democratic" revolutions are fated to eventually fall under the power of new elites. Far from being "self-evident truths" or "inalienable rights," the proclamations and declarations of equality enshrined in the revolutionary constitutions of America, France and elsewhere were, for Pareto, unrealizable myths which history had contradicted and falsified many times over.

One researcher (Higley 2001) labelled this disbelief in the possibility of democracy and social equality as the "futility thesis." For elite theorists who subscribe in one way or another to the futility thesis, even the supposedly democratic states of Western Europe and North America can be shown to be "sham democracies." Such theorists allege that the masses in these countries are manipulated by fraud, deception, propaganda, misinformation, intimidation and other material or symbolic pressures by a ruling elite, or set of elites. Along with Pareto, most elite theorists share a low opinion of the ordinary person in the street. Pareto concluded that the beliefs and actions of the masses are invariably motivated by irrational sentiments — strong emotions, passions and prejudices — which he called "residues." These residues — discussed in greater detail below — are best understood as non-logical or, according to Pareto, "irrational" sentiments or "mental states" that are rooted in basic human drives and emotions. These residues do not vary from one time or place to another and are found in all human societies. The two most significant residues that influence group action are those associated with innovation and reform (class I residues, the "instinct for combining") and those associated with conservatism and resistance to change (class 2 residues, the "persistence of aggregates"). Pareto believed that class I residues were expressed through experimentation, manipulation and innovation, while class 2 residues were expressed through a strong sense of loyalty, morality, discipline, honour, tradition and national security.

At the same time, Pareto suggested that although their beliefs and actions arise from irrational sources, the masses often find quasi-rational ways to justify and legitimize these beliefs and actions. These justifications are often expressed as ideologies, religious faiths, political doctrines and other public belief systems. Pareto refers to these forms of intellectual justification as "derivations." Derivations are the ways in which the masses try to clothe non-logical conduct and belief in a mantle of logic. Thus, although the drive to belong to a community and worship something larger than oneself has remained constant throughout history, Pareto suggests that the derivations used to justify or rationalize this drive are continually changing — from primitive beliefs, to the major world religions, to secular ideologies such as nationalism, socialism and humanitarianism. Thus, the residue for belonging remains constant, but the derivations corresponding to this residue are forever changing.

> The many varieties of Socialism, Syndicalism, Radicalism, Tolstoyism, pacifism, humanitarianism, Solidarism, and so on, form a sum that may be said to belong to the democratic religion, much as there was a sum of numberless sects in the early days of the Christian religion.... Socialism made room for itself by crowding back some of the prevailing faiths such as Catholicism and nationalism, and assimilating others, such as humanitarianism and a so-called Liberal Christianity and not at all liberal)... For many such people Christ has been stripped of all divine attributes and is to be applauded only as a Socialist or humanitarian leader. (Pareto 1935: 1145, 1294)

There has been a long tradition of disparaging the masses, or what we commonly refer to today as the "general public" or "electorate" — especially among elite theorists. Even the left-wing elite theorist C. Wright Mills (1956: 357), in his book *The Power Elite*, lamented what he called the "ostracism of mind from public affairs" and the apparent ability of media and political elites to turn modern citizens into "cheerful robots." Over the years, there has been much criticism directed at the political ignorance of the electorate, and growing concern is often expressed for the dangers that such public ignorance poses for the future of democracy. The U.S. right-wing Cato Institute, in a 1999 policy report, cited 1964 research data that revealed "more than 86 percent of the American people based their political decisions on criteria ranging from blind party loyalty and a candidate's perceived personal traits (is he smart? does he 'care about people like us?'), to such vague and dubious criteria as the 'nature of the times' (if there is prosperity and peace, the incumbent party must be responsible) and primitive judgments about the attitudes of political parties toward social groups such as races and classes" (Friedman 1999). Indeed, most voters appeared to be motivated more by irrational campaigns driven by values, rhetoric and misinformation than by real substantive political debates. Amazingly, a 1994 study found that "at the height of the Cold War, 62 percent of the U.S. public failed to realize that the U.S.S.R. was not a member of NATO" (Friedman 1999). None of this would have surprised Pareto.

As illustrated in the comedy mono-logue in Figure 12-2, public opinion surveys reveal an appalling level of prejudice and misinformation among Republican voters in the U.S. regard-ing the origins, beliefs and policies of President Barak Obama. Astonishing though this level of ignorance may ap-pear, it is far from unprecedented in the American electorate. Studies conducted during the 1950s at Columbia and Michigan universities and published in *The American Voter* (see Campbell et al. 1960; Lewis-Beck et al. 2008), revealed a woeful lack of knowledge among the American electorate regarding major political issues and a marked tendency for non-rational voter behaviour. These trends have been exacerbated by aggressive political campaigns, highly partisan media pundits and the internet. Within the past couple of decades, a volatile political climate has emerged in which attack-ads, conspiracy theories, malicious rumours and "wedge issues" have ratcheted up the level of public distrust and disinformation. Whether we are talking about the "birthers," who question President Obama's nationality; the "truthers," who question the official narrative of 9/11; or the moral panics raised by populist movements like the Tea Party over such wedge issues as abortion, same-sex marriage, gun control and school prayer, we are in a period when public passions and misinformation are running high. The spread of irrational ideas among the U.S. electorate is well documented in *Just How Stupid Are We?* (Shenkman 2008), *The Irrational Electorate* (Bartels 2008) and *Wingnuts: How the Lunatic Fringe Is Hijacking America* (Avlon 2010). Again, there is no doubt that Pareto would have felt vindicated by these findings.

> **Figure 12-2 The Irrational Public**
>
> **He May Be the Antichrist**
>
> A new Harris poll found that 57 percent of Republicans believe President Obama is a Muslim — 57 percent. 45 percent believe he was not born in the United States. 38 percent feel he's, quote, "doing many of the things that Hitler did." And 24 percent believe he may be the Antichrist. Oh, like Oprah would date the Antichrist.
>
> Jimmy Kimmel Monologue on *Jimmy Kimmel Live*.

We may find it difficult to accept Pareto's final verdict — that democracy and popular government is an impossible dream. Even knowing the outcome of past revolutions, we may not wish to abandon all hope in the possibility of greater social equality, social justice and social democracy — in our own society and around the world. But perhaps Pareto's arguments do not really require us to jettison our most cherished beliefs — even if these are only "derivations." At the very least, Pareto makes a compelling case against the possibility of democracy, a case that deserves to be taken seriously, and answered. If he has provoked us to reflect upon our own taken-for-granted assumptions, then he has performed a valuable service.

Pareto and the Italian Elite Theorists

The best way to understand Pareto's ideas is to see them as an outgrowth of the historical tradition of Italian social thought. Every tradition of social thought can be traced back to its historical roots. For example, classical French social theory can be traced back to Rousseau and other philosophers of the French Revolutionary period. In Germany, Kant and Hegel lay the foundations for the later development of classical social theory. While in Great Britain, the classical tradition can be traced back to Hobbes. In the case of Italy, the roots of classical social theory can be found in the works of Niccolo Machiavelli.

In his most famous work, *The Prince* (1961), which was written in 1513 as a treatise on government for the ruler of Florence, Machiavelli introduced what would become enduring themes of Italian social thought. Machiavelli suggested that, in the interests of social harmony, it was the duty of the ruler to govern effectively and the duty of the people to acquiesce to the authority of the ruler. Machiavelli believed that the social world was divisible into two fundamental categories — the rulers and the ruled. This division was the cornerstone of Machiavelli's theory of society and the hallmark of successive generations of Italian social theory. This tradition of social thought which analyzed society in terms of the relationship between the dominant political and economic elites and the subordinate masses, later became known as "elite theory." In his advice to rulers of his time, Machiavelli suggested that the most effective rulers were those who used a combination of force on the one hand, and fraud, deception and cunning on the other, to enforce their will. Today, we would refer to this distinction as the difference between "hard power " versus "soft power." Soft power — as a term of international diplomacy — refers to the ability of a state to secure the cooperation of another through non-coercive means — by providing a model for prosperity, political values or economic partnership. Hard power refers to the ability of a state to secure the compliance of another through coercive means — such as military force, sanctions or the withdrawal of economic aid (Nye 1990).

In Machiavelli's terms, rulers who relied primarily on the use of force to subjugate the masses were characterized as "lions," whereas rulers who relied primarily on the use of cunning were characterized as "foxes." Machiavelli believed that effective rulers needed to use the techniques of both the lion and the fox to maintain sovereignty. As we have seen, Pareto inherited these terms from Machiavelli and incorporated them into his own theory of society.

For Machiavelli, the purpose of social theory was essentially practical — it was intended to inform and refine the practice of government. Unlike the Enlightenment thinkers, who sought the liberation and emancipation of humanity, irrespective of whether these thinkers were monarchists, republicans, liberals, socialists, communists or feminists, Machiavelli's goals were far more pragmatic. He was primarily concerned with the theory and practice of effective governance — whether through force, or through manipulation. For this reason, Machiavelli's political philosophy may strike us today as unashamedly cynical. Indeed, the very term "Machiavellian" has come to mean "manipulative" in everyday discourse. But in his defence, Machiavelli was mostly concerned with formulating the principles of effective governance in the hope that these would eventually unify the Italian nation and put an end to the incessant wars between city-states. Machiavelli never lived to see the realization of this dream.

As mentioned, Machiavelli's political philosophy helped to shape the classical tradition of Italian social thought. Machiavelli believed that in every society, it was always the destiny of the few to rule and the destiny of many to be ruled. He also believed that the masses were largely motivated by irrational factors — such as myth, religion, political doctrine and other narratives which appealed to their uninformed passions. For Machiavelli, the basic division of society between elites and masses remained constant and unchanging. In every society, the elites would rise to the top and the masses would fall to the bottom, although a person of humble origins could become a member of these elites. Whether or not the elites were capable of producing stable authoritarian rule was largely dependent upon their skill in the art of domination.

Machiavelli formulated a theory of society that was greatly at odds with most of the Enlightenment philosophers. Unlike the Enlightenment thinkers, Machiavelli was not an optimist, nor did he believe in the doctrine of "human perfectibility." He scorned such ideals as liberty, equality and progress and was certainly skeptical of the concepts of democracy. Above all, Machiavelli saw himself as a realist. He believed that it was the fate of the majority to be ruled by the minority, and his main concern was that the minority learn to govern effectively in order to bring peace and stability to the nation. His ideas may appear to us as little more than an apologia for the autocratic ruler — the rule of the "strongman." But we should always remember that Machiavelli wrote in the sixteenth century and, as a counsellor to princes, was primarily concerned with the practice of stable and effective governance. In addition to Pareto, many Italian social theorists, for example, Gaetano Mosca and Robert Michels, were influenced by Machiavelli's elite theory. Even the Italian Marxist Antonio Gramsci — who was imprisoned by fascist leader Benito Mussolini during World War II — was partially influenced by Machiavelli. Although the Marxist theory of class struggle and revolution stands in sharp contrast to Machiavelli's theory, Gramsci incorporated some aspects of elite theory into his version of Marxism. He did this by introducing the concept of "hegemony" into his analysis of class relations. Hegemony refers to the cultural dominance exercised by a ruling class — through its

Figure 12-3 Italian Elite Theorists

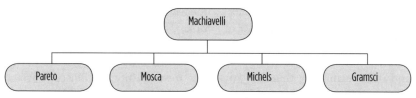

ideological control of the media, the schools, the politicians, the trade unions, the law and sometimes the churches — over an exploited or oppressed class, such as the working class.

Demystifying Social Life

One of the recurrent themes in Pareto's social theory is his stated intention to demystify social life. Pareto took great delight in unmasking what he regarded as the realities behind the appearances of social life. He was particularly concerned to show that most of the powerful systems of abstract thought that had supposedly influenced the course of human history, or had helped to shape society — such as religions, political ideologies and even philosophical systems — all drew their inspiration from underlying passions and irrational sentiments. In other words, nothing can ever be taken at face value, least of all, the intellectual justifications which are used by elites to consolidate their power and which are internalized by the masses as part of their own subordination. According to Pareto, if we probe beneath the surface of popular consciousness, we shall always find a deeper layer of irrational impulses and sentiments. The masses are always mobilized through an appeal to these irrational sentiments. For Pareto, it made little difference how elites succeeded in legitimizing their power and authority in society. Some elites have used the ideology of liberal capitalism, others, the ideologies of nationalism, fascism, socialism or communism. More recently, some elites have even used religious fundamentalism to seize and consolidate their power. While the name of the game may change — from religion to politics to ethnicity and race — the rules of the game remain the same: elites are destined to rule, and the masses are destined to be ruled.

Pareto was not alone in his urge to demystify social relations. Throughout the nineteenth century, many theorists and philosophers set out to expose the hidden content of social relations and uncover the underlying causal mechanisms that shape our social institutions and our individual identities. Thus, Marx probed beneath the surface of bourgeois society in order to reveal the underlying mechanism of labour exploitation. Sigmund Freud dug beneath the surface of bourgeois consciousness in order to expose the dark recesses of the sexualized unconscious mind. Even the philosopher

Friedrich Nietzsche explored the philosophies of his day in order to reveal the underlying will-to-power that he believed provided the real motives for human action in the world. And, of course, Charles Darwin discovered what he believed to be the underlying mechanism that explained the origin and development of the species — evolution through natural selection. In these and other examples, theorists attempted to demystify the illusory surface of appearances in order to expose an underlying causality. In this respect, the nineteenth century may be thought of as the "Age of Demystification."

Settling Accounts

Like other theorists, Pareto's ideas were influenced both positively and nega-tively by those who preceded him and his contemporaries. For Pareto, as for all social theorists, theory was an intellectual "conversation" conducted in part with the ghosts of past social thinkers, and in part with social thinkers of his own time. In Pareto's case, much of his conversation with other think-ers was essentially negative. As he aged, Pareto grew more dismissive of the prevailing theories and philosophies of his age. He became a controversialist who saw himself as a beacon of hard-nosed rationalism in a world mired in sentiment and illusion. That being said, Pareto was far from being a wholly original thinker, and many of his theoretical ideas were influenced by other social theorists.

Machiavelli

As already noted, Machiavelli was the most important source of the Italian tradition of social theory, and Pareto's intellectual debt to Machiavelli was profound. It was in Machiavelli's work that Pareto first encountered the elite theory of society, and it was also from Machiavelli that Pareto borrowed the metaphor of the lions and the foxes. Much of Pareto's own work may be seen as an attempt to place Machiavelli's ideas on a more contemporary and more scientific footing. Pareto tried to find an incontrovertible scientific explanation for the persistence of elites in society.

Figure 12-4 Pareto's Intellectual Influences

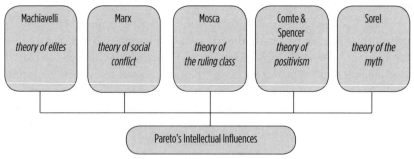

Marx

Pareto's relationship to Marx was far more ambivalent than was his relationship to Machiavelli. Much of Pareto's work was an extended attack on Marx's ideas and on the social movements inspired by these ideas. In many ways, Pareto assumed the role of an "anti-Marx." His criticism of what he regarded as Marx's utopian politics, and his withering contempt for the revolutionary aspirations of the socialists, are sarcastically recorded in many pages of his sociological writings. However, although Pareto rejected Marx's economic critique of capitalist society and ridiculed the doctrine of socialism as a secular religion designed for the uneducated and irrational masses, he was not unsympathetic to some of Marx's social analysis. While he discounted Marx as an economist, he partially accepted him as a sociologist. Pareto agreed with Marx that the working class lived in a state of "false consciousness" as a result of their internalization of the ideology of the ruling class. Both Marx and Pareto concluded that the working class was unable to recognize, or act according to, its own rational self-interest. The big difference between these two theorists was that Marx believed that the working class had the potential to correct its false consciousness and thereby come to a full understanding of its role as an agent of revolutionary change. Pareto, on the other hand, concluded that the masses were incapable of rational action in their own self-interest. For this reason, they were condemned to remain in a perpetual state of dependency and subordination to the elites in society. Even though some political ideologies try to conceal this fundamental social division through egalitarian rhetoric, according to Pareto, the evidence shows that in all societies the masses remain subordinated to the elite. However, Pareto remained attracted to Marx's theory of social conflict. Like Marx, Pareto saw human history as a conflict between antagonistic social groups — the elite versus the masses. But unlike Marx, Pareto believed that social conflict, especially class conflict, would remain an unchanging aspect of social relations. Whereas Marx believed that the revolutionary overthrow of capitalism would eventually eliminate class conflict, Pareto concluded that social and class conflict were here to stay.

Positivism

One of the strongest influences to shape Pareto's social theory was that of positivism. Throughout his career, Pareto saw himself as a "scientist" engaged in the rational study of society. His goal was to reduce the complexity of society to a set of abstract social and economic laws, much as Isaac Newton had reduced the complexity of nature to a set of abstract physical laws. "Above, far above the prejudices and passions of men soar the laws of nature. Eternal and immutable, they are the expression of the creative power they represent what is, what must be, what otherwise could not be. Man can come to understand them: he is incapable of changing them" (Pareto, [1896–1897] 1996: 122).

Although he recognized both Comte and Spencer as early champions of the positivist program in sociology, Pareto rejected what he perceived as the dogmatic and illogical elements of their work and ideas — especially those of Comte. "Comte becomes a prophet. The battle of ideas is over. So now he begins pronouncing dogma … and it is only natural that nothing but sentiments should now be left on the field — his own sentiments, of course" (Pareto 1935: 189).

Pareto's ambition was to develop a rigorous analytical science of society which was capable of generating universal laws of social behaviour. Compared to Comte and Spencer, Pareto advanced a rigorous, even extreme, conception of positivism. For this reason, he could be described as an "ultra-positivist." He insisted that all the basic assumptions contained in any theoretical perspective be based upon "factual observations." For Pareto, observable facts were the elementary building blocks of social theory. They formed the basis for any higher order generalizations. He believed that the hallmark of any rigorous science was its ability to logically progress from the collection of observable facts to the construction of universal generalizations that could eventually be formulated as abstract, mathematical laws.

Although Pareto insisted upon very strict logical and empirical rules for the practice of social science, he often broke these rules in his own research and studies. In this respect, he was just as inconsistent, or just as hypocritical, as many other social theorists who fail to practise what they preach. Pareto's most positivistic and abstract work is now celebrated more by economists than by sociologists. Pareto defined economics as the study of rational behaviour because economic behaviour was so strongly motivated by self-interest. He defined sociology, on the other hand, as the study of non-rational behaviour because so much social behaviour was strongly influenced by sentiments and non-logical passions. Because of its relative unpredictability and uncertainty, Pareto concluded that non-rational, or social, behaviour could not be studied as rigorously as rational, or economic, behaviour.

It was in his economic studies that Pareto came closest to formulating abstract laws that could be expressed as mathematical formulae. His best known example of an economic law is often called the Pareto Rule, or the 80%–20% Rule (also known as the "law of the vital few" and the "principle of factor sparsity"). This rule asserts that 80 percent of an output will be produced by 20 percent of the population. Pareto observed that in his own society, 80 percent of the wealth and income was owned by only 20 percent of the population. Today, we can test this rule by predicting that in a university, for example, 80 percent of the research will be produced by only 20 percent of the faculty members. In a business enterprise, 80 percent of the business normally comes from only 20 percent of the clients, or customers. We can also apply this rule to our own private lives. Thus, we are likely to wear only 20 percent of our favourite clothes for 80 percent of the time. Or we may spend 80 percent of our free time with only 20 percent of our friends and relations. Although Pareto aspired to explain all human behaviour in terms of abstract mathematical laws, he was only able to achieve this degree of rigour in his study of rational, economic behaviour. The study of non-rational, or social, behaviour proved too complex and unpredictable to reduce to abstract laws.

Other Intellectual Influences

Besides Machiavelli, Marx and the positivists, social theorists Gaetano Mosca and Georges Sorel were the most important influences on Pareto. In Mosca's famous work *The Ruling Class* (1939 [1836]), he outlined the view that in every society, power and authority would always be exercised by the minority over the majority. Mosca formulated a theory of elites which was similar to that advanced by Pareto. (For a discussion of the differences between the theories of Pareto, Mosca and Michels, see Femia, J. 2001). Mosca concluded that the concentration of power into the hands of an organized minority was an inevitable and natural aspect of social stratification.

It has been alleged by some writers (Ashley and Orenstein 2005: 329) that Mosca first coined the concept of circulation of elites, and Mosca himself accused Pareto of plagiarism, although Pareto strongly denied the charge. The other figure whose work partially influenced Pareto was French social theorist Georges Sorel. Although Sorel is often seen as a theorist of the revolutionary left, many of his ideas were later embraced by the revolutionary right. In other words, he was a theorist who influenced a number of violent political traditions — including anarchism, communism and fascism. He was a strong believer in the redemptive and liberating power of "direct action" as a form of political struggle. Direct action could include strikes, boycotts, sabotage, civil disobedience and even acts of terrorism. Sorel believed in the power of spontaneous action to bring about revolutionary changes in the political status quo.

> Proletarian violence comes upon the scene at the very moment when the conception

Figure 12-5 Mosca: On Elites

The domination of an organized minority, obeying a single impulse, over the unorganized majority is inevitable. The power of any minority is irresistible as against each single individual in the majority, who stands alone before the totality of the organized majority. At the same time, the minority is organized for the very reason that it is a minority. A hundred men acting uniformly in concert with a common understanding will triumph over a thousand men who are not in accord and can therefore be dealt with one by one.

Mosca (1939: 53).

of social peace claims to moderate disputes; proletarian violence confines employers to their role as producers and tends to restore the class structure just when they seemed on the point of intermingling in the democratic morass.... This violence compels capitalism to restrict its attentions solely to its material role and tends to restore to it the warlike qualities ... if a united and revolutionary proletariat confronts a rich bourgeoisie eager for conquest, capitalist society will reach its historical perfection. (Sorel 1999: 78–79)

Although he began his intellectual career as a Marxist, Sorel later collaborated with radical nationalist and fascist movements. Among other things, Sorel believed that the working class masses were driven largely by irrational impulses. Political leaders could best awaken the masses by appealing to their irrational sentiments — patriotism, racial and ethnic pride, class consciousness and other passionately held beliefs. Sorel contended that in order to arouse the masses, political leaders needed to construct popular myths — powerful stories which could be used to mobilize and energize the masses into collective action. Adolph Hitler later constructed the notorious myth of "the international Jewish conspiracy" to win support for the Nazi Party in Germany. Today, some would regard the "Axis of Evil" as a myth successfully constructed by the U.S. administration of George W. Bush to win support for its foreign policy — especially the global war on terrorism. Pareto was also attracted to the idea of the political myth, as it was a concept that helped to explain how elites manipulated the masses in modern societies.

Pareto's Conceptual Toolbox

Pareto's social theory assumes the impossibility of mass democratic politics. While not unsympathetic to the plight of "ordinary" people, Pareto argued that there are inherent, universal characteristics of human society that inevitably led to elite politics. In order to advance his theoretical narrative, Pareto employed a number of key concepts and basic assumptions — some of which were taken or modified from other theorists. Together, these concepts make up the basic toolbox that Pareto used throughout his long intellectual career.

The Irrational

As already discussed, Pareto placed great importance on the role of non-logical, or non-rational, action in society. He believed that most social action — especially among the masses — was motivated by non-logical factors such as traditional or customary sentiments, subconscious feelings and emotions, prejudices or other unexamined "psychic states." Much like Max Weber, Pareto distinguished three types of social action: logical, non-logical and illogical. For Pareto, as for Weber, logical, or rational, action is defined in

Figure 12-6 Pareto's Typology of Social Action

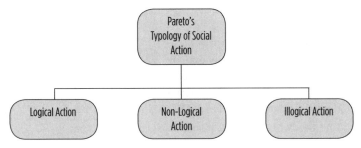

terms of a means/end calculus: logical action involves the selection of appropriate means to accomplish a practical end. The best examples of logical action — at least for Pareto — are to be found in strictly economic or scientific behaviours: "We apply the term *logical actions* ... to actions that are logical both subjectively and objectively.... Logical actions are very numerous among civilized peoples. Actions connected with the arts and sciences belong to that class, at least for artists and scientists" (Pareto 1935: 77–78).

Rational economic behaviour, which is normally driven by individual, collective or corporate self-interest, involves a rational calculation to bring about a specifically desired outcome. For example, a private business, such as a sporting goods company like Nike, Adidas or Reebok, may decide to outsource production to countries of the Global South in order to reduce its labour costs and to increase its profit margin. This would be regarded by Pareto as rational economic behaviour — that is, logical action. Similarly, the rational behaviour of scientists who collect and analyze their data under controlled conditions, and methodically test the validity of their hypotheses, is also regarded by Pareto as an example of logical action. Each of these examples is characterized by the rational calculation of means and ends.

It is important to remember that, in Pareto's typology, for an action to be defined as "logical" it has to be logical in two different aspects. It has first to be logical from the subjective viewpoint of the social actor, but it also has to be logical in its objective consequences. An action may be logical to an individual (according to their cultural beliefs) but may be non-logical according to its objective consequences. While it may be logical from the viewpoint of members of an indigenous community to perform a rain dance in order to bring rain for crop cultivation, this action is not regarded as logical — by scientific observers — in terms of its objective, meteorological, consequences. (For an interesting counter-argument on "rational magic," see Hendrix and Feltham 2011.) Action is only logical for Pareto if it can be objectively shown to have actually produced the desired ends. Logical action requires that both the subjectively logical motives of the actor and the objectively logical consequences of the action follow each other in a cause-effect relationship.

These two aspects of logical action were emphasized by Pareto throughout his discussions on this topic.

Pareto concluded that most social action in society is motivated by non-logical or even illogical factors which have little to do with rational calculation. In other words, Pareto believed that the actions of the masses in society were, for the most part, largely irrational. In any society, the actions of the majority are brought about either through fear of, or manipulation by, a dominant elite. Pareto dismissed the idea that most members of society were rational actors who logically calculated the consequences of their actions. On the contrary, he believed that most of us are like puppets — unaware that our strings are pulled by those who control us from above. For Pareto, all so-called "universal" principles and declarations were merely "rationalizations" (or "derivations") — elaborate excuses for actions that were motivated by deeply irrational and non-logical impulses. In the classical world of reason and optimism, Pareto held his own as an anti-rationalist — as a skeptic and a cynic.

> **Figure 12-7 Logical Action**
>
> From the subjective point of view nearly all human actions belong to the logical class. In the eyes of the Greek mariners, sacrifices to Poseidon and rowing with oars were equally logical means of navigation.... Suppose we apply the term logical actions to actions that logically conjoin means to ends not only from the standpoint of the subject performing them, but from the standpoint of other persons who have a more extensive knowledge-in other words, to actions that are logical both subjectively and objectively in the sense just explained. Other actions we shall call nonlogical (by no means the same as "illogical").
>
> Pareto 1935 [1916] *Mind and Society: A Treatise on General Sociology*, p. 77

Elites and Masses

Pareto was not a believer in democracies. For him, any society which proclaimed itself a democracy — "a government of the people, by the people, for the people" — was only fooling itself. Or more accurately, the elites in society were fooling the masses. He remained convinced that all societies were mechanisms for the rule of elites over the masses. This was the case irrespective of whether the society was described as a liberal democracy, a social democracy, a peoples' democracy, a republican democracy, a representative democracy, a participatory democracy, a direct democracy or any other permutation or combination of these ideological slogans. In other words, Pareto believed that all so-called democracies were, in fact, sham democracies in which the masses were dominated and manipulated by powerful political, economic, military, corporate and other elites in society. Pareto coined the term "pluto-democracy" to describe many of the European societies of his time. These societies were essentially "plutocracies" — societies governed by the rich — in which the masses were permitted to vote. But most of the candidates for political office came from the ranks of the wealthy. And although the masses enjoyed the right to vote, it was the rich and powerful who owned and operated the state. The idea of the pluto-democracy was later used by the Nazis to attack what they regarded as the corruption of the bourgeois state in Germany.

How does Pareto's theory of society compare with that of Marx? Both theorists believed that modern societies were based upon conflict, and in that sense, both were "conflict theorists." For Marx, modern society was based upon a conflict between the bourgeoisie and the proletariat. For Pareto, it was a conflict between the elite and the masses. Both theorists concluded that the lower classes in society were subordinated through force and through manipulation. Each theorist critiqued bourgeois democracy as a sham democracy in which the workers, or the masses, were dominated and exploited by the ruling classes, or the elites. However, although Marx declared the history of all societies to have been the history of class struggle, he recognized that the nature of class struggle was different for each historical period. In ancient societies, slavery formed the basis of class conflict, whereas in feudal societies, it was the military domination of the gentry and their private ownership of land. In capitalist societies, class conflict was based upon the economic domination of the working class by capitalists, through the exploitation of labour, and the private ownership and accumulation of capital. In other words, Marx proposed a theory of social conflict that was "historically specific." Every historical period produced its own unique class struggle which was distinct from those which preceded it and from those which would follow it. Pareto, on the other hand, proposed an abstract and trans-historical theory of social conflict which he believed had a universal validity — it was meant to hold true for all societies, at all times. As an ultra-positivist, Pareto tried to formulate his theory of elites as a universal social law. In any society, the elites rise to the top, and the masses fall to the bottom. The domination of the masses by the elite was, for Pareto, as natural and as inevitable as life itself. Pareto's own judgment of Marx and his followers was largely dismissive, although he credited Marx with recognizing the fundamental conflict between opposing social groups that lies at the root of all societies. But Pareto insisted that Marx's theory of class conflict was only a limited case of the universal conflict between elites and masses. Marx had mistakenly assumed that classes formed the basis of all social conflict, whereas — according to Pareto — class conflict was only one particular historical example of the more general social conflict between elites and masses. Marx had made the mistake of generalizing from the particular to the universal.

Pareto's major criticism of Marx and of Marxists concerned Marx's optimism and his "emancipatory narrative." Pareto dismissed as utopian the idea that the working class could ever liberate itself from domination through revolution and social recon-struction. Pareto believed that Marx was naive to deny the natural and in-evitable tendency for elites to dominate in all societies. Any suggestion that the natural domination of elites in society could be overcome, or transcended, seemed to Pareto to fly in the face of the facts and to challenge the nature of things. Socialist projects for reforming societies were completely untenable to Pareto and were contradicted by his-tory. Revolutions that had been fought in the names of reason, liberty and progress always resulted in the rise to power of new elites which continued to dominate and manipulate the masses. The more things changed, the more they remained the same. Although both Marx and Pareto believed that modern society was based upon a conflict of interest between antagonistic and un-equal social groups, they differed pro-foundly in their assumptions, concepts and theoretical conclusions. For Marx, the concept of a "ruling class" was always historically specific: a particular ruling class always dominated a particu-lar underclass in a particular historical society. For Pareto, on the other hand,

> ### Figure 12-8 Pareto on Marx's Concept of "Class Struggle"
>
> The class struggle, to which Marx has specially drawn attention, is a real factor, the tokens of which are to be found on every page of history. But the struggle is not confined only to two classes: the proletariat and the capitalist; it occurs be-tween an infinite number of groups with different interests, and above all between the elites contending for power. The exist-ence of these groups may vary in duration, they may be based on permanent or more or less temporary characteristics. In the most savage peoples, and perhaps in all, sex determines two of these groups. The oppression of which the proletariat com-plains, or had cause to complain of, is as nothing in comparison with that which the women of the Australian aborigines suffer. Characteristics to a greater or lesser degree real—nationality, religion, race, language, etc.—may give rise to these groups. In our own day the struggle of the Czechs and the Germans in Bohemia is more intense than that of the proletariat and the capitalists in England.
>
> Pareto, cited in Lyttelton 1975: 79–80.

the concept of "elite" was timeless and universal: all societies throughout recorded history had seen the domination of the masses by elites. While the names used to describe an elite may change, the underlying reality remains the same. Whereas Marx believed that class struggle could result in the democratic transformation of modern society, Pareto remained convinced that any society would be dominated by an elite and that conflict between social groups would never be eliminated from society. In his polemical writ-ings — such as *Les Systems Socialistes* — Pareto was unsparing in his attacks on Marxist social theory. Indeed, one commentator suggested that Pareto's savage critique of Marx even caused a revolutionary such as Lenin "many a sleepless night" (Hughes 1952: 16).

Non-logical Action: Sentiments, Residues and Derivations

As we have already seen, Pareto believed that most social action is driven by non-logical, or irrational, motives which arise from deep-seated impulses and biological urges. Pareto referred to these basic psychological drives as "sentiments" and suggested that most human conduct results from the need to express these powerful emotional and psychological drives. Although, according to Pareto, it is not possible to directly observe these sentiments, it is possible to observe their tangible effects, referred to as "residues." While sentiments can only be apprehended as deep-seated drives, residues can be directly observed — and described — as clearly definable "psychic states." In other words, sentiments manifest themselves as residues, and can only be observed and studied in this tangible form. Although Pareto listed six different classes of residue, the most important of these were the first two classes: class 1 — the instinct for combinations, and class 2 — group persistence, or persistence of aggregates.

> ### Figure 12-9 Pareto on Revolutionary Delusions
>
> All revolutionaries proclaim, in turn, that previous revolutions have ultimately ended up by deceiving the people; it is their revolution alone which is the true revolution ... "all previous historical movements" declared the Communist Manifesto of 1848, "were movements of minorities or in the interest of minorities. The proletarian movement is the self-conscious, independent movement of the immense majority, in the interest of the immense majority." Unfortunately this true revolution, which is to bring men an unmixed happiness, is only a deceptive mirage that never becomes a reality. It is akin to the golden age of the millenarians: for ever waited, it is for ever lost in the mists of the future, for ever eluding its devotees just when they think they have it.
>
> Pareto, cited in Lyttelton 1975: 86.

Pareto insisted that residues were grounded in human nature and, for this reason, were not likely to be changed or eliminated through education or re-socialization. In other words, he rejected any belief in "human perfectibility" through reason. Instead, he concluded that the essential nature of humankind was unchanging and unchangeable. In this respect, as in so many others, he stood against the Enlightenment thinkers and those who followed in their footsteps. The most interesting aspect of Pareto's theory of non-logical action relates to his concept of "derivations." While he remained convinced

Figure 12-10 Pareto's Elements of Non-Logical Action

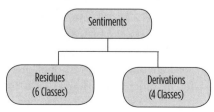

Sentiments

Residues
(6 Classes)

Derivations
(4 Classes)

that most social action is motivated by irrational sentiments, Pareto acknowledged that social actors normally offer apparently logical reasons, motives, causes and other pretexts to explain and justify their actions in society. The French revolutionaries, for example, fought their battles in the name of liberty, fraternity and equality, while the American revolutionaries went to war in the cause of independence and freedom from tyranny and unjust taxation. The former U.S.S.R. invaded nations (such as Hungary, Czechoslovakia and Afghanistan) in the name of international proletarian solidarity, and the U.S. invaded nations (such as Vietnam,

> **Figure 12-11 The Illusion of Equality**
>
> The sentiment of equality ... is not related to any abstraction, as a few naïve "intellectuals" still believe, but to direct interests of individuals who are bent on escaping certain inequalities not in their favor, and setting up new inequalities that will be in their favor, this latter being their chief concern (Section 1227).... What happens in the concrete is that people agitate for equality to get equality in general, and then go on to make countless distinctions to deny it in the particular. Equality is to belong to all — but it is granted only to the few.
>
> Pareto (1935) [1916]: 733).

Afghanistan and Iraq) in the cause of containing communism, exporting freedom and democracy and more recently, counter-terrorism, humanitarianism and nation-building. Pareto concluded that most of the explanations given for social action — whether these are expressed as political ideologies, religious doctrines, philosophical systems, common-sense accounts or other belief systems — are simply intellectualizations of underlying residues, which serve to mask the true motives. None of these derivations can be accepted at face value. In this respect, Pareto is the great debunker of proclamations, declarations and other grandiose political slogans and ideologies. He believed that he could see through the veil of hypocrisy and sanctimony that masked the real motives of social actions — whether these were acts of war, revolt and revolution, repression or fraud and deception. His critique of the doctrine of equality could, today, be just as easily applied to the doctrine of democracy — especially when this doctrine is imposed on others through force or through fraud and deception.

Circulation of Elites

As already discussed, Pareto argued that elites maintain their domination over the masses, and different elites periodically replace each other. Pareto concluded from his historical and empirical studies that every society contains several different types of elite, the most important distinction being between those which govern society and those which do not. In Western democracies, governing elites are those in charge of the ruling political party and those which dominate the parliamentary, congressional or other representative assemblies of the state. In more authoritarian and totalitarian societies, governing elites may include military and in some cases, even religious elites which, together, exercise total control over the masses. Pareto also recognized that there were non-governing elites, and in Western societies, these include industrial, financial, corporate and other types of economic elites, as well as scientific, media, military and education elites and also celebrity elites from the world of popular culture (Mills 1956; Domhoff 2006, 2009; Presthus 1973). In non-Western societies, religious and other traditional elites may form either part of governing or non-governing elites in society. Pareto's main thesis was that governing elites can only maintain their domination in society as long as they are willing and able to do what is necessary to impose their will on the masses. After a time —decades or centuries — all elites grow increasingly decadent and less willing, or able, to defend their prerogatives and impose their will. According to Pareto, when a governing elite has outlasted its ability to dominate the masses, it will be replaced by another elite in society which is able to seize power and install itself as the new governing elite. This circulation of elites is the story of the rise and fall of lions and foxes in an endless cycle of replacement.

According to Pareto, the foxes are typically characterized by class I residues — (the instinct for combinations, which are expressed as "an inclination to … combine things" (Pareto 1935: 519–23). These residues are manifested in individuals who prize innovation, calculation, imagination, inventiveness and a willingness to take risks and to experiment. It is found in inventors, speculators, entrepreneurs and politicians. In political terms, these residues are often translated into the politics of expediency, including the use of cunning and guile. The foxes maintain their power through diplomacy and skilful manipulation. On the other hand, the lions are typically characterized by class 2 residues — group persistence, or persistence of aggregates).

Figure 12-12 Circulation of Governing and non-Governing Elites

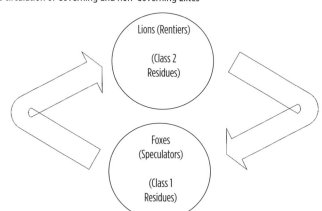

Lions (Rentiers)

(Class 2 Residues)

Foxes (Speculators)

(Class 1 Residues)

These residues are manifested in individuals who prize devotion to duty, protection of national honour, defence of traditional institutions, such as the crown, church, family, community, race, nation or the party) as well as the desire for social stability and continuity. Class 2 residues are typically found in religious leaders, military officers, family men and "good subordinates." These residues represent the more conservative side of the political spectrum, while class I residues reflect the more pragmatic and innovative side. Pareto concluded from his historical studies that every elite eventually succumbs to corruption and decadence and is overthrown by a more robust political elite. According to his view of the world, the history of human societies consists of the rise and fall of governing elites and their periodic replacement by a more aggressive or more cunning elite. Although societies may change over time, the battle between competing elites has always remained the same — the lions forever challenge the foxes, and the foxes forever challenge the lions. The political history of all societies can best be understood as the eternal struggle between elites and counter-elites for supremacy. These two types of elites may be illustrated in two types of government: a regime geared towards free trade, privatization and foreign investment versus a military junta committed to a restoration of national honour and morality, eradicating corruption and subversion, and rebuilding a sense of national community. Many countries have experienced abrupt *coups d'états* from relatively liberal to strongly conservative military regimes, for example, Chile (1973), Argentina (1976) and Pakistan (1977).

Today, there are plenty of examples of the circulation of elites. During the final years of the U.S.S.R., we saw the decline of the old governing elite, which had been based on force (the lions), and the rise of the new Gorbachev elite (the foxes), which was based more on diplomacy, pragmatism and expedience — Glasnost and Perestroika. The fall of the U.S.S.R. in 1989 signalled the rise to power of a new class of oligarchs under Boris Yeltsin and the growth of what some have called "gangster" or "bandit" capitalism. With the advent of Vladimir Putin, and the reassertion of state power in Russia, we may be witnessing a return to the lions

Pareto's theory of the circulation of elites runs counter to the Enlightenment tradition and to the assumptions of thinkers who followed in its wake. For most classical social theorists, human history played out in linear terms. History was the record of reason and progress, and historical change always moved forward from ignorance to knowledge, from barbarism to civilization. It is clear in the writings of Rousseau and the French rationalists, as well as those of Comte and the positivists. It is evident in Hegel's theory of historical idealism and in Marx's theory of historical materialism. It is also present in the evolutionist theories of Spencer, Durkheim and other nineteenth century social evolutionists. But Pareto's conception of history is very different. He proposed a cyclical theory of history, in which elites and counter-elites pursue their eternal struggle for power over the masses; nothing ever really changes. There is no forward movement, no linear progress and no assumption of human perfectibility. On the contrary, it is assumed that human nature is essentially fixed and unchanging and that the course of history is an endless cycle which always begins anew. This is a view which denies that social actors can ever emancipate themselves from their essential natures or that society can ever be radically reconstructed through reason. All attempts at social reconstruction — whether through moderate reforms, radical revolutions, free enterprise or state control — are reduced to the conflict between elites and counter-elites for power and control. For this reason, cyclical theories of history are often associated with ancient social theorists, such as the fourteenth-century Arabic historian Ibn Khaldun, or of Machiavelli in the fifteenth century, or, in the early twentieth century, with conservative historians Oswald Spengler and Arnold Toynbee. Above all else, Pareto regarded himself as a realist, or an objectivist, who unmasked what he believed to be the utopian, unrealizable and dangerous dreams of socialists and other social reformers.

Pareto's Contributions

Any assessment of Pareto's work, like that of all other social theorists, needs to acknowledge the strengths and the limitations of his contributions to social theory. It is never possible to provide an "objective" assessment of any social theorist. This is especially the case for Pareto, who was a provocative and controversial thinker.

Skepticism

Pareto encourages us to adopt a healthy skepticism towards the ideals of the Enlightenment and of the social reformers of this era. There can be little doubt that most of the major social engineering projects over the past three centuries have fallen short of the dreams of the social reformers who proposed these projects. Rousseau proposed a democratic social contract for France, but did not anticipate the Revolutionary Terror or Emperor Napoleon. Marx called for an end to class exploitation and social inequality, but did not anticipate the rise of Stalin, Mao Tse Tung and Pol Pot. Adam Smith hoped for free trade and global prosperity, but would not have endorsed the harsh neoliberal policies of Thatcher, Reagan and Bush, which widened social inequalities at home and escalated military adventures abroad. Pareto was a great debunker of ideologies, doctrines and other dogmas. He tried to alert us to what he believed were the real motives behind much human action, and he warned us against accepting at face value many of the reasons proffered by political elites for their decisions.

Conflict Theory

Pareto's work and ideas, much like those of Marx, contributed to the growth of conflict theory in sociology. His emphasis on the conflict of interests between the elites and the masses in society and on the circulation of elites provides an alternative perspective on social conflict to that of Marx and the Marxists. Whereas Marxism has always emphasized historically specific class conflict, Pareto argues that the basic conflicts in society are timeless and rooted in the depths of human nature. In capitalist societies, the existence of political and economic elites is widely acknowledged and to a certain extent even accepted. In supposedly more egalitarian socialist or communist societies, the existence of bureaucratic and state elites may remain hidden and largely unacknowledged. Pareto reminds us that not all conflict in society is reducible to class conflict. He was well aware, in his own time, of the growth of ethnic, racial and national conflicts throughout Europe. In some ways, little has changed. Since the end of the Cold War, we have also seen a resurgence of ethnic, racial religious and national conflicts around the world — in Europe (Chechnya, Bosnia, Kosovo, the former Yugoslavia), in Africa (Rwanda, Sierra Leone, Liberia, the Congo, Sudan and Somalia), in the Middle East (Palestine, Iraq,), in Central Asia (Afghanistan) and elsewhere. More recently, we have seen uprisings and unrest in Tunisia, Egypt and Libya, as well Yemen, Bahrain and Syria. Many of these conflict zones involve confrontations between contending elites. None of this would have surprised Pareto.

Systematic Theorist

One of the undoubted strengths of Pareto's social thought is that he was a systematic social theorist. In both his economic and his social studies, Pareto conceived of society as a system, which manifested a tendency towards maintaining a state of equilibrium. A system may generally be defined as a set of mutually interrelated parts in which a change in one part leads to a change in other parts. Pareto was influenced in this view of society by his earlier training as an engineer. He translated his study of mechanical systems into the study of economic systems, in which the forces of supply and demand were believed to strive for balance. In his later studies of society, Pareto concluded that non-logical sources of social action, or sentiments, also have a tendency to maintain a state of equilibrium. As an pioneer of the concept of "system" in the social sciences, Pareto laid the groundwork for later generations of system theorists. Throughout the first half of the twentieth century, the concept of "system" remained central to social theory, and even today, it retains some influence in contemporary social theory.

Criticizing Pareto

Pareto remains one of the least popular of the classical social theorists. This unpopularity derives in part from his alleged sympathies for the Italian fascist leader Benito Mussolini and from his purported intellectual links to the politics of fascism. However, although Pareto was undeniably a controversial figure — even during his own lifetime — this should not prevent us from examining his influence on the growth of social theory. While some commentators condemn Pareto for his proto-fascist sympathies, others dismiss these allegations as gross oversimplifications, which have only served to discredit his controversial and often provocative ideas.

Irrationalism

Although some sociologists, especially in the field of elite theory, have tried to build upon Pareto's work many others express criticisms of his theoretical ideas. One of the most common criticisms of Pareto is of his "irrationalism." For some social theorists, the assumption that most human conduct is non-logical, or non-rational, remains unproven. Because so much social theory is rooted in the Enlightenment tradition, many social theorists are committed to the assumption that social actors are fully capable of logical action. Indeed, much contemporary social theory is based on the assumption that social actors are able to make rational choices between alternative means and ends of action. For Pareto, with the exception of scientific practices, only economic action qualified as purely rational action, and, for this reason, he saw economics as the science which studied logical action, whereas sociology studied non-logical action. For many social theorists, Pareto's over-emphasis of non-logical action opened him up to charges of irrationalism. But as already noted, Pareto lived at a time when other social thinkers — such as Freud, Nietzsche and even Marx — concluded that much social action at the lower levels of society was motivated or manipulated by non-rational motives.

Anti-Humanism

Pareto is criticized for his alleged "anti-humanism," an accusation that has meant a number of different things. On the one hand, it refers to Pareto's rejection of the Enlightenment tradition — especially of those values such as reason, liberty and progress, which, in one way or another, were espoused by all Enlightenment thinkers and by all Enlightenment traditions. Pareto rejected the optimism of the Enlightenment, reflected in the doctrine of human perfectibility, in favour of a more cynical approach to the study of society. At the same time, the charge of anti-humanism has sometimes referred to more practical considerations — such as Pareto's apparent approval of the use of force and violence by elites in defence of their powers and privileges. Indeed, Pareto has acquired a notoriety for passages which may be interpreted as an approval for the use of violence.

Determinism

Because Pareto gave such prominence to the role of underlying psychological and biological factors in human behaviour, he is sometimes criticized for biological, or genetic, determinism. However while Pareto is condemned by some, he is also applauded by others — especially those who — like sociobiologists and evolutionary psychologists — seek to restore a biological context to the study of society.

Fascism

The combination of negative qualities — including Pareto's contempt for the pretensions of democracy, rejection of "humanitarianism" and apparent approval of the strategic use of force and violence, as well as his alleged admiration for Mussolini —lead some critics to conclude that Pareto was sympathetic to fascism. But the evidence supporting this charge is inconclusive, and reviewers continue to debate both sides of this controversy.

Figure 12-13 Pareto on Violence

Any people which has a horror of blood to the point of not knowing how to defend itself will sooner or later become the prey of some bellicose people or other.... Any elite which is not prepared to join in battle to defend its position is in full decadence, and all that is left to it is to give way to another elite having the virile qualities it lacks. It is pure day-dreaming to imagine that the humanitarian principles it may have proclaimed will be applied to it: its vanquishers will stun it with the implacable cry, "VaeVictis." The knife of the guillotine was being sharpened in the shadows when, at the end of the eighteenth century, the ruling classes in France were engrossed in developing their "sensibility." This idle and frivolous society, living like a parasite off the country, discoursed at its elegant supper parties of delivering the world from superstition and of crushing, all unsuspecting that it was itself going to be crushed.

Pareto cited in Lyttelton 1975: 79–81.

> It was not only Pareto's economic theories that influenced the course of the Fascist state, but especially the sociological theories…. Clearly, there was some agreement between Pareto and the new government. Pareto's theory of rule by elites, his authoritarian leanings, his uncompromising rejection of the liberal fixation with Economic Man, his hatred of disorder, his devotion to the hierarchical arrangement of society, and his belief in an aristocracy of merit are all ideas in harmony with Fascism. Let us keep in mind, however, that all of these ideas were formulated by Pareto decades before anyone had ever heard of Fascism and Mussolini. (Alexander 1994)

Imprecise Terminology

Pareto is criticized for his imprecise and inconsistent use of such key terms as sentiment, residue, instinct, drive and impulse. It is often unclear from his writings as to whether sentiments are psychic states, or biological instincts, or drives. As one frustrated reviewer (Faris 1936: 663) remarked, "The residues are manifestations of sentiments but the concept is not made as exact as possible, for Pareto's admirers are continually puzzling their brains over the meaning of the word 'sentiment.' The residues also manifest instincts…. But these manifested instincts are not defined as exactly as possible. They are not defined at all, but remain in the limbo of the vague." Moreover, Pareto, himself, appears to have knowingly contributed to this confusion when he declined to offer clear definitions for some of his terms: "I hope I shall be excused if I do not define this very sweet entity" (Pareto 1935: 1526). Although Pareto assigned great importance to his so-called "scientific" (or logico-experimental) approach to the study of society, his terminology remains confusing.

Pareto: Pariah or Prophet?

There can be little doubt that much of Pareto's notoriety as a social theorist derives from his alleged sympathies with fascism and from the popularity of his writings among leading fascist politicians — especially Mussolini. For this reason alone, Pareto is often vilified as a proto-fascist. But the issue of Pareto's politics has never been conclusively settled, although the question persists: did he flirt with fascist ideas, and did he indeed approve of fascist policies? In some ways, this remains a moot question as Pareto died in 1923, long before the full force of fascist policies were felt — either in Italy, or elsewhere in Europe. However, several indicators suggest that Pareto would not have wholeheartedly embraced the fascist cause and would probably have found many fascist policies repugnant and unacceptable. We know, for example, that in his younger days Pareto condemned the anti-Semitic campaign against Dreyfus in France and, like Durkheim, offered Dreyfus his sympathy and support. Even though Pareto welcomed the early policies of Mussolini, especially those that broke the back of the workers' movements and privatized former state enterprises, he later protested the fascists' clamp-down on freedom of speech and opposed their centralized model of state planning — or what he called the "crystallized" or "Byzantine" state (Finer 1968, 440–50). Pareto's later disillusionment with fascism is briefly summarized by Coser (1977: 407), who recalls that "when Mussolini muzzled the universities of Italy and restricted free speech, Pareto protested vehemently. Had Pareto lived it is unlikely that he would have endorsed the complete suppression of liberties during the later stages of Mussolini's regime, or that he would have looked with favour on the state-interventionist course of the fully matured fascist regime."

Pareto was, in the final analysis, too much of an individualist to ever become a hardcore fascist. He was, after all, deeply skeptical of all political doctrines — those of the right as well as those of the left. He would undoubtedly have dismissed the fascist slogans of "Blood and Soil" as derivations arising from irrational sentiments and residues. More than anything else, Pareto was a libertarian — a free-spirited controversialist and iconoclast — who sought to sweep away the cobwebs of superstition, prejudice and blind faith. But in one important respect his intellectual development paralleled that of Mussolini — at least in their early years. Both men began their careers as radical republican activists and as strong anti-imperialists; indeed, Mussolini was a socialist agitator in his youth. Both men later repudiated liberalism and socialism and expressed their disillusionment with the ideals of egalitarianism and social democracy. But at a crucial stage, their paths diverged: Mussolini chose the path of fascism, while Pareto chose the path of libertarianism.

Pareto's ideas make easy targets for criticism and condemnation. In an age that trumpets the ideals of reason, liberty, equality, democracy and progress, Pareto's ideas are bound to be unpopular. His cynical belief that the ideals of democracy (derivations) are simply myths for the masses which have little to do with the real practice of government, is clearly at odds with the official ideology of many modern societies. However, before we dismiss Pareto out of hand, we should evaluate some of his ideas in light of our own experiences. To what extent do our own democratic institutions appear to be dominated by elites? What have been the experiences of other countries in the process of transition? Is it often the case that one elite is simply replaced by another elite? Are many members of society often motivated or manipulated more by strong emotional or sentimental influences (such as patriotism, xenophobia, homophobia, racism, religion) than by more rational considerations? Is there a sense in which some aspects of human nature (such as conflict, aggression and territoriality) seem relatively durable over time and space? Are there deep-seated psychological or biological aspects to our behaviour which have remained largely unrecognized and unexamined — at least by social theorists?

If the answer to any of these questions appears to be "yes," or even "maybe," then we should hesitate before dismissing Pareto. In recent years, a number of contemporary social theories have emerged which may have some affinities with Pareto's ideas. For example: the traditions of sociobiology, evolutionary psychology and the sociology of emotions have each begun to emphasize the role of irrational factors in human behaviour. Similarly, some postmodernist theorists share Pareto's skepticism regarding the illusions of historical progress and the emancipatory project of the Enlightenment thinkers. Although Pareto challenges us to confront the ugliest and least acceptable sides of our selves and societies, this is not a valid reason to reject his ideas as "politically incorrect." When all is said and done, Pareto is still regarded as a controversial and provocative social thinker. There is no doubt that much of his social theory contradicts the main trends of Enlightenment social thought, and suggests a darker and less optimistic view of society and of humanity. It is also true that some reactionary political traditions — including the fascists in Italy and the Nazis in Germany —claim him as an intellectual ancestor. Whether or not Pareto would have fully sympathized with these political ideologies is still a matter for scholarly debate. However, in some important respects, Pareto was an original social thinker and, for that, his ideas are important.

References

Alexander, James. 1994. "Vilfredo Pareto: The Karl Marx of Fascism." *Journal of Historical Review* 14, 5 (September–October): 10–18. <library.flawlesslogic.com/pareto.htm>.

Avlon, John. 2010. *Wingnuts: How the Lunatic Fringe Is Hijacking America.* New York: Beast Books, co-published with Perseus Books.

Ashley, David, and David Michael Orenstein. 2005. *Sociological Theory: Classical Statements.* Sixth edition. Boston: Pearson Education.

Bartels, Larry M. 2008. "The Irrational Electorate." *Wilson Quarterly* (Autumn): 44–50.

Campbell, Angus, Philip E. Converse, Warren E. Miller and Donald E. Stokes. 1960. *The American Voter.* New York: John Wiley and Sons.

Cirillo, Renato. 2006. "Was Vilfredo Pareto Really a 'Precursor' of Fascism?" *American Journal of Economics and Sociology* 42, 2: 235–46.

Coser, Lewis. *1977. Masters of Sociological Thought: Ideas in the Historical and Sociological Context.* Second edition. San Diego, CA: Harcourt Brace Jonanovich.

Domhoff, G. William. 2006. "Mills's *The Power Elite* 50 Years Later." *Contemporary Sociology: A Journal of Reviews* 35 (November): 547–50.

___. 2009. *Who Rules America?* Sixth edition. New York: McGraw-Hill.

Faris, Ellsworth. 1936. "An Estimate of Pareto." *American Journal of Sociology* 41, 5: 657–68.

Femia, Joseph V. 2001. *Against the Masses: Varieties of Anti-Democratic Thought since the French Revolution.* London, Oxford University Press.

___. 2006. *Pareto and Political Theory.* Oxford, UK: Routledge.

Finer, S.E. 1968. "Pareto and Pluto-Democracy: The Retreat to Galapagos." *American Political Science Review* 62, 2: 440–50.

Friedman, Jeffrey. 1999. "Public Ignorance and Democracy." *Cato Policy Report* 21, 4 (July/August). <http://www.cato.org/pubs/policy_report/v21n4/cpr-21n4.html>.

Furman, Dmitri. 2008. "Imitation Democracies: The Post-Soviet Penumbra."*New Left Review* 54 (November–December): 29–47.

Greenhill, Sam. 2011. "Flying Proudly over the Birthplace of Libya's Revolution, the Flag of Al Qaeda." *The Daily Mail,* November 2. <www.dailymail.co.uk/news/article-2055630/Flying-proudly-birthplace-Libyas-revolution-flag-Al-Qaeda.

html#ixzz1jw8uVCV3>.

The Guardian (London). 2012. "Syrian Death Toll Tops 19,000, Say Activists." 22 July. <http://www.guardian.co.uk/world/2012/jul/22/syria-death-toll-tops-19000>.

Hale, Henry E. 2005. "Interpreting the Color Revolutions and Prospects for Post-Soviet Democratization Breaking the Cycles." *PONARS* Policy Memo No. 373 (December). <http://www.gwu.edu/~ieresgwu/assets/docs/ponars/pm_0373. pdf>.

Hendrix, Scott E., and Brian Feltham (eds.). 2011. *Rational Magic*. Oxford, UK: InterDisciplinary Press.

Higley, John. 2001. *Elites and Democracy: The "Futility Thesis" Today*. University of Texas at Austin. <Comenius-Elites-Democracy-Futility.doc>.

___. 2003. "Force to the Fore: The Bush Elite and America's Post-9/11 Democracy." *Australian Journal of American Studies* 22, 2 (December): 25–40.

___. 2011. "Introduction: Circulations and Qualities of Political Elites." *Comparative Sociology* 10: 829–39.

Higley, John, and Jan Pakulski. 2007. "Elite and Leadership Change in Liberal Democracies." *Comparative Sociology* 6 (1&2): 6–26.

___. 2011. "Do Ruling Elites Degenerate? American and British Elites Through Pareto's Lens." *Comparative Sociology* 10: 949–67.

Hughes, H. Stuart. 1952. *Oswald Spengler: A Critical Estimate*. NY: Charles Scribner & Sons.

Lewis-Beck, Michael S., William G. Jacoby, Helmut Norpoth and Herbert F. Weisberg. 2008. *The American Voter Revisited*. Ann Arbor, MI: University of Michigan Press.

Lopreato, Joseph. 1964. "A Functionalist Reappraisal of Pareto's Sociology." *American Journal of Sociology* 69: 639–46.

Lyttelton, Adrian (ed.). 1975. *Italian Fascisms: From Pareto to Gentile*. NY: Harper & Row.

Machiavelli, Niccolò. 1961. *The Prince*. Translated by George Bull. London: Penguin.

Mills, C. Wright. 1956. *The Power Elite and the State: How Policy Is Made in America*. New York: Oxford University Press.

___. 1959. *The Sociological Imagination*. London & Oxford: Oxford University Press.

Mosca, Gaetano. 1939 [1836]. *The Ruling Class*. New York: McGraw-Hill.

Nye, Joseph. 1990. *Bound to Lead: The Changing Nature of American Power*. New York: Basic Books.

Pareto, Vilfredo. [1896–1897] 1996. *Cours d'economie politique*. Lausanne: F. Rouge.

___. 1902. *Les Systèmes Socialistes*. Paris: V. Giard and E. Brière.

___. 1935 [1916]. *The Mind and Society: A Treatise on General Sociology*. Translated by A. Bongiorno and A. Livingston. New York: Dover Publications.

Presthus, Robert. 1973. *Elite Accommodation in Canadian politics*. Cambridge, UK: Cambridge University Press.

Shenkman, Rick. 2008. *Just How Stupid Are We? Facing the Truth about the American Voter*. New York: Basic Books.

Sorel, Georges. 1999. *Reflections on Violence*. Edited by Jeremy Jennings. Cambridge, England: Cambridge University Press.

Spector, J. Brooks. 2011. "Analysis: Revolutionary Cycle or Repeat Play — Where

Will 2011 Take Us?" <thedailymaverick.co.za/article/2011-03-07-analysis-revolutionary-cycle-or-repeat-play-where-will-2011-take-us>.

Srebrnik, Henry. 2011. "Who Will Replace Today's Middle Eastern Rulers?" *The Guardian*, February 24. <http://www.theguardian.pe.ca/Opinion/Letters-to-editor/2011-02-24/article-2275973/Who-will-replace-today%26rsquo%3Bs-Middle-Eastern-rulers%3F/1>.

Stacher, Joshua. 2011. "Egypt's Democratic Mirage: How Cairo's Authoritarian Regime Is Adapting to Preserve Itself." *The New Arab Revolt. NY: Council on Foreign Relations.*

___. 2012. *Adaptable Autocrats: Regime Power in Egypt and Syria.* (Stanford Studies in Middle Eastern and I). Palo Alto: Stanford University Press.

Thornton, Bruce. 2012. *The Arab Spring: An Obituary.* Frontpagemag.com. January 5. <http://frontpagemag.com/2012/01/05/the-arab-spring-an-obituary >

van den Berghe, Pierre L. 1967. *South Africa, A Study in Conflict.* Berkeley & Los Angeles: University of California Press. <http://ark.cdlib.org/ark:/13030/ft5x0nb3tg/>.

van Wyk, Jo Ansie. 2009. *Cadres, Capitalists and Coalitions: The ANC, Business and Development in South Africa.* Discussion Paper No. 46. February. University of South Africa, Nordiska Afrikainstitutet (The Nordic Africa Institute). <http://www.google.ca/url?sa=t&rct=j&q=&esrc=s&source=web&cd=1&ved=0CCQQFjAA&url=http%3A%2F%2Fnai.diva-portal.org%2Fsmash%2Fget%2Fdiva2%3A278764%2FFULLTEXT01&ei=PkCRUP20DMzcqAHglID4Ag&usg=AFQjCNFyF0TQZwikp1aRt2rhIumrllKyyQ>.

Epilogue

The Living Classics

Taking Theory Seriously

At first glance, nothing seems to be more remote from the hustle and bustle of our daily lives than social theory — especially classical social theory. Almost by definition, "theory" refers to abstract ideas, often associated with "dead white guys," that may appear to have little or nothing to do with our present concerns. If anything, learning about classical social theory may have some historical value, in the same way that a museum is useful for preserving the artefacts of the past. But when is the last time you visited a museum?

This book tries to show how even today, classical social theories have much to teach us. Far from being irrelevant, they still speak to some of the central issues in our lives: big, public issues such as war, inequality, sexism, religion, environmental degradation and crime; and smaller, more personal troubles such as the pace of life in the consumer rat-race, how we interact with family and friends, and how to survive sensory overload in the digital age (see also Mills 1959: 24). Everything that happens to us can be analyzed and often clarified through the use of theory. Theories help to make sense of the modern world by providing us with languages to describe and analyze our experiences. Theories provide us with arguments and concepts that can be used to find explanations for the causes of social events. By finding new ways to talk about our worlds, we can also learn to observe our worlds in fresh and unaccustomed ways. Novel ideas can lead to new ways of seeing.

Picking up an item from the local supermarket, such as a chocolate bar, we can use Marx's concept of "exploitation" to track the human labour that went into making this commodity. Most of the major brands of chocolate are produced by underpaid workers and trafficked child labourers who toil all their lives on the cocoa farms in Ivory Coast and similar places — for next to nothing (see the 2010 documentary film *The Dark Side of Chocolate*;

Figure Ep-1

The ideas of economists and political philosophers, both when they are right and when they are wrong, are more powerful than is commonly understood. Indeed the world is ruled by little else. Practical men, who believe themselves to be quite exempt from any intellectual influence, are usually the slaves of some defunct economist. Madmen in authority, who hear voices in the air, are distilling their frenzy from some academic scribbler of a few years back.

Source: John Maynard Keynes 1935: 383.

also Off 2008). Many other products in our stores are produced by cheap labour, and as consumers we may be unaware of this. Marx's concept of "surplus value" gives us a framework to understand why the accumulation of wealth in many societies is always distributed so unequally between workers and the corporations that employ them. Visualizing these conditions from Marx's perspective may well encourage us to support fair trade products in our local stores.

Durkheim's concept of "altruistic suicide" gives us a language to comprehend, if not to condone, why suicide bombers, who are bound to their communities by strong ties of social solidarity and moral regulation, engage in "martyrdom operations" against those they regard as invaders of their lands and cultures. Rather than simply demonizing these acts, we may use Durkheim's theoretical language to reach beyond the media headlines for deeper explanations of events that make the daily news.

The Power of Theories

Sometimes theories may be imposed upon us from above — by governments, corporations and other powerful organizations in the form of ideologies, policies and laws. All policy is encoded with theory, even though the underlying theory is often unacknowledged and invisible. When politicians tell us that we need to "reform" our health-care system by privatizing hospitals, clinics and insurance providers, they are invoking a particular theoretical language. By speaking about health care as though it were just another commodity in the marketplace of goods and services — rather than a basic human right — they are using the theoretical language of neoclassical economics to make their point. The language of commodities is very different from that of human rights.

Theory can also influence the conduct of conflict between nations. The United States used the "domino theory" of creeping communism during the late 1950s and early 1960s to rationalize a decade-long war in Indo-China that resulted in millions of civilian deaths. Other theories have had even more baleful consequences. Stalin's genocidal policy of the forced collectivization of Soviet agriculture during the early 1930s resulted from a dogmatic interpretation of Marxist-Leninist theory (Conquest 1986: 20–24). The urbanization policy known as the "Great Leap Forward," which led to the deaths of millions of Chinese, was similarly inspired by the theories of Mao Zedung. And, of course, the Holocaust was partly inspired and justified by Hitler's theory of Aryan racial supremacy. Closer-to-home, social Darwinian racial theories laid the groundwork for discriminatory Canadian and U.S. immigration policy until the early 1960s and, even today, seem to cast a shadow over policies concerning immigration and refugees.

The neoliberal theories pursued by many transnational organizations, such as the International Monetary Fund, World Bank and World Trade Organization, have proven disastrous for ordinary people in many parts of the developing world. Yet it often appears as though these theories are pursued without regard to their factual consequences. As the former chief economist for the World Bank observed: "The IMF was so certain about the correctness of its dogmatic position that it had little interest in looking at actual experiences" (see Stiglitz 2002: 32).

Sometimes, our urge to theorize will bring us into confrontation with others. Theories may even get us into trouble and earn us the dislike — or even the hatred — of our friends and colleagues, especially when the ideas challenge commonly cherished beliefs. This is what happened during the famous 1925 Scopes' "monkey trial" in Tennessee, when religious fundamentalists fought against the teaching of the theory of evolution in high schools because they regarded it as an assault on their community beliefs and values. Several centuries earlier, in sixteenth-century Italy, Galileo was imprisoned for teaching the "heretical" doctrine that the earth revolves around the sun (for details about the trial of Galileo, see De Santillana 1962 [1955]; Ginzburg 1980). Giordarno Bruno had been burned at the stake thirty-three years earlier for the same offence. Several centuries later, Jean-Jacques Rousseau had warrants out for his arrest in France, Geneva and Bern, and the Council of Geneva condemned his book *The Social Contract* to be publicly burned. Karl Marx also spent part of his life "on the run." Exiled to Brussels he became a leading figure of the Communist League, before moving back to Cologne, where he founded his own newspaper. In 1849 he was exiled again and moved to London with his wife and children. Even Charles Darwin was vehemently attacked by the Church of England after the publication of his famous book, *On the Origin of Species by Means of Natural Selection*, in 1859. And in 1933, as Hitler and the Nazi Party seized power in Germany, all of the books of Sigmund Freud were publicly burnt by Hitler's Stormtroopers. While theories may appear to be little more than abstract ideas, they are capable of rattling the rafters and shaking the walls. "Theories have the power to transform societies."

Practising Theory

Most of the time, we view the world and our lives through our own taken-for-granted theories. Like spectacles that we wear "behind our eyes," our understandings of our social world are based upon our own implicit theories. But unlike the more formal theories of the sociologist, or philosopher, our home-grown theories are rarely tested for their validity. Most of us assume that our knowledge is based on practical experience, even on common sense. We certainly do not think of our everyday knowledge as "theoretical" in any obvious sense.

Theories have always been used to reduce the complexity of the "real world" — whether we are talking about the origins of the universe, the evolution of humankind or how consumers behave. And sometimes, social theories can be useful in helping us to understand our own social worlds and those of others. By showing us that there are many different social worlds, social theory has an important role to play in expanding our horizons of understanding and our margins of tolerance. In this respect, social theory has a crucial and largely unacknowledged ethical dimension. In its own way, it can help us to appreciate the wide range of opinions, beliefs and worldviews that reflect the diversity of humanity.

But it is also the role of social theory — and the responsibility of the theorist — to remain critical of our institutions and skeptical of our inherited beliefs. In this respect, there is something essentially noble, even heroic, in the task of the theorist. Edward Said, the Palestinian writer, suggested that the task of the intellectual is to "speak the truth to power" (Said 1994: xvi). In much the same way, the role of the social theorist is to question what most of us take for granted and to pioneer new ways of looking at the familiar and the unremarkable. The role of the theorist is to turn all of us into strangers, or outsiders, in our own lands. Or as Said (1994: 63) also suggested, the "true" intellectual is always defined by a sense of marginality and intellectual exile: "A condition of marginality, which might seem irresponsible, or flippant, frees you from having always to proceed with caution, afraid to overturn the applecart, anxious about upsetting fellow members of the same corporation."

Learning to fight with ideas is an important part of growing up. Many of us first became interested in public issues and current affairs as a result of a clash of opinion — often with somebody close to us. Over time, the "argumentative impulse" normally grows more refined. Instead of competing for the louder voice, or the greater dramatic effect, winning arguments becomes more a matter of intellectual organization. Good debaters are always able to organize their ideas in logical, deductive statements without ever contradicting themselves and, most importantly, are able to present relevant "facts" in support of their arguments. After a while, many of us, without necessarily realizing it, are well on our way to becoming practical theorists.

Sometimes, our experience as practical theorists may be put to use in public debates on controversial topics. For example, if the province or municipality decides to run an oil pipeline through our community or locate a waste treatment plant in our home town, or even to finance a major sporting event like the Olympic Games in the face of strong local opposition, we will need to criticize these proposed projects by contesting the ideas on which they are based. These tasks often require the intellectual skills of a theorist. In the world of power politics, public and private sector administrators will always defend their plans and proposals in the name of "realism" and concern for the "facts." Those who oppose their ideas will invariably find themselves labelled "idealists," "utopians" or even "spoilers" and "trouble-makers." (For a discussion of how the politics of knowledge can influence what are accepted, and what are rejected as "facts," see the case of an environmental impact assessment hearing in Alberta, by Richardson, Sherman and Gismondi 1993.)

The ideas of the powerful in any particular situation are normally represented as factual, while those of the critics are typically dismissed as "ideological" or "speculative," "unrealistic" or "utopian." It is only by theorizing these debates that the tables can sometimes be turned: and the ideas of the powerful can be seen for what they really are — arguments driven by an ideological agenda. Neither the powerful nor their critics have a monopoly over the use of "facts." For facts are never raw representations of reality; they are always observation statements connected directly or indirectly to a theory language. Arguments and debates, therefore, should be seen as the breeding ground for theories. If we want to learn anything important about theories, we need to know something about arguments. And the classical theorists were nothing if not argumentative.

Rebooting the Classics

The task of identifying the classics in sociology has become increasingly politicized. The more conservative custodians of the discipline continue to insist upon the centrality of the traditional classics — especially the Holy Trinity of Marx, Durkheim and Weber — and resist any broadening of the canon. For some commentators, these long established classics still represent the highest standards of scholarship and research within the discipline. "I consider the writings of Marx, Durkheim, and Weber indispensable, in the sense that we shall not be able to put them on forgotten library shelves as easily as chemists or physics do with their own classical texts. This is because they inform current research, scholarship and debate" (Mouzelis 1997: 1). Attempts to incorporate women theorists, theorists of non-European descent and other forgotten social theorists into the classical canon are resisted on a number of grounds. Appeals for the rediscovery of neglected theorists may be dismissed as evidence of a "creeping relativism," often seen to be driven by external political pressures or by a general lowering of standards within the discipline. A couple of commentators observe: "The radicalization of the curriculum and the pressure from suppressed groups for recognition of 'their' classics forced an examination of how the canon was constructed, why some forms of literature or art were included, and others excluded, why few women and African-American authors or artists were included in the then acceptable curricula" (Davis and Zald 2008: 638).

For conservatives, the traditional classics represent the highest standards of research and scholarship. Demands for the inclusion of such figures as Charlotte Perkins Gillman or African American sociologist W.B Dubois, for example, are seen, not as opportunities to rediscover lost social theorists, but as special pleading by political movements. For this reason, attempts to broaden the historical canon of social theory have often been seen as illegitimate. Thus, one defender of the status quo (Mouzelis 1997: 3) has candidly admitted: "I do not at all see why WE.B. Du Bois or Charlotte Perkins Gilman should be admitted to the club.... Until I am presented with more convincing arguments, I am bound to assume that his proposal is based less on intrinsic/cognitive and more on extrinsic values. (For those unfamiliar with their names, Du Bois is black and Gilman is a feminist)."

But in many ways, the conservative defenders of the traditional canon are swimming against the tide. Today, there appears to be a growing sentiment among sociologists and across the social sciences in favour of a more inclusive definition of the classics. In part, this new wave coincides with the rise of theoretical perspectives such as postmodernism and poststructuralism, and with the corresponding growth of interdisciplinary areas such as women's studies, cultural studies, global studies and postcolonial studies. A fresh generation of scholars are critically re-evaluating the historical narrative of sociology. Many of these critics conclude that traditional histories of social thought remain severely compromised by androcentric (i.e., male-oriented) perspectives, as well as by Eurocentric assumptions of Western superiority over non-Western societies and cultures, what some call the "imperial gaze." As one writer declared, "Sociology was formed within the culture of imperialism and embodied a cultural response to the colonized world. This fact is crucial in understanding the content and method of sociology as well as the discipline's cultural significance" (Connell 1997: 1519).

There has never been a better time to broaden our understanding of our shared global heritage of social theory and to rediscover some of the lost classics of past social thinkers. Several scholars are already reclaiming some of these neglected masterpieces from Western societies and beyond (see Abdo,1996; Alatas and Sinha 2001; Alatas 2006; Churchill 1995). Indeed, this process is also underway in many other disciplines (Naidoo 1996; Ramose 2002; Thiong'o 1986). In this book, I advance a conception of social theory as a "debate" between theorists. All theories were originally formulated as responses — sometimes explicit, often implicit — to previous and contemporary theories. Most classical theorists "settled their accounts" with their predecessors and with their contemporaries. In this sense, theories are all about argument, debate and polemic; they never fall out of a clear blue sky.

Much as theorizing may be thought of as a debate or an argument with an opponent, the same holds true for all definitions of the classics. Although the chronology of social theory may appear as a simple matter of historical record, the inclusion of theorists in this record remains a contested terrain. Indeed, it would be accurate to say that the classics are constructed rather than simply discovered, or even reclaimed. This is because the criteria used to select the classics are unavoidably ideological and are liable to change from one generation to the next. The canon of social theory, therefore, is not only a living legacy, subject to periodic change and transformation, it is also a reflection of the struggles and conflicts of social groups for recognition and respect. The early histories of social thought, published at the turn of the twentieth century, faithfully reflected, for the most part, the worldview of the predominantly white, patriarchal, heterosexual, middle-class professoriate of that time. The construction of the classics during this early period conformed to the predilections and prejudices of the educated elite in Europe and North America. For many years, even the works of Karl Marx were either trivialized or excluded from many standard histories of social and economic thought (Williams 1964). Indeed, Marx was contemptuously dismissed by one famous economist as a "minor post-Ricardian" (Samuelson 1962; Brewer,1995). Although, to be fair to Samuelson, he later added the following qualification: "Marx's bold economic or materialistic theory of history, his political theories of the class struggle, his transmutations of Hegelian philosophy, have an importance for the historian of 'ideas' that far transcends his facade of economics" (1962: 14).

Today, things are changing. Postcolonial scholars are deconstructing and reconstructing the traditional canon of social theory. Past social thinkers who were overlooked because they were women or because they came from non-Western cultures and civilizations are now being taken seriously and incorporated into an expanding global conception of our shared intellectual heritage. Once again, the historical canon is an object of contestation, negotiation and revision. Earlier criteria for inclusion in the canon are being expanded; the new criteria are more open and more cosmopolitan than ever before. The intellectual excitement of these times is well captured by one recent commentator: "The classics and the canon evolve.... We have no idea whether there are hidden jewels out there, just waiting for some scholar to make claims about their importance for current or future thinking" (Davis and Zald 2008: 644).

This is the spirit of the present volume. In addition to the usual list of classical social thinkers, we focus on some of those thinkers — such as the first wave feminists and Ibn Khaldun — who have received short shrift in many standard textbooks. Our focus on two generations of feminists reflects a growing recognition of the historical and contemporary significance of women's social issues in the world — not only for women but for all humanity. The inclusion of Ibn Khaldun attempts to redress the appalling ignorance in the West of the venerable traditions of Islamic social thought and other non-European traditions of social thought. Every reconstruction of the classics is a sign of the changing times; we always view the past through the prism of the present.

At the same time, there is no easy way to correct the parochialism of the past and to recover the unknown classics of forgotten social thinkers. Even the best intentioned attempts at reconstructing the historical canon of social theory still suffer from what is sometimes called the "Anglo-centric gaze": an over-reliance on Anglo-American sources to the virtual exclusion of other cultural contributions. As one eminent critic suggests: "What we need is to broaden out to the formation of canons in other disciplines and in other parts of the world.... Perhaps some day there will be a genuinely cosmopolitan account" (Collins 1997: 1564). Some critics even downplay the importance of "revising the story of 'great men' to include Ibn Khaldun among the classics" (Connell 1997: 1546), in favour of more cross-cultural studies of how different civilizations have produced their own classics of social thought. When viewed through the eyes of another civilization or another gender, even such theorists as Marx, Durkheim and Weber exemplify the many cultural and gender prejudices of their age. While this is not a reason to disregard their works entirely, it is a reason to recognize their inevitable historical limitations. As in many things, we can only take one step at a time — even when dismantling the past legacy of Eurocentism, Orientalism and sexism.

Decoding the Classics

Now that we have nearly reached the end of this book, it is time to offer some practical advice on how to use the classics to better understand the world we live in and to analyze our own life experiences. For most of us who lead busy and complex lives, the traditional ways of studying social theory may sometimes seem unrewarding. What is the point, we may well ask, of learning about long-departed thinkers if the only use we make of their ideas is to complete required courses and pass examinations? There has to be more to learning social theory than this.

In practical terms, there are a number of ways in which we can appreciate social theories. In order to more fully appreciate the classical theories outlined

Figure EP-2 Dimensions of Social Theory

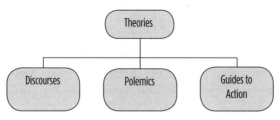

in this book, each theory may be viewed from a number of dimensions (see also Craib 1992: 15–17). Each of these dimensions will tell us more about how theories work — how they can teach us new languages, introduce us to new arguments and sometimes, even cause us to change our ways of acting in the world.

Theories as Discourses

Social theories are specialized languages. Many of the classical theorists reviewed in this book invented or adapted their own vocabularies. Marx's theoretical language included such key concepts as "alienation," "exploitation," "surplus value," "class consciousness" and so on. Weber introduced "rationalization," "bureaucracy" and "disenchantment," among others. Ibn Khaldun focused on the role of *"asabiyya"* in social life, while Pareto introduced us to the "circulation of elites" and the perpetual struggle between the "lions" and the "foxes." Studying a social theory is akin to learning a new language. To become proficient in the use of a theoretical language, we should be able to define and explain its key concepts and show how they are related to each other. In time, as we learn to apply the key concepts of the theory to relevant social situations, we will be able to adapt the theory to our personal circumstances. This is what it means to become a "practical theorist."

How we speak about social relations will greatly influence how we observe these relations. What we see, and how we observe, are greatly dependent upon the concepts and categories we use to organize our experiences. In other words, as practical theorists, our observation languages are greatly influenced by our theoretical languages. When speaking the language of Marx, for example, we are more likely to observe examples of "class struggle," "exploitation" and "immiseration" in the world. If we shift to the language of Durkheim, we may well begin to see subtle evidence of "anomie" in our own society, or examples of "altruistic suicide" in some of the combat zones in the world today. We may even understand the euphoria of hockey fans as a form of what Durkheim described as "collective effervescence" — the powerful and uplifting collective emotional excitement or delirium that may be experienced by a social group when assembled together for religious, mystical, patriotic or even secular events — including highly dramatized sporting events (see Tiryakian 1995).

The language of theory allows us a specialized frame of reference to focus our attention on crucial aspects of our experience. But while theories can illuminate some aspects of our social worlds, they can also obscure or overlook other aspects. In this respect, theories can only ever offer us partial and incomplete windows on our lives. However, without some kind of language it is difficult to impose any conceptual order on the world.

The languages of different classical theories may also produce different "facts." What counts as a fact in one theoretical language, may not in another. As a general rule of thumb, a fact is best understood as a "highly confirmed observation statement" — a statement that can be shown to be true or false through direct or indirect observation. But different theories often have different criteria for deciding what is observable. In this sense, facts and theories are perpetually engaged in an intimate dance, one that is often hidden and unrecognized. Theories without facts are empty; facts without theories are blind. Or, as the philosopher Immanuel Kant [1871] observed: "Thoughts without content are empty, intuitions without concepts are blind." Part of the purpose of this book is to reveal the hidden dialectical relationship that has always existed between facts and theories and to render the process of social observation more reflexive and self-conscious.

Observation terms are normally defined in the context of a particular theory. For Durkheim, the study of society began with the observation of "social facts." He meant by this term, any type of social code that was external to and which regulated the behaviour of the individual. Social facts refer to collective patterns of social relations, whether these are embodied in suicide rates, legal systems, languages or currencies. For Weber, on the other hand, the observation of society began with the study of "subjectively meaningful social action." Whereas for Durkheim, the language of observation referred to collective patterns of social relations, for Weber it referred to the subjective states of the individual. In these examples — as in other social theories discussed in this book — observation terms are always defined within the context of a theory and its vocabulary of concepts.

We can begin to appreciate more fully the influence of social theories on our lives and identities when we view them as specialized languages. In ways that are often subtle and taken for granted, social theories provide us with categories and concepts that structure our observations of the world. They also influence the ways in which we define our social selves and the selves of others with whom we interact. The study of social theory, therefore, can help us to become more self-critical and reflexive about out own attitudes and opinions and about the assumptions that guide the views and opinions of others.

When we examine the languages of different classical theories, there are a number of questions that we should ask ourselves. Together, these questions will help us to examine social theories as languages — with their own vocabularies of key concepts, their own observation terms and basic assumptions. In this way, we can better understand that how we speak about our social world strongly influences how we perceive it:

• what are the key concepts of the theory, and how are they interrelated?

- where do these concepts come from: what is their genealogy?
- what count as "facts," or socially significant observations in the language?

Theories as Polemics

Besides seeing theories as specialized languages, classical theories can also be seen as arguments and counter-arguments between particular theorists. Most, if not all, classical theories came into the world as critical responses to earlier, established theories. Every theory carries within it its own historical birthmarks. These often include the vocabulary of political and ideological struggle drawn from particular social movements. Marx's language, for example, was clearly indebted, as well as addressed, to the nineteenth-century revolutionary workers' movements. Rousseau's language both echoed and incited the radical democrats of the Enlightenment. Spencer refined his ideas and language from several different sources, including the French positivists and the British liberals. At the same time, these movements were, in turn, influenced by the theoretical languages of each of these prominent theorists. In other words, the relations between social theories and society are essentially dialectical and reciprocal. Each influences the other.

Most social theories have arisen as critiques of earlier intellectual traditions. Marx used the expression "settling of accounts" to justify his critiques of Hegel, Adam Smith and Ricardo, as well as of Charles Fourier and Robert Owen. And while he may have built upon their foundations, he saw his own work both as a critique and a transcendence of these earlier traditions. Similarly, Pareto's ideas developed, in no small part, as a critique of Marx and of the rising socialist movements of the early twentieth century.

When we examine the arguments of classical social theorists, we need to clarify the following:

- which social theories are being challenged by the current theory?
- how does a particular theory refute, modify or transcend earlier theories?

Theories as Guides to Action

Social theories may also be understood is as guides to social action. Many theories contain some, explicit or implicit, recommendations for public policy or political action. Some theories may be explicitly programmatic in their political content. Marx's popular writings sounded a clarion call to the working class for revolutionary political action. The early feminists campaigned for women's suffrage. And much of Herbert Spencer's work reads like a manifesto for a free-market economy and an uncompromising defence of the rights of private property. Other social theories may carry more subtle recommendations.

While many social theories contain some explicit or implicit guides for collective action, it is not always an easy task to decipher these ideological agendas. When examining social theories as practical guides to action, ask the following questions:

- who are the major players represented in the theory?
- whose interests are being served by these theoretical ideas, that is, "cui bono," or who profits?

There are many ways to appreciate social theories. This conclusion shows how theories are more than simply sets of abstract ideas. They are languages that influence how we see our social worlds. They are guides to action that may influence our social conduct. And when adopted by social movements or nation states as ideologies, they may be converted into powerful collective forces, with real consequences — both good and ill — for societies and for the world. Theories often have practical consequences. Becoming a practical theorist involves not only learning how to use theories to expand your range of observation and your depth of understanding of the world, but also learning how theories may influence the beliefs and actions of others. The goal of this book is to encourage you to become a practical theorist. As you learn more and more how to flex your theoretical muscles, you will find that the whole world is grist for your theoretical mill.

References

Abdo, Nahla. 1996. *Sociological Thought: Beyond Eurocentric Theory*. Toronto: Canadian Scholars Press.

Alatas, Farid. 2006. *Alternative Discourses in Asian Social Science*. Thousand Oaks, CA: Sage Publications.

Alatas, Syed Farid, and Vineeta Sinha. 2001. "Teaching Classical Sociological Theory in Singapore: The Context of Eurocentrism." *Teaching Sociology 29*, 3: 316–31.

Brewer, Anthony. 1995. "A Minor Post Ricardian: Marx as an Economist." *History of Political Economy* 27, 1: 111–45.

Churchill, Ward. 1995. "White Studies: The Intellectual Imperialism of U.S. Higher Education." In S. Jackson and J. Solis (eds.), *Beyond Comfort Zones in Multiculturalism: Confronting the Politics of Privilege*. Westport: Bergin & Garvey.

Collins, Randall. 1997. "A Sociological Guilt Trip: Comment on Connell." *American Journal of Sociology* 102, 6: 1558–64.

Connell, R.W. 1997. "Why Is Classical Theory Classical?" *American Journal of Sociology* 102, 6: 1511–57.

Conquest, Robert. 1986. *The Harvest of Sorrow: Soviet Collectivization and the Terror-Famine*. New York: Oxford University Press.

Craib, Ian. 1992. *Modern Social Theory: from Parsons to Habermas*. New York: St. Martin's Press.

Dark Side of Chocolate. 2010. 45 minute documentary by Miki Mistrati and U. Roberto

Romano.16 March (Denmark).

Darwin, Charles. 1859. *The Origin of Species by Means of Natural Selection*. London: John Murray.

Davis, Gerald F., and Mayer N. Zald. 2008. *Afterworld: Sociological Classics and the Cannon in the Study of Organizations*. In Paul S. Adler (ed.), *Oxford Handbook of Sociology and Organization Studies: Classical Resources*: Oxford: Oxford University Press.

Dawes, Milton. 2012. "Theories in Everyday Situations." <miltondawes.com/formal-essays-handouts/theories-in-everyday-situations/>.

De Santillana, Giorgio. 1955. *The Crime of Galileo*. Chicago: University of Chicago Press.

Ginzburg, Carlo. 1980. *The Cheese and the Worms: The Cosmos of a Sixteenth Century Miller*. Baltimore: Johns Hopkins University Press.

Kant, Immanuel. 1965 [1781]. *Critique of Pure Reason*. Translated by Norman Kemp Smith. New York: St. Martins.

Keynes, John Maynard. 1935. *The General Theory of Employment, Interest and Money*. London: Macmillan.

Mills, C. Wright. 1959. *The Sociological Imagination*. London: Oxford University Press

Mouzelis, Nicos. 1997. "In Defence of the Sociological Canon: A reply to David Parker." *Sociological Review* 45: 244–53.

Naidoo, A.V. 1996. "Challenging the Hegemony of Eurocentric Psychology." *The Journal of Community and Health Sciences* 2, 2: 9–16.

Off, Carol. 2008. *Bitter Chocolate: The Dark Side of the World's Most Seductive Sweet*. New York: New Press.

Plato. 1993. *Apology: The Last Days of Socrates: Euthyphro; The Apology;Crito; Phaedo*. Harmondsworth, Middlesex: Penguin.

Ramose, M.B. 2002. *African Philosophy Through Ubuntu*. Harare, Zimbabwe: Mond Books.

Richardson, Mary, Joan Sherman and Michael Gismondi. 1993. *Winning Back the Words*. Toronto: Garamond Press.

Rousseau, Jean-Jacques. 2008 [1962]. *The Social Contract*. New York: Cosimo Inc.

Said, Edward. 1994. *Representations of the Intellectual: The 1993 Reith Lectures*. New York: Pantheon Books.

Samuelson, Paul A. 1962. "Economists and the History of Ideas." *American Economic Review* 52, 1: 1–18.

Saul, John Ralston. 1992. *Voltaire's Bastards: The Dictatorship of Reason in the West*. Toronto: Penguin Books Canada.

Smith, Dorothy. 1999. *Writing the Social: Critique, Theory, and Investigations*. Toronto: University of Toronto Press.

Stiglitz Joseph. 2002. *Globalization and Its Discontents*. New York: W.W. Norton.

Thiong'o, Ngugi wa. 1986. *Decolonising the Mind — The Politics of Language in African Literature*. London: James Currey.

Tiryakian, Edward A. 1995. "Collective Effervescence, Social Change and Charisma: Durkheim, Weber and 1989." *International Sociology* 10, 3: 269–81.

Williams, William Appleton. 1964. *The Great Evasion: An Essay on the Contemporary Relevance of Karl Marx and on the Wisdom of Admitting the Heretic Into the Dialogue About America's Future*. Chicago: Quadrangle Books.

Zeitlin, Irving. 2000. *Ideology and the development of Sociological Theory*. Seventh edition. New Jersey: Prentice Hall.

Glossary

alienation — central to Marx's theory of society alienation is the process by which those who labour for a livelihood (whether in field, factory or office) lose control over the products of their labour and the conditions of their work. Workers are not only alienated from the products they produce, they are also alienated from other workers and from themselves. The philosophical concept of "alienation" in the works of Hegel, Feuerbach and the early Marx was later transformed by Marx into the economic concept of "exploitation" (see below).

altruism — the willingness of individuals to sacrifice themselves for the greater good of the collectivity — whether this collectivity is a national, racial or ethnic, religious or tribal, or other social group. Altruistic suicide, according to Durkheim, is normally caused by the over-integration of the individual in the collectivity.

androcentrism — the adoption of a male-oriented worldview, a masculin-ized viewpoint that tacitly privileges the experiences and perspectives of men over those of women, children and gay, lesbian or transgendered people.

anomie — a state of moral confusion, a condition of normlessness or moral de-regulation, associated with the weakening of the conscience collec-tive — the set of beliefs and values that guide the conduct of individu-als in traditional societies. Anomie was diagnosed by Durkheim as a pathological condition of hyper-individualism. He believed that it is especially acute during periods of rapid economic change — whether downward cycles of recession or depression, or upward cycles of rapid growth and sudden prosperity. Both contribute to a weakening of col-lective norms. Durkheim also suggested that anomie may be recognized as "the malady of infinite aspiration," whereby the individual falls prey to the unlimited possibilities for satisfying the infinite desires and needs of modern society.

asabiyya — the strong bonds of social cohesion that unite and integrate nomadic groups in their hostile and often unforgiving wilderness envi-ronments. For Ibn Khaldun, asabiyya represented the virtues of cour-age, hardiness, self-reliance and independence, as well as a puritanical capacity for hard work and asceticism. Asabiyya, is the powerful sense of group identity and social cohesion that enables a vigorous and virile people to conquer and dominate more sedentary and less robust cultures.

Asiatic mode of production — an alternative path of historical development of Eastern, non-European societies. For Marx, the most important factor distinguishing the Asiatic from the European mode of production was the central importance of irrigation. Those who controlled the systems of irrigation in the Asian "hydraulic civilizations" (of India and China) effectively controlled the populations, which were totally dependent for their survival upon these systems, often referred to in the eighteenth- and nineteenth-century European literature as "Oriental despotism."

authority — those cases of the exercise of power in which a social actor is able to secure the voluntary consent and compliance of others in the achievement of their goals. In other words, authority is based upon the consent by those who are dominated of the right of others to dominate them. The motives for compliance may include fear, duty, custom and tradition, self-interest or even love. This process is referred to by Weber as "legitimation." Authority can best be understood as "legitimated power," inasmuch as authority rests upon the compliance of the governed in the conditions of their governance.

base — the "real" material foundation of all societies, based on the "mode of production"; how real individuals make their livelihood and produce their subsistence. For Marx, the mode of production was a complex concept that can be broken down into the *forces of production* and the *relations of production*. The forces of production refer to the technology (the tools and techniques) of production, while the relations of production refer to the division of social classes, the technical division of labour and the property relations in society. Taken together, the mode of production constitutes the "real" or material economic base of society.

bureaucracy — "government by officials," a large, formal and complex structure which is organized around an elaborate division of labour, under hierarchical authority and operating according to explicit rules and procedures. Weber provided his own definition: "Administration of government through departments and subdivisions managed by a set of appointed officials following an inflexible routine."

charismatic authority — authority based upon some extraordinary abilities, or personal qualities, of an individual leader. The very term "charisma" from the Greek means "magic" or "grace." Charismatic leaders may sometimes be regarded as supernatural, superhuman or having excep- tional, exemplary or outstanding personal qualities.

circulation of elites — the cyclic theory of the periodic rise and fall of politi- cal elites, or ruling dynasties. In many ways, this theory can be thought of as a theory of regime change. According to Pareto, the history of regime change is best understood as the periodic replacement of one political elite by another. Some elites rule through the use of coercive force and harsh methods of social control (hard power), while other elites rule through the use of manipulation, deception and cunning (soft power). For Pareto, elites using "hard" power were lions, while those using "soft" power were foxes (taken from Machiavelli). Pareto believed that the role of the masses was destined to remain that of followers or supporters of particular elites because they were motivated by irrational sentiments. However hard the masses may fight for social change from below, all political change ultimately results in the installation of a new political elite from above.

class-in-itself — a social class in which all members share a common objective relationship to the means of production but have not as yet developed any subjective consciousness of their own common class interests, or of their relationship to other social classes. This term is a simple objective definition of class that refers only to the economic position of a group in society.

class-for-itself — members of a social class who have become fully conscious of their own common class interests and of their relationship to other social classes. For Marx, class consciousness could be developed by any class and was a necessary precondition for collective action. Without class consciousness, a class-in-itself is doomed to remain a passive aggregate of individuals with only a latent potential for class formation and class struggle.

commodity — any object that acquires its value through the process of exchange. In capitalist societies, commodities are those objects that are sold and bought in the marketplace. And in capitalist societies, the labour power of the worker is also a commodity. Money is the universal commodity in a capitalist society, used to express the values of all other commodities.

communism — a society in which private property has been abolished and the means of production, distribution and exchange have been nationalized and placed under public ownership and state control. Marx famously described communism as a society in which wealth and basic resources would be redistributed "from each according to his ability, to each according to his need." That is, in a communist society, every person should contribute to the best of their ability and consume in proportion to their needs.

conscience collective — the set of beliefs, values and shared sentiments that hold a society together. In traditional societies, based on mechanical solidarity, there is typically a very strong and well-defined conscience collective. However, in modern societies, based on organic solidarity, the conscience collective grows weaker, more diffuse, more abstract and less commanding.

conservatism — is a political and social philosophy committed to the preservation of traditional social institutions. The first political use of the term was by François-René de Chateaubriand in the aftermath of the

French Revolution. While some conservatives have sought to preserve things as they are, emphasizing stability and continuity, others have strongly opposed modernism and have sought to restore an earlier social order — a *status quo ante* or *"ancien régime."* Conservatives — both past and present — have all claimed to defend those customary beliefs and practices that have proven their value over time against the encroachments of innovations which threaten to destabilize the traditional social order. Their ideological battles have proclaimed the need to preserve the best of the old and to resist the worst of the new. At heart, they remain nostalgic for a simpler, often mythological, age, governed by traditional beliefs and practices that have stood the test of time.

deductivism — the idea that all knowledge is based upon the logical relations between cause and effect. Deductive reasoning entails the application of general laws or principles to explanations for the occurrence of specific or particular events. The normal form of a deductive explanation is: "if ... then," such as "If water is heated to boiling point, then it will begin to evaporate."

derivations — refer to the ways in which the masses try to clothe non-logical conduct and belief in a mantle of logic. While he remained convinced that most social action is motivated by irrational sentiments, Pareto acknowledged that social actors normally offer apparently logical reasons, motives, causes, ideologies, doctrines and other pretexts to "explain" and justify their actions in society.

dialectics — the idea that historical change results from the gradual accumulation of minor changes which lead eventually to sudden major transformations. Historical changes are the result of internal oppositions, or contradictions, which arise between conflicting elements in the historical process. These contradictions are finally resolved through a unification, or synthesis, of opposing elements into a new form. Over time, however, this new form (which Hegel called a thesis) will generate its own opposing form (an antithesis), and together these two opposing forms will ultimately unite into a third new form (a synthesis). Inevitably, the synthesis will eventually generate a new antithesis, which means that — according to Hegel — the dialectical process of historical change is endless.

domestic sphere of production — the political economy of the household, or the family. Much of the work, or "production," in the domestic sphere is performed by women — traditionally for no wage or financial remuneration. Women produce use-values rather than exchange-values in the household economy because their products and services are not bought and sold on the open market, but are consumed by family members. Later feminist writers reproached Marx and other economists for concluding that women's labour is "non-productive," simply because it does not produce exchange-value. Socialist feminists argue that women's domestic labour is essential to the reproduction and maintenance of the labour force — even though this household labour is unwaged.

egoism — a state of social isolation and detachment experienced by the individual in modern society. Egoism is often described as a condition of detachment or social dis-integration, associated with the weakening of the conscience collective. Like anomie, egoism was also diagnosed by Durkheim as a pathological condition of hyper-individualism. Whereas anomie led to the moral confusion (normlessness), egoism led to melancholy and depression. Anomie was caused by low moral regulation, egoism by low social integration. In practice, many commentators conclude that Durkheim's distinction between these pathological states is fuzzy; they are different sides of the same coin.

empiricism — the belief that valid and reliable knowledge of the world can only be gained through sensory experience — as opposed to theoretical or metaphysical speculation.

Enlightenment — a period of exceptional intellectual creativity and social upheaval that lasted from the mid-seventeenth to the late eighteenth century in Europe. It was a time during which philosophers began to question and critique many of the established doctrines of their day — especially those sanctified by religious faith or tradition. It was an age of unprecedented skepticism and radical doubt that paved the way for the revolutions of the eighteenth century, but also an age of unparalleled innovation and invention — especially in the fields of science and technology. The Enlightenment was an intellectual and political movement that proclaimed the values of reason, liberty, equality and progress.

Eurocentrism — a Western-oriented worldview that tacitly privileges the experiences and perspectives of Westerners over those of non-European, immigrant or formerly colonized nationalities.

evolutionism — the belief that all species of organisms develop from relatively simple to increasingly more complex forms of biological organization. As organisms evolve, each structural part becomes more differentiated from its other parts and more specialized in its function. Whereas for Darwin, the process of evolution was driven by random mutation and natural selection, pre-Darwinian biologists, such as Lamarck, believed that organic traits were acquired or lost through use or disuse and that acquired characteristics could be genetically transmitted from one generation to the next. Lamarck believed that evolution was driven by necessity, whereas Darwin believed that it was driven largely by chance.

exchange value — the value that a product has for the seller when it is sold to a consumer in the marketplace. Or, to put it another way, exchange value is the value realized through commodity exchange. Exchange value is normally expressed in a money price.

exploitation — the process whereby surplus value is extracted from the worker during commodity production. Surplus value is the value produced by the worker above and beyond their wages, the value produced during that part of the working day for which the worker remains unpaid. Thus, for Marx, "exploitation" is much more than a term of moral condemnation. It is the hidden mechanism by which wealth is accumulated in capitalist society.

false consciousness — the inability of members of a social class to correctly identify their position in society and their relation to other social classes — especially to the dominant or ruling class. For Marx, false consciousness describes the situation of those social classes in society which accept the ideology of the ruling class even when their own material interests were structurally opposed to those of the ruling class.

fatalism — the over-regulation of the individual in society and the consequent abandonment of all hope or possibility of freedom or emancipation. Fatalistic suicide, according to Durkheim, is typically committed by heavily over-regulated individuals — such as prisoners, slaves, women in forced marriages and others whose spirits are crushed by oppression or poverty. Fatalistic suicide results in individuals whose "passions [were] violently choked by oppressive discipline."

feminism — refers to the broad social and political movement struggling for gender equality and for the emancipation of women from the political, legal, economic and cultural constraints of patriarchy. Feminism also refers to the intellectual tradition of thought that criticizes, analyses and transcends male-centred, (i.e., androcentric) discourse in the humanities, social and biological sciences. The feminist movement is usually broken down into three distinctive "waves": the first wave of the eighteenth, nineteenth and early twentieth century; the second wave of the mid-twentieth century; and the third wave of the late twentieth century.

fetishism of commodities — the loss of connection between commodities and the human labour that is incorporated in them. Our failure to recognize any human dimension to commodities means remaining ignorant of the underlying social relations that connect us to the products and services that we buy and consume. Marx recognized the growing influence of this disconnected consumerism in the culture of capitalism.

forces of production — according to Marx and Engels, the term "forces of production" can refer to the technology (the machinery, tools and techniques) of production, to land and infrastructure, to human labor power, to capital (as accumulated labor power) and to sources of fuel and energy. It may also refer to human knowledge, especially knowledge applied to the process of production.

formal rationality — instrumental logic that emphasizes above all else the drive for greater efficiency which has been responsible for the rationalization of our worldview and our institutions. Formal rationality is associated with rational-purposive, or goal-oriented, action, which is based upon the need to select the most efficient means in order to accomplish a specific end. Weber believed that modern science was one of the highest expressions of formal rationality — the most efficient means for discovering valid knowledge of the material world.

forms — the elementary units of interaction (sociation), the basic societal building blocks, to which all higher and more complex social structures can be reduced. The most basic forms, according to Simmel, are the dyad and the triad — combinations of two, and of three, individuals in a pattern of social interaction.

hierarchy of the sciences — Comte's belief that the sciences formed both a historical and a logical hierarchy of knowledge. The historical hierarchy was based on the order in which the sciences first developed: the early physical sciences laid the foundations for the later development of the biological and social sciences. The logical hierarchy was based on the different levels of abstraction of each of the sciences. Thus, mathematics and then astronomy were regarded as the most abstract sciences, while sociology was regarded as the most concrete and practical.

hegemony — the cultural dominance exercised by a ruling class over an exploited or oppressed class — such as the working class. According to the Marxist theorist Antonio Gramsci, this cultural dominance may be transmitted through the mass media, schooling, religion, politics, law and other institutions positioned to disseminate the ideology and propaganda of the ruling class.

historical materialism — the theory of history and society first systematically expounded by Karl Marx and Friedrich Engels. The primary focus for understanding human history should be on how communities and societies make their livelihoods and produce their subsistence — that is, their mode of production. Each mode of production develops its own corresponding political and cultural superstructure, which is always determined by the mode of production. From this framework, Marx derived his theory of class conflict and his periodization of history into stages, or epochs, of historical development.

historiography — refers to the study of the methods and analytical perspectives used by historians in their narratives of past events. In other words, historiography refers to the study of the way history is written. Unlike history itself, which purports to document the record of past events, historiography does not directly study these events but rather the changing interpretations of these events by historians. Thus, historiography is concerned with the reliability of the sources used in historical scholarship, the credibility of the historian and the authenticity of historical texts. One of the earliest scholars to evaluate the methods used by historians to record past events was Ibn Khaldun.

holism (sometimes known as realism)— the belief that society and all large-scale social structures have a reality that is above and beyond the sum of the individuals who compose these structures. Also known as ontological or metaphysical realism, sociological holism is based upon the assumption that society exists at a level of independent reality that cannot be reduced to, or explained in terms of, other psychological or biological levels of reality.

idealism — the belief that the reality of the world is based upon our consciousness. Only ideas are real: the world is constructed from them. Idealists believe that we can only "know" reality indirectly through our mental categories and concepts — that we can never have direct knowledge of a raw or uninterpreted reality.

ideal types — a method of social research popularized and refined by Max Weber, although some previous social thinkers — such as Montesquieu — had already made use of this method in their own studies. An ideal type is an abstract description of some aspect of society (such as a structure, a process or an event), constructed from observations made from a number of real cases. An ideal-type never completely corresponds to any real case, but rather is typical of most cases. Ideal types may help us to compare and contrast societies in different ways.

ideology — a set of ideas that influence the beliefs, perceptions and actions of individuals and groups in society irrespective of whether these ideas are expressed as philosophical systems, political doctrines, economic theories, laws and policies or other well established forms of social thought. An ideology is a comprehensive vision, or worldview, which is often applied to politics and public policy. Every political or economic perspective entails an ideology, whether it is explicitly propounded as a formal system of ideas or implicitly accepted as a statement of common sense. Marx believed that ideologies distorted the ability of individuals and social classes to accurately perceive their true position in society and their true relation to other social classes. He maintained that that the ruling ideas, or ideology, of any age always reflect the material interests of the ruling class. He concluded that every dominant class in history has claimed to represent a universal ideology and had sought to extend its ideas to all other classes and groups in society.

inductivism — the process of inferring a general law or principle from observation of particular instances. Inductive reasoning entails the idea that knowledge is based not on the logical relations between things but on the pattern of past, or customary, relations. In other words, induction is the formation of a generalization derived from examination of a set of particulars.

labour theory of value — the belief that the value of any commodity is equal to the amount of average or "socially necessary" mental and manual labour time used to produce it. All commodities derive their value, as opposed to their price, from the amount of labour used to produce them. The labour theory of value was generally accepted by the classical school of political economy — Adam Smith, David Ricardo and, of course, Karl Marx.

Laffer curve — an economic formula that shows a relationship between tax rates and tax revenue collected by governments. This formula suggests that, as taxes increase, the tax revenue collected by the government also increases. However, if tax rates increase beyond a certain point, the higher tax rate becomes a disincentive for people to work as hard as previously, thereby reducing tax revenue. The Laffer curve suggests that relatively low rates of taxation tend to stimulate consumer demand and investor confidence — thereby leading to higher tax revenues. Although this idea can be traced back to Ibn Khaldun, the modern version of this theorem is associated with economist Arthur Laffer.

laissez-faire — ("let it be" in French), usually refers to the absence, or proposed absence, of government regulation of, or intervention in, trade and commerce — beyond the minimum necessary for a free-enterprise system to operate according to its own economic laws. Originating with the liberal tradition of classical political economy, *laissez-faire* classical liberals oppose any economic policies — such as tariffs, excessive taxes, government subsidies and enforced monopolies — which they believe will inhibit the growth of free and open economic markets, or prevent the development of "perfect competition." The *laissez-faire* economic philosophy was strongly advocated by Scottish economist Adam Smith in his 1776 classic *The Wealth of Nations*, in which he argued that the forces of supply and demand allow a market economy to self-regulate and that prices, wages and employment are automatically adjusted by an "invisible hand."

law of tendency — a law which predicts the development of a particular trend, or tendency — a declining rate of profit or an increasing polarization of classes. The law remains valid only when the conditions which produced this trend remain unchanged. Laws of tendency, therefore, are probabilistic laws based on the assumption of "other things being equal." Marx always acknowledged that if conditions changed, then the trends he predicted could also change.

law of the three stages — Comte's periodization of history into three evolving stages of human consciousness — the theological, the metaphysical and the positive (or scientific).

liberalism — the ideas associated with the Enlightenment, emphasizing the importance of individual liberty and equality, as well as the power of reason to guide human affairs and promote economic efficiency. Classical liberalism of the nineteenth century promoted the values of personal liberty through freedom of speech, freedom of assembly, freedom of (religious) conscience and freedom of the press. The political economist Adam Smith promoted free trade, while other liberals — such as David Hume — campaigned for limited government, constitutionalism and the separation of powers between the executive, legislative and judicial branches of government. Many liberals — such as John Stuart Mill — were also committed to the idea of natural rights. In Britain, liberalism was closely associated with the doctrine of utilitarianism — especially in the work of Jeremy Bentham. During the 1980s, many of the ideas of classical liberalism were resurrected as neoliberalism.

liquid modernity — the peculiar conditions of transience, changeability and flexibility that characterize developed societies in the late twentieth and early twenty-first centuries. In the words of Zygmunt Bauman, a liquid modern society is one "in which the conditions under which its members act change faster than it takes the ways of acting to consolidate into habits and routines." Liquid modernity implies the need for the individual to continually adapt and re-adapt to the ever-changing and rapid pace of technological and social change in the postmodern world.

Maghreb — the territories of North Africa.

Mashreq — the territories of the Middle East.

materialism — the belief that all our ideas are reflections of the material world. The world exists independently of our ideas.

mechanical solidarity — traditional societies characterized by a relatively simple division of labour. One example would be a hunting and gathering society in which work is assigned on the basis of age and sex. Societies based on mechanical solidarity also have a very strong conscience collective.

militant and industrial societies — the basic distinction, first introduced by Saint-Simon and then Comte, but later popularized by Herbert Spencer, between societies organized for war and defence versus societies organized for peace and productivity. Militant societies tend to be strongly hierarchical; the interests of the collectivity prevail over those of the individual; and the ideological values of loyalty and patriotism are strongly emphasized. Industrial societies are more decentralized; the interests of the individual prevail over those of the collectivity; and mobility, trade and intercultural contact are strongly encouraged.

mode of production — the way in which a society is organized to produce its own subsistence and livelihood. Every society, according to Marx, is characterized by a historically specific mode of production. Primitive societies produce their subsistence through hunting and gathering; ancient societies produce their subsistence through slavery; feudal societies produce their subsistence through agriculture; and industrial capitalist societies produce their subsistence through machine production. Marx proposed that every mode of production can be analyzed in terms of the forces of production and the relations of production. He also concluded that the mode of production — as the basis of material life — strongly influences all other — cultural, political and artistic — aspects of social life.

natural rights — the idea, first popularized by the philosophers and political leaders of the Enlightenment, that all human beings have inalienable, universal "rights" that are valid for all times and places, thus, not dependent upon the authority of a crown or the state, upon custom or tradition or upon particular cultural or religious beliefs. Many revolutionary and republican states, inspired by the ideals of the Enlightenment, have enshrined what they regard as natural rights into their constitutions. Thus, the United States Declaration of Independence enshrined the rights of "Life, Liberty and the Pursuit of Happiness," while in France these rights were expressed in the national motto *"Liberte, Egalite, Fraternite"* — and were later codified into the Declaration of the Rights of Man and the Citizen.

neoconservatism — is a relatively recent branch of the political ideology of conservatism that combines aspects of traditional conservatism with political and economic liberalism, as well as an aggressive commitment to a "muscular" foreign policy. Although neoconservatives (or neocons) may share certain ideas in common with neoliberals — such as a belief in the efficacy of free trade, privatization, de-regulation, full marketization, low taxes and a down-sized government — they often depart from neoliberals in their socially conservative domestic and foreign policy agendas. Unlike neoliberals, neoconservatives are more likely to endorse policies such as a restoration of patriotism and national honor (and opposition to multiculturalism), a return to religion, support for family values (and opposition to abortion and gay rights), as well as the aggressive export of democracy and free markets to other nations. Neoconservatism arose in the United States in the 1970s among strongly anti-communist intellectuals. After 9-11, neoconservatives supported and initiated the invasions of Afghanistan and Iraq and promulgated the doctrine of the "clash of civilizations" — between the "liberal West" and the "intolerant" Muslim world.

neoliberalism — the late twentieth-century doctrine that economic prosperity is best achieved through such policies as free trade, privatization, deregulation, low taxes, reduced government spending and full marketization. Neoliberalism was closely associated with the economic policies of Margaret Thatcher (in the UK) and Ronald Reagan (in the US). It is sometimes referred to as monetarism, or supply side economics.

nominalism — the belief that the structures of society (or the economy) are fully reducible to the individuals who compose these structures. This view is sometimes known as metaphysical or ontological "individualism."

objectification — the process whereby the local subjective activities of individuals are collectively transformed into larger more objective societal structures and processes which often come to dominate and control individual members of society. In his writings, Georg Simmel remained preoccupied with how the practices of individual culture were inevitably transformed into the (material and ideological) products of objective culture.

organicism — the view of society as a social organism, made up of a set of interrelated parts. This view of society is based on the analogy of a biological organism — in particular, the human body, made up of interrelated vital organs.

organic solidarity — a modern society with a relatively weak conscience collective and a highly specialized division of labour. Whereas the mechanical solidarity of a traditional society is derived from the sameness and similarity of its members, the organic solidarity of a modern society is derived from the interdependence of its members within a complex division of labour. Similarly, whereas the strong conscience collective of traditional society is based upon a common set of long held beliefs and practices, the weaker conscience collective of a modern society is expressed in more universal and abstract terms.

Orientalism — the view of the late Palestinian-American scholar Edward Said that the Western image of the "Orient" has long been based upon a set of stereotypes and presuppositions which actually tell us much more about the arrogance, ignorance and insecurities of Western colonial societies than they do about the colonized Eastern societies. In other words, the Orient has always been an elaborate fiction, or "imaginary," conjured up from the narratives of colonial officials, military officers, missionaries, travel writers, novelists and other Western observers. The Orient, as represented in the Western imagination has never really existed.

Pashtunwali — the ancestral tribal code of the Pashtun peoples, who live in Afghanistan and Pakistan. This unwritten traditional code of conduct emphasizes such values as honour, justice, loyalty, protection and sanctuary, and retribution, and is based upon a long held set of ethical beliefs and traditional practices.

Pareto rule — also known as the 80 percent–20 percent rule, asserts that 80 percent of an output will be produced by 20 percent of the population. The Pareto rule is also sometimes referred to as the law of the vital few.

perfectibility — the highly optimistic belief of the Enlightenment that through the application of reason, humans possess an infinite capacity for progress. Enlightenment theorists believed that the power of reason could overcome the prejudices and superstitions of the past and also ensure the progressive development and evolution of human society.

pluto-democracy — a hybrid state in which society is run by the rich and powerful with the consent of the masses. According to Pareto, most so-called democracies are essentially pluto-democracies, in which the masses are permitted to vote, but the rich and powerful own and operate the state. Most of the candidates for political office in a pluto-democracy come from the ranks of the wealthy.

positivism — the belief, initially advanced by Comte, that there are laws of society in much the same as there are laws of nature. Once these laws of society are discovered through social science, knowledge of these laws can be used to predict and explain the occurrence of future social events. Today, however, positivism refers more to a broad philosophical tendency than to a rigorously formulated theory of knowledge. It has often been used to refer inclusively to classical positivism, classical empiricism, logical positivism, logical empiricism and critical rationalism.

power — the ability of a social actor to achieve their goals even when opposed by others.

profane — those aspects of social life which are part of the practical everyday mundane world.

pure sociology — the most basic micro-sociological level of analysis. Simmel also included in pure sociology his studies of the forms and the types of social interaction.

rationalism — both a theory of knowledge and a theory of politics. As a theory of knowledge, rationalism argues that the power of reason can overcome superstition and prejudice in the realm of ideas. As a theory of politics, rationalists believe that the power of reason can also overthrow tyranny and despotism and reconstruct society along the principles of reason and justice.

rationalization — an irreversible historical trend in society towards modernization and to ever greater efficiency, standardization and uniformity. At the same time, rationalization also leads to increasing impersonality, regimentation and conformity. Weber famously described this as "disenchantment of the world." Rationalization is a process that renders all pre-modern practices and beliefs — based on tradition or religion — progressively obsolete.

reactionaries — extreme conservatives who seek turn back the historical clock and restore the institutions and practices of the past. After the French Revolution, the extreme conservatives tended to idealize and romanticize the past, and would have been happy to have re-imposed mediaeval social relations onto what they perceived as the degenerate, corrupt and anarchic state of post-revolutionary French society.

reification — the mystification of consciousness in capitalist society whereby the relations between people are misperceived as relations between things. Thus, individuals may come to believe that their lives are controlled by large, impersonal forces — such as the market forces of supply and demand — over which they can't exercise any significant control. Reification thus becomes a means whereby large numbers of people are rendered passive and quiescent, and are subordinated to indirect and increasingly abstract forms of domination. Reification is the social equivalent of the economic process of commodity fetishism. Reification can also entail attributing to abstract concepts the properties of concrete things. Thus, an abstraction such as "society" may be said to have concrete "needs" or "goals."

relations of production — according to Marx and Engels, relations of production refers to the sum total of social relationships that it is necessary for individuals to enter into in order to produce and reproduce their subsistence and their livelihood. The totality of these relationships constitutes a relatively stable and permanent structure, the economic structure of society. More specifically, however, the relations of production may also refer to the division of social classes, the property relations in society or the technical division of labour within a workplace.

residues — arise from the fact that the masses are fundamentally irrational. Their beliefs and actions are invariably motivated by irrational sentiments — the residues of strong emotions, passions and prejudices, based to a large extent upon misinformation, misunderstanding and ignorance.

sacred — those aspects of social life which are set apart and become the objects of ritualized reverence and veneration.

scientism — the belief that only the natural, or physical, sciences provide an appropriate model for all other humanistic and social disciplines of inquiry.

sentiments — the non-logical, or irrational, motives that arise from deep-seated impulses and biological urges that drive social action. Pareto suggested that most human conduct results from the need to express these powerful emotional and psychological drives.

social contract — the voluntary social order that is necessary for individuals to live cooperatively together in large numbers. Rousseau believed that it was necessary for individuals to sacrifice some of the liberties they had formerly enjoyed when living separately in a state of nature. Individual liberties had to be sacrificed in order to ensure the greater good of the larger society.

social Darwinism — a doctrine that envisaged the social world as a competitive struggle for existence in which only the "fittest" were destined to survive. For social Darwinists, the principles of natural selection were used to explain the rise and fall of different human populations in their respective struggles for existence. This focus often made invidious comparisons between the presumed "civilized races" of the West versus the "primitive races" of Africa, Asia and South America. Herbert Spencer's notion of "survival of the fittest" was influenced far more by Jean-Baptiste Lamarck than by Charles Darwin.

social facts — those facts that have an independent social existence which cannot be fully reduced to psychological or biological explanations. For Durkheim, social facts were real things (whether these were social structures, social processes or social events) that existed or occurred in society due to social causes, not reducible to non-social causes. Durkheim suggested that social facts were, by definition, external to the individual, coercive or constraining of the individual, and independent of the individual (i.e., objective rather than subjective).

social physics — the early name given by Comte to the scientific study of society, although this term was first used by Belgian statistician Adolphe Quetelet.

social theory — may sometimes be defined in very formal terms that emphasize the strict methodological requirements of theory construction. One such definition is provided by Michael Faia, who defines a social theory as "a set of interrelated propositions that allow for the systematization of knowledge, explanation and prediction of social life, and generation of new research hypotheses" (1986: 134). Other sociologists define social theory more loosely and informally in order to include those ideas that have proven influential but cannot always be formally defined according to such strict and narrow methodological criteria. Such a definition is provided by George Ritzer, who defines a sociological theory as a system of ideas "that have a wide range of application, deal with centrally important social issues, and have stood the test of time" (2008: 2). Throughout this book, social theories are analyzed first as "discourses," or mini-languages composed of a vocabulary of concepts; second as "polemics," or arguments and counter-arguments to other theories; and third, as "guides to social and political action."

socialism — the egalitarian political ideology that seeks to nationalize the means of production, distribution and exchange, and place the major institutions that produce wealth under public ownership and control by the state. Unlike communists, many of whom seek to achieve these ends through revolution, many socialists seek to achieve these ends through gradual evolutionary means.

sociation — the process of social interaction, especially the "subjectively meaningful" aspects of social interaction. Actually, "sociation" (in English) may be understood as a contraction of "social association." Simmel, who introduced this term, believed that the defining property of human interaction lay in the fact that individuals (unlike other animals) possess consciousness and self-awareness. Human actions and interactions are motivated by goals and intentions and above all by self-consciousness. For Simmel and for Weber, the study of society begins with the study of "subjectively meaningful" action.

sociologism — the belief in the autonomous nature of social reality: namely, that social phenomena (social structures, processes and events) have a real and independent existence that is not reducible to biological or psychological levels of reality. Sociologism is closely related to the notion of "social facts" and is sometimes known as "sociological realism" or "sociological holism."

standpoint theory — the idea that any view of society is always grounded in a definite social position. A social position may be defined by membership in a recognizable social group — whether this group is defined by race, ethnicity, religion, gender, sexual orientation, language, lifestyle, politics or some other basis for collective identity. A standpoint is composed of the experiences, beliefs and observations which together contribute to an individual's sense of identity. The main message of standpoint theory is that any standpoint is always conditioned by the social position occupied by the human subject.

status — the evaluations which others make of the relative position of an individual, or a social group. The status of a social group is measured by the amount of "social honour" or "prestige" shown to that group relative to other groups in society. Status, therefore, is related to tradition, lifestyle and the subjective differences between social groups.

substantive rationality — actions that are oriented, not towards an instrumental goal of efficiency (formal rationality), but to the realization of certain expressive values for their own sake. These values may be religious, political, ideological or personal in nature. Thus, individuals may be motivated to act in the name of patriotism, religious or political ideals, or to uphold basic civil or human rights.

sui-generis — structures that are self-produced, self-sufficient and independent forms of reality. Durkheim believed that social structures had their own independent existence that could not be reduced to psychological or biological explanations.

superstructure — those social relations and forms of social consciousness that are involved in such institutions and practices as the state and politics, law, ideology, religion, art, science and culture, and other non-economic activities. The superstructure represents those parts of society that are determined by the material base in Marx's binary structure of society.

surplus value — the value that is extracted from the worker during the process of commodity production and realized by the capitalist as profit. The process of extracting surplus value from the worker is referred to by Marx as "exploitation" (see above).

system — a set of mutually interrelated parts in which a change in one part leads to a change in other parts. Systems may be biological organisms or physical machines.

transition crisis — the rapid shift from traditional to modern lifestyles that occurred in many European societies between the eighteenth and nineteenth centuries and which included the Agricultural, Industrial and Demographic revolutions.

totem — an emblem which is used to represent a clan or lineage group. A totemic emblem may portray an animal, bird or even plant or other natural object — such the sun, moon or stars. While a totem may appear to signify a special relationship between a clan, or lineage group, and its object of reverence, anthropologist Levi-Strauss believed that a totem expresses a metaphorical relationship between a social group and its deity. Totems may also function as taboos; it is often prohibited for anyone to kill, eat or even touch a totemic animal or plant.

totemism — a set of religious beliefs and practices common to many traditional and non-literate societies in which an animal, or plant or other natural object, is given special reverence and veneration. Totemism is distinct from other traditional belief systems such as animism, naturism or polytheism.

utilitarianism — the belief that the greatest good for the largest number of people is best advanced through the unregulated pursuit of individual rational self-interest through the market. This is sometimes known as the doctrine of *laissez-faire*, or non-intervention, in the private sector or market). This principle, which was advanced by philosopher Jeremy Bentham, among others, is also sometimes referred to as the principle of "rational egoism."

Ummah — the global community of Muslim believers.

use value — the value that a product, or any other item, has for the consumer who derives satisfaction from using it. Use value is normally distinguished from exchange value.

utopian socialists — those early socialists — such as Pierre-Joseph Proudhon, Charles Fourier, Robert Owen, among others — who constructed speculative philosophical models of socialism which, according to Marx, and Engels, were not based upon any concrete or materialist analysis of social life. In many ways, the utopian socialists based their models of socialism on pre-modern models of society.

verstehen — a method for analyzing the subjective meaning of social action from the perspective of the individual social actor. Weber believed that in order to understand the meanings of unique and unrepeatable historical events, it was necessary for the social theorist to re-experience these events in the imagination through the process of *verstehen* — or "interpretative understanding." For this reason, Weber concluded that the historical methods of interpretation and understanding were absolutely necessary for the proper study of society.

References

Faia, Michael. 1986. *Dynamic Functionalism: Strategy and Tactics*. London: Cambridge University Press.

Ritzer, George. 2008. *Modern Sociological Theory*. Boston: McGraw-Hill.

Index

Name Index